KSOB IUPUI BUS K201 The Computer in Business

New Perspectives Microsoft® Office 365 & Access 2016: Intermediate

1st EDITION

Sasha Vodnik | Mark Shellman

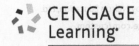

Australia • Brazil • Japan • Korea • Mexico • Singapore • Spain • United Kingdom • United States

KSOB IUPUI BUS K201 The Computer in Business: New Perspectives Microsoft® Office 365 & Access 2016: Intermediate, 1st Edition

New Perspectives Microsoft® Office 365 & Access 2016: Intermediate, 1st Edition

Mark Shellman | Sasha Vodnik

© 2017 Cengage Learning. All rights reserved.

This book contains select works from existing Cengage Learning resources and was produced by Cengage Learning Custom Solutions for collegiate use. As such, those adopting and/or contributing to this work are responsible for editorial content accuracy, continuity and completeness.

Compilation © 2017 Cengage Learning

ISBN: 978-1-337-30044-5

Cengage Learning
20 Channel Center Street
Boston, MA 02210
USA

Cengage Learning is a leading provider of customized learning solutions with office locations around the globe, including Singapore, the United Kingdom, Australia, Mexico, Brazil, and Japan. Locate your local office at:
www.international.cengage.com/region.

Cengage Learning products are represented in Canada by Nelson Education, Ltd.

For your lifelong learning solutions, visit **www.cengage.com/custom.**

Visit our corporate website at **www.cengage.com.**

TABLE OF CONTENTS

ACCESS MODULES

Module 1 Creating a Database
Tracking Animal, Visit, and Billing Data .... **AC 1**

Session 1.1 Visual Overview:
The Access Window ....AC 2

Introduction to Database Concepts .... AC 4

   Organizing Data ....AC 4

   Databases and Relationships ....AC 4

   Relational Database Management
   Systems ....AC 6

Starting Access and Creating a Database .... AC 7

   Working in Touch Mode ....AC 9

Creating a Table in Datasheet View .... AC 11

   Renaming the Default Primary
   Key Field ....AC 12

   Changing the Data Type of the Default Primary
   Key Field ....AC 13

   Adding New Fields ....AC 14

   Entering Records ....AC 16

   Saving a Table ....AC 19

   Opening a Table ....AC 22

Closing a Table and Exiting Access .... AC 22

Session 1.1 Quick Check ....AC 23

Session 1.2 Visual Overview:
The Create Tab Options ....AC 24

Copying Records from Another Access
Database ....AC 26

Navigating a Datasheet ....AC 29

Creating a Simple Query ....AC 30

Creating a Simple Form ....AC 33

Creating a Simple Report ....AC 35

   Printing a Report ....AC 39

Viewing Objects in the Navigation Pane .... AC 40

Using Microsoft Access Help ....AC 40

Managing a Database ....AC 41

   Compacting and Repairing a Database ....AC 42

   Backing Up and Restoring a Database ....AC 43

Session 1.2 Quick Check ....AC 44

Review Assignments ....AC 45

Case Problems ....AC 46

Module 2 Building a Database and Defining Table Relationships
*Creating the Billing, Owner, and Animal
Tables* .... **AC 51**

Session 2.1 Visual Overview:
Table Window in Design View ....AC 52

Guidelines for Designing Databases .... AC 54

Guidelines for Setting Field Properties .... AC 56

   Naming Fields and Objects ....AC 56

   Assigning Field Data Types ....AC 56

   Setting Field Sizes ....AC 57

   Setting the Caption Property for Fields ....AC 58

Creating a Table in Design View .... AC 59

   Defining Fields ....AC 59

   Specifying the Primary Key ....AC 67

   Saving the Table Structure ....AC 68

Modifying the Structure of an Access Table ...... AC 68

   Moving a Field in Design View ....AC 69

   Adding a Field in Design View ....AC 69

Modifying Field Properties ....AC 71

   Changing the Format Property in
   Datasheet View ....AC 71

   Changing Properties in Design View ....AC 73

Session 2.1 Quick Check ....AC 75

Session 2.2 Visual Overview:
Modified Visit table in Datasheet view ....AC 76

Adding Records to a New Table. . . . . AC 78

Importing Data from an Excel Worksheet . . . . AC 80

Creating a Table by Importing an Existing Table
or Table Structure . . . . AC 83

    Importing an Existing Table Structure . . . . AC 84

    Importing an Existing Table . . . . AC 86

Adding Fields to a Table Using the Data
Type Gallery . . . . AC 86

Modifying the Structure of an
Imported Table . . . . AC 88

    Deleting Fields from a Table Structure. . . . . . . .AC 88

    Renaming Fields in Design View. . . . . .AC 90

    Changing the Data Type for a Field in
    Design View . . . . .AC 90

Setting the Default Value Property for a Field. . . . AC 93

Adding Data to a Table by Importing a
Text File. . . . . AC 95

Defining Table Relationships. . . . . AC 97

    One-to-Many Relationships . . . . .AC 98

    Referential Integrity . . . . .AC 99

    Defining a Relationship Between Two
    Tables . . . . .AC 99

Session 2.2 Quick Check. AC 104

Review Assignments . . . . AC 105

Case Problems . . . . AC 106

Module 3 Maintaining and Querying a Database
*Updating Tables and Retrieving Care Center
Information* . . . . **AC 115**

Session 3.1 Visual Overview:
Query Window in Design View . . . . AC 116

Updating a Database . . . . AC 118

    Modifying Records . . . . .AC 118

    Hiding and Unhiding Fields . . . . .AC 119

    Finding Data in a Table. . . . . .AC 121

Deleting Records . . . . AC 122

Introduction to Queries . . . . AC 124

Creating and Running a Query. . . . . AC 125

Updating Data Using a Query . . . . AC 128

Creating a Multitable Query. . . . . AC 129

Sorting Data in a Query . . . . AC 131

    Using an AutoFilter to Sort Data . . . . .AC 131

    Sorting on Multiple Fields in Design View. . . . .AC 132

Filtering Data . . . . AC 136

Session 3.1 Quick Check. AC 139

Session 3.2 Visual Overview:
Selection Criteria in Queries . . . . .AC 140

Defining Record Selection Criteria for
Queries . . . . AC 142

    Specifying an Exact Match . . . . .AC 142

    Modifying a Query . . . . .AC 144

    Using a Comparison Operator to Match a
    Range of Values. . . . . .AC 147

Defining Multiple Selection Criteria for
Queries . . . . AC 149

    The And Logical Operator . . . . .AC 150

    The Or Logical Operator . . . . .AC 152

Changing a Datasheet's Appearance. . . . . AC 154

    Modifying the Font Size . . . . .AC 154

    Changing the Alternate Row Color in a
    Datasheet . . . . .AC 154

Creating a Calculated Field . . . . AC 156

    Formatting a Calculated Field . . . . .AC 160

Using Aggregate Functions . . . . AC 161

    Working with Aggregate Functions Using
    the Total Row . . . . .AC 162

    Creating Queries with Aggregate
    Functions. . . . . .AC 163

    Using Record Group Calculations. . . . . .AC 166

Working with the Navigation Pane . . . . AC 167

Session 3.2 Quick Check . . . . AC 170

Review Assignments . . . . AC 171

Case Problems . . . . AC 172

Module 4 Creating Forms and Reports
*Using Forms and Reports to Display
Owner, Animal, and Visit Data . . . .* **AC 179**

Session 4.1 Visual Overview:
Form Displayed in Form View . . . . AC 180

Creating a Form Using the Form Wizard . . . . AC 182

Modifying a Form's Design in Layout View . . . . . AC 185

    Applying a Theme to a Database
    Object . . . . AC 185

    Adding a Picture to a Form . . . . AC 189

    Changing the Color of Text on a Form . . . . AC 191

Navigating a Form . . . . AC 193

Finding Data Using a Form . . . . AC 194

Maintaining Table Data Using a Form . . . . AC 197

Previewing and Printing Selected Form
Records . . . . AC 198

Creating a Form with a Main Form
and a Subform . . . . AC 200

Session 4.1 Quick Check . . . . AC 205

Session 4.2 Visual Overview:
Report Displayed in Print Preview . . . . AC 206

Creating a Report Using the
Report Wizard . . . . AC 208

Modifying a Report's Design in
Layout View . . . . AC 212

    Applying a Theme to a Report . . . . AC 212

    Changing the Alignment of Field Values . . . . . AC 213

    Moving and Resizing Fields on a
    Report . . . . AC 214

    Changing the Font Color and Inserting a
    Picture in a Report . . . . AC 217

Using Conditional Formatting in a Report . . . . . . AC 218

Session 4.2 Quick Check . . . . AC 222

Review Assignments . . . . AC 223

Case Problems . . . . AC 225

**Module 5 Creating Advanced Queries and
Enhancing Table Design**
*Making the CareCenter Database
Easier to Use . . . .* **AC 233**

Session 5.1 Visual Overview:
Calculated Field . . . . AC 234

Reviewing the CareCenter Database . . . . AC 236

Using a Pattern Match in a Query . . . . AC 237

Using a List-of-Values Match in a Query . . . . AC 240

Using the Not Logical Operator in a Query . . . . . AC 241

    Using an AutoFilter to Filter Data . . . . AC 242

Assigning a Conditional Value to a
Calculated Field . . . . AC 245

Creating a Parameter Query . . . . AC 249

    Creating a More Flexible Parameter Query . . . . AC 251

Session 5.1 Quick Check . . . . AC 253

Session 5.2 Visual Overview:
Advanced Query Wizards . . . . AC 254

Creating a Crosstab Query . . . . AC 256

Creating a Find Duplicates Query . . . . AC 263

Creating a Find Unmatched Query . . . . AC 265

Creating a Top Values Query . . . . AC 267

Session 5.2 Quick Check . . . . AC 269

Session 5.3 Visual Overview:
Lookup Fields and Input Masks . . . . AC 270

Creating a Lookup Field . . . . AC 272

Using the Input Mask Wizard . . . . AC 276

Identifying Object Dependencies . . . . AC 281

Defining Data Validation Rules . . . . AC 282

    Defining Field Validation Rules . . . . AC 283

Defining Table Validation Rules . . . . .AC 284

Working with Long Text Fields . . . . AC 286

Designating a Trusted Folder . . . . AC 289

Session 5.3 Quick Check. . . . . AC 291

Review Assignments . . . . AC 292

Case Problems . . . . AC 294

Module 6 Using Form Tools and Creating Custom Forms
Creating Forms for Riverview Veterinary Care Center. . . . . **AC 301**

Session 6.1 Visual Overview:
Anchoring Controls . . . . .AC 302

Designing Forms. . . . . AC 304

Changing a Lookup Field to a
Short Text field . . . . .AC 304

Creating a Relationship Report and Using the
Documenter . . . . AC 307

Creating Forms Using Form Tools . . . . AC 311

Creating a Form Using the Datasheet Tool . . .AC 311

Creating a Form Using the Multiple
Items Tool . . . . AC 313

Creating a Form Using the Split Form Tool . . .AC 314

Modifying a Split Form in Layout View. . . . . . .AC 315

Anchoring Controls in a Form. . . . . .AC 319

Session 6.1 Quick Check. . . . . AC 321

Session 6.2 Visual Overview:
Custom Form in Design View . . . . .AC 322

Planning and Designing a Custom Form . . . . . . AC 324

Creating a Custom Form in Design View . . . . . . AC 324

Working in the Form Window in
Design View . . . . .AC 325

Adding Fields to a Form . . . . .AC 327

Selecting, Moving, and Aligning
Form Controls. . . . . AC 329

Resizing and Deleting Controls. . . . . AC 333

Adding a Combo Box Control to a Form . . . . AC 336

Using Form Headers and Form Footers . . . . AC 342

Adding a Title to a Form. . . . . .AC 343

Session 6.2 Quick Check. . . . . AC 345

Session 6.3 Visual Overview:
Custom Form in Form View . . . . .AC 346

Adding a Combo Box to Find Records. . . . . AC 348

Adding a Subform to a Form . . . . AC 352

Displaying a Subform's Calculated Controls in the
Main Form. . . . . AC 356

Adding Calculated Controls to a Subform's
Form Footer Section. .AC 356

Adding Calculated Controls to a
Main Form. . . . . .AC 358

Resizing, Moving, and Formatting
Calculated Controls . . . . .AC 361

Changing the Tab Order in a Form. . . . . AC 364

Improving a Form's Appearance. . . . . AC 367

Adding a Line to a Form . . . . .AC 367

Adding a Rectangle to a Form . . . . .AC 368

Modifying the Visual Effects of the Controls
in a Form . . . . .AC 370

Session 6.3 Quick Check. . . . . AC 372

Review Assignments . . . . AC 373

Case Problems . . . . AC 375

Module 7 Creating Custom Reports

Modifying a Report in Design View . . . . AC 381

Creating Mailing Labels . . . . AC 385

INDEX. . . . . REF 1

ACCESS

Creating a Database

Tracking Animal, Visit, and Billing Data

OBJECTIVES

Session 1.1
- Learn basic database concepts and terms
- Start and exit Access
- Explore the Microsoft Access window and Backstage view
- Create a blank database
- Create and save a table in Datasheet view
- Enter field names and records in a table datasheet
- Open a table using the Navigation Pane

Session 1.2
- Open an Access database
- Copy and paste records from another Access database
- Navigate a table datasheet
- Create and navigate a simple query
- Create and navigate a simple form
- Create, preview, navigate, and print a simple report
- Use Help in Access
- Learn how to compact, back up, and restore a database

Case | *Riverview Veterinary Care Center*

Riverview Veterinary Care Center, a veterinary care center in Cody, Wyoming, provides care for pets and livestock in the greater Cody area. In addition to caring for household pets, such as dogs and cats, the center specializes in serving the needs of livestock on ranches in the surrounding area. Kimberly Johnson, the office manager for Riverview Veterinary Care Center, oversees a small staff and is responsible for maintaining the medical records for all of the animals the care center serves.

In order to best manage the center, Kimberly and her staff rely on electronic medical records for information on the animals and their owners, billing, inventory control, purchasing, and accounts payable. Several months ago, the center upgraded to **Microsoft Access 2016** (or simply **Access**), a computer program used to enter, maintain, and retrieve related data in a format known as a database. Kimberly and her staff want to use Access to store information about the animals, their owners, billing, vendors, and products. She asks for your help in creating the necessary Access database.

STARTING DATA FILES

Access1 → Module
Kimberly.accdb

Review
Company.accdb

Case1
BeautyToGo.accdb

Case2
ProgPros.accdb

Case3
Diane.accdb

Case4
HikeApp.accdb

Session 1.1 Visual Overview:

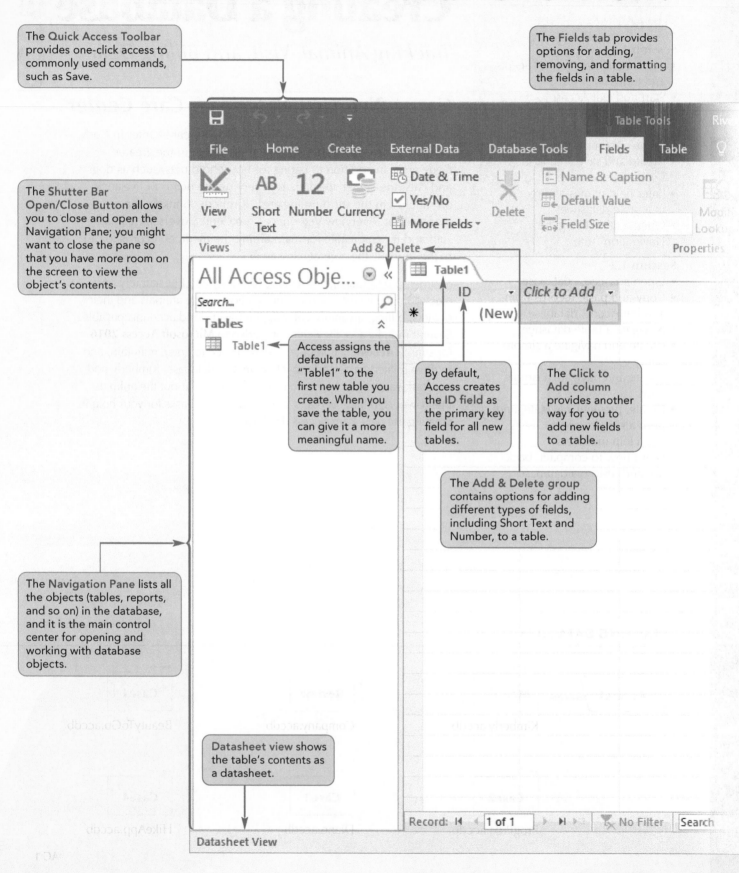

The **Quick Access Toolbar** provides one-click access to commonly used commands, such as Save.

The **Fields** tab provides options for adding, removing, and formatting the fields in a table.

The **Shutter Bar Open/Close Button** allows you to close and open the Navigation Pane; you might want to close the pane so that you have more room on the screen to view the object's contents.

Access assigns the default name "Table1" to the first new table you create. When you save the table, you can give it a more meaningful name.

By default, Access creates the ID field as the primary key field for all new tables.

The **Click to Add** column provides another way for you to add new fields to a table.

The **Add & Delete** group contains options for adding different types of fields, including Short Text and Number, to a table.

The **Navigation Pane** lists all the objects (tables, reports, and so on) in the database, and it is the main control center for opening and working with database objects.

Datasheet view shows the table's contents as a datasheet.

The Access Window

The Access window is the program window that appears when you create a new database or open an existing database.

You use the window buttons to minimize, maximize, and close the Access window.

If you are signed in to your Office account, your name appears here. If you are not signed in, the Sign in link will appear here, and you can click it to sign into your Office account.

Riverview : Database- E:\Access1\Module\Riverview.acc...   ?   —   ▢   ✕

♀ Tell me what you want to do...   Your Name

Modify Lookups   ƒx Modify Expression   ab| Memo Settings ▾   Data Type: Format: Formatting ▾ $ % , ←.0 .00 →   ☐ Required   ☐ Unique   ☐ Indexed   Validation ▾

Properties   Formatting   Field Validation

The ribbon provides the main Access commands organized by task into tabs and groups.

The title bar displays the name of the open file and the program.

A datasheet displays the table's contents in rows and columns, similar to a table that you create in a Word document or an Excel worksheet. Each row will be a separate record in the table, and each column will contain the field values for one field in the table.

The status bar provides information about the program or open file, as well as buttons for working with the file. At the far left, the status bar indicates the current view, in this case, Datasheet view.

Search

Introduction to Database Concepts

Before you begin using Access to create the database for Kimberly, you need to understand a few key terms and concepts associated with databases.

Organizing Data

Data is a valuable resource to any business. At Riverview Veterinary Care Center, for example, important data includes the names of the animals, owners' contact information, visit dates, and billing information. Organizing, storing, maintaining, retrieving, and sorting this type of data are critical activities that enable a business to find and use information effectively. Before storing data on a computer, however, you must organize the data.

Your first step in organizing data is to identify the individual fields. A **field** is a single characteristic or attribute of a person, place, object, event, or idea. For example, some of the many fields that Riverview Veterinary Care Center tracks are the animal ID, animal name, animal type, breed, visit date, reason for visit, and invoice amount.

Next, you group related fields together into tables. A **table** is a collection of fields that describes a person, place, object, event, or idea. Figure 1-1 shows an example of an Animal table that contains the following four fields: AnimalID, AnimalName, AnimalType, and AnimalBreed. Each field is a column in the table, with the field name displayed as the column heading.

Figure 1-1	Data organization for a table of animals

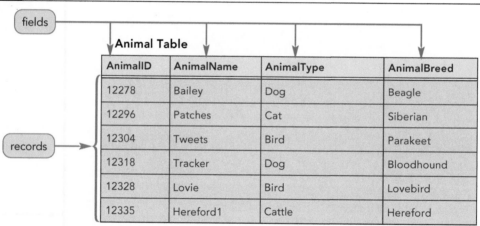

The specific content of a field is called the **field value**. In Figure 1-1, the first set of field values for AnimalID, AnimalName, AnimalType, and AnimalBreed are, respectively: 12278; Bailey; Dog; and Beagle. This set of field values is called a **record**. In the Animal table, the data for each animal is stored as a separate record. Figure 1-1 shows six records; each row of field values in the table is a record.

Databases and Relationships

A collection of related tables is called a **database**, or a **relational database**. In this module, you will create the database for Riverview Veterinary Care Center, and within that database, you'll create a table named Visit to store data about animal visits. Later on, you'll create three more tables, named Animal, Owner, and Billing, to store related information about animals, their owners, and invoices related to their care.

As Kimberly and her staff use the database that you will create, they will need to access information about animals and their visits. To obtain this information, you must have a way to connect records in the Animal table to records in the Visit table. You connect the records in the separate tables through a **common field** that appears in both tables.

In the sample database shown in Figure 1-2, each record in the Animal table has a field named AnimalID, which is also a field in the Visit table. For example, the beagle named Bailey is the first animal in the Animal table and has an AnimalID field value of 12278. This same AnimalID field value, 12278, appears in two records in the Visit table. Therefore, the beagle named Bailey is the animal that was seen at these two visits.

| Figure 1-2 | Database relationship between tables for animals and visits |

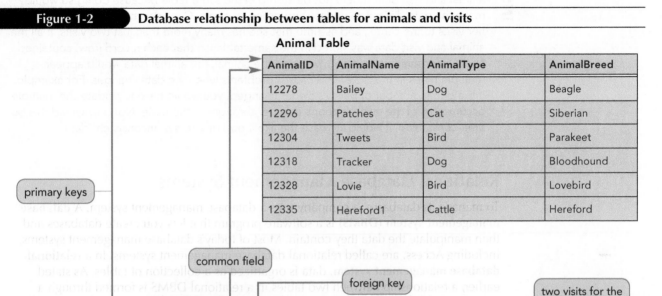

Each AnimalID value in the Animal table must be unique so that you can distinguish one animal from another. These unique AnimalID values also identify each animal's specific visits in the Visit table. The AnimalID field is referred to as the primary key of the Animal table. A **primary key** is a field, or a collection of fields, whose values uniquely identify each record in a table. No two records can contain the same value for the primary key field. In the Visit table, the VisitID field is the primary key because Riverview Veterinary Care Center assigns each visit a unique identification number.

When you include the primary key from one table as a field in a second table to form a relationship between the two tables, it is called a **foreign key** in the second table, as shown in Figure 1-2. For example, AnimalID is the primary key in the Animal table and a foreign key in the Visit table. The AnimalID field must have the same characteristics in both tables. Although the primary key AnimalID contains unique values in the Animal table, the same field as a foreign key in the Visit table does not necessarily contain unique values. The AnimalID value 12278, for example, appears two times in the Visit table because the beagle named Bailey made two visits to the center. Each foreign key value, however, must match one of the field values for the primary key in the other table. In the example shown in Figure 1-2, each AnimalID value in the Visit table must match an AnimalID value in the Animal table. The two tables are related, enabling users to connect the facts about animals with the facts about their visits to the center.

Storing Data in Separate Tables

When you create a database, you must create separate tables that contain only fields that are directly related to each other. For example, in the Riverview database, the animal and visit data should not be stored in the same table because doing so would make the data difficult to update and prone to errors. Consider the beagle Bailey and her visits to the center, and assume that she has many more than just two visits. If all the animal and visit data was stored in the same table, so that each record (row) contained all the information about each visit and the animal, the animal data would appear multiple times in the table. This causes problems when the data changes. For example, if the phone number of Bailey's owner changed, you would have to update the multiple occurrences of the owner's phone number throughout the table. Not only would this be time-consuming, it would increase the likelihood of errors or inconsistent data.

Relational Database Management Systems

To manage its databases, a company uses a database management system. A **database management system (DBMS)** is a software program that lets you create databases and then manipulate the data they contain. Most of today's database management systems, including Access, are called relational database management systems. In a **relational database management system**, data is organized as a collection of tables. As stated earlier, a relationship between two tables in a relational DBMS is formed through a common field.

A relational DBMS controls the storage of databases and facilitates the creation, manipulation, and reporting of data, as illustrated in Figure 1-3.

Figure 1-3	Relational database management system

Specifically, a relational DBMS provides the following functions:

- It allows you to create database structures containing fields, tables, and table relationships.
- It lets you easily add new records, change field values in existing records, and delete records.
- It contains a built-in query language, which lets you obtain immediate answers to the questions (or queries) you ask about your data.
- It contains a built-in report generator, which lets you produce professional-looking, formatted reports from your data.
- It protects databases through security, control, and recovery facilities.

An organization such as Riverview Veterinary Care Center benefits from a relational DBMS because it allows users working in different groups to share the same data. More than one user can enter data into a database, and more than one user can retrieve and analyze data that other users have entered. For example, the database for Riverview Veterinary Care Center will contain only one copy of the Visit table, and all employees will use it to access visit information.

Finally, unlike other software programs, such as spreadsheet programs, a DBMS can handle massive amounts of data and can be used to create relationships among multiple tables. Each Access database, for example, can be up to two gigabytes in size, can contain up to 32,768 objects (tables, reports, and so on), and can have up to 255 people using the database at the same time. For instructional purposes, the databases you will create and work with throughout this text contain a relatively small number of records compared to databases you would encounter outside the classroom, which would likely contain tables with very large numbers of records.

Starting Access and Creating a Database

Now that you've learned some database terms and concepts, you're ready to start Access and create the Riverview database for Kimberly.

To start Access:

▶ **1.** On the Windows taskbar, click the **Start** button ⊞. The Start menu opens.

▶ **2.** Click **All apps** on the Start menu, and then click **Access 2016**. Access starts and displays the Recent screen in Backstage view. See Figure 1-4.

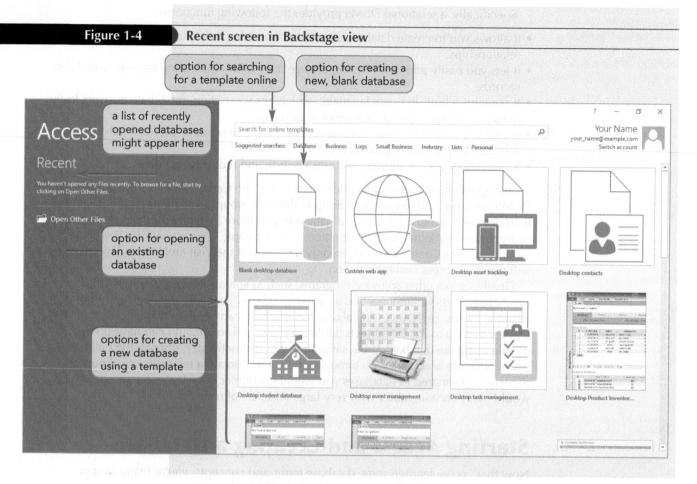

Figure 1-4 Recent screen in Backstage view

option for searching for a template online

option for creating a new, blank database

a list of recently opened databases might appear here

option for opening an existing database

options for creating a new database using a template

When you start Access, the first screen that appears is Backstage view, which is the starting place for your work in Access. **Backstage view** contains commands that allow you to manage Access files and options. The Recent screen in Backstage view provides options for you to create a new database or open an existing database. To create a new database that does not contain any data or objects, you use the Blank desktop database option. If the database you need to create contains objects that match those found in common databases, such as databases that store data about contacts or tasks, you can use one of the templates provided with Access. A **template** is a predesigned database that includes professionally designed tables, reports, and other database objects that can make it quick and easy for you to create a database. You can also search for a template online using the Search for online templates box.

In this case, the templates provided do not match Kimberly's needs for the center's database, so you need to create a new, blank database from scratch.

To create the new Riverview database:

1. Make sure you have the Access starting Data Files on your computer.

   Trouble? If you don't have the starting Data Files, you need to get them before you can proceed. Your instructor will either give you the Data Files or ask you to obtain them from a specified location (such as a network drive). If you have any questions about the Data Files, see your instructor or technical support person for assistance.

2. On the Recent screen, click **Blank desktop database** (see Figure 1-4). The Blank desktop database screen opens.

Be sure to type **Riverview** or you'll create a database named Database1.

3. In the File Name box, type **Riverview** to replace the selected database name provided by Access, Database1. Next you need to specify the location for the file.

4. Click the **Browse** button to the right of the File Name box. The File New Database dialog box opens.

5. Navigate to the drive and folder where you are storing your files, as specified by your instructor.

6. Make sure the Save as type box displays "Microsoft Access 2007–2016 Databases."

   Trouble? If your computer is set up to show filename extensions, you will see the Access filename extension ".accdb" in the File name box.

TIP

If you don't type the filename extension, Access adds it automatically.

7. Click the **OK** button. You return to the Blank desktop database screen, and the File Name box now shows the name Riverview.accdb. The filename extension ".accdb" identifies the file as an Access 2007–2016 database.

8. Click the **Create** button. Access creates the new database, saves it to the specified location, and then opens an empty table named Table1.

   Trouble? If you see only ribbon tab names and no buttons, click the Home tab to expand the ribbon, and then in the bottom-right corner of the ribbon, click the Pin the ribbon button.

Refer back to the Session 1.1 Visual Overview and spend some time becoming familiar with the components of the Access window.

INSIGHT

Understanding the Database File Type

Access 2016 uses the .accdb file extension, which is the same file extension used for databases created with Microsoft Access 2007, 2010, and 2013. To ensure compatibility between these earlier versions and the Access 2016 software, new databases created using Access 2016 have the same file extension and file format as Access 2007, Access 2010, and Access 2013 databases. This is why the File New Database dialog box provides the Microsoft Access 2007–2016 Databases option in the Save as type box. In addition, the notation "(Access 2007–2016 file format)" appears in the title bar next to the name of an open database in Access 2016, confirming that database files with the .accdb extension can be used in Access 2007, Access 2010, Access 2013, and Access 2016.

Working in Touch Mode

TIP

On a touch device, you tap instead of *click*.

If you are working on a touch device, such as a tablet, you can switch to Touch Mode in Access to make it easier for you to tap buttons on the ribbon and perform other touch actions. Your screens will not match those shown in the book exactly, but this will not cause any problems.

Note: The following steps assume that you are using a mouse. If you are instead using a touch device, please read these steps but don't complete them, so that you remain working in Touch Mode.

To switch to Touch Mode:

▶ **1.** On the Quick Access Toolbar, click the **Customize Quick Access Toolbar** button ▾. A menu opens listing buttons you can add to the Quick Access Toolbar as well as other options for customizing the toolbar.

Trouble? If the Touch/Mouse Mode command on the menu has a checkmark next to it, press the Esc key to close the menu, and then skip to Step 3.

▶ **2.** Click **Touch/Mouse Mode**. The Quick Access Toolbar now contains the Touch/Mouse Mode button 🖱, which you can use to switch between Mouse Mode, the default display, and Touch Mode.

▶ **3.** On the Quick Access Toolbar, click the **Touch/Mouse Mode** button 🖱. A menu opens with two commands: Mouse, which shows the ribbon in the standard display and is optimized for use with the mouse; and Touch, which provides more space between the buttons and commands on the ribbon and is optimized for use with touch devices. The icon next to Mouse is shaded red to indicate that it is selected.

Trouble? If the icon next to Touch is shaded red, press the Esc key to close the menu and skip to Step 5.

▶ **4.** Click **Touch**. The display switches to Touch Mode with more space between the commands and buttons on the ribbon. See Figure 1-5.

Figure 1-5 ▶ **Ribbon displayed in Touch Mode**

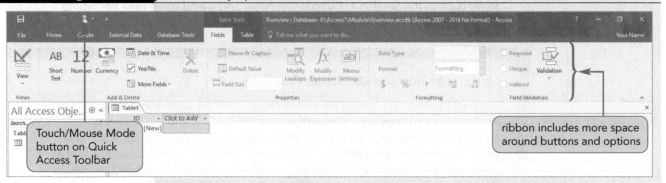

The figures in this text show the standard Mouse Mode display, and the instructions assume you are using a mouse to click and select options, so you'll switch back to Mouse Mode.

Trouble? If you are using a touch device and want to remain in Touch Mode, skip Steps 5 and 6.

▶ **5.** On the Quick Access Toolbar, click the **Touch/Mouse Mode** button 🖱, and then click **Mouse**. The ribbon returns to the standard display, as shown in the Session 1.1 Visual Overview.

▶ **6.** On the Quick Access Toolbar, click the **Customize Quick Access Toolbar** button ▾, and then click **Touch/Mouse Mode** to deselect it. The Touch/Mouse Mode button is removed from the Quick Access Toolbar.

Creating a Table in Datasheet View

Tables contain all the data in a database and are the fundamental objects for your work in Access. There are different ways to create a table in Access, including entering the fields and records for the table directly in Datasheet view.

Creating a Table in Datasheet View

- On the ribbon, click the Create tab.
- In the Tables group, click the Table button.
- Rename the default ID primary key field and change its data type, if necessary; or accept the default ID field with the AutoNumber data type.
- In the Add & Delete group on the Fields tab, click the button for the type of field you want to add to the table (for example, click the Short Text button), and then type the field name; or, in the table datasheet, click the Click to Add column heading, click the type of field you want to add from the list that opens, and then press the Tab or Enter key to move to the next column in the datasheet. Repeat this step to add all the necessary fields to the table.
- In the first row below the field names, enter the value for each field in the first record, pressing the Tab or Enter key to move from one field to the next.
- After entering the value for the last field in the first record, press the Tab or Enter key to move to the next row, and then enter the values for the next record. Continue this process until you have entered all the records for the table.
- On the Quick Access Toolbar, click the Save button, enter a name for the table, and then click the OK button.

For Riverview Veterinary Care Center, Kimberly needs to track information about each animal visit at the center. She asks you to create the Visit table according to the plan shown in Figure 1-6.

| Figure 1-6 | Plan for the Visit table |

Field	Purpose
VisitID	Unique number assigned to each visit; will serve as the table's primary key
AnimalID	Unique number assigned to each animal; common field that will be a foreign key to connect to the Animal table
VisitDate	Date on which the animal visited the center or was seen offsite
Reason	Reason/diagnosis for the animal visit
OffSite	Whether the animal visit was offsite at a home or ranch

As shown in Kimberly's plan, she wants to store data about visits in five fields, including fields to contain the date of each visit, the reason for the visit, and if the visit was offsite. These are the most important aspects of a visit and, therefore, must be tracked. Also, notice that the VisitID field will be the primary key for the table; each visit at Riverview Veterinary Care Center has a unique number assigned to it, so this field is the logical choice for the primary key. Finally, the AnimalID field is needed in the Visit table as a foreign key to connect the information about visits to animals. The data about animals, as well as the data about their owners, and the bills for the animals' care, will be stored in separate tables, which you will create later.

Notice the name of each field in Figure 1-6. You need to name each field, table, and object in an Access database.

PROSKILLS

Decision Making: Naming Fields in Access Tables

One of the most important tasks in creating a table is deciding what names to specify for the table's fields. Keep the following guidelines in mind when you assign field names:

- A field name can consist of up to 64 characters, including letters, numbers, spaces, and special characters, except for the period (.), exclamation mark (!), grave accent ('), and square brackets ([ ]).
- A field name cannot begin with a space.
- Capitalize the first letter of each word in a field name that combines multiple words, for example VisitDate.
- Use concise field names that are easy to remember and reference and that won't take up a lot of space in the table datasheet.
- Use standard abbreviations, such as Num for Number, Amt for Amount, and Qty for Quantity, and use them consistently throughout the database. For example, if you use Num for Number in one field name, do not use the number sign (#) for Number in another.
- Give fields descriptive names so that you can easily identify them when you view or edit records.
- Although Access supports the use of spaces in field names (and in other object names), experienced database developers avoid using spaces because they can cause errors when the objects are involved in programming tasks.

By spending time obtaining and analyzing information about the fields in a table, and understanding the rules for naming fields, you can create a well-designed table that will be easy for others to use.

Renaming the Default Primary Key Field

As noted earlier, Access provides the ID field as the default primary key for a new table you create in Datasheet view. Recall that a primary key is a field, or a collection of fields, whose values uniquely identify each record in a table. However, according to Kimberly's plan, the VisitID field should be the primary key for the Visit table. You'll begin by renaming the default ID field to create the VisitID field.

To rename the ID field to the VisitID field:

TIP

A **shortcut menu** opens when you right-click an object and provides options for working with that object.

1. Right-click the **ID** column heading to open the shortcut menu, and then click **Rename Field**. The column heading ID is selected, so that whatever text you type next will replace it.

2. Type **VisitID** and then click the row below the heading. The column heading changes to VisitID, and the insertion point moves to the row below the heading. The **insertion point** is a flashing cursor that shows where text you type will be inserted. In this case, it is hidden within the selected field value (New). See Figure 1-7.

   Trouble? If you make a mistake while typing the field name, use the Backspace key to delete characters to the left of the insertion point or the Delete key to delete characters to the right of the insertion point. Then type the correct text. To correct a field name by replacing it entirely, press the Esc key, and then type the correct text.

Figure 1-7   **ID field renamed to VisitID**

Table Tools contextual tab is active

AutoNumber data type assigned to the default primary key field (ID)

VisitID field name entered in the column heading

option for specifying the data type for a field

Notice that the Table Tools tab is active on the ribbon. This is an example of a **contextual tab**, which is a tab that appears and provides options for working with a specific object that is selected—in this case, the table you are creating. As you work with other objects in the database, other contextual tabs will appear with commands and options related to each selected object.

> **INSIGHT**
>
> ### Buttons and Labels on the Ribbon
>
> Depending on the size of the monitor you are using and your screen resolution settings, you might see more or fewer buttons on the ribbon, and you might not see labels next to certain buttons. The screenshots in these modules were created using a screen resolution setting of 1366 x 768 with the program window maximized. If you are using a smaller monitor or a lower screen resolution, some buttons will appear only as icons, with no labels next to them, because there is not enough room on the ribbon to display the labels.

You have renamed the default primary key field, ID, to VisitID. However, the VisitID field still retains the characteristics of the ID field, including its data type. Your next task is to change the data type of this field.

Changing the Data Type of the Default Primary Key Field

Notice the Formatting group on the Table Tools Fields tab. One of the options available in this group is the Data Type option (see Figure 1-7). Each field in an Access table must be assigned a data type. The **data type** determines what field values you can enter for the field. In this case, the AutoNumber data type is displayed. Access assigns the AutoNumber data type to the default ID primary key field because the **AutoNumber** data type automatically inserts a unique number in this field for every record, beginning with the number 1 for the first record, the number 2 for the second record, and so on. Therefore, a field using the AutoNumber data type can serve as the primary key for any table you create.

Visit numbers at the Riverview Veterinary Care Center are specific, four-digit numbers, so the AutoNumber data type is not appropriate for the VisitID field, which is the primary key field in the table you are creating. A better choice is the **Short Text** data type, which allows field values containing letters, digits, and other characters, and which is appropriate for identifying numbers, such as visit numbers, that are never used in calculations. So, Kimberly asks you to change the data type for the VisitID field from AutoNumber to Short Text.

To change the data type for the VisitID field:

▶ **1.** Make sure that the VisitID column is selected. A column is selected when you click a field value, in which case the background color of the column heading changes to orange (the default color) and the insertion point appears in the field value. You can also click the column heading to select a column, in which case the background color of both the column heading and the field value changes (the default colors are gray and blue, respectively).

▶ **2.** On the Table Tools Fields tab, in the Formatting group, click the **Data Type arrow**, and then click **Short Text**. The VisitID field is now a Short Text field. See Figure 1-8.

Figure 1-8	Short Text data type assigned to the VisitID field

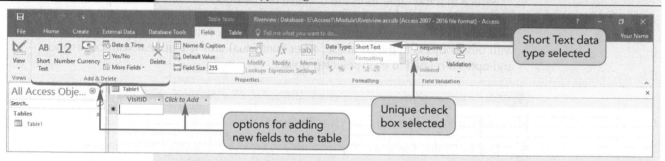

Note the Unique check box in the Field Validation group. This check box is selected because the VisitID field assumed the characteristics of the default primary key field, ID, including the fact that each value in the field must be unique. Because this check box is selected, no two records in the Visit table will be allowed to have the same value in the VisitID field.

With the VisitID field created and established as the primary key, you can now enter the rest of the fields in the Visit table.

Adding New Fields

When you create a table in Datasheet view, you can use the options in the Add & Delete group on the Table Tools Fields tab to add fields to your table. You can also use the Click to Add column in the table datasheet to add new fields. (See Figure 1-8.) You'll use both methods to add the four remaining fields to the Visit table. The next field you need to add is the AnimalID field. Similar to the VisitID field, the AnimalID field will contain numbers that will not be used in calculations, so it should be a Short Text field.

To add the rest of the fields to the Visit table:

▶ **1.** On the Table Tools Fields tab, in the Add & Delete group, click the **Short Text** button. A new field named "Field1" is added to the right of the VisitID field. See Figure 1-9.

Figure 1-9	New Short Text field added to the table

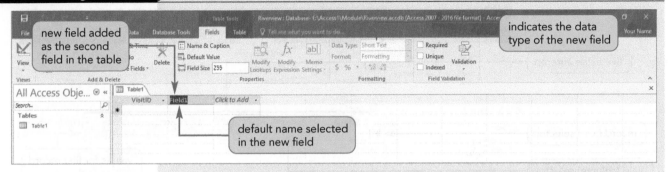

The text "Field1" is selected, so you can simply type the new field name to replace it.

2. Type **AnimalID**. The second field is added to the table. Next, you'll add the VisitDate field. Because this field will contain date values, you'll add a field with the **Date/Time** data type, which allows field values in a variety of date and time formats.

3. In the Add & Delete group, click the **Date & Time** button. Access adds a third field to the table, this time with the Date/Time data type.

4. Type **VisitDate** to replace the selected name "Field1." The fourth field in the Visit table is the Reason field, which will contain brief descriptions of the reason for the visit to the center. You'll add another Short Text field—this time using the Click to Add column.

5. Click the **Click to Add** column heading. Access displays a list of available data types from which you can choose the data type for the new field you're adding.

6. Click **Short Text** in the list. Access adds a fourth field to the table.

7. Type **Reason** to replace the highlighted name "Field1," and then press the **Enter** key. The Click to Add column becomes active and displays the list of field data types.

The fifth and final field in the Visit table is the OffSite field, which will indicate whether or not the visit was at an offsite venue, such as at a home or ranch (that is, not within the center). The **Yes/No** data type is suitable for this field because it is used to define fields that store values representing one of two options—true/false, yes/no, or on/off.

TIP

You can also type the first letter of a data type to select it and close the Click to Add list.

8. Click **Yes/No** in the list, and then type **OffSite** to replace the highlighted name "Field1."

Trouble? If you pressed the Tab or Enter key after typing the OffSite field name, press the Esc key to close the Click to Add list.

9. Click in the row below the VisitID column heading. All five fields are now entered for the Visit table. See Figure 1-10.

Figure 1-10   **Table with all fields entered**

five fields entered

record (row) selector

field (column) selector

values for first record will go in this row

The table contains three Short Text fields (VisitID, AnimalID, and Reason), one Date/Time field (VisitDate), and one Yes/No field (OffSite). You'll learn more about field data types in the next module.

As noted earlier, Datasheet view shows a table's contents in rows (records) and columns (fields). Each column is headed by a field name inside a field selector, and each row has a record selector to its left (see Figure 1-10). Clicking a **field selector** or a **record selector** selects that entire column or row (respectively), which you then can manipulate. A field selector is also called a **column selector**, and a record selector is also called a **row selector**.

Entering Records

With the fields in place for the table, you can now enter the field values for each record. Kimberly requests that you enter eight records in the Visit table, as shown in Figure 1-11.

Figure 1-11   **Visit table records**

VisitID	AmimalID	VisitDate	Reason	OffSite
1072	12356	12/12/2016	Vaccinations	Yes
1169	12278	1/20/2017	Spaying	No
1184	12443	1/25/2017	Neutering	No
1016	12345	11/18/2016	Vaccinations	Yes
1196	12455	2/1/2017	Vaccinations	No
1098	12296	1/3/2017	Declawing	No
1178	12362	1/24/2017	Injured leg and hoof	Yes
1044	12278	12/2/2016	Vaccinations	No

To enter records in a table datasheet, you type the field values below the column headings for the fields. The first record you enter will go in the first row (see Figure 1-10).

To enter the first record for the Visit table:

Be sure to type the numbers "0" and "1" and not the letters "O" and "I" in the field value.

1. In the first row for the VisitID field, type **1072** (the VisitID field value for the first record), and then press the **Tab** key. Access adds the field value and moves the insertion point to the right, into the AnimalID column. See Figure 1-12.

Figure 1-12 | **First field value entered**

pencil symbol

star symbol

first VisitID field value entered

insertion point positioned in the AnimalID field

Trouble? If you make a mistake when typing a value, use the Backspace key to delete characters to the left of the insertion point or the Delete key to delete characters to the right of the insertion point. Then type the correct value. To correct a value by replacing it entirely, press the Esc key, and then type the correct value.

Notice the pencil symbol that appears in the row selector for the new record. The **pencil symbol** indicates that the record is being edited. Also notice the star symbol that appears in the row selector for the second row. The **star symbol** identifies the second row as the next row available for a new record.

2. Type **12356** (the AnimalID field value for the first record), and then press the **Tab** key. Access enters the field value and moves the insertion point to the VisitDate column.

3. Type **12/12/16** (the VisitDate field value for the first record), and then press the **Tab** key. Access displays the year as "2016" even though you entered only the final two digits of the year. This is because the VisitDate field has the Date/Time data type, which automatically formats dates with four-digit years.

4. Type **Vaccinations** (the Reason field value for the first record), and then press the **Tab** key to move to the OffSite column.

Recall that the OffSite field is a Yes/No field. Notice the check box displayed in the OffSite column. By default, the value for any Yes/No field is "No"; therefore, the check box is initially empty. For Yes/No fields with check boxes, you press the Tab key to leave the check box unchecked, or you press the spacebar to insert a checkmark in the check box. The record you are entering in the table is for an offsite visit, so you need to insert a checkmark in the check box to indicate "Yes."

TIP

You can also click a check box in a Yes/No field to insert or remove a checkmark.

5. Press the **spacebar** to insert a checkmark, and then press the **Tab** key. The first record is entered into the table, and the insertion point is positioned in the VisitID field for the second record. The pencil symbol is removed from the first row because the record in that row is no longer being edited. The table is now ready for you to enter the second record. See Figure 1-13.

| Figure 1-13 | Datasheet with first record entered |

next row available
for a new record

field values for the
first record entered

value displayed with
a four-digit year

Now you can enter the remaining seven records in the Visit table.

To enter the remaining records in the Visit table:

1. Referring to Figure 1-11, enter the values for records 2 through 8, pressing the **Tab** key to move from field to field and to the next row for a new record. Keep in mind that you do not have to type all four digits of the year in the VisitDate field values; you can enter only the final two digits, and Access will display all four. Also, for any OffSite field values of "No," be sure to press the Tab key to leave the check box empty.

   Trouble? If you enter a value in the wrong field by mistake, such as entering a Reason field value in the VisitDate field, a menu might open with options for addressing the problem. If this happens, click the "Enter new value" option in the menu. You'll return to the field with the incorrect value selected, which you can then replace by typing the correct value.

   Notice that not all of the Reason field values are fully displayed. To see more of the table datasheet and the full field values, you'll close the Navigation Pane and resize the Reason column.

2. At the top of the Navigation Pane, click the **Shutter Bar Open/Close Button** ⟪. The Navigation Pane closes, and only the complete table datasheet is displayed.

3. Place the pointer on the vertical line to the right of the Reason field name until the pointer changes to ↔, and then double-click the vertical line. All the Reason field values are now fully displayed. See Figure 1-14.

Figure 1-14 **Datasheet with eight records entered**

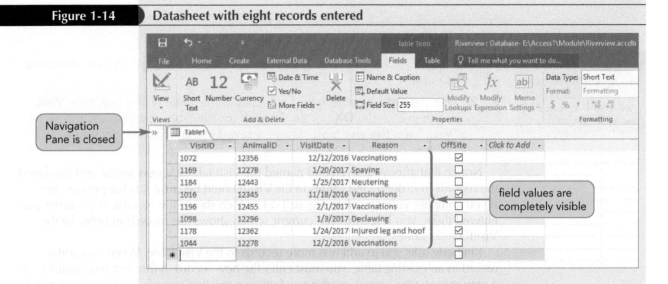

> Navigation Pane is closed

> field values are completely visible

When you resize a datasheet column by double-clicking the column dividing line, you are sizing the column to its **best fit**—that is, so the column is just wide enough to display the longest visible value in the column, including the field name.

4. Compare your table to the one in Figure 1-14. If any of the field values in your table do not match those shown in the figure, you can correct a field value by clicking to position the insertion point in the value, and then using the Backspace key or Delete key to delete incorrect text. Then type the correct text and press the Enter key. To correct a value in the OffSite field, simply click the check box to add or remove the checkmark as appropriate. Also, be sure the spelling and capitalization of field names in your table match those shown in the figure exactly and that there are no spaces between words. To correct a field name, double-click it to select it, and then type the correct name; or use the Rename Field option on the shortcut menu to rename a field with the correct name.

> Carefully compare your VisitID and AnimalID values with those in the figure, and correct any errors before continuing.

Saving a Table

The records you enter are immediately stored in the database as soon as you enter them; however, the table's design—the field names and characteristics of the fields themselves, plus any layout changes to the datasheet—are not saved until you save the table. When you save a new table for the first time, you should give it a name that best identifies the information it contains. Like a field name, a table name can contain up to 64 characters, including spaces.

REFERENCE

Saving a Table

- Make sure the table you want to save is open.
- On the Quick Access Toolbar, click the Save button. The Save As dialog box opens.
- In the Table Name box, type the name for the table.
- Click the OK button.

According to Kimberly's plan, you need to save the table with the name "Visit."

To save and name the Visit table:

1. On the Quick Access Toolbar, click the **Save** button 🖫. The Save As dialog box opens.

2. With the default name Table1 selected in the Table Name box, type **Visit**, and then click the **OK** button. The tab for the table now displays the name "Visit," and the Visit table design is saved in the Riverview database.

Notice that after you saved and named the Visit table, Access sorted and displayed the records in order by the values in the VisitID field because it is the primary key. If you compare your screen to Figure 1-11, which shows the records in the order you entered them, you'll see that the current screen shows the records in order by the VisitID field values.

Kimberly asks you to add two more records to the Visit table. When you add a record to an existing table, you must enter the new record in the next row available for a new record; you cannot insert a row between existing records for the new record. In a table with just a few records, such as the Visit table, the next available row is visible on the screen. However, in a table with hundreds of records, you would need to scroll the datasheet to see the next row available. The easiest way to add a new record to a table is to use the New button, which scrolls the datasheet to the next row available so you can enter the new record.

To enter additional records in the Visit table:

1. If necessary, click the first record's VisitID field value (**1016**) to make it the current record.

2. On the ribbon, click the **Home** tab.

3. In the Records group, click the **New** button. The insertion point is positioned in the next row available for a new record, which in this case is row 9. See Figure 1-15.

Figure 1-15   **Entering a new record**

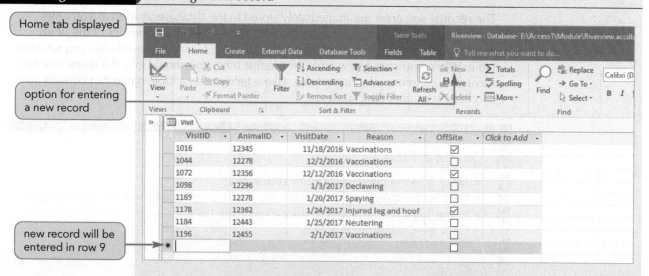

Home tab displayed

option for entering a new record

new record will be entered in row 9

4. With the insertion point in the VisitID field for the new record, type **1036** and then press the **Tab** key.

5. Complete the entry of this record by entering each value shown below, pressing the **Tab** key to move from field to field:

AnimalID = **12294**

VisitDate = **11/29/2016**

Reason = **Declawing**

OffSite = **No (unchecked)**

6. Enter the values for the next new record, as follows, and then press the **Tab** key after entering the OffSite field value:

VisitID = **1152**

AnimalID = **12318**

VisitDate = **1/13/2017**

Reason = **Not eating**

OffSite = **No (unchecked)**

Your datasheet should now look like the one shown in Figure 1-16.

Figure 1-16   Datasheet with additional records entered

The new records you added appear at the end of the table, and are not sorted in order by the primary key field values. For example, VisitID 1036 should be the second record in the table, placed between VisitID 1016 and VisitID 1044. When you add records to a table datasheet, they appear at the end of the table. The records are not displayed in primary key order until you either close and reopen the table or switch between views.

7. Click the **Close 'Visit'** button ☒ on the object tab (see Figure 1-16 for the location of this button). The Visit table closes, and the main portion of the Access window is now blank because no database object is currently open. The Riverview database file is still open, as indicated by the filename in the Access window title bar.

Opening a Table

The tables in a database are listed in the Navigation Pane. You open a table, or any Access object, by double-clicking the object name in the Navigation Pane. Next, you'll open the Visit table so you can see all the records you've entered in the correct primary key order.

To open the Visit table:

▶ **1.** On the Navigation Pane, click the **Shutter Bar Open/Close Button** 〉〉 to open the pane. Note that the Visit table is listed.

▶ **2.** Double-click **Visit** to open the table in Datasheet view. See Figure 1-17.

| Figure 1-17 | Table with 10 records entered and displayed in primary key order |

The two records you added, with VisitID field values of 1036 and 1152, now appear in the correct primary key order. The table now contains a total of 10 records, as indicated by the Current Record box at the bottom of the datasheet. The **Current Record box** displays the number of the current record as well as the total number of records in the table.

Each record contains a unique VisitID value because this field is the primary key. Other fields, however, can contain the same value in multiple records; for example, note the four values of "Vaccinations" in the Reason field.

Closing a Table and Exiting Access

When you are finished working in an Access table, it's a good idea to close the table so that you do not make unintended changes to the table data. You can close a table by clicking its Close button on the object tab, as you did earlier. Or, if you want to close the Access program as well, you can click the program's Close button. When you do, any open tables are closed, the active database is closed, and you exit the Access program.

TIP

To close a database without exiting Access, click the File tab to display Backstage view, and then click Close.

To close the Visit table and exit Access:

1. Click the **Close** button ☒ on the program window title bar. The Visit table and the Riverview database close, and then the Access program closes.

INSIGHT

Saving a Database

Unlike the Save buttons in other Office programs, the Save button on the Quick Access Toolbar in Access does not save the active document (database). Instead, you use the Save button to save the design of an Access object, such as a table (as you saw earlier), or to save datasheet format changes, such as resizing columns. Access does not have a button or option you can use to save the active database.

Access saves changes to the active database automatically when you change or add a record or close the database. If your database is stored on a removable storage device, such as a USB drive, you should never remove the device while the database file is open. If you do, Access will encounter problems when it tries to save the database, which might damage the database. Make sure you close the database first before removing the storage device.

Now that you've become familiar with database concepts and Access, and created the Riverview database and the Visit table, Kimberly wants you to add more records to the table and work with the data stored in it to create database objects including a query, form, and report. You'll complete these tasks in the next session.

REVIEW

Session 1.1 Quick Check

1. A(n) _____ is a single characteristic of a person, place, object, event, or idea.

2. You connect the records in two separate tables through a(n) _____ that appears in both tables.

3. The _____, whose values uniquely identify each record in a table, is called a(n) _____ when it is placed in a second table to form a relationship between the two tables.

4. The _____ is the area of the Access window that lists all the objects in a database, and it is the main control center for opening and working with database objects.

5. What is the name of the field that Access creates, by default, as the primary key field for a new table in Datasheet view?

6. Which group on the Fields tab contains the options you use to add new fields to a table?

7. What does a pencil symbol at the beginning of a record represent? What does a star symbol represent?

8. Explain how the saving process in Access is different from saving in other Office programs.

Session 1.2 Visual Overview:

The Create tab provides options for creating various database objects, including tables, forms, and reports. The options appear on the tab grouped by object type.

The Forms group contains options for creating a form, which is a database object you use to enter, edit, and view records in a database.

The Query Wizard button opens a dialog box with different types of wizards that guide you through the steps to create a query. One of these, the Simple Query Wizard, allows you to select records and fields quickly to display in the query results.

You use the options in the Tables group to create a table in Datasheet view or in Design view.

The Form tool quickly creates a form containing all the fields in the table (or query) on which you're basing the form.

The Form Wizard guides you through the process of creating a form.

The Queries group contains options for creating a query, which is a question you ask about the data stored in a database. In response to a query, Access displays the specific records and fields that answer your question.

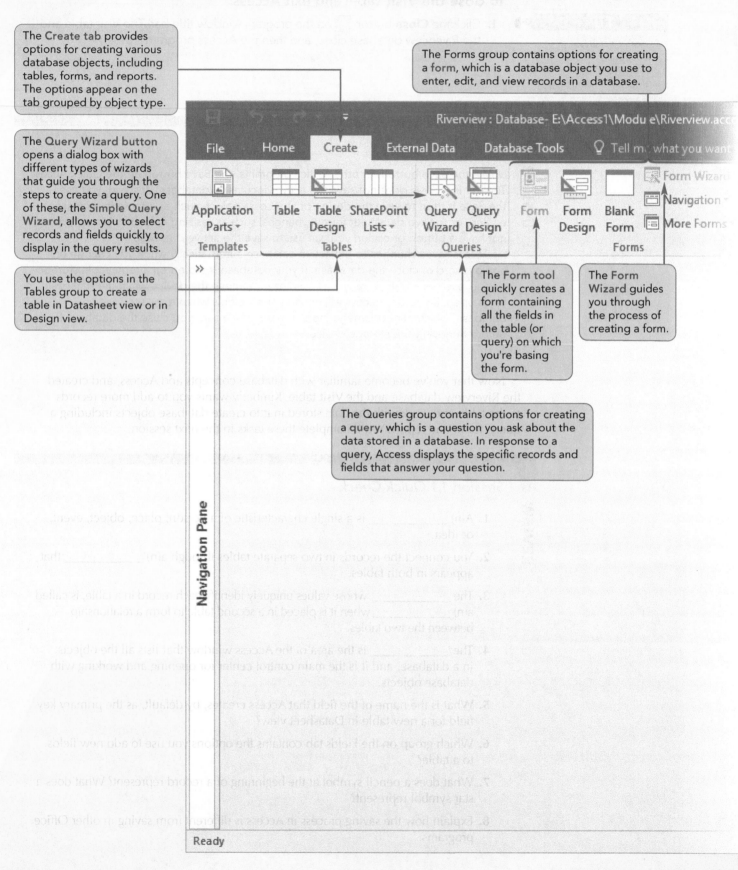

The Create Tab Options

The Reports group contains options for creating a **report**, which is a formatted printout (or screen display) of the contents of one of more tables (or queries) in a database.

The Microsoft Access Help button opens the **Access 2016 Help** window, where you can find information about Access commands and features as well as instructions for using them.

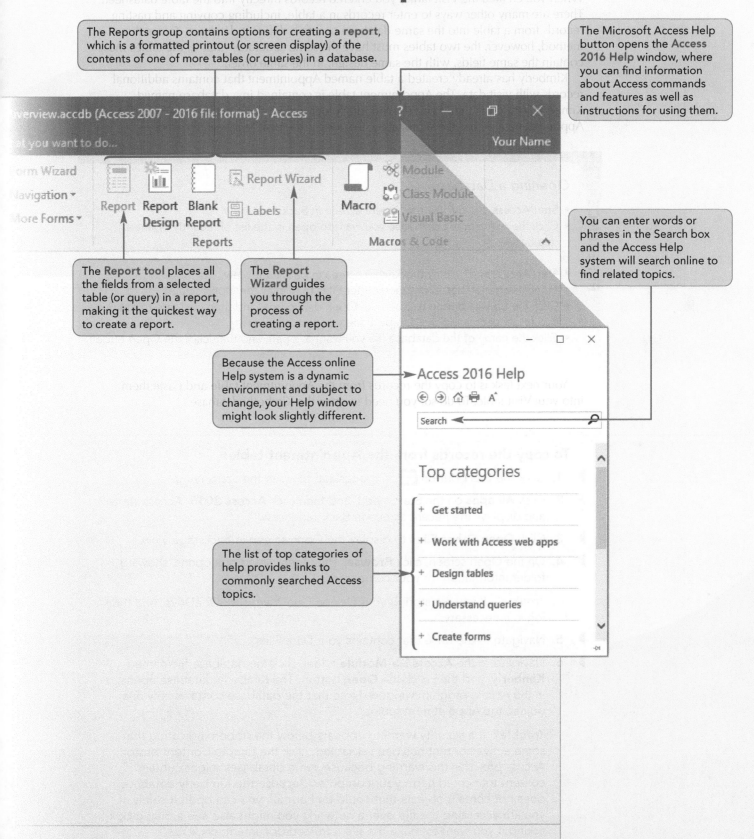

The **Report tool** places all the fields from a selected table (or query) in a report, making it the quickest way to create a report.

The **Report Wizard** guides you through the process of creating a report.

You can enter words or phrases in the Search box and the Access Help system will search online to find related topics.

Because the Access online Help system is a dynamic environment and subject to change, your Help window might look slightly different.

The list of top categories of help provides links to commonly searched Access topics.

Copying Records from Another Access Database

When you created the Visit table, you entered records directly into the table datasheet. There are many other ways to enter records in a table, including copying and pasting records from a table into the same database or into a different database. To use this method, however, the two tables must have the same structure—that is, the tables must contain the same fields, with the same design, in the same order.

Kimberly has already created a table named Appointment that contains additional records with visit data. The Appointment table is contained in a database named Kimberly located in the Access1 > Module folder included with your Data Files. The Appointment table has the same table structure as the Visit table you created.

REFERENCE

Opening a Database

- Start Access and display the Recent screen in Backstage view.
- Click the name of the database you want to open in the list of recently opened databases.

or

- Start Access and display the Recent screen in Backstage view.
- In the navigation bar, click Open Other Files to display the Open screen.
- Click the Browse button to open the Open dialog box, and then navigate to the drive and folder containing the database file you want to open.
- Click the name of the database file you want to open, and then click the Open button.

Your next task is to copy the records from the Appointment table and paste them into your Visit table. To do so, you need to open the Kimberly database.

To copy the records from the Appointment table:

▶ **1.** Click the **Start** button ⊞ on the taskbar to open the Start menu.

▶ **2.** Click **All apps** on the Start menu, and then click **Access 2016**. Access starts and displays the Recent screen in Backstage view.

▶ **3.** Click **Open Other Files** to display the Open screen in Backstage view.

▶ **4.** On the Open screen, click **Browse**. The Open dialog box opens, showing folder information for your computer.

   Trouble? If you are storing your files on OneDrive, click OneDrive, and then log in if necessary.

▶ **5.** Navigate to the drive that contains your Data Files.

▶ **6.** Navigate to the **Access1 > Module** folder, click the database file named **Kimberly**, and then click the **Open** button. The Kimberly database opens in the Access program window. Note that the database contains only one object, the Appointment table.

   Trouble? If a security warning appears below the ribbon indicating that some active content has been disabled, click the Enable Content button. Access provides this warning because some databases might contain content that could harm your computer. Because the Kimberly database does not contain objects that could be harmful, you can open it safely. If you are accessing the file over a network, you might also see a dialog box asking if you want to make the file a trusted document; click Yes.

7. In the Navigation Pane, double-click **Appointment** to open the Appointment table in Datasheet view. The table contains 65 records and the same five fields, with the same characteristics, as the fields in the Visit table. See Figure 1-18.

| Figure 1-18 | Appointment table in the Kimberly database |

Kimberly wants you to copy all the records in the Appointment table. You can select all the records by clicking the **datasheet selector**, which is the box to the left of the first field name in the table datasheet, as shown in Figure 1-18.

8. Click the **datasheet selector** to the left of the VisitID field. All the records in the table are selected.

9. On the Home tab, in the Clipboard group, click the **Copy** button. All the records are copied to the Clipboard.

10. Click the **Close 'Appointment'** button ☒ on the object tab. A dialog box opens asking if you want to save the data you copied to the Clipboard. This dialog box opens only when you copy a large amount of data to the Clipboard.

11. Click the **Yes** button. The dialog box closes, and then the Appointment table closes.

With the records copied to the Clipboard, you can now paste them into the Visit table. First you need to close the Kimberly database while still keeping the Access program open, and then open the Riverview database.

To close the Kimberly database and then paste the records into the Visit table:

1. Click the **File** tab to open Backstage view, and then click **Close** in the navigation bar to close the Kimberly database. You return to a blank Access program window, and the Home tab is the active tab on the ribbon.

2. Click the **File** tab to return to Backstage view, and then click **Open** in the navigation bar. Recent is selected on the Open screen, and the recently opened database files are listed. This list should include the Riverview database.

3. Click **Riverview** to open the Riverview database file.

   Trouble? If the Riverview database file is not in the list of recent files, click Browse. In the Open dialog box, navigate to the drive and folder where you are storing your files, and then open the Riverview database file.

   Trouble? If the security warning appears below the ribbon, click the Enable Content button, and then, if necessary, click Yes to identify the file as a trusted document.

4. In the Navigation Pane, double-click **Visit** to open the Visit table in Datasheet view.

5. On the Navigation Pane, click the **Shutter Bar Open/Close Button** ⟪ to close the pane.

6. Position the pointer on the star symbol in the row selector for row 11 (the next row available for a new record) until the pointer changes to ➡, and then click to select the row.

7. On the Home tab, in the Clipboard group, click the **Paste** button. The pasted records are added to the table, and a dialog box opens asking you to confirm that you want to paste all the records (65 total).

   Trouble? If the Paste button isn't active, click the ➡ pointer on the row selector for row 11, making sure the entire row is selected, and then repeat Step 7.

8. Click the **Yes** button. The dialog box closes, and the pasted records are selected. See Figure 1-19. Notice that the table now contains a total of 75 records—10 records that you entered previously and 65 records that you copied and pasted.

Figure 1-19   Visit table after copying and pasting records

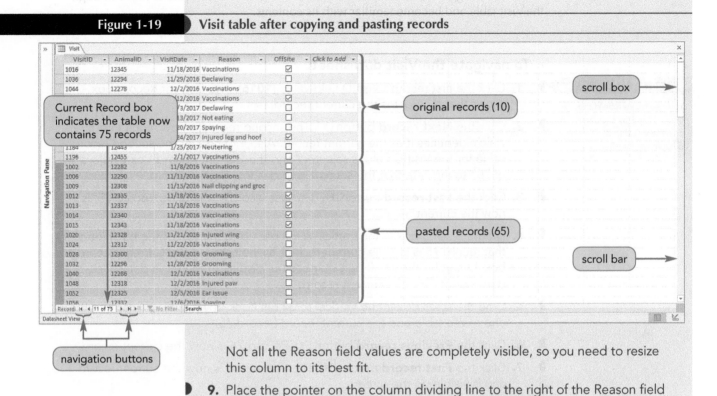

Not all the Reason field values are completely visible, so you need to resize this column to its best fit.

9. Place the pointer on the column dividing line to the right of the Reason field name until the pointer changes to ↔, and then double-click the column dividing line. The Reason field values are now fully displayed.

Navigating a Datasheet

The Visit table now contains 75 records, but only some of the records are visible on the screen. To view fields or records not currently visible on the screen, you can use the horizontal and vertical scroll bars to navigate the data. The **navigation buttons**, shown in Figure 1-19 and also described in Figure 1-20, provide another way to move vertically through the records. The Current Record box appears between the two sets of navigation buttons and displays the number of the current record as well as the total number of records in the table. Figure 1-20 shows which record becomes the current record when you click each navigation button. Note the New (blank) record button, which works in the same way as the New button on the Home tab you used earlier to enter a new record in the table.

Figure 1-20   Navigation buttons

Navigation Button	Record Selected	Navigation Button	Record Selected
⏮	First record	⏭	Last record
◀	Previous record	⏭▸	New (blank) record
▶	Next record		

Kimberly suggests that you use the various navigation techniques to move through the Visit table and become familiar with its contents.

To navigate the Visit datasheet:

TIP

You can make a field the current field by clicking anywhere within the column for that field.

1. Click the first record's VisitID field value (**1016**). The Current Record box shows that record 1 is the current record.

2. Click the **Next record** button ▶. The second record is now highlighted, which identifies it as the current record. Also, notice that the second record's value for the VisitID field is selected, and the Current Record box displays "2 of 75" to indicate that the second record is the current record.

3. Click the **Last record** button ▶|. The last record in the table, record 75, is now the current record.

4. Drag the scroll box in the vertical scroll bar up to the top of the bar. Notice that record 75 is still the current record, as indicated in the Current Record box. Dragging the scroll box changes the display of the table datasheet, but does not change the current record.

5. Drag the scroll box in the vertical scroll bar back down until you can see the end of the table and the current record (record 75).

6. Click the **Previous record** button ◀. Record 74 is now the current record.

7. Click the **First record** button |◀. The first record is now the current record and is visible on the screen.

   Earlier you resized the Reason column to its best fit, to ensure all the field values were visible. However, when you resize a column to its best fit, the column expands to fully display only the field values that are visible on the screen at that time. If you move through the complete datasheet and notice that not all of the field values are fully displayed after conducting the resizing process on the records initially visible, you need to repeat the resizing process.

8. Scroll down through the records and observe if the field values are fully displayed. In this case, all of the fields are fully visible, so there is no need to resize any of the field columns.

The Visit table now contains all the data about animal visits for Riverview Veterinary Care Center. To better understand how to work with this data, Kimberly asks you to create simple objects for the other main types of database objects—queries, forms, and reports.

Creating a Simple Query

As noted earlier, a query is a question you ask about the data stored in a database. When you create a query, you tell Access which fields you need and what criteria it should use to select the records that will answer your question. Then Access displays only the information you want, so you don't have to navigate through the entire database for the information. In the Visit table, for example, Kimberly might create a query to display only those records for visits that occurred in a specific month. Even though a query can display table information in a different way, the information still exists in the table as it was originally entered.

Kimberly wants to see a list of all the visit dates and reasons for visits in the Visit table. She doesn't want the list to include all the fields in the table, such as AnimalID and OffSite. To produce this list for Kimberly, you'll use the Simple Query Wizard to create a query based on the Visit table.

To start the Simple Query Wizard:

▶ **1.** On the ribbon, click the **Create** tab.

▶ **2.** In the Queries group, click the **Query Wizard** button. The New Query dialog box opens.

▶ **3.** Make sure **Simple Query Wizard** is selected, and then click the **OK** button. The first Simple Query Wizard dialog box opens. See Figure 1-21.

| **Figure 1-21** | First Simple Query Wizard dialog box |

Because the Visit table is the only object in the Riverview database, it is listed in the Tables/Queries box by default. If the database contained more objects, you could click the Tables/Queries arrow and choose another table or a query as the basis for the new query you are creating. The Available Fields box lists all the fields in the Visit table.

You need to select fields from the Available Fields box to include them in the query. To select fields one at a time, click a field and then click the | > | button. The selected field moves from the Available Fields box on the left to the Selected Fields box on the right. To select all the fields, click the | >> | button. If you change your mind or make a mistake, you can remove a field by clicking it in the Selected Fields box and then clicking the | < | button. To remove all fields from the Selected Fields box, click the | << | button.

Each Simple Query Wizard dialog box contains buttons on the bottom that allow you to move to the previous dialog box (Back button), move to the next dialog box (Next button), or cancel the creation process (Cancel button). You can also finish creating the object (Finish button) and accept the wizard's defaults for the remaining options.

Kimberly wants her query results to list to include data from only the following fields: VisitID, VisitDate, and Reason. You need to select these fields to include them in the query.

To create the query using the Simple Query Wizard:

TIP

You can also double-click a field to move it from the Available Fields box to the Selected Fields box.

1. Click **VisitID** in the Available Fields box to select the field (if necessary), and then click the | **>** | button. The VisitID field moves to the Selected Fields box.

2. Repeat Step 1 for the fields **VisitDate** and **Reason**, and then click the **Next** button. The second, and final, Simple Query Wizard dialog box opens and asks you to choose a name (title) for your query. The suggested name is "Visit Query" because the query you are creating is based on the Visit table. You'll change the suggested name to "VisitList."

3. Click at the end of the suggested name, use the **Backspace** key to delete the word "Query" and the space, and then type **List**. Now you can view the query results.

4. Click the **Finish** button to complete the query. The query results are displayed in Datasheet view, on a new tab named "VisitList." A query datasheet is similar to a table datasheet, showing fields in columns and records in rows—but only for those fields and records you want to see, as determined by the query specifications you select.

5. Place the pointer on the column divider line to the right of the Reason field name until the pointer changes to ✛, and then double-click the column divider line to resize the Reason field. See Figure 1-22.

Figure 1-22 **Query results**

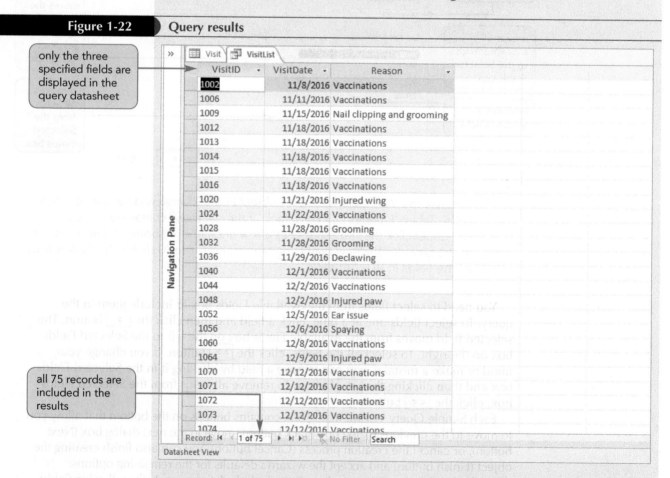

only the three specified fields are displayed in the query datasheet

all 75 records are included in the results

The VisitList query datasheet displays the three fields in the order you selected them in the Simple Query Wizard, from left to right. The records are listed in order by the primary key field, VisitID. Even though the query datasheet displays only the three fields you chose for the query, the Visit table still includes all the fields for all records.

Notice that the navigation buttons are located at the bottom of the window. You navigate a query datasheet in the same way that you navigate a table datasheet.

▶ **6.** Click the **Last record** button ▶|. The last record in the query datasheet is now the current record.

▶ **7.** Click the **Previous record** button ◀. Record 74 in the query datasheet is now the current record.

▶ **8.** Click the **First record** button |◀. The first record is now the current record.

▶ **9.** Click the **Close 'VisitList'** button ✕ on the object tab. A dialog box opens asking if you want to save the changes to the layout of the query. This dialog box opens because you resized the Reason column.

▶ **10.** Click the **Yes** button to save the query layout changes and close the query.

The query results are not stored in the database; however, the query design is stored as part of the database with the name you specified. You can re-create the query results at any time by opening the query again. When you open the query at a later date, the results displayed will reflect up-to-date information to include any new records entered in the Visit table.

Next, Kimberly asks you to create a form for the Visit table so that Riverview Veterinary Care Center staff can use the form to enter and work with data in the table easily.

Creating a Simple Form

As noted earlier, you use a form to enter, edit, and view records in a database. Although you can perform these same functions with tables and queries, forms can present data in many customized and useful ways.

Kimberly wants a form for the Visit table that shows all the fields for one record at a time, with fields listed one below another in a column. This type of form will make it easier for her staff to focus on all the data for a particular visit. You'll use the Form tool to create this form quickly and easily.

To create the form using the Form tool:

▶ **1.** Make sure the Visit table is still open in Datasheet view. The table or other database object you're using as the basis for the form must either be open or selected in the Navigation Pane when you use the Form tool.

Trouble? If the Visit table is not open, click the Shutter Bar Open/Close Button ≫ to open the Navigation Pane. Then double-click Visit to open the Visit table in Datasheet view. Click the Shutter Bar Open/Close Button ≪ to close the pane.

▶ **2.** On the ribbon, click the **Create** tab if necessary.

3. In the Forms group, click the **Form** button. The Form tool creates a simple form showing every field in the Visit table and places it on a tab named "Visit" because the form is based on the Visit table. See Figure 1-23.

Figure 1-23   **Form created by the Form tool**

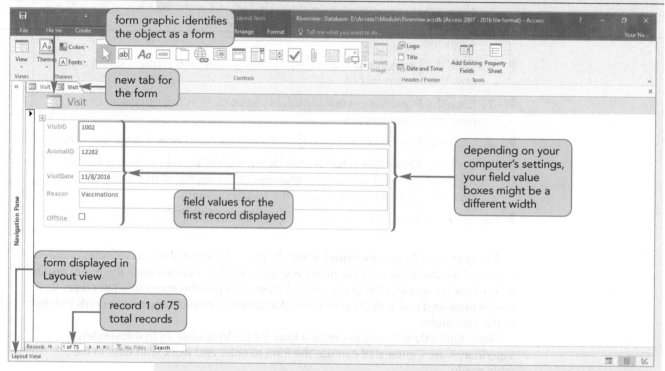

> form graphic identifies the object as a form

> new tab for the form

> field values for the first record displayed

> depending on your computer's settings, your field value boxes might be a different width

> form displayed in Layout view

> record 1 of 75 total records

Trouble? Depending on the size of your monitor and your screen resolution settings, the fields in your form might appear in multiple columns instead of a single column. This difference will not present any problems.

The form displays one record at a time in the Visit table, providing another view of the data that is stored in the table and allowing you to focus on the values for one record. Access displays the field values for the first record in the table and selects the first field value (VisitID) as indicated by the border that appears around the value. Each field name appears on a separate line and on the same line as its field value, which appears in a box to the right. Depending on your computer's settings, the field value boxes in your form might be wider or narrower than those shown in the figure. As indicated in the status bar, the form is displayed in Layout view. In **Layout view**, you can make design changes to the form while it is displaying data, so that you can see the effects of the changes you make immediately.

To view, enter, and maintain data using a form, you must know how to move from field to field and from record to record. Notice that the form contains navigation buttons, similar to those available in Datasheet view, which you can use to display different records in the form. You'll use these now to navigate the form; then you'll save and close the form.

To navigate, save, and close the form:

▶ 1. Click the **Next record** button ▶. The form now displays the values for the second record in the Visit table.

▶ 2. Click the **Last record** button ▶| to move to the last record in the table. The form displays the information for VisitID 1196.

▶ 3. Click the **Previous record** button ◀ to move to record 74.

▶ 4. Click the **First record** button |◀ to return to the first record in the Visit table.

▶ 5. Next, you'll save the form with the name "VisitData" in the Riverview database. Then the form will be available for later use.

▶ 6. On the Quick Access Toolbar, click the **Save** button 🔲. The Save As dialog box opens.

▶ 7. In the Form Name box, click at the end of the selected name "Visit," type **Data**, and then press the **Enter** key. The dialog box closes and the form is saved as VisitData in the Riverview database. The tab containing the form now displays the name VisitData.

▶ 8. Click the **Close 'VisitData'** button ☒ on the object tab to close the form.

INSIGHT

Saving Database Objects

In general, it is best to save a database object—query, form, or report—only if you anticipate using the object frequently or if it is time-consuming to create, because all objects use storage space and increase the size of the database file. For example, you most likely would not save a form you created with the Form tool because you can re-create it easily with one mouse click. (However, for the purposes of this text, you usually need to save the objects you create.)

Kimberly would like to see the information in the Visit table presented in a more readable and professional format. You'll help Kimberly by creating a report.

Creating a Simple Report

As noted earlier, a report is a formatted printout (or screen display) of the contents of one or more tables or queries. You'll use the Report tool to quickly produce a report based on the Visit table for Kimberly. The Report tool creates a report based on the selected table or query.

To create the report using the Report tool:

▶ 1. On the ribbon, click the **Create** tab.

▶ 2. In the Reports group, click the **Report** button. The Report tool creates a simple report showing every field in the Visit table and places it on a tab named "Visit" because the object you created (the report) is based on the Visit table. See Figure 1-24.

Figure 1-24   **Report created by the Report tool**

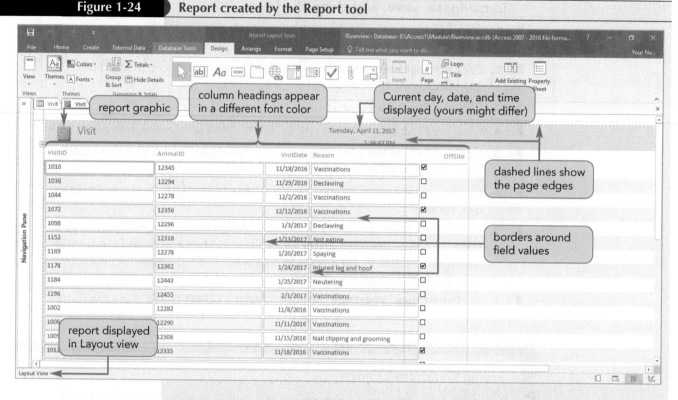

Trouble? The records in your report might appear in a different order from the records shown in Figure 1-24. This difference will not cause any problems.

The report shows each field in a column, with the field values for each record in a row, similar to a table or query datasheet. However, the report offers a more visually appealing format for the data, with the column headings in a different color, borders around each field value, a graphic of a report at the top left, and the current day, date, and time at the top right. Also notice the dashed horizontal and vertical lines on the top and right, respectively; these lines mark the edges of the page and show where text will print on the page.

The report needs some design changes to better display the data. The columns are much wider than necessary for the VisitID and AnimalID fields, and the Reason and OffSite field values and borders are not completely displayed within the page area defined by the dashed lines, which means they would not appear on the same page as the rest of the fields in the printed report. You can resize the columns easily in Layout view.

To resize the VisitID and AnimalID columns:

1. Position the pointer on the right border of any field value in the VisitID column until the pointer changes to ↔.

2. Click and drag the mouse to the left. Notice the dark outlines surrounding the field names and field values indicating the changing column width.

3. Drag to the left until the column is slightly wider than the VisitID field name, and then release the mouse button. The VisitID column is now narrower, and the other four columns have shifted to the left. The Reason and OffSite fields, values, and borders are now completely within the page area. See Figure 1-25.

Figure 1-25	Report after resizing the VisitID column

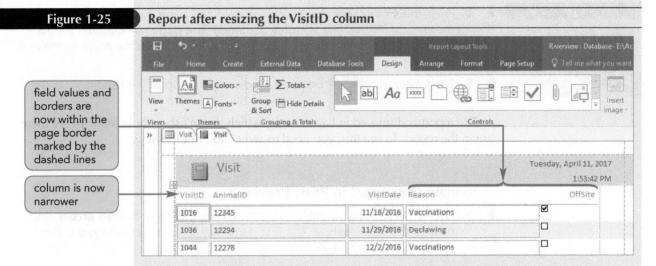

field values and borders are now within the page border marked by the dashed lines

column is now narrower

4. Click the first field value for AnimalID. AnimalID is now the current field.

5. Position the pointer on the right border of the first value in the AnimalID column until the pointer changes to ↔, click and drag to the left until the column is slightly wider than its field name, and then release the mouse button.

6. Drag the scroll box on the vertical scroll bar down to the bottom of the report to check its entire layout.

   The Report tool displays the number "75" at the bottom left of the report, showing the total number of records in the report and the table on which it is based—the Visit table. The Report tool also displays the page number at the bottom right, but the text "Page 1 of 1" appears cut off through the vertical dashed line. This will cause a problem when you print the report, so you need to move this text to the left.

7. Click anywhere on the words **Page 1 of 1**. An orange outline appears around the text, indicating it is selected. See Figure 1-26.

Figure 1-26	Report page number selected

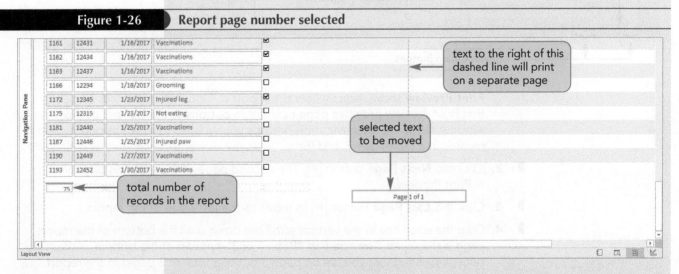

text to the right of this dashed line will print on a separate page

selected text to be moved

total number of records in the report

With the text selected, you can use the keyboard arrow keys to move it.

TIP

You can also use the mouse to drag the selected page number, but the arrow key is more precise.

8. Press the ← key repeatedly until the selected page number is to the left of the vertical dashed line (roughly 35 times). The page number text is now completely within the page area and will print on the same page as the rest of the report.

9. Drag the vertical scroll box up to redisplay the top of the report.

The report is displayed in Layout view, which doesn't show how many pages there are in the report. To see this, you need to switch to Print Preview.

To view the report in Print Preview:

1. On the Design tab, in the Views group, click the **View button arrow**, and then click **Print Preview**. The first page of the report is displayed in Print Preview. See Figure 1-27.

Figure 1-27 First page of the report in Print Preview

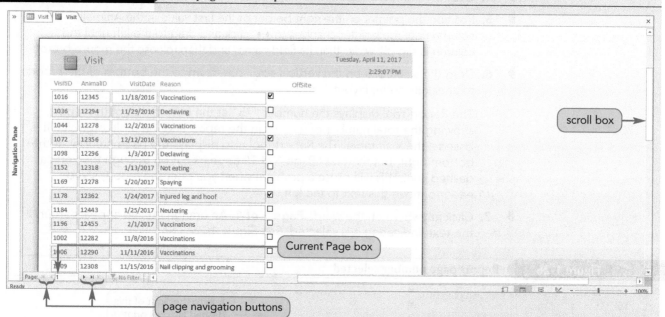

Print Preview shows exactly how the report will look when printed. Notice that Print Preview provides page navigation buttons at the bottom of the window, similar to the navigation buttons you've used to move through records in a table, query, and form.

2. Click the **Next Page** button ▶. The second page of the report is displayed in Print Preview.

3. Click the **Last Page** button ▶| to move to the last page of the report.

4. Drag the scroll box in the vertical scroll bar down until the bottom of the report page is displayed. The notation "Page 3 of 3" appears at the bottom of the page, indicating that you are on page 3 out of a total of 3 pages in the report.

Trouble? Depending on the printer you are using, your report might have more or fewer pages, and some of the pages might be blank. If so, don't worry. Different printers format reports in different ways, sometimes affecting the total number of pages and the number of records printed per page.

5. Click the **First Page** button ⏮ to return to the first page of the report, and then drag the scroll box in the vertical scroll bar up to display the top of the report.

Next you'll save the report as VisitDetails, and then print it.

6. On the Quick Access Toolbar, click the **Save** button 🖫. The Save As dialog box opens.

7. In the Report Name box, click at the end of the selected word "Visit," type **Details**, and then press the **Enter** key. The dialog box closes and the report is saved as VisitDetails in the Riverview database. The tab containing the report now displays the name "VisitDetails."

Printing a Report

After creating a report, you might need to print it to distribute it to others who need to view the report's contents. You can print a report without changing any print settings, or display the Print dialog box and select options for printing.

REFERENCE

Printing a Report

- Open the report in any view, or select the report in the Navigation Pane.
- Click the File tab to display Backstage view, click Print, and then click Quick Print to print the report with the default print settings.

or

- Open the report in any view, or select the report in the Navigation Pane.
- Click the File tab, click Print, and then click Print (or, if the report is displayed in Print Preview, click the Print button in the Print group on the Print Preview tab). The Print dialog box opens, in which you can select the options you want for printing the report.

Kimberly asks you to print the entire report with the default settings, so you'll use the Quick Print option in Backstage view.
Note: To complete the following steps, your computer must be connected to a printer. Check with your instructor first to see if you should print the report.

To print the report and then close it:

1. On the ribbon, click the **File** tab to open Backstage view.

2. In the navigation bar, click **Print** to display the Print screen, and then click **Quick Print**. The report prints with the default print settings, and you return to the report in Print Preview.

Trouble? If your report did not print, make sure that your computer is connected to a printer, and that the printer is turned on and ready to print. Then repeat Steps 1 and 2.

3. Click the **Close 'VisitDetails'** button ☒ on the object tab to close the report.

4. Click the **Close 'Visit'** button ☒ on the object tab to close the Visit table.

Trouble? If you are asked to save changes to the layout of the table, click the Yes button.

You can also use the Print dialog box to print other database objects, such as table and query datasheets. Most often, these objects are used for viewing and entering data, and reports are used for printing the data in a database.

Viewing Objects in the Navigation Pane

The Riverview database now contains four objects—the Visit table, the VisitList query, the VisitData form, and the VisitDetails report. When you work with the database file—such as closing it, opening it, or distributing it to others—the file includes all the objects you created and saved in the database. You can view and work with these objects in the Navigation Pane.

To view the objects in the Riverview database:

> **1.** On the Navigation Pane, click the **Shutter Bar Open/Close Button** ≫ to open the pane. See Figure 1-28.

Figure 1-28 **First page of the report in Print Preview**

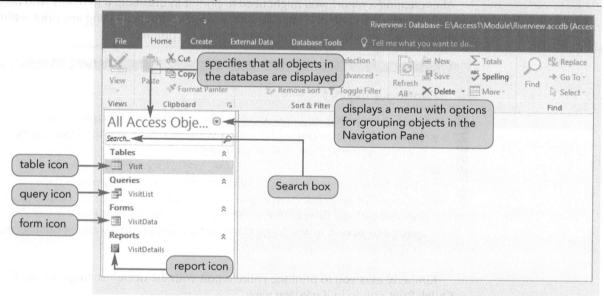

The Navigation Pane currently displays the default category, **All Access Objects**, which lists all the database objects in the pane. Each object type (Tables, Queries, Forms, and Reports) appears in its own group. Each database object (the Visit table, the VisitList query, the VisitData form, and the VisitDetails report) has a unique icon to its left to indicate the type of object. This makes it easy for you to identify the objects and choose which one you want to open and work with.

The arrow on the All Access Objects bar displays a menu with options for various ways to group and display objects in the Navigation Pane. The Search box enables you to enter text for Access to find; for example, you could search for all objects that contain the word "Visit" in their names. Note that Access searches for objects only in the categories and groups currently displayed in the Navigation Pane.

As you continue to build the Riverview database and add more objects to it in later modules, you'll use the options in the Navigation Pane to manage those objects.

Using Microsoft Access Help

Access includes a Help system you can use to search for information about specific program features. You start Help by clicking the Microsoft Access Help button in the top right of the Access window, or by pressing the F1 key.

You'll use Help now to learn more about the Navigation Pane.

To search for information about the Navigation Pane in Help:

TIP

You can also get help by typing keywords in the Tell Me box on the ribbon to access information about topics related to those words in the Access Help window.

1. Click the **Microsoft Access Help** button [?] on the title bar. The Access 2016 Help window opens, as shown earlier in the Session 1.2 Visual Overview.

2. Click in the **Search** box, type **Navigation Pane**, and then press the **Enter** key. The Access 2016 Help window displays a list of topics related to the Navigation Pane.

3. Click the topic **Manage Access database objects in the Navigation Pane**. The Access Help window displays the article you selected. See Figure 1-29.

Figure 1-29	Article displayed in the Access Help window

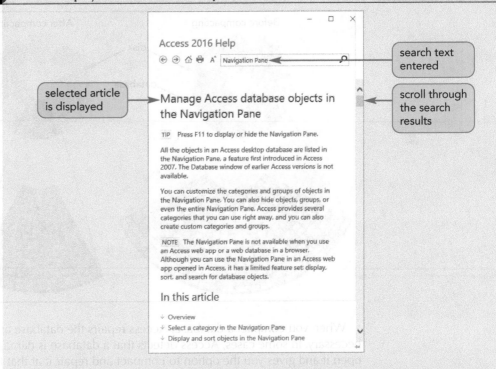

4. Scroll through the article to read detailed information about working with the Navigation Pane.

Trouble? If the article on managing database objects is not listed in your Help window, choose another article related to the Navigation Pane to read.

5. When finished, click the **Close** button [X] on the Access 2016 Help window to close it.

The Access Help system is an important reference tool for you to use if you need additional information about databases in general, details about specific Access features, or support with problems you might encounter.

Managing a Database

One of the main tasks involved in working with database software is managing your databases and the data they contain. Some of the activities involved in database management include compacting and repairing a database and backing up and restoring a database. By managing your databases, you can ensure that they operate in the most efficient way, that the data they contain is secure, and that you can work with the data effectively.

Compacting and Repairing a Database

Whenever you open an Access database and work in it, the size of the database increases. Further, when you delete records or when you delete or replace database objects—such as queries, forms, and reports—the storage space that had been occupied by the deleted or replaced records or objects does not automatically become available for other records or objects. To make the space available, and also to increase the speed of data retrieval, you must compact the database. **Compacting** a database rearranges the data and objects in a database to decrease its file size, thereby making more storage space available and enhancing the performance of the database. Figure 1-30 illustrates the compacting process.

Figure 1-30   **Compacting a database**

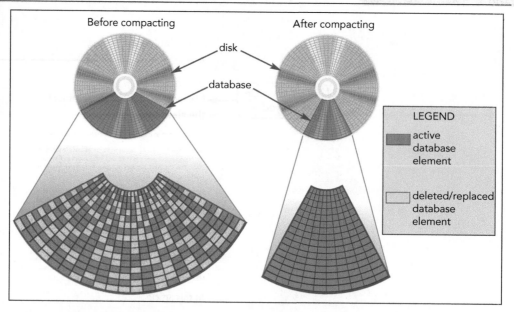

When you compact a database, Access repairs the database at the same time, if necessary. In some cases, Access detects that a database is damaged when you try to open it and gives you the option to compact and repair it at that time. For example, the data in your database might become damaged, or corrupted, if you exit the Access program suddenly by turning off your computer. If you think your database might be damaged because it is behaving unpredictably, you can use the Compact & Repair Database option to fix it.

REFERENCE

Compacting and Repairing a Database

- Make sure the database file you want to compact and repair is open.
- Click the File tab to display the Info screen in Backstage view.
- Click the Compact & Repair Database button.

Access also allows you to set an option to compact and repair a database file automatically every time you close it. The Compact on Close option is available in the Current Database section of the Access Options dialog box, which you open from

Backstage view by clicking the Options command in the navigation bar. By default, the Compact on Close option is turned off.

Next, you'll compact the Riverview database manually using the Compact & Repair Database option. This will make the database smaller and allow you to work with it more efficiently. After compacting the database, you'll close it.

To compact and repair the Riverview database:

▶ **1.** On the ribbon, click the **File** tab to open the Info screen in Backstage view.

▶ **2.** Click the **Compact & Repair Database** button. Although nothing visible happens on the screen, the Riverview database is compacted, making it smaller, and repairs it at the same time. The Home tab is again the active tab on the ribbon.

▶ **3.** Click the **File** tab to return to Backstage view, and then click **Close** in the navigation bar. The Riverview database closes.

Backing Up and Restoring a Database

Backing up a database is the process of making a copy of the database file to protect your database against loss or damage. The Back Up Database command enables you to back up your database file from within the Access program, while you are working on your database. To use this option, click the File tab to display the Info screen in Backstage view, click Save As in the navigation bar, click Back Up Database in the Advanced section of the Save Database As pane, and then click the Save As button. In the Save As dialog box that opens, a default filename is provided for the backup copy that consists of the same filename as the database you are backing up (for example, "Riverview"), and an underscore character, plus the current date. This filenaming system makes it easy for you to keep track of your database backups and when they were created. To restore a backup database file, you simply copy the backup from the location where it is stored to your hard drive, or whatever device you use to work in Access, and start working with the restored database file. (You will not actually back up the Riverview database in this module unless directed by your instructor to do so.)

Planning and Performing Database Backups

INSIGHT

Experienced database users make it a habit to back up a database before they work with it for the first time, keeping the original data intact. They also make frequent backups while continuing to work with a database; these backups are generally on flash drives, recordable CDs or DVDs, external or network hard drives, or cloud-based storage (such as OneDrive). Also, it is recommended to store the backup copy in a different location from the original. For example, if the original database is stored on a flash drive, you should not store the backup copy on the same flash drive. If you lose the drive or the drive is damaged, you would lose both the original database and its backup copy.

If the original database file and the backup copy have the same name, restoring the backup copy might replace the original. If you want to save the original file, rename it before you restore the backup copy. To ensure that the restored database has the most current data, you should update the restored database with any changes made to the original between the time you created the backup copy and the time the original database became damaged or lost.

By properly planning for and performing backups, you can avoid losing data and prevent the time-consuming effort required to rebuild a lost or damaged database.

Decision Making: When to Use Access vs. Excel

Using a spreadsheet application like Microsoft Excel to manage lists or tables of information works well when the data is simple, such as a list of contacts or tasks. As soon as the data becomes complex enough to separate into tables that need to be related, you start to see the limitations of using a spreadsheet application. The strength of a database application such as Access is in its ability to easily relate one table of information to another. Consider a table of contacts that includes home addresses, with a separate row for each person living at the same address. When an address changes, it's too easy to make a mistake and not update the home address for each person who lives there. To ensure you have the most accurate data at all times, it's important to have only one instance of each piece of data. By creating separate tables that are related and keeping only one instance of each piece of data, you'll ensure the integrity of the data. Trying to accomplish this in Excel is a complex process, whereas Access is specifically designed for this functionality.

Another limitation of using Excel instead of Access to manage data has to do with the volume of data. Although a spreadsheet can hold thousands of records, a database can hold millions. A spreadsheet containing thousands of pieces of information is cumbersome to use. Think of large-scale commercial applications such as enrollment at a college or tracking customers for a large company. It's hard to imagine managing such information in an Excel spreadsheet. Instead, you'd use a database. Finally, with an Access database, multiple users can access the information it contains at the same time. Although an Excel spreadsheet can be shared, there can be problems when users try to open and edit the same spreadsheet at the same time.

When you're trying to decide whether to use Excel or Access, ask yourself the following questions.

1. Do you need to store data in separate tables that are related to each other?
2. Do you have a very large amount of data to store?
3. Will more than one person need to access the data at the same time?

If you answer "yes" to any of these questions, an Access database is most likely the appropriate application to use.

In the following modules, you'll help Kimberly complete and maintain the Riverview database, and you'll use it to meet the specific information needs of the employees of the care center.

Session 1.2 Quick Check

1. To copy the records from a table in one database to another table in a different database, the two tables must have the same _____.

2. A(n) _____ is a question you ask about the data stored in a database.

3. The quickest way to create a form is to use the _____.

4. Which view enables you to see the total number of pages in a report and navigate through the report pages?

5. In the Navigation Pane, each database object has a unique _____ to its left that identifies the object's type.

6. _____ a database rearranges the data and objects in a database to decrease its file size and enhance the speed and performance of the database.

7. _____ a database is the process of making a copy of the database file to protect the database against loss or damage.

Review Assignments

PRACTICE

Data File needed for the Review Assignments: Company.accdb

For Riverview Veterinary Care Center, Kimberly asks you to create a new database to contain information about the vendors that the care center works with to obtain supplies, equipment, and resale items, and the vendors who service and maintain the equipment. Complete the following steps:

1. Create a new, blank database named **Vendor** and save it in the folder where you are storing your files, as specified by your instructor.
2. In Datasheet view for the Table1 table, rename the default ID primary key field to **SupplierID**. Change the data type of the SupplierID field to Short Text.
3. Add the following 10 fields to the new table in the order shown; all of them are Short Text fields *except* InitialContact, which is a Date/Time field: **Company**, **Category**, **Address**, **City**, **State**, **Zip**, **Phone**, **ContactFirst**, **ContactLast**, and **InitialContact**. Resize the columns as necessary so that the complete field names are displayed. Save the table as **Supplier**.
4. Enter the records shown in Figure 1-31 in the Supplier table. For the first record, be sure to enter your first name in the ContactFirst field and your last name in the ContactLast field.
   Note: When entering field values that are shown on multiple lines in the figure, do not try to enter the values on multiple lines. The values are shown on multiple lines in the figure for page spacing purposes only.

Figure 1-31	Supplier table records

SupplierID	Company	Category	Address	City	State	Zip	Phone	ContactFirst	ContactLast	InitialContact
YUM345	Yummy Dog Food	Resale	345 Riverside Dr	Charlotte	NC	28201	704-205-8725	*Student First*	*Student Last*	2/1/2017
FTS123	Flea & Tick Supplies	Resale	123 Overlook Ln	Atlanta	GA	30301	404-341-2981	Robert	Jackson	3/6/2017
PMC019	Pet Medical	Equipment	19 Waverly Ct	Blacksburg	VA	24061	540-702-0098	Julie	Baxter	2/21/2017
APL619	A+ Labs	Equipment	619 West Dr	Omaha	NE	68022	531-219-7206	Jacques	Dupont	4/10/2017
CWI444	Cat World Inc.	Supplies	444 Boxcar Way	San Diego	CA	92110	619-477-9482	Amelia	Kline	5/1/2017

5. Kimberly created a database named Company that contains a Business table with supplier data. The Supplier table you created has the same design as the Business table. Copy all the records from the **Business** table in the **Company** database (located in the Access1 > Review folder provided with your Data Files) and then paste them at the end of the Supplier table in the Vendor database.
6. Resize all datasheet columns to their best fit, and then save the Supplier table.
7. Close the Supplier table, and then use the Navigation Pane to reopen it. Note that the records are displayed in primary key order by the values in the SupplierID field.
8. Use the Simple Query Wizard to create a query that includes the Company, Category, ContactFirst, ContactLast, and Phone fields (in that order) from the Supplier table. Name the query **SupplierList**, and then close the query.
9. Use the Form tool to create a form for the Supplier table. Save the form as **SupplierInfo**, and then close it.

10. Use the Report tool to create a report based on the Supplier table. In Layout view, resize all fields except the Company field, so that each field is slightly wider than the longest entry (either the field name itself or an entry in the field). Display the report in Print Preview and verify that all the fields fit across one page in the report. Save the report as **SupplierDetails**, and then close it.

11. Close the Supplier table, and then compact and repair the Vendor database.

12. Close the Vendor database.

Case Problem 1

APPLY

Data File needed for this Case Problem: BeautyToGo.accdb

Beauty To Go   Sue Miller, an owner of a nail and hair salon in Orlando, Florida, regularly checks in on her grandmother, who resides in a retirement community. On some of her visits, Sue does her grandmother's hair and nails. Her grandmother recently asked if Sue would also be willing to do the hair and nails of some of her friends in her retirement community and other surrounding communities. She said that these friends would happily pay for her services. Sue thinks this is an excellent way to expand her current business and serve the needs of the retirement community at the same time. In discussing the opportunity with some of the members of the retirement community, she found that the ladies would very much like to pay Sue in advance for her services and have them scheduled on a regular basis; however, the frequency and types of the services vary from person to person. Sue decides to come up with different options that would serve the needs of the ladies in the retirement community. Sue wants to use Access to maintain information about the customers and the types of options offered. She needs your help in creating this database. Complete the following:

1. Create a new, blank database named **Beauty** and save it in the folder where you are storing your files, as specified by your instructor.

2. In Datasheet view for the Table1 table, rename the default primary key ID field to **OptionID**. Change the data type of the OptionID field to Short Text.

3. Add the following three fields to the new table in the order shown: **OptionDescription** (a Short Text field), **OptionCost** (a Currency field), and **FeeWaived** (a Yes/No field). Save the table as **Option**.

4. Enter the records shown in Figure 1-32 in the Option table. *Hint*: When entering the OptionCost field values, you do not have to type the dollar signs, commas, or decimal places; they will be entered automatically.

Figure 1-32   **Option table records**

OptionID	OptionDescription	OptionCost	FeeWaived
136	Wash/cut bi-weekly for 6 months	$500.00	Yes
101	Manicure weekly for 1 month	$125.00	No
124	Manicure/pedicure weekly for 3 months	$700.00	Yes
142	Wash/cut/color monthly for 6 months	$600.00	Yes
117	Pedicure bi-weekly for 3 months	$190.00	No

when entering currency values, you do not have to type the dollar signs, commas, or decimal places

5. Sue created a database named BeautyToGo that contains a MoreOptions table with plan data. The Option table you created has the same design as the MoreOptions table. Copy all the records from the **MoreOptions** table in the **BeautyToGo** database (located in the Access1 > Case1 folder provided with your Data Files), and then paste them at the end of the Option table in the Beauty database.

6. Resize all datasheet columns to their best fit, and then save the Option table.

7. Close the Option table, and then use the Navigation Pane to reopen it. Note that the records are displayed in primary key order by the values in the OptionID field.

8. Use the Simple Query Wizard to create a query that includes the OptionID, OptionDescription, and OptionCost fields from the Option table. In the second Simple Query Wizard dialog box, select the Detail option if necessary. (This option appears because the query includes a Currency field.) Save the query as **OptionData**, and then close the query.

9. Use the Form tool to create a form for the Option table. Save the form as **OptionInfo**, and then close it.

10. Use the Report tool to create a report based on the Option table. In Layout view, resize the OptionID field so it is slightly wider than the longest entry, which is the field name in this case. Resize the OptionDescription field so there are no entries with multiple lines. Also, resize the box containing the total amount that appears below the OptionCost column by clicking the box and then dragging its bottom border down so that the amount is fully displayed. (The Report Tool calculated this total automatically.) Display the report in Print Preview; then verify that all the fields are within the page area and all field values are fully displayed. Save the report as **OptionList**, print the report (only if asked by your instructor to do so), and then close it.

11. Close the Option table, and then compact and repair the Beauty database.

12. Close the Beauty database.

Case Problem 2

APPLY

Data File needed for this Case Problem: ProgPros.accdb

Programming Pros While in college obtaining his bachelor's degree in Raleigh, North Carolina, Brent Hovis majored in computer science and learned programming. Brent found that many of his fellow classmates found it difficult to write code, and he was constantly assisting them with helpful tips and techniques. Prior to graduating, Brent began tutoring freshman and sophomore students in programming to make some extra money. As his reputation grew, high school students began contacting him for help with their programming classes. When Brent entered graduate school, he started Programming Pros, a company offering expanded tutoring service for high school and college students through group, private, and semi-private tutoring sessions. As demand for the company's services grew, Brent hired many of his fellow classmates to assist him. Brent wants to use Access to maintain information about the tutors who work for him, the students who sign up for tutoring, and the contracts they sign. He needs your help in creating this database. Complete the following steps:

1. Create a new, blank database named **Programming** and save it in the folder where you are storing your files, as specified by your instructor.

2. In Datasheet view for the Table1 table, rename the default primary key ID field to **TutorID**. Change the data type of the TutorID field to Short Text.

3. Add the following five fields to the new table in the order shown; all of them are Short Text fields *except* HireDate, which is a Date/Time field: **FirstName**, **LastName**, **Major**, **YearInSchool**, **School**, and **HireDate**. Resize the columns, if necessary, so that the complete field names are displayed. Save the table as **Tutor**.

4. Enter the records shown in Figure 1-33 in the Tutor table. For the first record, be sure to enter your first name in the FirstName field and your last name in the LastName field.

Figure 1-33   Tutor table records

TutorID	FirstName	LastName	Major	YearInSchool	School	HireDate
1060	*Student First*	*Student Last*	Computer Science	Senior	Ellings College	2/14/2017
1010	Cathy	Cowler	Computer Engineering	Graduate	Eikenville College	2/1/2017
1051	Donald	Gallager	Computer Science	Graduate	Hogan University	1/18/2017
1031	Nichole	Schneider	Computer Science	Junior	Switzer University	2/28/2017
1018	Fredrik	Karlsson	Mechatronics	Junior	Smith Technical College	2/6/2017

5. Brent created a database named ProgPros that contains a MoreTutors table with tutor data. The Tutor table you created has the same design as the MoreTutors table. Copy all the records from the **MoreTutors** table in the **ProgPros** database (located in the Access1 > Case2 folder provided with your Data Files), and then paste them at the end of the Tutor table in the Programming database.

6. Resize all datasheet columns to their best fit, and then save the Tutor table.

7. Close the Tutor table, and then use the Navigation Pane to reopen it. Note that the records are displayed in primary key order by the values in the TutorID field.

8. Use the Simple Query Wizard to create a query that includes the FirstName, LastName, and HireDate fields from the Tutor table. Save the query as **StartDate**, and then close the query.

9. Use the Form tool to create a form for the Tutor table. Save the form as **TutorInfo**, and then close it.

10. Use the Report tool to create a report based on the Tutor table. In Layout view, resize the TutorID, FirstName, LastName, Major, YearInSchool, School, and HireDate fields so they are slightly wider than the longest entry (either the field name itself or an entry in the field). All seven fields should fit within the page area after you resize the fields. At the bottom of the report, move the text "Page 1 of 1" to the left so it is within the page area. Display the report in Print Preview; then verify that the fields and page number fit within the page area and that all field values are fully displayed. Save the report as **TutorList**, print the report (only if asked by your instructor to do so), and then close it.

11. Close the Tutor table, and then compact and repair the Programming database.

12. Close the Programming database.

Case Problem 3

CHALLENGE

Data File needed for this Case Problem: Diane.accdb

Diane's Community Center   Diane Coleman is a successful businesswoman in Dallas, Georgia, but things were not always that way. Diane experienced trying times and fortunately had people in the community come into her life to assist her and her children when times were difficult. Diane now wants to give back to her community and support those in need, just as she was supported many years ago, by creating a community center in Dallas where those in need can come in for goods and services. Diane plans to open a thrift store as well to sell donated items to support the center. Diane has been contacted by many people in the community wishing to donate materials to the center as well as items to be sold at the thrift store. Diane has asked you to create an Access database to manage information about the center's patrons and donations. Complete the following steps:

1. Create a new, blank database named **Center** and save it in the folder where you are storing your files, as specified by your instructor.

2. In Datasheet view for the Table1 table, rename the default primary key ID field to **PatronID**. Change the data type of the PatronID field to Short Text.

3. Add the following five Short Text fields to the new table in the order shown: **Title**, **FirstName**, **LastName**, **Phone**, and **Email**. Save the table as **Patron**.

4. Enter the records shown in Figure 1-34 in the Patron table. For the first record, be sure to enter your title in the Title field, your first name in the FirstName field, and your last name in the LastName field.

Figure 1-34   Patron table records

PatronID	Title	FirstName	LastName	Phone	Email
3001	Student Title	Student First	Student Last	404-987-1234	student@example.com
3030	Mr.	David	Hampton	404-824-3381	thehamptons@example.net
3006	Dr.	Elbert	Schneider	678-492-9101	countrydoc@example.com
3041	Mr.	Frank	Miller	404-824-3431	frankmiller12@example.net
3019	Mrs.	Jane	Michaels	706-489-3310	jjmichaels@example.com

5. Diane created a database named Diane that contains a MorePatrons table with data about additional patrons. The Patron table you created has the same design as the MorePatrons table. Copy all the records from the **MorePatrons** table in the **Diane** database (located in the Access1 > Case3 folder provided with your Data Files), and then paste them at the end of the Patron table in the Center database.

6. Resize all datasheet columns to their best fit, and then save the Patron table.

7. Close the Patron table, and then use the Navigation Pane to reopen it. Note that the records are displayed in primary key order by the values in the PatronID field.

✪ **Explore** 8. Use the Simple Query Wizard to create a query that includes all the fields in the Patron table *except* the Title field. (*Hint*: Use the >> and < buttons to select the necessary fields.) Save the query using the name **PatronContactList**.

✪ **Explore** 9. The query results are displayed in order by the PatronID field values. You can specify a different order by sorting the query. Display the Home tab. Then, click the insertion point anywhere in the LastName column to make it the current field. In the Sort & Filter group on the Home tab, click the Ascending button. The records are now listed in order by the values in the LastName field. Save and close the query.

✪ **Explore** 10. Use the Form tool to create a form for the Patron table. In the new form, navigate to record 13 (the record with PatronID 3028), and then print the form *for the current record only*. (*Hint*: You must use the Print dialog box in order to print only the current record. Go to Backstage view, click Print in the navigation bar, and then click Print to open the Print dialog box. Click the Selected Record(s) option button, and then click the OK button to print the current record.) Save the form as **PatronInfo**, and then close it.

11. Use the Report tool to create a report based on the Patron table. In Layout view, resize each field so it is slightly wider than the longest entry (either the field name itself or an entry in the field). All six fields should fit within the page area after resizing. At the bottom of the report, move the text "Page 1 of 1" to the left so it is within the page area. Display the report in Print Preview, then verify that the fields and page number fit within the page area and that all field values are fully displayed. Save the report as **PatronList**. Print the report (only if asked by your instructor to do so), and then close it.

12. Close the Patron table, and then compact and repair the Center database.

13. Close the Center database.

Case Problem 4

Data File needed for this Case Problem: HikeApp.accdb

CHALLENGE

Hike Appalachia   Molly and Bailey Johnson grew up in the Blue Ridge Mountains of North Carolina. Their parents were avid outdoors people and loved to take the family on long hikes and teach the girls about the great outdoors. During middle school and high school, their friends would ask them to guide them in the surrounding area because it could be quite dangerous. One summer, the girls had an idea to expand their hiking clientele beyond their friends and help earn money for college; this was the start of their business, which they named Hike Appalachia. The girls advertised in local and regional outdoor magazines and were flooded with requests from people all around the region. They would like you to build an Access database to manage information about the hikers they guide, the tours they provide, and tour reservations. Complete the following:

1. Create a new, blank database named **Appalachia** and save it in the folder where you are storing your files, as specified by your instructor.

2. In Datasheet view for the Table1 table, rename the default primary key ID field to **HikerID**. Change the data type of the HikerID field to Short Text.

3. Add the following seven Short Text fields to the new table in the order shown: **HikerFirst**, **HikerLast**, **Address**, **City**, **State**, **Zip**, and **Phone**. Save the table as **Hiker**.

4. Enter the records shown in Figure 1-35 in the Hiker table. For the first record, be sure to enter your first name in the HikerFirst field and your last name in the HikerLast field.

Figure 1-35 Hiker table records

HikerID	HikerFirst	HikerLast	Address	City	State	Zip	Phone
501	*Student First*	*Student Last*	123 Jackson St	Boone	NC	28607	828-497-9128
547	Heather	Smith	412 Sentry Ln	Gastonia	NC	28052	704-998-0987
521	Zack	Hoskins	2 Hope Rd	Atlanta	GA	30301	404-998-2381
535	Elmer	Jackson	99 River Rd	Blacksburg	SC	29702	864-921-2384
509	Sarah	Peeler	32 Mountain Ln	Ridgeview	WV	25169	703-456-9381

5. Molly and Bailey created a database named HikeApp that contains a MoreHikers table with data about hikers. The Hiker table you created has the same design as the MoreHikers table. Copy all the records from the **MoreHikers** table in the **HikeApp** database (located in the Access1 > Case4 folder provided with your Data Files), and then paste them at the end of the Hiker table in the Appalachia database.

6. Resize all datasheet columns to their best fit, and then save the Hiker table.

7. Close the Hiker table, and then use the Navigation Pane to reopen it. Note that the records are displayed in primary key order.

8. Use the Simple Query Wizard to create a query that includes the following fields from the Hiker table, in the order shown: HikerID, HikerLast, HikerFirst, State, and Phone. Name the query **HikerData**.

⊕ **Explore** 9. The query results are displayed in order by the HikerID field values. You can specify a different order by sorting the query. Display the Home tab. Then, click the insertion point anywhere in the State column to make it the current field. In the Sort & Filter group on the Home tab, click the Ascending button. The records are now listed in order by the values in the State field. Save and close the query.

⊕ **Explore** 10. Use the Form tool to create a form for the Hiker table. In the new form, navigate to record 10 (the record with HikerID 527), and then print the form *for the current record only*. (*Hint*: You must use the Print dialog box in order to print only the current record. Go to Backstage view, click Print in the navigation bar, and then click Print to open the Print dialog box. Click the Selected Record(s) option button, and then click the OK button to print the current record.) Save the form as **HikerInfo**, and then close it.

11. Use the Report tool to create a report based on the Hiker table. In Layout view, resize each field so it is slightly wider than the longest entry (either the field name itself or an entry in the field). At the bottom of the report, move the text "Page 1 of 1" to the left so it is within the page area on the report's first page. All fields should fit on one page. Save the report as **HikerList**.

12. Print the report (only if asked by your instructor to do so), and then close it.

   a. Close the Hiker table, and then compact and repair the Appalachia database.

   b. Close the Appalachia database.

ACCESS

Building a Database and Defining Table Relationships

Creating the Billing, Owner, and Animal Tables

OBJECTIVES

Session 2.1
- Learn the guidelines for designing databases and setting field properties
- Create a table in Design view
- Define fields, set field properties, and specify a table's primary key
- Modify the structure of a table
- Change the order of fields in Design view
- Add new fields in Design view
- Change the Format property for a field in Datasheet view
- Modify field properties in Design view

Session 2.2
- Import data from Excel
- Import an existing table structure
- Add fields to a table with the Data Type gallery
- Delete and rename fields
- Change the data type for a field in Design view
- Set the Default Value property for a field
- Import a text file
- Define a relationship between two tables

Case | *Riverview Veterinary Care Center*

The Riverview database currently contains one table, the Visit table. Kimberly Johnson also wants to track information about the clinic's animals, their owners, and the invoices sent to them for services provided by Riverview Veterinary Care Center. This information includes such items as each owner's name and address, animal information, and the amount and billing date for each invoice.

In this module, you'll create three new tables in the Riverview database—named Billing, Owner, and Animal—to contain the additional data Kimberly wants to track. You will use two different methods for creating the tables, and learn how to modify the fields. After adding records to the tables, you will define the necessary relationships between the tables in the Riverview database to relate the tables, enabling Kimberly and her staff to work with the data more efficiently.

STARTING DATA FILES

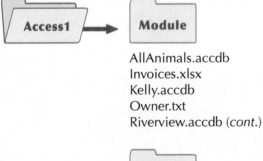

Access1 → **Module**

AllAnimals.accdb
Invoices.xlsx
Kelly.accdb
Owner.txt
Riverview.accdb (*cont.*)

Review

Supplies.xlsx
Vendor.accdb (*cont.*)

Case1

Beauty.accdb (*cont.*)
Customers.txt

Case2

Agreements.xlsx
Client.accdb
Programming.accdb (*cont.*)
Students.txt

Case3

Auctions.txt
Center.accdb (*cont.*)
Donations.xlsx

Case4

Appalachia.accdb (*cont.*)
Bookings.txt
Travel.accdb

Session 2.1 Visual Overview:

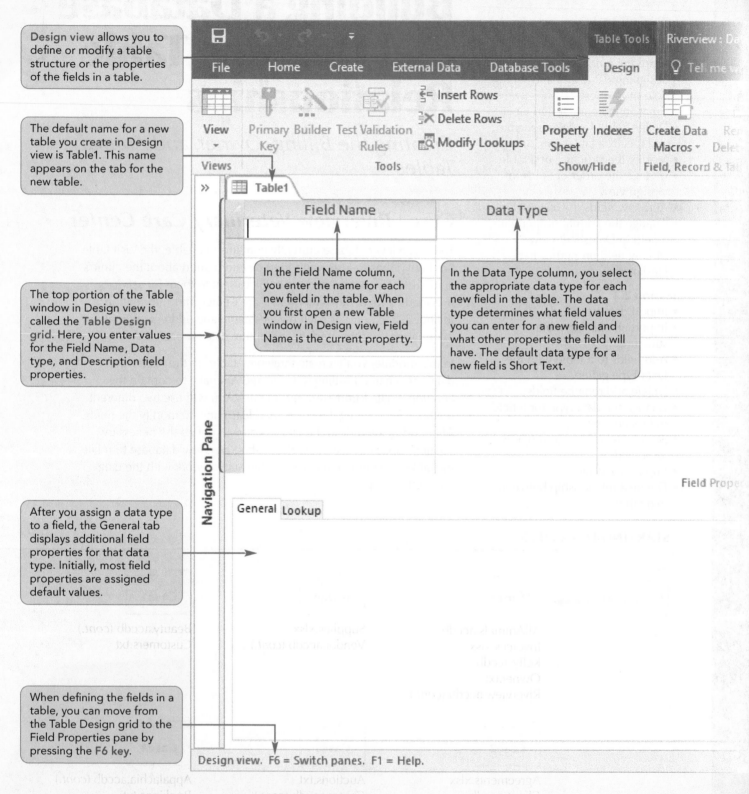

Design view allows you to define or modify a table structure or the properties of the fields in a table.

The default name for a new table you create in Design view is Table1. This name appears on the tab for the new table.

The top portion of the Table window in Design view is called the Table Design grid. Here, you enter values for the Field Name, Data type, and Description field properties.

After you assign a data type to a field, the General tab displays additional field properties for that data type. Initially, most field properties are assigned default values.

When defining the fields in a table, you can move from the Table Design grid to the Field Properties pane by pressing the F6 key.

In the Field Name column, you enter the name for each new field in the table. When you first open a new Table window in Design view, Field Name is the current property.

In the Data Type column, you select the appropriate data type for each new field in the table. The data type determines what field values you can enter for a new field and what other properties the field will have. The default data type for a new field is Short Text.

Table Tools   Riverview : D

File   Home   Create   External Data   Database Tools   Design   Tell me wi

View   Primary Key   Builder   Test Validation Rules   Insert Rows   Delete Rows   Modify Lookups   Property Sheet   Indexes   Create Data Macros   Re   Dele

Views   Tools   Show/Hide   Field, Record & Ta

Table1

Field Name   Data Type

Navigation Pane

Field Prope

General   Lookup

Design view. F6 = Switch panes. F1 = Help.

Table Window in Design View

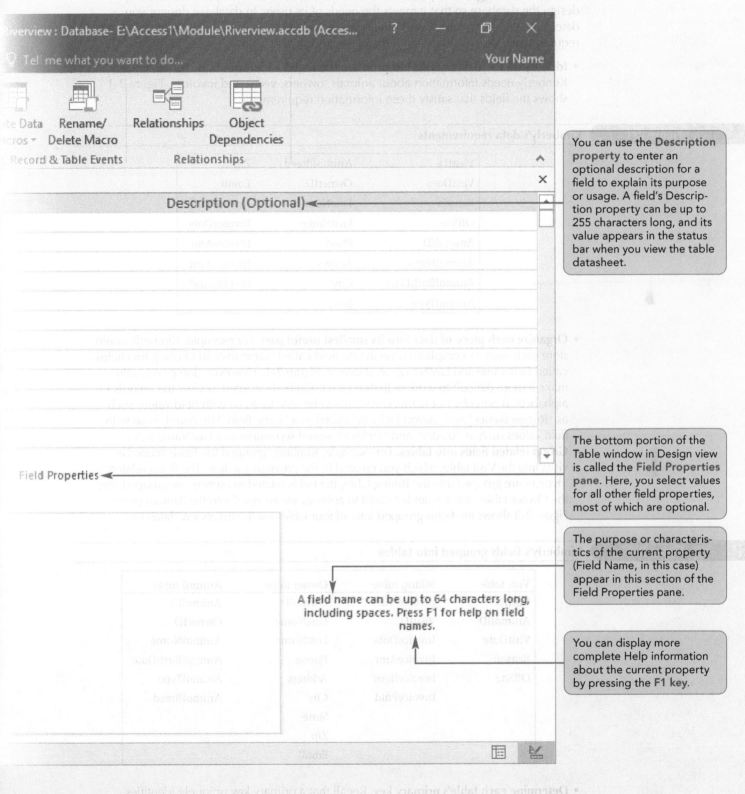

You can use the **Description property** to enter an optional description for a field to explain its purpose or usage. A field's Description property can be up to 255 characters long, and its value appears in the status bar when you view the table datasheet.

The bottom portion of the Table window in Design view is called the **Field Properties pane**. Here, you select values for all other field properties, most of which are optional.

The purpose or characteristics of the current property (Field Name, in this case) appear in this section of the Field Properties pane.

You can display more complete Help information about the current property by pressing the **F1 key**.

*(image labels)*

Riverview : Database- E:\Access1\Module\Riverview.accdb (Acces...

Tell me what you want to do...   Your Name

Rename/ Delete Macro   Relationships   Object Dependencies

Record & Table Events   Relationships

Description (Optional)

Field Properties

A field name can be up to 64 characters long, including spaces. Press F1 for help on field names.

Guidelines for Designing Databases

A database management system can be a useful tool, but only if you first carefully design the database so that it meets the needs of its users. In database design, you determine the fields, tables, and relationships needed to satisfy the data and processing requirements. When you design a database, you should follow these guidelines:

- **Identify all the fields needed to produce the required information.** For example, Kimberly needs information about animals, owners, visits, and invoices. Figure 2-1 shows the fields that satisfy these information requirements.

Figure 2-1	Kimberly's data requirements

VisitID	AnimalBreed	Zip
VisitDate	OwnerID	Email
Reason	FirstName	InvoiceNum
OffSite	LastName	InvoiceDate
AnimalID	Phone	InvoiceAmt
AnimalName	Address	InvoiceItem
AnimalBirthDate	City	InvoicePaid
AnimalType	State	

- **Organize each piece of data into its smallest useful part.** For example, Kimberly could store each owner's complete name in one field called Name instead of using two fields called FirstName and LastName, as shown in Figure 2-1. However, doing so would make it more difficult to work with the data. If Kimberly wanted to view the records in alphabetical order by last name, she wouldn't be able to do so with field values such as "Reggie Baxter" and "Aaron Jackson" stored in a Name field. She could do so with field values such as "Baxter" and "Jackson" stored separately in a LastName field.
- **Group related fields into tables.** For example, Kimberly grouped the fields related to visits into the Visit table, which you created in the previous module. The fields related to invoices are grouped into the Billing table, the fields related to owners are grouped into the Owner table, and the fields related to animals are grouped into the Animal table. Figure 2-2 shows the fields grouped into all four tables for the Riverview database.

Figure 2-2	Kimberly's fields grouped into tables

Visit table	Billing table	Owner table	Animal table
VisitID	InvoiceNum	OwnerID	AnimalID
AnimalID	VisitID	FirstName	OwnerID
VisitDate	InvoiceDate	LastName	AnimalName
Reason	InvoiceAmt	Phone	AnimalBirthDate
OffSite	InvoiceItem	Address	AnimalType
	InvoicePaid	City	AnimalBreed
		State	
		Zip	
		Email	

- **Determine each table's primary key.** Recall that a primary key uniquely identifies each record in a table. For some tables, one of the fields, such as a credit card number, naturally serves the function of a primary key. For other tables, two or more fields might be needed to function as the primary key. In these cases, the primary key is called a **composite key**. For example, a school grade table would use a combination of student number, term, and course code to serve as the primary key. For a third category of tables, no single field or combination of fields can uniquely identify a record in a table. In these cases, you need to add a field whose sole purpose is to serve as the table's primary key. For Kimberly's tables, VisitID is the primary key for the Visit table, InvoiceNum is the primary key for the Billing table, OwnerID is the primary key for the Owner table, and AnimalID is the primary key for the Animal table.

- **Include a common field in related tables.** You use the common field to connect one table logically with another table. For example, Kimberly's Visit and Animal tables include the AnimalID field as a common field. Recall that when you include the primary key from one table as a field in a second table to form a relationship, the field in the second table is called a foreign key; therefore, the AnimalID field is a foreign key in the Visit table. With this common field, Kimberly can find all visits to the clinic made by a particular animal; she can use the AnimalID value for an animal and search the Visit table for all records with that AnimalID value. Likewise, she can determine which animal made a particular visit by searching the Animal table to find the one record with the same AnimalID value as the corresponding value in the Visit table. Similarly, the VisitID field is a common field, serving as the primary key in the Visit table and a foreign key in the Billing table. Since animals have owners responsible for their bills, there must be a relationship between the animals and owners for the clinic to contact; therefore, the OwnerID field is a foreign key in the Animal table.
- **Avoid data redundancy.** When you store the same data in more than one place, **data redundancy** occurs. With the exception of common fields to connect tables, you should avoid data redundancy because it wastes storage space and can cause inconsistencies. An inconsistency would exist, for example, if you type a field value one way in one table and a different way in the same table or in a second table. Figure 2-3, which contains portions of potential data stored in the Animal and Visit tables, shows an example of incorrect database design that has data redundancy in the Visit table. In Figure 2-3, the AnimalName field in the Visit table is redundant, and one value for this field was entered incorrectly, in three different ways.

Figure 2-3	Incorrect database design with data redundancy

AnimalID	AnimalName	AnimalBirthDate	AnimalType
12286	Lady	8/12/2015	Dog
12304	Tweets	11/12/2010	Bird
12332	Smittie	5/19/2014	Cat
12345	Herford5	4/28/2015	Cattle
12359	Merino4	8/2/2014	Sheep

data redundancy

VisitID	AnimalID	AnimalName	VisitDate	OffSite
1202	12500	Bonkers	12/11/2016	No
1250	12332	Smitty	12/19/2016	No
1276	12492	Bessie	1/10/2017	Yes
1308	12332	Smity	1/23/2017	No
1325	12612	Tweets	2/6/2017	No
1342	12595	Angus	2/27/2017	Yes
1367	12332	Smittee	3/7/2017	No

Inconsistent data

- **Determine the properties of each field.** You need to identify the **properties**, or characteristics, of each field so that the DBMS knows how to store, display, and process the field values. These properties include the field's name, data type, maximum number of characters or digits, description, valid values, and other field characteristics. You will learn more about field properties later in this module.

The Billing, Owner, and Animal tables you need to create will contain the fields shown in Figure 2-2. Before creating these new tables in the Riverview database, you first need to learn some guidelines for setting field properties.

Guidelines for Setting Field Properties

As just noted, the last step of database design is to determine which values to assign to the properties, such as the name and data type, of each field. When you select or enter a value for a property, you **set** the property. Access has rules for naming fields and objects, assigning data types, and setting other field properties.

Naming Fields and Objects

You must name each field, table, and other object in an Access database. Access stores these items in the database, using the names you supply. It's best to choose a field or object name that describes the purpose or contents of the field or object so that later you can easily remember what the name represents. For example, the four tables in the Riverview database are named Visit, Billing, Owner, and Animal because these names suggest their contents. Note that a table or query name must be unique within a database. A field name must be unique within a table, but it can be used again in another table.

Assigning Field Data Types

Each field must have a data type, which is either assigned automatically by Access or specifically by the table designer. The data type determines what field values you can enter for the field and what other properties the field will have. For example, the Billing table will include an InvoiceDate field, which will store date values, so you will assign the Date/Time data type to this field. Then Access will allow you to enter and manipulate only dates or times as values in the InvoiceDate field.

Figure 2-4 lists the most commonly used data types in Access, describes the field values allowed for each data type, explains when you should use each data type, and indicates the field size of each data type. You can find more complete information about all available data types in Access Help.

| Figure 2-4 | Common data types |

Data Type	Description	Field Size
Short Text	Allows field values containing letters, digits, spaces, and special characters. Use for names, addresses, descriptions, and fields containing digits that are *not used in calculations*.	0 to 255 characters; default is 255
Long Text	Allows field values containing letters, digits, spaces, and special characters. Use for long comments and explanations.	1 to 65,535 characters; exact size is determined by entry
Number	Allows positive and negative numbers as field values. A number can contain digits, a decimal point, commas, a plus sign, and a minus sign. Use for fields that will be used in calculations, except those involving money.	1 to 15 digits
Date/Time	Allows field values containing valid dates and times from January 1, 100 to December 31, 9999. Dates can be entered in month/day/year format, several other date formats, or a variety of time formats, such as 10:35 PM. You can perform calculations on dates and times, and you can sort them. For example, you can determine the number of days between two dates.	8 bytes
Currency	Allows field values similar to those for the Number data type, but is used for storing monetary values. Unlike calculations with Number data type decimal values, calculations performed with the Currency data type are not subject to round-off error.	Accurate to 15 digits on the left side of the decimal point and to 4 digits on the right side
AutoNumber	Consists of integer values created automatically by Access each time you create a new record. You can specify sequential numbering or random numbering, which guarantees a unique field value, so that such a field can serve as a table's primary key.	9 digits
Yes/No	Limits field values to yes and no, on and off, or true and false. Use for fields that indicate the presence or absence of a condition, such as whether an order has been filled or whether an invoice has been paid.	1 character
Hyperlink	Consists of text used as a hyperlink address, which can have up to four parts: the text that appears in a field or control; the path to a file or page; a location within the file or page; and text displayed as a ScreenTip.	Up to 65,535 characters total for the four parts of the hyperlink

Setting Field Sizes

The **Field Size property** defines a field value's maximum storage size for Short Text, Number, and AutoNumber fields only. The other data types have no Field Size property because their storage size is either a fixed, predetermined amount or is determined automatically by the field value itself, as shown in Figure 2-4. A Short Text field has a default field size of 255 characters; you can also set its field size by entering a number from 0 to 255. For example, the FirstName and LastName fields in the Owner table will be Short Text fields with sizes of 20 characters and 25 characters, respectively. These field sizes will accommodate the values that will be entered in each of these fields.

PROSKILLS

Decision Making: Specifying the Field Size Property for Number Fields

When you use the Number data type to define a field, you need to decide what the Field Size setting should be for the field. You should set the Field Size property based on the largest value that you expect to store in that field. Access processes smaller data sizes faster, using less memory, so you can optimize your database's performance and its storage space by selecting the correct field size for each field. Field Size property settings for Number fields are as follows:

- **Byte**: Stores whole numbers (numbers with no fractions) from 0 to 255 in one byte
- **Integer**: Stores whole numbers from –32,768 to 32,767 in two bytes
- **Long Integer** (default): Stores whole numbers from –2,147,483,648 to 2,147,483,647 in four bytes
- **Single**: Stores positive and negative numbers to precisely seven decimal places in four bytes
- **Double**: Stores positive and negative numbers to precisely 15 decimal places in eight bytes
- **Replication ID**: Establishes a unique identifier for replication of tables, records, and other objects in databases created using Access 2003 and earlier versions in 16 bytes
- **Decimal**: Stores positive and negative numbers to precisely 28 decimal places in 12 bytes

Choosing an appropriate field size is important to optimize efficiency. For example, it would be wasteful to use the Long Integer field size for a Number field that will store only whole numbers ranging from 0 to 255 because the Long Integer field size uses four bytes of storage space. A better choice would be the Byte field size, which uses one byte of storage space to store the same values. By first gathering and analyzing information about the number values that will be stored in a Number field, you can make the best decision for the field's Field Size property and ensure the most efficient user experience for the database.

Setting the Caption Property for Fields

The **Caption property** for a field specifies how the field name is displayed in database objects, including table and query datasheets, forms, and reports. If you don't set the Caption property, Access displays the field name as the column heading or label for a field. For example, field names such as InvoiceAmt and InvoiceDate in the Billing table can be difficult to read. Setting the Caption property for these fields to "Invoice Amt" and "Invoice Date" would make it easier for users to read the field names and work with the database.

INSIGHT

Setting the Caption Property vs. Naming Fields

Although Access allows you to include spaces in field names, this practice is not recommended because the spaces cause problems when you try to perform more complex tasks with the data in your database. Setting the Caption property allows you to follow best practices for naming fields, such as not including spaces in field names, while still providing users with more readable field names in datasheets, forms, and reports.

In the previous module, you created the Riverview database file and, within that file, you created the Visit table working in Datasheet view. According to her plan for the Riverview database, Kimberly also wants to track information about the invoices the care center sends to the owners of the animals. Next, you'll create the Billing table for Kimberly—this time, working in Design view.

Creating a Table in Design View

Creating a table in Design view involves entering the field names and defining the properties for the fields, specifying a primary key for the table, and then saving the table structure. Kimberly documented the design for the new Billing table by listing each field's name and data type; each field's size and description (if applicable); and any other properties to be set for each field. See Figure 2-5.

| Figure 2-5 | Design for the Billing table |

Field Name	Data Type	Field Size	Description	Other
InvoiceNum	Short Text	5	Primary key	Caption = Invoice Num
VisitID	Short Text	4	Foreign key	Caption = Visit ID
InvoiceAmt	Currency			Format = Currency
				Decimal Places = 2
				Caption = Invoice Amt
InvoiceDate	Date/Time			Format = mm/dd/yyyy
				Caption = Invoice Date
InvoicePaid	Yes/No			Caption = Invoice Paid

You'll use Kimberly's design as a guide for creating the Billing table in the Riverview database.

To begin creating the Billing table:

▶ **1.** Start Access and open the **Riverview** database you created in the previous module.

   Trouble? If the security warning is displayed below the ribbon, click the **Enable Content** button.

▶ **2.** If the Navigation Pane is open, click the **Shutter Bar Open/Close Button** ⟪ to close it.

▶ **3.** On the ribbon, click the **Create** tab.

▶ **4.** In the Tables group, click the **Table Design** button. A new table named Table1 opens in Design view. Refer to the Session 2.1 Visual Overview for a complete description of the Table window in Design view.

Defining Fields

When you first create a table in Design view, the insertion point is located in the first row's Field Name box, ready for you to begin defining the first field in the table. You enter values for the Field Name, Data Type, and Description field properties, and then select values for all other field properties in the Field Properties pane. These other properties will appear when you move to the first row's Data Type box.

REFERENCE

Defining a Field in Design View

- In the Field Name box, type the name for the field, and then press the Tab key.
- Accept the default Short Text data type, or click the arrow and select a different data type for the field. Press the Tab key.
- Enter an optional description for the field, if necessary.
- Use the Field Properties pane to type or select other field properties, as appropriate.

The first field you need to define is the InvoiceNum field. This field will be the primary key for the Billing table. Each invoice at Riverview Veterinary Care Center is assigned a specific five-digit number. Although the InvoiceNum field will contain these number values, the numbers will never be used in calculations; therefore, you'll assign the Short Text data type to this field. Any time a field contains number values that will not be used in calculations—such as phone numbers, zip codes, and so on—you should use the Short Text data type instead of the Number data type.

To define the InvoiceNum field:

TIP

You can also press the Enter key to move from one property to the next in the Table Design grid.

1. Type **InvoiceNum** in the first row's Field Name box, and then press the **Tab** key to advance to the Data Type box. The default data type, Short Text, is selected in the Data Type box, which now also contains an arrow, and the field properties for a Short Text field appear in the Field Properties pane. See Figure 2-6.

Figure 2-6 Table window after entering the first field name

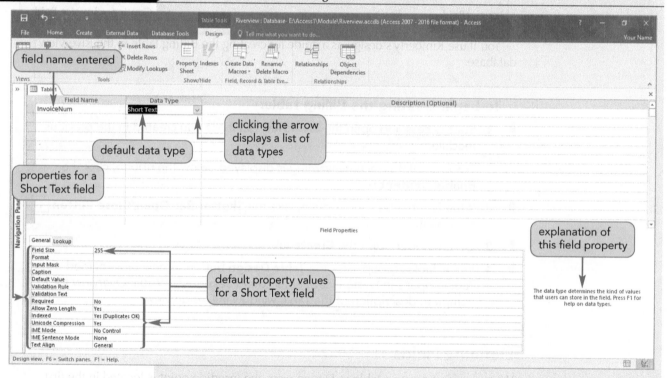

Notice that the right side of the Field Properties pane now provides an explanation for the current property, Data Type.

Trouble? If you make a typing error, you can correct it by clicking to position the insertion point, and then using either the Backspace key to delete characters to the left of the insertion point or the Delete key to delete characters to the right of the insertion point. Then type the correct text.

Because the InvoiceNum field values will not be used in calculations, you will accept the default Short Text data type for the field.

2. Press the **Tab** key to accept Short Text as the data type and to advance to the Description (Optional) box.

3. Next you'll enter the Description property value as "Primary key." The value you enter for the Description property will appear in the status bar when you view the table datasheet. Note that specifying "Primary key" for the Description property does *not* establish the current field as the primary key; you use a button on the ribbon to specify the primary key in Design view, which you will do later in this session.

4. Type **Primary key** in the Description (Optional) box.

Notice the Field Size property for the field. The default setting of 255 for Short Text fields is displayed. You need to change this number to 5 because all invoice numbers at Riverview Veterinary Care Center contain only five digits.

5. Double-click the number **255** in the Field Size property box to select it, and then type **5**.

Finally, you need to set the Caption property for the field so that its name appears with a space, as "Invoice Num."

6. Click the **Caption** property box, and then type **Invoice Num**. The definition of the first field is complete. See Figure 2-7.

Figure 2-7   **InvoiceNum field defined**

Kimberly's Billing table design (Figure 2-5) shows VisitID as the second field. Because Kimberly and other staff members need to relate information about invoices to the visit data in the Visit table, the Billing table must include the VisitID field, which is the Visit table's primary key. Recall that when you include the primary key from one table as a field in a second table to connect the two tables, the field is a foreign key in the second table. The field must be defined in the same way in both tables—that is, the field properties, including field size and data type, must match exactly.

Next, you will define VisitID as a Short Text field with a field size of 4. Later in this session, you'll change the Field Size property for the VisitID field in the Visit table to 4 so that the field definition is the same in both tables.

To define the VisitID field:

▶ 1. In the Table Design grid, click the second row's **Field Name** box, type **VisitID**, and then press the **Tab** key to advance to the Data Type box.

▶ 2. Press the **Tab** key to accept Short Text as the field's data type. Because the VisitID field is a foreign key to the Visit table, you'll enter "Foreign key" in the Description (Optional) box to help users of the database understand the purpose of this field.

▶ 3. Type **Foreign key** in the Description (Optional) box. Next, you'll change the Field Size property.

▶ 4. Press the **F6** key to move to the Field Properties pane. The current entry for the Field Size property, 255, is selected.

▶ 5. Type **4** to set the Field Size property. Finally, you need to set the Caption property for this field.

▶ 6. Press the **Tab** key three times to position the insertion point in the Caption box, and then type **Visit ID** (be sure to include a space between the two words). You have completed the definition of the second field.

The third field in the Billing table is the InvoiceAmt field, which will display the dollar amount of each invoice the clinic sends to the animals' owners. Kimberly wants the values to appear with two decimal places because invoice amounts include cents. She also wants the values to include dollar signs, so that the values will be formatted as currency when they are printed in bills sent to owners. The Currency data type is the appropriate choice for this field.

To define the InvoiceAmt field:

▶ 1. Click the third row's **Field Name** box, type **InvoiceAmt** in the box, and then press the **Tab** key to advance to the Data Type box.

▶ 2. Click the **Data Type** arrow, click **Currency** in the list, and then press the **Tab** key to advance to the Description (Optional) box. According to Kimberly's design (Figure 2-5), you do not need to enter a description for this field. If you've assigned a descriptive field name and the field does not fulfill a special function (such as primary key), you usually do not enter a value for the optional Description property. InvoiceAmt is a field that does not require a value for its Description property.

Kimberly wants the InvoiceAmt field values to be displayed with two decimal places. The **Decimal Places property** specifies the number of decimal places that are displayed to the right of the decimal point.

TIP

You can display the arrow and the list simultaneously by clicking the right side of a box.

3. In the Field Properties pane, click the **Decimal Places** box to position the insertion point there. An arrow appears on the right side of the Decimal Places box, which you can click to display a list of options.

4. Click the **Decimal Places** arrow, and then click **2** in the list to specify two decimal places for the InvoiceAmt field values.

5. Press the **Tab** key twice to position the insertion point in the Caption box, and then type **Invoice Amt**. The definition of the third field is now complete. Notice that the Format property is set to "Currency," which formats the values with dollar signs. See Figure 2-8.

| Figure 2-8 | Table window after defining the first three fields |

current field

property values set for the current field

The fourth field in the Billing table is the InvoiceDate field. This field will contain the dates on which invoices are generated for the animals in the care center. You'll define the InvoiceDate field using the Date/Time data type. Also, according to Kimberly's design (Figure 2-5), the date values should be displayed in the format mm/dd/yyyy, which is a two-digit month, a two-digit day, and a four-digit year.

To define the InvoiceDate field:

1. Click the fourth row's **Field Name** box, type **InvoiceDate**, and then press the **Tab** key to advance to the Data Type box.

   You can select a value from the Data Type list as you did for the InvoiceAmt field. Alternately, you can type the property value in the box or type just the first character of the property value.

2. Type **d**. Access completes the entry for the fourth row's Data Type box to "date/Time," with the letters "ate/Time" selected. See Figure 2-9.

Figure 2-9	Selecting a value for the Data Type property

completed entry for Data Type

3. Press the **Tab** key to advance to the Description (Optional) box. Note that the value for the Data Type property changes to "Date/Time."

   Kimberly wants the values in the InvoiceDate field to be displayed in a format showing the month, the day, and a four-digit year, as in the following example: 03/10/2017. You use the Format property to control the display of a field value.

4. In the Field Properties pane, click the right side of the **Format** box to display the list of predefined formats for Date/Time fields. See Figure 2-10.

Figure 2-10	Displaying available formats for Date/Time fields

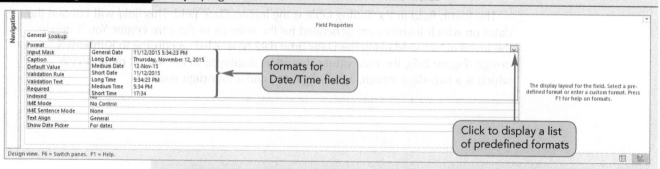

formats for Date/Time fields

Click to display a list of predefined formats

Trouble? If you see an arrow instead of a list of predefined formats, click the arrow to display the list.

As noted in the right side of the Field Properties pane, you can either choose a predefined format or enter a custom format. Even though the Short Date format seems to match the format Kimberly wants, it displays only one digit for months that contain only one digit. For example, it would display the month of March with only the digit "3"—as in 3/10/2017—instead of displaying the month with two digits, as in 03/10/2017.

Because none of the predefined formats matches the exact layout Kimberly wants for the InvoiceDate values, you need to create a custom date format. Figure 2-11 shows some of the symbols available for custom date and time formats.

| Figure 2-11 | Symbols for some custom date formats |

Symbol	Description
/	date separator
d	day of the month in one or two numeric digits, as needed (1 to 31)
dd	day of the month in two numeric digits (01 to 31)
ddd	first three letters of the weekday (Sun to Sat)
dddd	full name of the weekday (Sunday to Saturday)
w	day of the week (1 to 7)
ww	week of the year (1 to 53)
m	month of the year in one or two numeric digits, as needed (1 to 12)
mm	month of the year in two numeric digits (01 to 12)
mmm	first three letters of the month (Jan to Dec)
mmmm	full name of the month (January to December)
yy	last two digits of the year (01 to 99)
yyyy	full year (0100 to 9999)

Kimberly wants the dates to be displayed with a two-digit month (mm), a two-digit day (dd), and a four-digit year (yyyy).

5. Click the **Format** arrow to close the list of predefined formats, and then type **mm/dd/yyyy** in the Format box.

6. Press the **Tab** key twice to position the insertion point in the Caption box, and then type **Invoice Date**. See Figure 2-12.

Figure 2-12 Specifying the custom date format

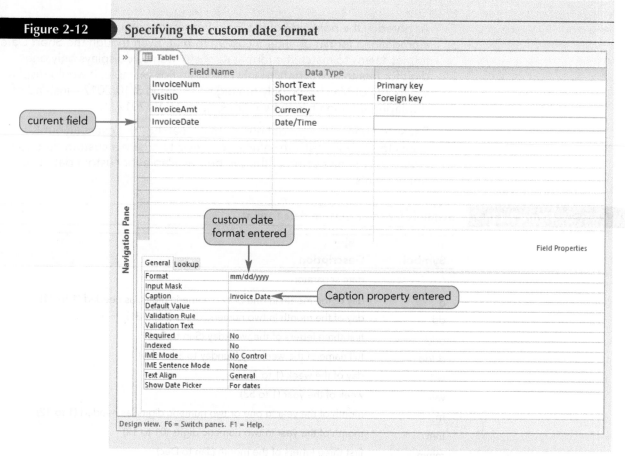

The fifth and final field to be defined in the Billing table is InvoicePaid. This field will be a Yes/No field to indicate the payment status of each invoice record stored in the Billing table. Recall that the Yes/No data type is used to define fields that store true/false, yes/no, and on/off field values. When you create a Yes/No field in a table, the default Format property is set to Yes/No.

To define the InvoicePaid field:

1. Click the fifth row's **Field Name** box, type **InvoicePaid**, and then press the **Tab** key to advance to the Data Type box.

2. Type **y**. Access completes the data type as "yes/No".

3. Press the **Tab** key to select the Yes/No data type and move to the Description (Optional) box. In the Field Properties pane, note that the default format of "Yes/No" is selected, so you do not have to change this property.

4. In the Field Properties pane, click the **Caption** box, and then type **Invoice Paid**.

You've finished defining the fields for the Billing table. Next, you need to specify the primary key for the table.

Specifying the Primary Key

As you learned earlier, the primary key for a table uniquely identifies each record in the table.

Specifying a Primary Key in Design View

- Display the table in Design view.
- Click in the row for the field you've chosen to be the primary key to make it the active field. If the primary key will consist of two or more fields, click the row selector for the first field, press and hold the Ctrl key, and then click the row selector for each additional primary key field.
- In the Tools group on the Table Tools Design tab, click the Primary Key button.

According to Kimberly's design, you need to specify InvoiceNum as the primary key for the Billing table. You can do so while the table is in Design view.

To specify InvoiceNum as the primary key:

1. Click in the row for the InvoiceNum field to make it the current field.

TIP

This button is a toggle; you can click it to remove the key symbol.

2. On the Table Tools Design tab, in the Tools group, click the **Primary Key** button. The Primary Key button in the Tools group is now selected, and a key symbol appears in the row selector for the first row, indicating that the InvoiceNum field is the table's primary key. See Figure 2-13.

Figure 2-13	InvoiceNum field selected as the primary key

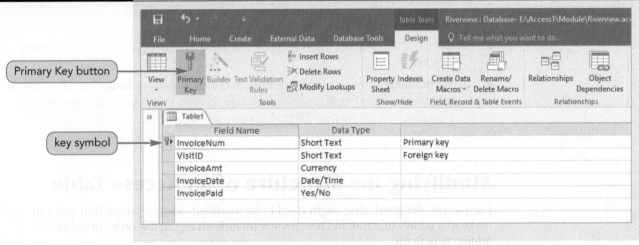

Primary Key button

key symbol

Field Name	Data Type	
InvoiceNum	Short Text	Primary key
VisitID	Short Text	Foreign key
InvoiceAmt	Currency	
InvoiceDate	Date/Time	
InvoicePaid	Yes/No	

INSIGHT

Understanding the Importance of the Primary Key

Although Access does not require a table to have a primary key, including a primary key offers several advantages:

- A primary key uniquely identifies each record in a table.
- Access does not allow duplicate values in the primary key field. For example, if a record already exists in the Visit table with a VisitID value of 1550, Access prevents you from adding another record with this same value in the VisitID field. Preventing duplicate values ensures the uniqueness of the primary key field.
- When a primary key has been specified, Access forces you to enter a value for the primary key field in every record in the table. This is known as **entity integrity**. If you do not enter a value for a field, you have actually given the field a **null value**. You cannot give a null value to the primary key field because entity integrity prevents Access from accepting and processing that record.
- You can enter records in any order, but Access displays them by default in order of the primary key's field values. If you enter records in no specific order, you are ensured that you will later be able to work with them in a more meaningful, primary key sequence.
- Access responds faster to your requests for specific records based on the primary key.

Saving the Table Structure

The last step in creating a table is to name the table and save the table's structure. When you save a table structure, the table is stored in the database file (in this case, the Riverview database file). Once the table is saved, you can enter data into it. According to Kimberly's plan, you need to save the table you've defined as "Billing."

To name and save the Billing table:

▶ **1.** On the Quick Access Toolbar, click the **Save** button 🖫. The Save As dialog box opens.

▶ **2.** Type **Billing** in the Table Name box, and then press the **Enter** key. The Billing table is saved in the Riverview database. Notice that the tab for the table now displays the name "Billing" instead of "Table1."

Modifying the Structure of an Access Table

Even a well-designed table might need to be modified. Some changes that you can make to a table's structure in Design view include changing the order of fields and adding new fields.

After meeting with her assistant, Kelly Flannagan, and reviewing the structure of the Billing table, Kimberly has changes she wants you to make to the table. First, she wants the InvoiceAmt field to be moved so that it appears right before the InvoicePaid field. Then, she wants you to add a new Short Text field named InvoiceItem to the table to include information about what the invoice is for, such as office visits, lab work, and so on. Kimberly would like the InvoiceItem field to be inserted between the InvoiceAmt and InvoicePaid fields.

Moving a Field in Design View

To move a field, you use the mouse to drag it to a new location in the Table Design grid. Although you can move a field in Datasheet view by dragging its column heading to a new location, doing so rearranges only the *display* of the table's fields; the table structure is not changed. To move a field permanently, you must move the field in Design view.

Next, you'll move the InvoiceAmt field so that it is before the InvoicePaid field in the Billing table.

To move the InvoiceAmt field:

▶ **1.** Position the pointer on the row selector for the InvoiceAmt field until the pointer changes to ➡.

▶ **2.** Click the **row selector** to select the entire InvoiceAmt row.

▶ **3.** Place the pointer on the row selector for the InvoiceAmt field until the pointer changes to ⌖, press and hold the mouse button and then drag to the row selector for the InvoicePaid field. Notice that as you drag, the pointer changes to ⌖. See Figure 2-14.

Figure 2-14	Moving the InvoiceAmt field in the table structure

▶ **4.** Release the mouse button. The InvoiceAmt field now appears between the InvoiceDate and InvoicePaid fields in the table structure.

Trouble? If the InvoiceAmt field did not move, repeat Steps 1 through 4, making sure you hold down the mouse button during the drag operation.

Adding a Field in Design View

To add a new field between existing fields, you must insert a row. You begin by selecting the row below where you want the new field to be inserted.

REFERENCE

Adding a Field Between Two Existing Fields

- In the Table window in Design view, select the row below where you want the new field to be inserted.
- In the Tools group on the Table Tools Design tab, click the Insert Rows button.
- Define the new field by entering the field name, data type, optional description, and any property specifications.

Next, you need to add the InvoiceItem field to the Billing table structure between the InvoiceAmt and InvoicePaid fields.

To add the InvoiceItem field to the Billing table:

1. Click the **InvoicePaid Field Name** box. You need to establish this field as the current field so that the row for the new record will be inserted above this field.

2. On the Table Tools Design tab, in the Tools group, click the **Insert Rows** button. A new, blank row is added between the InvoiceAmt and InvoicePaid fields. The insertion point is positioned in the Field Name box for the new row, ready for you to type the name for the new field. See Figure 2-15.

Figure 2-15   **Table structure after inserting a row**

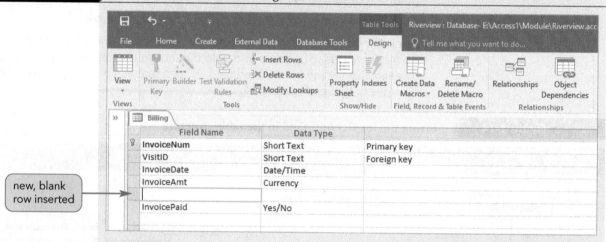

Trouble? If you selected the InvoicePaid field's row selector and then inserted the new row, you need to click the new row's Field Name box to position the insertion point in it.

You'll define the InvoiceItem field in the new row of the Billing table. This field will be a Short Text field with a field size of 40, and you need to set the Caption property to include a space between the words in the field name.

3. Type **InvoiceItem**, press the **Tab** key to move to the Data Type property, and then press the **Tab** key again to accept the default Short Text data type.

4. Press the **F6** key to select the default field size in the Field Size box, and then type **40**.

5. Press the **Tab** key three times to position the insertion point in the Caption box, and then type **Invoice Item**. The definition of the new field is complete. See Figure 2-16.

Figure 2-16   **InvoiceItem field added to the Billing table**

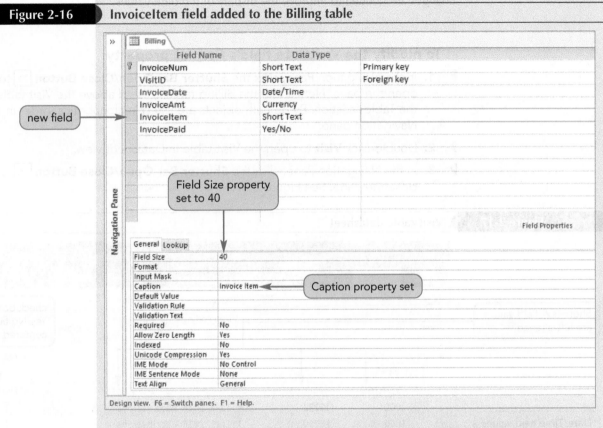

6. On the Quick Access Toolbar, click the **Save** button 🖫 to save the changes to the Billing table structure.

7. Click the **Close 'Billing'** button ✖ on the object tab to close the Billing table.

Modifying Field Properties

With the Billing table design complete, you can now go back and modify the properties of the fields in the Visit table you created in the previous module, as necessary. You can make some changes to properties in Datasheet view; for others, you'll work in Design view.

Changing the Format Property in Datasheet View

The Formatting group on the Table Tools Fields tab in Datasheet view allows you to modify some formatting for certain field types. When you format a field, you change the way data is displayed, but not the actual values stored in the table.

Next, you'll check the properties of the VisitDate field in the Visit table to see if any changes are needed to improve the display of the date values.

To modify the VisitDate field's Format property:

▶ 1. In the Navigation Pane, click the **Shutter Bar Open/Close Button** 〉〉 to open the pane. Notice that the Billing table is listed above the Visit table in the Tables section. By default, objects are listed in alphabetical order in the Navigation pane.

▶ 2. Double-click **Visit** to open the Visit table in Datasheet view.

▶ 3. In the Navigation Pane, click the **Shutter Bar Open/Close Button** 〈〈 to close the pane. See Figure 2-17.

| Figure 2-17 | Visit table datasheet |

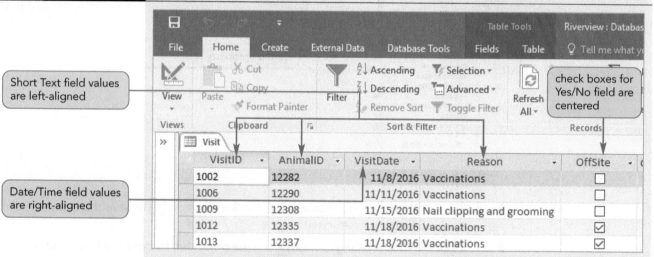

Short Text field values are left-aligned

Date/Time field values are right-aligned

check boxes for Yes/No field are centered

Notice that the values in the three Short Text fields—VisitID, AnimalID, and Reason—appear left-aligned within their boxes, and the values in the Date/Time field (VisitDate) appear right-aligned. In Access, values for Short Text fields are left-aligned, and values for Number, Date/Time, and Currency fields are right-aligned. The Offsite field is a Yes/No field, so its values appear in check boxes that are centered within the column.

▶ 4. On the ribbon, click the **Table Tools Fields** tab.

▶ 5. Click the **first field value** in the VisitDate column. The Data Type option shows that this field is a Date/Time field.

By default, Access assigns the General Date format to Date/Time fields. Note the Format box in the Formatting group, which you use to set the Format property (similar to how you set the Format property in the Field Properties pane in Design view.) Even though the Format box is empty, the VisitDate field has the General Date format applied to it. The General Date format includes settings for date or time values, or a combination of date and time values. However, Kimberly wants *only date values* to be displayed in the VisitDate field, so she asks you to specify the Short Date format for the field.

▶ 6. In the Formatting group, click the **Format** arrow, and then click **Short Date**. See Figure 2-18.

| Figure 2-18 | VisitDate field after modifying the format |

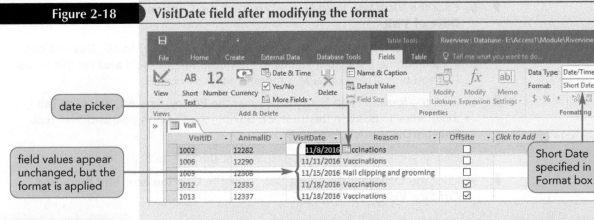

date picker

field values appear unchanged, but the format is applied

Short Date format specified in the Format box

TIP

When working with date values, you can type dates directly or click the date picker shown in Figure 2-18 to select a date from an interactive calendar.

Although no change is apparent in the datasheet—the VisitDate field values already appear with the Short Date setting (for example, 11/8/2016), as part of the default General Date format—the field now has the Short Date format applied to it. This ensures that only date field values, and not time or date/time values, are allowed in the field.

Changing Properties in Design View

Recall that each of the Short Text fields in the Visit table—VisitID, AnimalID, and Reason—still has the default field size of 255, which is too large for the data contained in these fields. Also, the VisitID and AnimalID fields need descriptions to identify them as the primary and foreign keys, respectively, in the table. Finally, each of these fields needs a caption either to include a space between the words in the field name or to make the name more descriptive. You can make all of these property changes more easily in Design view.

TIP

You can also click the Design View button on the far right end of the status bar to switch to Design view.

To modify the Field Size, Description, and Caption field properties:

1. On the Table Tools Fields tab, in the Views group, click the **View** button. The table is displayed in Design view with the VisitID field selected. You need to enter a Description property value for this field, the primary key in the table, and change its Field Size property to 4 because each visit number at Riverview Veterinary Care Center consists of four digits.

2. Press the **Tab** key twice to position the insertion point in the Description (Optional) box, and then type **Primary key**.

3. Press the **F6** key to move to and select the default setting of 255 in the Field Size box in the Fields Properties pane, and then type **4**. Next you need to set the Caption property for this field.

4. Press the **Tab** key three times to position the insertion point in the Caption box, and then type **Visit ID**.

   Next you need to enter a Description property value for the AnimalID field, a foreign key in the table, and set its Field Size property to 5 because each AnimalID number at Riverview Veterinary Care Center consists of five digits. You also need to set this field's Caption property.

5. Click the **VisitDate** Field Name box, click the **Caption** box, and then type **Date of Visit**.

For the Reason field, you will set the Field Size property to 60. This size can accommodate the longer values in the Reason field. You'll also set this field's Caption property to provide a more descriptive name.

6. Click the **Reason** Field Name box, press the **F6** key, type **60**, press the **Tab** key three times to position the insertion point in the Caption box, and then type **Reason/Diagnosis**.

Finally, you'll set the Caption property for the OffSite field.

7. Click the **OffSite** Field Name box, click the **Caption** box, and then type **Off-Site Visit?**. See Figure 2-19.

Figure 2-19	Visit table after modifying field properties

Notice that the OffSite field's Default Value property is automatically set to "No," which means the check box for this field will be empty for each new record. This is the default for this property for any Yes/No field. You can set the Default Value property for other types of fields to make data entry easier. You'll learn more about setting this property in the next session.

The changes to the Visit table's properties are now complete, so you can save the table and view the results of your changes in Datasheet view.

To save and view the modified Visit table:

1. On the Quick Access Toolbar, click the **Save** button 💾 to save the modified table. A dialog box opens informing you that some data may be lost because you decreased the field sizes. Because all of the values in the VisitID, AnimalID, and Reason fields contain the same number of or fewer characters than the new Field Size properties you set for each field, you can ignore this message.

2. Click the **Yes** button.

3. On the Table Tools Design tab, in the Views group, click the **View** button to display the Visit table in Datasheet view. Notice that each column (field) heading now displays the text you specified in the Caption property for that field. However, now the Off-Site Visit? field caption doesn't fully display.

4. Place the pointer on the column border to the right of the Off-Site Visit? field name until the pointer changes to ✛, and then double-click the column border to fully display this field name. See Figure 2-20.

| Figure 2-20 | Modified Visit table in Datasheet view |

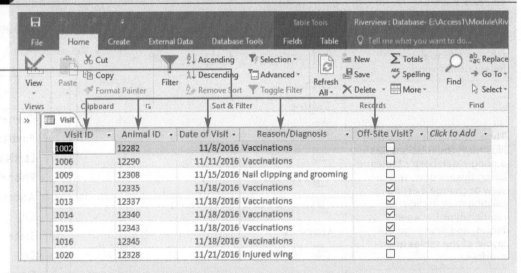

5. Click the **Close 'Visit'** button ☒ on the object tab to close the Visit table, and click **Yes** to save the changes to the Visit table.

6. If you are not continuing to Session 2.2, click the **File** tab, and then click **Close** in the navigation bar of Backstage view to close the Riverview database.

You have created the Billing table and made modifications to its design. In the next session, you'll add records to the Billing table and create the Animal and Owner tables in the Riverview database.

Session 2.1 Quick Check

REVIEW

1. What guidelines should you follow when designing a database?

2. What is the purpose of the Data Type property for a field?

3. The _____ property specifies how a field's name is displayed in database objects, including table and query datasheets, forms, and reports.

4. For which three types of fields can you assign a field size?

5. The default Field Size property setting for a Short Text field is _____.

6. In Design view, which key do you press to move from the Table Design grid to the Field Properties pane?

7. List three reasons why you should specify a primary key for an Access table.

Session 2.2 Visual Overview:

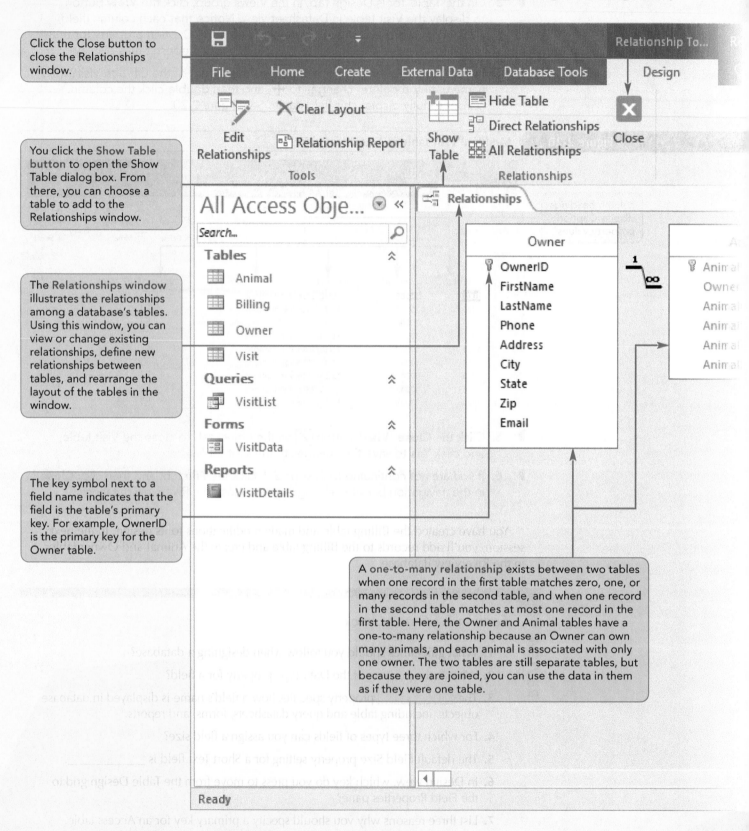

Click the Close button to close the Relationships window.

You click the Show Table button to open the Show Table dialog box. From there, you can choose a table to add to the Relationships window.

The Relationships window illustrates the relationships among a database's tables. Using this window, you can view or change existing relationships, define new relationships between tables, and rearrange the layout of the tables in the window.

The key symbol next to a field name indicates that the field is the table's primary key. For example, OwnerID is the primary key for the Owner table.

A one-to-many relationship exists between two tables when one record in the first table matches zero, one, or many records in the second table, and when one record in the second table matches at most one record in the first table. Here, the Owner and Animal tables have a one-to-many relationship because an Owner can own many animals, and each animal is associated with only one owner. The two tables are still separate tables, but because they are joined, you can use the data in them as if they were one table.

Modified Visit table in Datasheet view

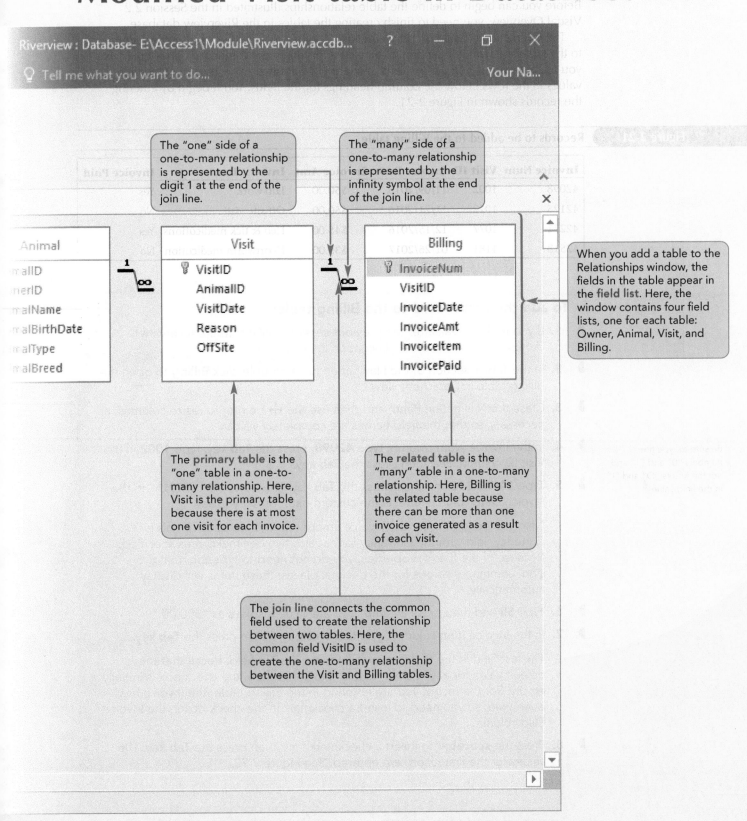

Riverview : Database- E:\Access1\Module\Riverview.accdb...   ?   —   □   ✕

💡 Tell me what you want to do...   Your Na...

The "one" side of a one-to-many relationship is represented by the digit 1 at the end of the join line.

The "many" side of a one-to-many relationship is represented by the infinity symbol at the end of the join line.

Animal
- allD
- nerID
- alName
- alBirthDate
- alType
- alBreed

Visit
- 🔑 VisitID
- AnimalID
- VisitDate
- Reason
- OffSite

Billing
- 🔑 InvoiceNum
- VisitID
- InvoiceDate
- InvoiceAmt
- InvoiceItem
- InvoicePaid

When you add a table to the Relationships window, the fields in the table appear in the **field list**. Here, the window contains four field lists, one for each table: Owner, Animal, Visit, and Billing.

The **primary table** is the "one" table in a one-to-many relationship. Here, Visit is the primary table because there is at most one visit for each invoice.

The **related table** is the "many" table in a one-to-many relationship. Here, Billing is the related table because there can be more than one invoice generated as a result of each visit.

The **join line** connects the common field used to create the relationship between two tables. Here, the common field VisitID is used to create the one-to-many relationship between the Visit and Billing tables.

Adding Records to a New Table

Before you can begin to define the table relationships illustrated in the Session 2.2 Visual Overview, you need to finish creating the tables in the Riverview database.

The Billing table design is complete. Now, Kimberly would like you to add records to the table so it will contain the invoice data for Riverview Veterinary Care Center. As you learned earlier, you add records to a table in Datasheet view by typing the field values in the rows below the column headings for the fields. You'll begin by entering the records shown in Figure 2-21.

| Figure 2-21 | Records to be added to the Billing table |

Invoice Num	Visit ID	Invoice Date	Invoice Amt	Invoice Item	Invoice Paid
42098	1002	11/09/2016	$50.00	Lab work	Yes
42125	1012	11/21/2016	$50.00	Off-site visit	No
42271	1077	12/15/2016	$45.00	Flea & tick medications	Yes
42518	1181	01/26/2017	$35.00	Heartworm medication	No

To add the first record to the Billing table:

1. If you took a break after the previous session, make sure the Riverview database is open and the Navigation Pane is open.

2. In the Tables section of the Navigation Pane, double-click **Billing** to open the Billing table in Datasheet view.

3. Close the Navigation Pane, and then use the ✛ pointer to resize columns, as necessary, so that the field names are completely visible.

> Be sure to type the numbers "0" and "1" and *not* the letters "O" and "I" in the field values.

4. In the Invoice Num column, type **42098**, press the **Tab** key, type **1002** in the Visit ID column, and then press the **Tab** key.

5. Type **11/9/2016** and then press the **Tab** key. The date "11/09/2016" in the Invoice Date column reflects the custom date format you set.

   Next you need to enter the invoice amount for the first record. This is a Currency field with the Currency format and two decimal places specified. Because of the field's properties, you do not need to type the dollar sign, comma, or zeroes for the decimal places; these items will display automatically.

6. Type **50** and then press the **Tab** key. The value displays as "$50.00."

7. In the Invoice Item column, type **Lab work**, and then press the **Tab** key.

   The last field in the table, InvoicePaid, is a Yes/No field. Recall that the default value for any Yes/No field is "No"; therefore, the check box is initially empty. For the record you are entering in the Billing table, the invoice has been paid, so you need to insert a checkmark in the check box in the Invoice Paid column.

8. Press the **spacebar** to insert a checkmark, and then press the **Tab** key. The values for the first record are entered. See Figure 2-22.

Figure 2-22 | First record entered in the Billing table

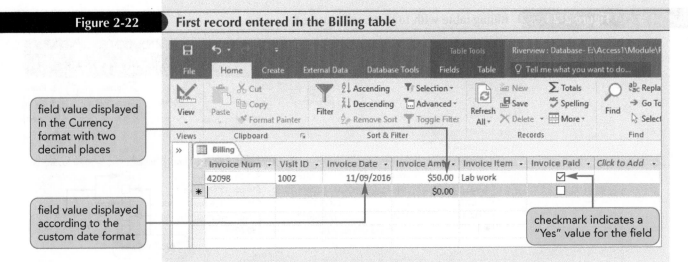

field value displayed in the Currency format with two decimal places

field value displayed according to the custom date format

checkmark indicates a "Yes" value for the field

Now you can add the remaining three records. As you do, you'll learn a keyboard shortcut for inserting the value from the same field in the previous record. A **keyboard shortcut** is a key or combination of keys you press to complete an action more efficiently.

To add the next three records to the Billing table:

▶ **1.** Refer to Figure 2-21 and enter the values in the second record's Invoice Num, Visit ID, and Invoice Date columns.

Notice that the value in the second record's Invoice Amt column is $50.00. This value is the exact same value as in the first record. You can quickly insert the value from the same column in the previous record using the Ctrl + ' (apostrophe) keyboard shortcut. To use this shortcut, you press and hold the Ctrl key, press the ' key once, and then release both keys. (The plus sign in the keyboard shortcut indicates you're pressing two keys at once; you do not press the + key.)

▶ **2.** With the insertion point in the Invoice Amt column, press the **Ctrl + ' keys**. The value "$50.00" is inserted in the Invoice Amt column for the second record.

▶ **3.** Press the **Tab** key to move to the Invoice Item column, and then type **Off-site visit**.

▶ **4.** Press the **Tab** key to move to the Invoice Paid column, and then press the **Tab** key to leave the Invoice Paid check box unchecked to indicate the invoice has not been paid. The second record is entered in the Billing table.

▶ **5.** Refer to Figure 2-21 to enter the values for the third and fourth records. Your table should look like the one in Figure 2-23.

Figure 2-23 Billing table with four records entered

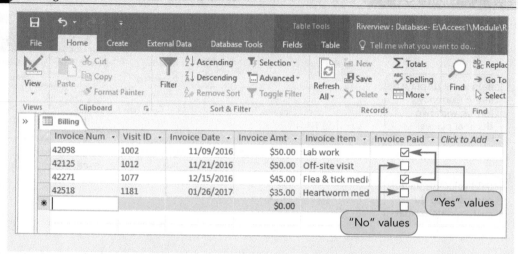

To finish entering records in the Billing table, you'll use a method that allows you to import the data.

Importing Data from an Excel Worksheet

Often, the data you want to add to an Access table exists in another file, such as a Word document or an Excel workbook. You can bring the data from other files into Access in different ways. For example, you can copy and paste the data from an open file, or you can **import** the data, which is a process that allows you to copy the data from a source without having to open the source file.

Kimberly had been using Excel to track invoice data for Riverview Veterinary Care Center and already created a worksheet, named "Invoices," containing this data. You'll import this Excel worksheet into your Billing table to complete the entry of data in the table. To use the import method, the columns in the Excel worksheet must match the names and data types of the fields in the Access table.

The Invoices worksheet contains the following columns: InvoiceNum, VisitID, InvoiceDate, InvoiceAmt, InvoiceItem, and InvoicePaid. These column headings match the field names in the Billing table exactly, so you can import the data. Before you import data into a table, you need to close the table.

TIP

Caption property values set for fields are not considered in the import process. Therefore make sure that the field names match the Excel worksheet column headings. If there are differences, change the column headings in the Excel worksheet to match the Access table field names.

To import the Invoices worksheet into the Billing table:

1. Click the **Close 'Billing'** button ⊠ on the object tab to close the Billing table, and then click the **Yes** button in the dialog box asking if you want to save the changes to the table layout.

2. On the ribbon, click the **External Data** tab.

3. In the Import & Link group, click the **Excel** button. The Get External Data - Excel Spreadsheet dialog box opens. See Figure 2-24.

Figure 2-24	Get External Data – Excel Spreadsheet dialog box

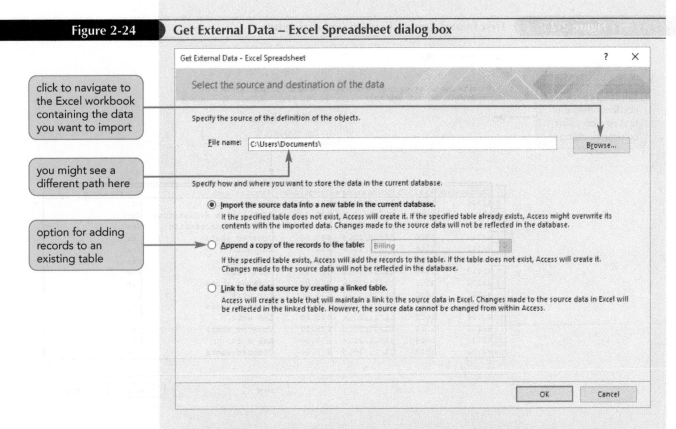

click to navigate to the Excel workbook containing the data you want to import

you might see a different path here

option for adding records to an existing table

The dialog box provides options for importing the entire worksheet as a new table in the current database, adding the data from the worksheet to an existing table, or linking the data in the worksheet to the table. You need to add, or append, the worksheet data to the Billing table.

4. Click the **Browse** button. The File Open dialog box opens. The Excel workbook file is named "Invoices" and is located in the Access1 > Module folder provided with your Data Files.

5. Navigate to the **Access1 > Module** folder, where your Data Files are stored, and then double-click the **Invoices** Excel file. You return to the dialog box.

6. Click the **Append a copy of the records to the table** option button. The box to the right of this option becomes active and displays the Billing table name, because it is the first table listed in the Navigation Pane.

7. Click the **OK** button. The first Import Spreadsheet Wizard dialog box opens. The dialog box confirms that the first row of the worksheet you are importing contains column headings. The bottom section of the dialog box displays some of the data contained in the worksheet. See Figure 2-25.

Figure 2-25 First Import Spreadsheet Wizard dialog box

selected check box confirms that the first row contains column headings

8. Click the **Next** button. The second, and final, Import Spreadsheet Wizard dialog box opens. Notice that the Import to Table box shows that the data from the spreadsheet will be imported into the Billing table.

9. Click the **Finish** button. A dialog box opens asking if you want to save the import steps. If you needed to repeat this same import procedure many times, it would be a good idea to save the steps for the procedure. However, you don't need to save these steps because you'll be importing the data only one time. Once the data is in the Billing table, Kimberly will no longer use Excel to track invoice data.

10. Click the **Close** button in the dialog box to close it without saving the steps.

The data from the Invoices worksheet has been added to the Billing table. Next, you'll open the table to view the new records.

To open the Billing table and view the imported data:

1. Open the Navigation Pane, and then double-click **Billing** in the Tables section to open the table in Datasheet view.

2. Resize the Invoice Item column to its best fit, scrolling the worksheet and resizing, as necessary.

> **3.** Press the **Ctrl + Home** keys to scroll to the top of the datasheet. Notice that the table now contains a total of 204 records—the four records you entered plus 200 records imported from the Invoices worksheet. The records are displayed in primary key order by the values in the Invoice Num column. See Figure 2-26.

Figure 2-26	Billing table after importing data from Excel

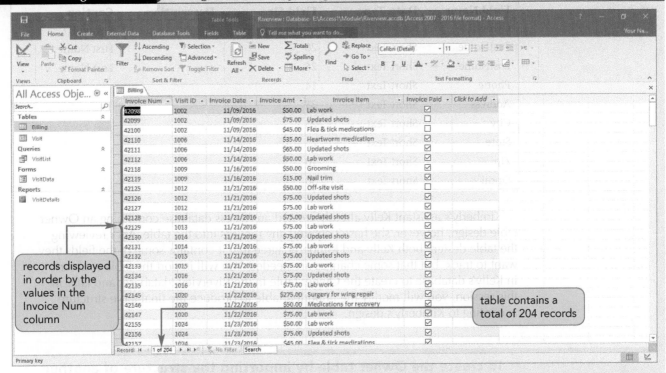

records displayed in order by the values in the Invoice Num column

table contains a total of 204 records

> **4.** Save and close the Billing table, and then close the Navigation Pane.

Two of the tables—Visit and Billing—are now complete. According to Kimberly's plan for the Riverview database, you still need to create the Owner and Animal tables. You'll use a different method to create these tables.

Creating a Table by Importing an Existing Table or Table Structure

If another Access database contains a table—or even just the design, or structure, of a table—that you want to include in your database, you can import the table and any records it contains or import only the table structure into your database. To create the new Owner and Animal tables per Kimberly's plan shown in Figure 2-2, you will import a table structure from a different Access database to create the Owner table and an existing table structure and records from another database to create the Animal table.

Importing an Existing Table Structure

Kimberly documented the design for the new Owner table by listing each field's name and data type, as well as any applicable field size, description, and caption property values, as shown in Figure 2-27. Note that each field in the Owner table will be a Short Text field, and the OwnerID field will be the table's primary key.

| Figure 2-27 | Design for the Owner table |

Field Name	Data Type	Field Size	Description	Caption
OwnerID	Short Text	4	Primary key	Owner ID
FirstName	Short Text	20		First Name
LastName	Short Text	25		Last Name
Phone	Short Text	14		
Address	Short Text	35		
City	Short Text	25		
State	Short Text	2		
Zip	Short Text	10		
Email	Short Text	50		

Kimberly's assistant Kelly already created an Access database containing an Owner table design, however, she hasn't entered any records into the table. After reviewing the table design, both Kelly and Kimberly agree that it contains some of the fields they want to track, but that some changes are needed. You will import the table structure in Kelly's database to create the Owner table in the Riverview database, and later in this session, you will modify the imported table to produce the final table structure according to Kimberly's design.

To create the Owner table by importing the structure of another table:

1. Make sure the External Data tab is the active tab on the ribbon.

2. In the Import & Link group, click the **Access** button. The Get External Data - Access Database dialog box opens. This dialog box is similar to the one you used earlier when importing the Excel spreadsheet.

3. Click the **Browse** button. The File Open dialog box opens. The Access database file from which you need to import the table structure is named "Kelly" and is located in the Access1 > Module folder provided with your Data Files.

4. Navigate to the **Access1 > Module** folder, where your Data Files are stored, and then double-click the **Kelly** database file. You return to the dialog box.

5. Make sure the **Import tables, queries, forms, reports, macros, and modules into the current database** option button is selected, and then click the **OK** button. The Import Objects dialog box opens. The dialog box contains tabs for importing all the different types of Access database objects—tables, queries, forms, and so on. The Tables tab is the current tab.

6. Click the **Options** button in the dialog box to see all the options for importing tables. See Figure 2-28.

Figure 2-28	Import Objects dialog box

tabs for importing other
types of database objects

table object to be
imported

this option imports
the table structure
and the table

Import Objects   ?   ✕

Tables   Queries   Forms   Reports   Macros   Modules

Owner

    OK

    Cancel

    Select All

    Deselect All

    Options >>

Import   Import Tables   Import Queries
☑ Relationships   ◉ Definition and Data   ◉ As Queries
☐ Menus and Toolbars   ○ Definition Only   ○ As Tables
☐ Import/Export Specs
☐ Nav Pane Groups
☐ All Images and Themes

this option imports the
table structure only

7. On the Tables tab, click **Owner** to select this table.

8. In the Import Tables section of the dialog box, click the **Definition Only** option button, and then click the **OK** button. Access creates the Owner table in the Riverview database using the structure of the Owner table in the Kelly database, and opens a dialog box asking if you want to save the import steps.

9. Click the **Close** button to close the dialog box without saving the import steps.

10. Open the Navigation Pane, double-click **Owner** in the Tables section to open the table, and then close the Navigation Pane. The Owner table opens in Datasheet view. The table contains no records. See Figure 2-29.

Figure 2-29	Imported Owner table in Datasheet view

Before you add records to the Owner table and fine-tune its design, you need to first add the Animal table to the Riverview database. You will do this by importing a table and its data from another database.

Importing an Existing Table

Kelly has already created a database called "AllAnimals" that contains a table called "Animal." To import this Animal table into the Riverview database, you will follow the same process you used to import the table structure from the Kelly database to create the Owner table; however, this time you will choose the Definition and Data option, instead of the Definition only option in the Import Objects dialog box. This will import the structure and the data that Kelly has created and verified in the Animal table in the AllAnimals database.

To create the Animal table by importing the structure and data of another table:

▶ 1. Close the Owner table, make sure the External Data tab is the active tab on the ribbon, and then in the Import & Link group, click the **Access** button. The Get External Data - Access Database dialog box opens.

▶ 2. Click the **Browse** button. The File Open dialog box opens. The Access database file from which you need to import the table is named "AllAnimals" and is located in the Access1 > Module folder provided with your Data Files.

▶ 3. Navigate to the **Access1 > Module** folder, where your Data Files are stored, and then double-click the **AllAnimals** database file. You return to the dialog box.

▶ 4. Make sure the **Import tables, queries, forms, reports, macros, and modules into the current database** option button is selected, and then click the **OK** button to open the Import Objects dialog box opens. The Tables tab is the current tab.

▶ 5. Click **Animal** to select this table, click the **Options** button to display the options for importing tables, and then, in the Import Tables section, make sure the **Definition and Data** option button is selected.

▶ 6. Click the **OK** button, and then click the **Close** button to close the dialog box without saving the import steps. Access creates the Animal table in the Riverview database using the records and structure of the Animal table in the AllAnimals database.

▶ 7. Open the Navigation Pane, double-click **Animal** in the Tables section to open the table, and then close the Navigation Pane. The Animal table opens in Datasheet view. Kimberly reviews the new Animal table and is satisfied with its structure and the records it contains, so you can close this table.

▶ 8. Close the Animal table.

Now Kimberly asks you to complete the Owner table. She notes that the table structure you imported earlier for this table contains some of the fields she wants, but not all (see Figure 2-27); it also contains some fields she does not want in the Owner table. You can add the missing fields using the Data Type gallery.

Adding Fields to a Table Using the Data Type Gallery

The **Data Type gallery**, available from the More Fields button located on the Add & Delete group on the Table Tools Fields tab, allows you to add a group of related fields to a table at the same time, rather than adding each field to the table individually.

The group of fields you add is called a **Quick Start selection**. For example, the **Address Quick Start selection** adds a collection of fields related to an address, such as Address, City, State, and so on, to the table at one time. When you use a Quick Start selection, the fields added already have properties set. However, you need to review and possibly modify the properties to ensure the fields match your design needs for the database.

Next, you'll use the Data Type gallery to add the missing fields to the Owner table.

To add fields to the Owner table using the Data Type gallery:

1. Open the **Owner** table, and then on the ribbon, click the **Table Tools Fields** tab. Before inserting fields from the Data Type gallery, you need to place the insertion point in the field to the right of where you want to insert the new fields. According to Kimberly's design, the Address field should come after the Phone field, so you need to make the next field, Email, the active field.

2. Click the **first row** in the Email field to make it the active field.

3. In the Add & Delete group, click the **More Fields** button. The Data Type gallery opens and displays options for different types of fields you can add to your table.

4. Scroll down the gallery until the Quick Start section is visible. See Figure 2-30.

> Make sure the correct field is active before adding new fields.

Figure 2-30	Owner table with the Data Type gallery displayed

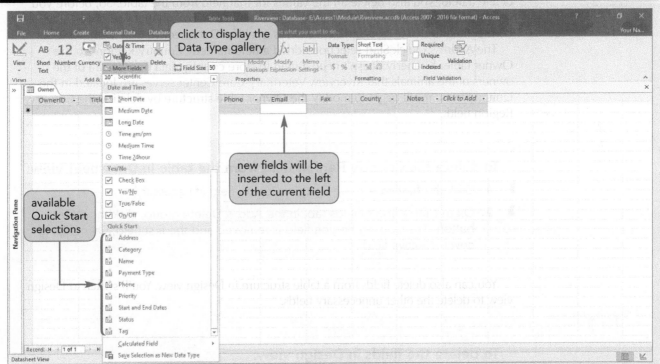

The Quick Start section provides options that will add multiple, related fields to the table at one time. The new fields will be inserted to the left of the current field.

5. In the Quick Start section, click **Address**. Five fields are added to the table: Address, City, State Province, ZIP Postal, and Country Region. See Figure 2-31.

Figure 2-31   Owner table after adding fields from the Data Type gallery

Modifying the Structure of an Imported Table

Refer back to Kimberly's design for the Owner table (Figure 2-27). To finalize the table design, you need to modify the imported table by deleting fields, renaming fields, and changing field data types. You'll begin by deleting fields.

Deleting Fields from a Table Structure

After you've created a table, you might need to delete one or more fields. When you delete a field, you also delete all the values for that field from the table. So, before you delete a field, you should make sure that you want to do so and that you choose the correct field to delete. You can delete fields in either Datasheet view or Design view.

The Address Quick Start selection added a field named "Country Region" to the Owner table. Kimberly doesn't need a field to store country data because all of the owners of the animals that Riverview Veterinary Care Center serves are located in the United States. You'll begin to modify the Owner table structure by deleting the Country Region field.

To delete the Country Region field from the table in Datasheet view:

1. Click the **first row** in the Country Region field (if necessary).

2. On the Table Tools Fields tab, in the Add & Delete group, click the **Delete** button. The Country Region field is removed and the first field, OwnerID, is now the active field.

You can also delete fields from a table structure in Design view. You'll switch to Design view to delete the other unnecessary fields.

To delete the fields in Design view:

1. On the Table Tools Fields tab, in the Views group, click the **View** button. The Owner table opens in Design view. See Figure 2-32.

Figure 2-32   Owner table in Design view

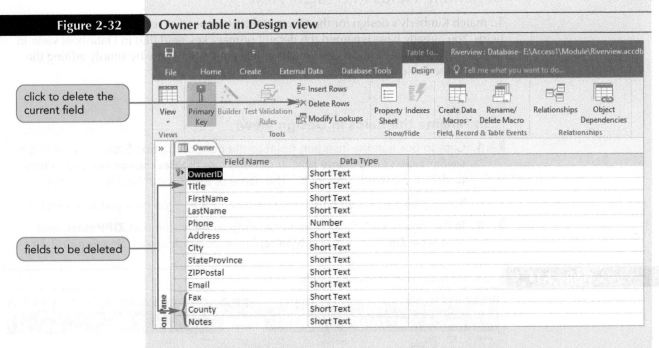

click to delete the current field

fields to be deleted

2. Click the **Title** Field Name box to make it the current field.

3. On the Table Tools Design tab, in the Tools group, click the **Delete Rows** button. The Title field is removed from the Owner table structure. You'll delete the Fax, County, and Notes fields next. Instead of deleting these fields individually, you'll select and delete them at the same time.

4. On the row selector for the **Fax** field, press and hold the mouse button and then drag the mouse to select the **County** and **Notes** fields.

5. Release the mouse button. The rows for the three fields are outlined in red, indicating all three fields are selected.

6. In the Tools group, click the **Delete Rows** button. See Figure 2-33.

Figure 2-33   Owner table after deleting fields

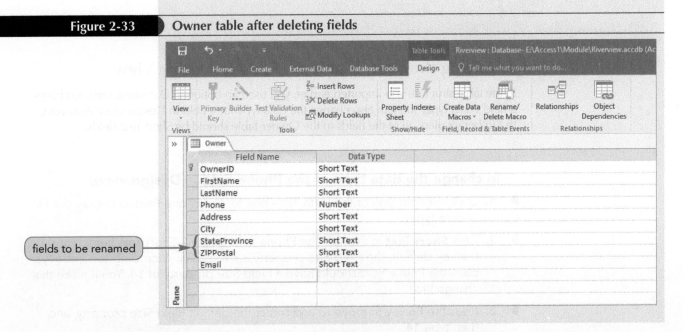

fields to be renamed

Renaming Fields in Design View

To match Kimberly's design for the Owner table, you need to rename some of the fields. You already have renamed the default primary key field (ID) in Datasheet view in the previous module. You can also rename fields in Design view by simply editing the names in the Table Design grid.

To rename the fields in Design view:

▶ 1. Click to position the insertion point to the right of the text StateProvince in the seventh row's Field Name box, and then press the **Backspace** key eight times to delete the word "Province." The name of the seventh field is now State.

   You can also select an entire field name and then type new text to replace it.

▶ 2. In the eighth row's Field Name box, drag to select the text **ZIPPostal**, and then type **Zip**. The text you type replaces the original text. See Figure 2-34.

Figure 2-34 Owner table after renaming fields

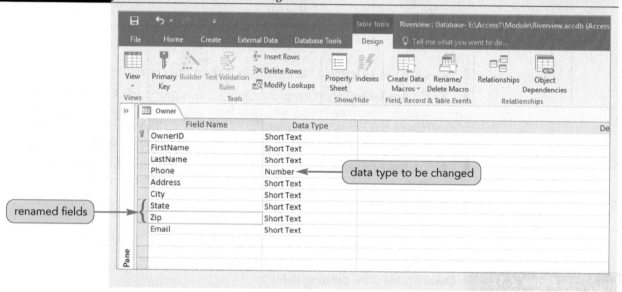

Changing the Data Type for a Field in Design View

In the table structure you imported earlier, you used an option in Datasheet view to change a field's data type. You can also change the data type for a field in Design view. According to Kimberly's plan, all of the fields in the Owner table should be Short Text fields.

To change the data type of the Phone field in Design view:

▶ 1. Click the right side of the Data Type box for the Phone field to display the list of data types.

▶ 2. Click **Short Text** in the list. The Phone field is now a Short Text field. Note that, by default, the Field Size property is set to 255. According to Kimberly's plan, the Phone field should have a Field Size property of 14. You'll make this change next.

▶ 3. Press the **F6** key to move to and select the default Field Size property, and then type **14**.

Each of the remaining fields you added using the Address Quick Start selection—Address, City, State, and Zip—also has the default field size of 255. You need to change the Field Size property for these fields to match Kimberly's design. You'll also delete any Caption property values for these fields because the field names match how Kimberly wants them displayed, so captions are unnecessary.

To change the Field Size and Caption properties for the fields:

▶ 1. Click the **Address Field Name** box to make it the current field.

▶ 2. Press the **F6** key to move to and select the default Field Size property, and then type **35**. Note that the Caption property setting for this field is the same as the field name. This field doesn't need a caption, so you can delete this value.

▶ 3. Press the **Tab** key three times to select Address in the Caption box, and then press the **Delete** key. The Caption property value is removed.

▶ 4. Repeat Steps 1 through 3 for the City field to change the Field Size property to **25** and delete its Caption property value.

▶ 5. Change the Field Size property for the State field to **2**, and then delete its Caption property value.

▶ 6. Change the Field Size property for the Zip field to **10**, and then delete its Caption property value.

▶ 7. On the Quick Access Toolbar, click the **Save** button 🖫 to save your changes to the Owner table.

Finally, Kimberly would like you to set the Description property for the OwnerID field and the Caption property for the OwnerID, FirstName, and LastName fields. You'll make these changes now.

To enter the Description and Caption property values:

▶ 1. Click the **Description (Optional)** box for the OwnerID field, and then type **Primary key**.

▶ 2. In the Field Properties pane, click the **Caption** box.

After you leave the Description (Optional) box, the Property Update Options button 🖅 appears below this box for the OwnerID field. When you change a field's property in Design view, you can use this button to update the corresponding property on forms and reports that include the modified field. For example, if the Riverview database included a form that contained the OwnerID field, you could choose to propagate, or update, the modified Description property in the form by clicking the Property Update Options button, and then choosing the option to make the update everywhere the field is used. The ScreenTip on the Property Update Options button and the options it lists vary depending on the task; in this case, if you click the button, the option is "Update Status Bar Text everywhere OwnerID is used." Because the Riverview database does not include any forms or reports that are based on the Owner table, you do not need to update the properties, so you can ignore the button for now. In most cases, however, it is a good idea to perform the update.

▶ 3. In the Caption box for the OwnerID field, type **Owner ID**.

▶ 4. Click the **FirstName** Field Name box to make it the current field, click the **Caption** box, and then type **First Name**.

5. Click the **LastName** Field Name box to make it the current field, click the **Caption** box, and then type **Last Name**. See Figure 2-35.

Figure 2-35 **Owner table after entering descriptions and captions**

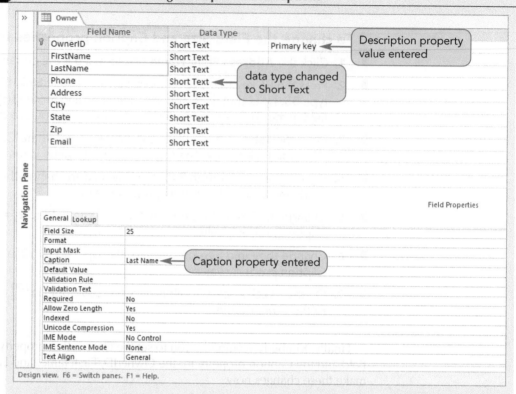

6. On the Quick Access Toolbar, click the **Save** button 🖫 to save your changes to the Owner table.

7. On the Table Tools Design tab, in the Views group, click the **View** button to display the table in Datasheet view.

8. Resize each column to its best fit, and then click in the first row for the **Owner ID** column. See Figure 2-36.

Figure 2-36 **Modified Owner table in Datasheet view**

Kimberly feels that data entry would be made easier if the State field value of "WY" was automatically filled in for each new record added to the table, because all of the owners live in Wyoming. You can accomplish this by setting the Default Value property for the field.

Setting the Default Value Property for a Field

The **Default Value property** for a field specifies what value will appear, by default, for the field in each new record you add to a table.

Because all of the owners at Riverview Veterinary Care Center live in Wyoming, you'll specify a default value of "WY" for the State field in the Owner table. With this setting, each new record in the Owner table will have the correct State field value entered automatically.

To set the Default Value property for the State field:

▶ **1.** On the Home tab, in the Views group, click the **View** button to display the Owner table in Design view.

▶ **2.** Click the **State** Field Name box to make it the current field.

▶ **3.** In the Field Properties pane, click the **Default Value** box, type **WY**, and then press the **Tab** key. See Figure 2-37.

Figure 2-37	Specifying the Default Value property for the State field

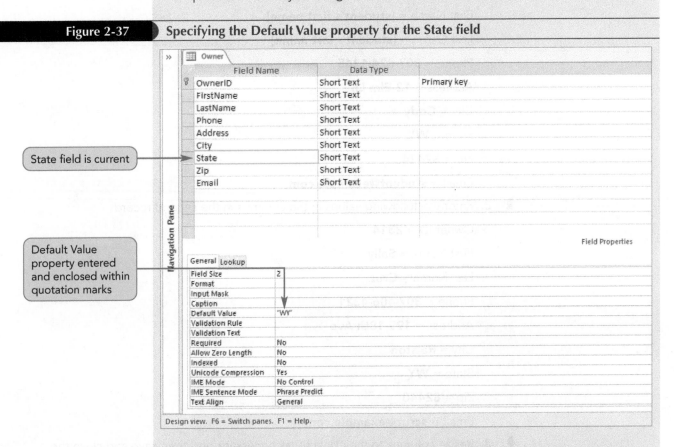

State field is current

Default Value property entered and enclosed within quotation marks

Note that a text entry in the Default Value property must be enclosed within quotation marks. If you do not type the quotation marks, Access adds them for you. However, for some entries, you would receive an error message indicating invalid syntax if you omitted the quotation marks. In such cases, you have to enter the quotation marks yourself.

▶ **4.** On the Quick Access Toolbar, click the **Save** button to save your changes to the Owner table.

TIP

You can change the value in a record from the default value to another value, if necessary.

5. Display the table in Datasheet view. Note that the State field for the first row now displays the default value "WY" as specified by the Default Value property. Each new record entered in the table will automatically have this State field value entered.

With the Owner table design set, you can now enter records in it. You'll begin by entering two records, and then you'll use a different method to add the remaining records.

Note: Be sure to enter your last name and first name where indicated.

To add two records to the Owner table:

1. Enter the following values in the columns in the first record; note that you can press **Tab** to move past the default State field value:

   Owner ID = **2310**

   First Name = **[student's first name]**

   Last Name = **[student's last name]**

   Phone = **307-824-1245**

   Address = **12 Elm Ln**

   City = **Cody**

   State = **WY**

   Zip = **82414**

   Email = **student@example.com**

2. Enter the following values in the columns in the second record:

   Owner ID = **2314**

   First Name = **Sally**

   Last Name = **Cruz**

   Phone = **307-406-4321**

   Address = **199 18th Ave**

   City = **Ralston**

   State = **WY**

   Zip = **82440**

   Email = **scruz@example.com**

3. Resize columns to their best fit, as necessary, and then save and close the Owner table.

Before Kimberly decided to store data using Access, Kelly managed the owner data for the care center in a different system. She exported that data into a text file and now asks you to import it into the new Owner table. You can import the data contained in this text file to add the remaining records to the Owner table.

Adding Data to a Table by Importing a Text File

There are many ways to import data into an Access database. So far, you've learned how to add data to an Access table by importing an Excel spreadsheet, and you've created a new table by importing the structure of an existing table. You can also import data contained in text files.

To complete the entry of records in the Owner table, you'll import the data contained in Kelly's text file. The file is named "Owner" and is located in the Access1 > Module folder provided with your Data Files.

To import the data contained in the Owner text file:

 1. On the ribbon, click the **External Data** tab.

 2. In the Import & Link group, click the **Text File** button. The Get External Data - Text File dialog box opens. This dialog box is similar to the one you used earlier when importing the Excel spreadsheet and the Access table structure.

 3. Click the **Browse** button. The File Open dialog box opens.

 4. Navigate to the **Access1 > Module** folder, where your Data Files are stored, and then double-click the **Owner** file. You return to the dialog box.

 5. Click the **Append a copy of the records to the table** option button. The box to the right of this option becomes active. Next, you need to select the table to which you want to add the data.

 6. Click the arrow on the box, and then click **Owner**.

 7. Click the **OK** button. The first Import Text Wizard dialog box opens. The dialog box indicates that the data to be imported is in a delimited format. A **delimited text file** is one in which fields of data are separated by a character such as a comma or a tab. In this case, the dialog box shows that data is separated by the comma character in the text file.

 8. Make sure the **Delimited** option button is selected in the dialog box, and then click the **Next** button. The second Import Text Wizard dialog box opens. See Figure 2-38.

Figure 2-38) **Second Import Wizard dialog box**

fields in the text file are separated by commas

preview of the data being imported

This dialog box asks you to confirm the delimiter character that separates the fields in the text file you're importing. Access detects that the comma character is used in the Owner text file and selects this option. The bottom area of the dialog box provides a preview of the data you're importing.

9. Make sure the **Comma** option button is selected, and then click the **Next** button. The third and final Import Text Wizard dialog box opens. Notice that the Import to Table box shows that the data will be imported into the Owner table.

10. Click the **Finish** button, and then click the **Close** button in the dialog box that opens to close it without saving the import steps.

Kimberly asks you to open the Owner table in Datasheet view so she can see the results of importing the text file.

To view the Owner table datasheet:

1. Open the Navigation Pane, and then double-click **Owner** to open the Owner table in Datasheet view. The Owner table contains a total of 25 records.

2. Close the Navigation Pane, and then resize columns to their best fit, scrolling the table datasheet as necessary, so that all field values are displayed. When finished, scroll back to display the first fields in the table, and then click the first row's **Owner ID** field, if necessary. See Figure 2-39.

| Figure 2-39 | Owner table after importing data from the text file |

3. Save and close the Owner table, and then open the Navigation Pane.

The Riverview database now contains four tables—Visit, Billing, Owner, and Animal—and the tables contain all the necessary records. Your final task is to complete the database design by defining the necessary relationship between its tables.

Defining Table Relationships

One of the most powerful features of a relational database management system is its ability to define relationships between tables. You use a common field to relate one table to another. The process of relating tables is often called performing a **join**. When you join tables that have a common field, you can extract data from them as if they were one larger table. For example, you can join the Animal and Visit tables by using the AnimalID field in both tables as the common field. Then you can use a query, form, or report to extract selected data from each table, even though the data is contained in two separate tables, as shown in Figure 2-40. The AnimalVisits query shown in Figure 2-40 includes the AnimalID, AnimalName, AnimalType, and AnimalBreed fields from the Animal table, and the VisitDate and Reason fields from the Visit table. The joining of records is based on the common field of AnimalID. The Animal and Visit tables have a type of relationship called a one-to-many relationship.

Figure 2-40	One-to-many relationship and sample query

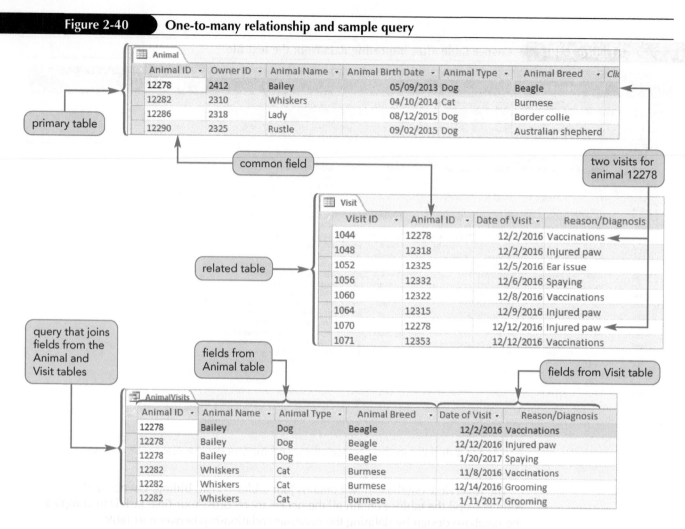

One-to-Many Relationships

As shown earlier in the Session 2.2 Visual Overview, a one-to-many relationship exists between two tables when one record in the first table matches zero, one, or many records in the second table, and when one record in the second table matches at most one record in the first table. For example, as shown in Figure 2-40, Animal 12278 has two visits in the Visit table. Other animals have one or more visits. Every visit has a single matching animal.

In Access, the two tables that form a relationship are referred to as the primary table and the related table. The primary table is the "one" table in a one-to-many relationship; in Figure 2-40, the Animal table is the primary table because there is only one animal for each visit. The related table is the "many" table; in Figure 2-40, the Visit table is the related table because an animal can have zero, one, or many visits.

Because related data is stored in two tables, inconsistencies between the tables can occur. Referring to Figure 2-40, consider the following three scenarios:

- Kimberly adds a record to the Visit table for a new animal, Fluffy (a Siberian cat), using Animal ID 12500. She did not first add the new animal's information to the animal table, so this visit does not have a matching record in the animal table. The data is inconsistent, and the visit record is considered to be an **orphaned record**.
- In another situation, Kimberly changes the AnimalID in the Animal table for Bailey the beagle from 12278 to 12510. Because there is no longer an animal with the AnimalID 12278 in the Animal table, this change creates two orphaned records in the Visit table, and the database is inconsistent.

- In a third scenario, Kimberly deletes the record for Bailey the beagle, Animal 12278, from the Animal table because this animal and its owner have moved and so the animal no longer receives care from Riverview. The database is again inconsistent; two records for Animal 12278 in the Visit table have no matching record in the Animal table.

You can avoid these types of problems and avoid having inconsistent data in your database by specifying referential integrity between tables when you define their relationships.

Referential Integrity

Referential integrity is a set of rules that Access enforces to maintain consistency between related tables when you update data in a database. Specifically, the referential integrity rules are as follows:

- When you add a record to a related table, a matching record must already exist in the primary table, thereby preventing the possibility of orphaned records.
- If you attempt to change the value of the primary key in the primary table, Access prevents this change if matching records exist in a related table. However, if you choose the **Cascade Update Related Fields option**, Access permits the change in value to the primary key and changes the appropriate foreign key values in the related table, thereby eliminating the possibility of inconsistent data.
- When you attempt to delete a record in the primary table, Access prevents the deletion if matching records exist in a related table. However, if you choose the **Cascade Delete Related Records option**, Access deletes the record in the primary table and also deletes all records in related tables that have matching foreign key values. However, you should rarely select the Cascade Delete Related Records option because doing so might cause you to inadvertently delete records you did not intend to delete. It is best to use other methods for deleting records that give you more control over the deletion process.

Defining a Relationship Between Two Tables

At the Riverview Veterinary Care Center, the owners own animals, the animals visit the clinic, and the owner receives the bill for the visits. It is important to understand these relationships in order to determine which owner to send the bill to for the visit each animal makes. Understanding these relationships also allows you to establish relationships between the tables of records in the Riverview database. When two tables have a common field, you can define a relationship between them in the Relationships window, as shown in the Session 2.2 Visual Overview.

Next, you need to define a series of relationships in the Riverview database. First, you will define a one-to-many relationship between the Owner and Animal tables, with Owner as the primary table and Animal as the related table and with OwnerID as the common field (primary key in the Owner table and a foreign key in the Animal table). Second, you will define a one-to-many relationship between the Animal and Visit tables, with Animal as the primary table and Visit as the related table and with AnimalID as the common field (the primary key in the Animal table and a foreign key in the Visit table). Finally, you will define a one-to-many relationship between the Visit and Billing tables, with Visit as the primary table and Billing as the related table and with VisitID as the common field (the primary key in the Visit table and a foreign key in the Billing table).

To define the one-to-many relationship between the Owner and Animal tables:

1. On the ribbon, click the **Database Tools** tab.

2. In the Relationships group, click the **Relationships** button to display the Relationship window and open the Show Table dialog box. See Figure 2-41.

Figure 2-41	Show Table dialog box

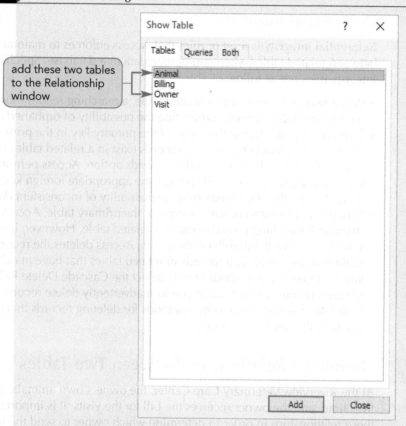

add these two tables to the Relationship window

You must add each table participating in a relationship to the Relationships window. Because the Owner table is the primary table in the relationship, you'll add it first.

TIP

You can also double-click a table in the Show Table dialog box to add it to the Relationships window.

3. Click **Owner**, and then click the **Add** button. The Owner table's field list is added to the Relationships window.

4. Click **Animal**, and then click the **Add** button. The Animal table's field list is added to the Relationships window.

5. Click the **Close** button in the Show Table dialog box to close it.

So that you can view all the fields and complete field names, you'll resize the Owner table field list.

6. Position the mouse pointer on the bottom border of the Owner table field list until it changes to ↕, and then drag the bottom of the Owner table field list to lengthen it until the vertical scroll bar disappears and all the fields are visible.

To form the relationship between the two tables, you drag the common field of OwnerID from the primary table to the related table. Then Access opens the Edit Relationships dialog box, in which you select the relationship options for the two tables.

7. Click **OwnerID** in the Owner field list, and then drag it to **OwnerID** in the Animal field list. When you release the mouse button, the Edit Relationships dialog box opens. See Figure 2-42.

| Figure 2-42 | Edit Relationships dialog box |

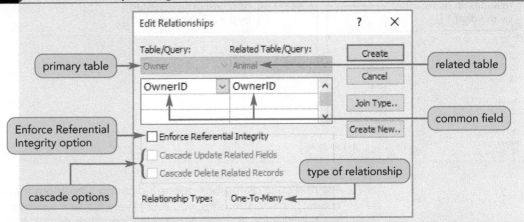

The primary table, related table, common field, and relationship type (One-To-Many) appear in the dialog box. Note that Access correctly identifies the "One" side of the relationship and places the primary table Owner in the Table/Query section of the dialog box; similarly, Access correctly identifies the "Many" side of the relationship and places the related table Animal in the Related Table/Query section of the dialog box.

8. Click the **Enforce Referential Integrity** check box. After you click the Enforce Referential Integrity check box, the two cascade options become available. If you select the Cascade Update Related Fields option, Access will update the appropriate foreign key values in the related table when you change a primary key value in the primary table. You will *not* select the Cascade Delete Related Records option because doing so could cause you to delete records that you do not want to delete; this option is rarely selected.

9. Click the **Cascade Update Related Fields** check box.

10. Click the **Create** button to define the one-to-many relationship between the two tables and to close the dialog box. The completed relationship appears in the Relationships window, with the join line connecting the common field of OwnerID in each table. See Figure 2-43.

Figure 2-43   Defined relationship in the Relationship window

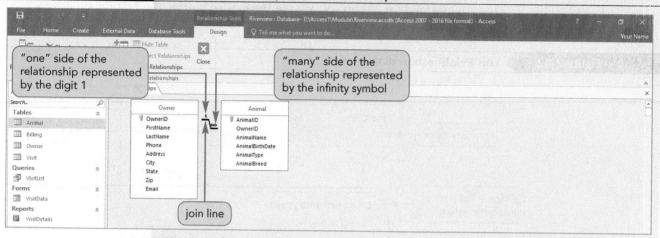

Trouble? If a dialog box opens indicating a problem that prevents you from creating the relationship, you most likely made a typing error when entering the two records in the Owner table. If so, click the OK button in the dialog box and then click the Cancel button in the Edit Relationships dialog box. Refer back to the earlier steps instructing you to enter the two records in the Owner table and carefully compare your entries with those shown in the text, especially the OwnerID field values. Make any necessary corrections to the data in the Owner table, and then repeat Steps 7 through 10. If you still receive an error message, ask your instructor for assistance.

The next step is to define the one-to-many relationship between the Animal and Visit tables. In this relationship, Animal is the primary ("one") table because there is at most one animal for each visit. Visit is the related ("many") table because there are zero, one, or many visits that are generated for each animal. Similarly, you need to define the one-to-many relationship between the Visit and Billing tables. In this relationship, Visit is the primary ("one") table because there is at most one visit for each invoice. Billing is the related ("many") table because there are zero, one, or many invoices that are generated for each animal visit. For example, some visits require lab work, which is invoiced separately.

To define the relationship between the Animal and Visit tables and to define the relationship between the Visit and billing tables:

1. On the Relationship Tools Design tab, in the Relationships group, click the **Show Table** button to open the Show Table dialog box.

2. Click **Visit** on the Tables tab, click the **Add** button, and then click the **Close** button to close the Show Table dialog box. The Visit table's field list appears in the Relationships window to the right of the Animal table's field list.

    Because the Animal table is the primary table in this relationship, you need to drag the AnimalID field from the Animal field list to the Visit field list.

3. Drag the **AnimalID** field in the Animal field list to the **AnimalID** field in the Visit field list. When you release the mouse button, the Edit Relationships dialog box opens.

TIP

You can also use the mouse to drag a table from the Navigation Pane to add it to the Relationships window.

4. Click the **Enforce Referential Integrity** check box, click the **Cascade Update Related Fields** check box, and then click the **Create** button. The Edit Relationships dialog box closes and the completed relationship appears in the Relationships window.

   Finally, you will define the relationship between the Visit and Billing tables.

5. On the Relationship Tools Design tab, in the Relationships group, click the **Show Table** button to open the Show Table dialog box.

6. Click **Billing** on the Tables tab, click the **Add** button, and then click the **Close** button to close the Show Table dialog box. The Billing table's field list appears in the Relationships window to the right of the Visit table's field list.

7. Click and drag the **VisitID** field in the Visit field list to the **VisitID** field in the Billing field list. The Edit Relationships dialog box opens.

8. In the Edit Relationships dialog box, click the **Enforce Referential Integrity** check box, click the **Cascade Update Related Fields** check box, and then click the **Create** button to define the one-to-many relationship between the two tables and to close the dialog box. The completed relationships for the Riverview database appear in the Relationships window. See Figure 2-44.

Figure 2-44 — All three relationships now defined

9. On the Quick Access Toolbar, click the **Save** button to save the layout in the Relationships window.

10. On the Relationship Tools Design tab, in the Relationships group, click the **Close** button to close the Relationships window.

11. Compact and repair the Riverview database, and then close the database.

PROSKILLS

Problem Solving: Creating a Larger Database

The Riverview database is a relatively small database containing only a few tables, and the data and the reports you will generate from it will be fairly simple. A larger database would most likely have many more tables and different types of relationships that can be quite complex. When creating a large database, follow this standard process:

- Consult people who will be using the data to gain an understanding of how it will be used. Gather sample reports and representative data if possible.
- Plan the tables, fields, data types, other properties, and the relationships between the tables.
- Create the tables and define the relationships between them.
- Populate the tables with sample data.
- Design some queries, forms, and reports that will be needed, and then test them.
- Modify the database structure, if necessary, based on the results of your tests.
- Enter the actual data into the database tables.

Testing is critical at every stage of creating a database. Once the database is finalized and implemented, it's not actually finished. The design of a database evolves as new functionality is required and as the data that is gathered changes.

REVIEW

Session 2.2 Quick Check

1. What is the keyboard shortcut for inserting the value from the same field in the previous record into the current record?

2. _____ data is a process that allows you to copy the data from a source without having to open the source file.

3. The _____ gallery allows you to add a group of related fields to a table at the same time, rather than adding each field to the table individually.

4. What is the effect of deleting a field from a table structure?

5. A(n) _____ text file is one in which fields of data are separated by a character such as a comma or a tab.

6. The _____ is the "one" table in a one-to-many relationship, and the _____ is the "many" table in the relationship.

7. _____ is a set of rules that Access enforces to maintain consistency between related tables when you update data in a database.

Review Assignments

PRACTICE

Data File needed for the Review Assignments: Vendor.accdb (*cont. from Module 1*) and Supplies.xlsx

In addition to tracking information about the vendors Riverview Veterinary Care Center works with, Kimberly also wants to track information about their products and services. First, Kimberly asks you to modify the necessary properties in the existing Supplier table in the Vendor database; then she wants you to create a new table in the Vendor database to contain product data. Complete the following:

1. Open the **Vendor** database you created in the previous module.
2. Open the **Supplier** table in Design view, and set the field properties as shown in Figure 2-45.

Figure 2-45   **Field properties for the Supplier table**

Field Name	Data Type	Description	Field Size	Other
SupplierID	Short Text	Primary key	6	Caption = Supplier ID
Company	Short Text		50	
Category	Short Text		15	
Address	Short Text		35	
City	Short Text		25	
State	Short Text		2	
Zip	Short Text		10	
Phone	Short Text		14	Caption = Contact Phone
ContactFirst	Short Text		20	Caption = Contact First Name
ContactLast	Short Text		25	Caption = Contact Last Name
InitialContact	Date/Time			Format = Short Date
				Caption = Initial Contact

3. Save the Supplier table. Click the **Yes** button when a message appears, indicating some data might be lost. Switch to Datasheet view and resize columns, as necessary, to their best fit. Then save and close the Supplier table.
4. Create a new table in Design view, using the table design shown in Figure 2-46.

Figure 2-46   **Design for the Product table**

Field Name	Data Type	Description	Field Size	Other
ProductID	Short Text	Primary key	5	Caption = Product ID
SupplierID	Short Text	Foreign key	6	Caption = Supplier ID
ProductName	Short Text		75	Caption = Product Name
Price	Currency			Format = Standard
				Decimal Places = 2
TempControl	Yes/No			Caption = Temp Controlled?
Sterile	Yes/No			Caption = Sterile?
Units	Number		Integer	Decimal Places = 0
				Caption = Units/Case
				Default Value = [no entry]

5. Specify ProductID as the primary key, and then save the table as **Product**.

6. Modify the table structure by adding a new field between the Price and TempControl fields. Name the new field **Weight** (data type: **Number**; field size: **Single**; Decimal Places: **2**; Caption: **Weight in Lbs**; Default Value: [no entry]). Then move the **Units** field so that it is positioned between the Price and Weight fields.

7. Enter the records shown in Figure 2-47 in the Product table. Resize all datasheet columns to their best fit. When finished, save and close the Product table.

Figure 2-47   Records for the Product table

Product ID	Supplier ID	Product Name	Price	Units/Case	Weight in Lbs	Temp Controlled?	Sterile?
PT100	KLS321	Paper tape roll	20.00	12	3	No	No
TC050	QLS002	Thermometer covers	27.00	50	1	No	Yes

8. Use the Import Spreadsheet Wizard to add data to the Product table. The data you need to import is contained in the Supplies workbook, which is an Excel file located in the Access1 > Review folder provided with your Data Files.

   a. Specify the Supplies workbook as the source of the data.

   b. Select the option for appending the data.

   c. Select Product as the table.

   d. In the Import Spreadsheet Wizard dialog boxes, make sure Access confirms that the first row contains column headings, and import to the Product table. Do not save the import steps.

9. Open the **Product** table in Datasheet view, and resize columns to their best fit, as necessary. Then save and close the Product table.

10. Define a one-to-many relationship between the primary Supplier table and the related Product table. Resize the table field lists so that all field names are visible. Select the referential integrity option and the cascade updates option for the relationship.

11. Save the changes to the Relationships window and close it, compact and repair the Vendor database, and then close the database.

Case Problem 1

Data Files needed for this Case Problem: Beauty.accdb (cont. from Module 1) **and Customers.txt**

Beauty To Go   Sue Miller wants to use the Beauty database to track information about customers who subscribe to her business, which provides a variety of salon services on a subscription basis, and the plans in which customers are enrolled. She asks you to help maintain this database. Complete the following:

1. Open the **Beauty** database you created in the previous module, open the **Option** table in Design view, and then change the following field properties:

   a. OptionID: Enter **Primary key** for the description, change the field size to **3**, and enter **Option ID** for the caption.

   b. OptionDescription: Change the field size to **45** and enter **Option Description** for the caption.

   c. OptionCost: Change the format to **Standard**, specify **0** decimal places, enter **Option Cost** for the caption, no default value.

   d. FeeWaived: Enter **Fee Waived** for the caption.

2. Save and close the Option table. Click the Yes button when a message appears, indicating some data might be lost.

3. Create a new table in Design view, using the table design shown in Figure 2-48.

Figure 2-48	Design for the Member table

Field Name	Data Type	Description	Field Size	Other
MemberID	Short Text	Primary key	4	Caption = Member ID
OptionID	Short Text	Foreign key	3	Caption = Option ID
FirstName	Short Text		20	Caption = First Name
LastName	Short Text		25	Caption = Last Name
Phone	Short Text		14	
OptionEnd	Date/Time	Date Option Ends		Format = Short Date
				Caption = Option Ends

4. Specify **MemberID** as the primary key, and then save the table as **Member**.

5. Use the Address Quick Start selection in the Data Type gallery to add five fields between the LastName and Phone fields.

6. Switch to Design view, and then make the following changes to the Member table design:

   a. Address field: Change the name of this field to **Street**, change the field size to **40**, and delete the entry for the caption.

   b. City field: Change the field size to **25**, and delete the entry for the caption.

   c. StateProvince field: Change the name of this field to **State**, change the field size to **2**, delete the entry for the caption, and enter **FL** for the default value.

   d. ZIPPostal field: Change the name of this field to **Zip**, change the field size to **10**, and delete the entry for the caption.

   e. Delete the **CountryRegion** field from the Member table structure.

   f. Between the Phone and OptionEnd fields, add a new field named **OptionBegin** (data type: **Date/Time**; format: **Short Date**; Caption: **Option Begins**).

7. Enter the records shown in Figure 2-49 in the Member table. Resize all datasheet columns to their best fit. When finished, save and close the Member table. Be sure to enter your first and last name in the appropriate fields in the first record.

Figure 2-49	Records for the Member table

Member ID	Option ID	First Name	Last Name	Street	City	State	Zip	Phone	Option Begins	Option Ends
2103	123	*Student First*	*Student Last*	22 Oak St	Orlando	FL	32801	407-832-3944	2/1/17	3/1/17
2118	120	Susan	Reyes	3 Balboa St	Orlando	FL	32804	407-216-0091	11/2/16	2/2/17

8. Use the Import Text File Wizard to add data to the Member table. The data you need to import is contained in the Customers text file, which is located in the Access1 > Case1 folder provided with your Data Files.

   a. Specify the Customers text file as the source of the data.

   b. Select the option for appending the data.

   c. Select Member as the table.

   d. In the Import Text File Wizard dialog boxes, choose the options to import delimited data, to use a comma delimiter, and to import the data into the Member table. Do not save the import steps.

9. Open the **Member** table in Datasheet view and resize columns to their best fit, as necessary. Then save and close the Member table.

10. Define a one-to-many relationship between the primary Option table and the related Member table. Resize the Member table field list so that all field names are visible. Select the referential integrity option and the cascade updates option for this relationship.

11. Save the changes to the Relationships window and close it, compact and repair the Beauty database, and then close the database.

Case Problem 2

Data Files needed for this Case Problem: Programming.accdb *(cont. from Module 1)*, **Client.accdb, Students.txt, and Agreements.xlsx**

Programming Pros Brent Hovis plans to use the Programming database to maintain information about the students, tutors, and contracts for his tutoring services company. Brent asks you to help him build the database by updating one table and creating two new tables in the database. Complete the following:

1. Open the **Programming** database you created in the previous module, open the **Tutor** table in Design view, and then set the field properties as shown in Figure 2-50.

Figure 2-50 Field properties for the Tutor table

Field Name	Data Type	Description	Field Size	Other
TutorID	Short Text	Primary key	4	Caption = Tutor ID
FirstName	Short Text		20	Caption = First Name
LastName	Short Text		25	Caption = Last Name
Major	Short Text		25	
YearInSchool	Short Text		12	Caption = Year In School
School	Short Text		30	
HireDate	Date/Time			Format = Short Date
				Caption = Hire Date

2. Add a new field as the last field in the Tutor table with the field name **Groups**, the **Yes/No** data type, and the caption **Groups Only**.

3. Save the Tutor table. Click the **Yes** button when a message appears, indicating some data might be lost.

4. In the table datasheet, specify that the following tutors conduct group tutoring sessions only: Carey Billings, Fredrik Karlsson, Ellen Desoto, and Donald Gallager. Close the Tutor table.

5. Brent created a table named Student in the Client database that is located in the Access1 > Case2 folder provided with your Data Files. Import the structure of the Student table in the Client database into a new table named Student in the Programming database. Do not save the import steps.

6. Open the **Student** table in Datasheet view, and then add the following two fields to the end of the table: **BirthDate** (Date/Time field) and **Gender** (Short Text field).

7. Use the Phone Quick Start selection in the Data Type gallery to add four fields related to phone numbers between the Zip and BirthDate fields. (*Hint:* Be sure to make the BirthDate field the active field before adding the new fields.)

8. Display the Student table in Design view, delete the BusinessPhone and FaxNumber fields, and then save and close the Student table.

9. Reopen the Student table and modify its design so that it matches the design in Figure 2-51, *including the revised field names and data types*.

Figure 2-51   Field properties for the Student table

Field Name	Data Type	Description	Field Size	Other
StudentID	Short Text	Primary key	7	Caption = Student ID
LastName	Short Text		25	Caption = Last Name
FirstName	Short Text		20	Caption = First Name
Address	Short Text		35	
City	Short Text		25	
State	Short Text		2	Default Value = NC
Zip	Short Text		10	
HomePhone	Short Text		14	Caption = Home Phone
CellPhone	Short Text		14	Caption = Cell Phone
BirthDate	Date/Time			Format = Short Date Caption = Birth Date
Gender	Short Text		1	

10. Move the LastName field so it follows the FirstName field.
11. Save your changes to the table design, and then add the records shown in Figure 2-52 to the Student table.

Figure 2-52   Records for the Student table

Student ID	First Name	Last Name	Address	City	State	Zip	Home Phone	Cell Phone	Date of Birth	Gender
LOP4015	Henry	Lopez	19 8th St	Raleigh	NC	27601	919-264-9981	919-665-8110	2/19/1998	M
PER4055	Rosalyn	Perez	421 Pine Ln	Cary	NC	27511	984-662-4761	919-678-0012	4/12/1996	F

12. Resize the fields to their best fit, and then save and close the Student table.
13. Use the Import Text File Wizard to add data to the Student table. The data you need to import is contained in the Students text file, which is located in the Access1 > Case2 folder provided with your Data Files.
   a. Specify the Students text file as the source of the data.
   b. Select the option for appending the data.
   c. Select Student as the table.
   d. In the Import Text File Wizard dialog boxes, choose the options to import delimited data, to use a comma delimiter, and to import the data into the Student table. Do not save the import steps.
14. Open the **Student** table in Datasheet view, resize columns in the datasheet to their best fit (as necessary), and then save and close the table.
15. Create a new table in Design view, using the table design shown in Figure 2-53.

Figure 2-53   Design for the Contract table

Field Name	Data Type	Description	Field Size	Other
ContractID	Short Text	Primary key	4	Caption = Contract ID
StudentID	Short Text	Foreign key	7	Caption = Student ID
TutorID	Short Text	Foreign key	4	Caption = Tutor ID
SessionType	Short Text		15	Caption = Session Type
Length	Number		Integer	Decimal Places = 0
				Caption = Length (Hrs)
				Default Value = [no entry]
NumSessions	Number		Integer	Decimal Places = 0
				Caption = Number of Sessions
				Default Value = [no entry]
Cost	Currency			Format = Currency
				Decimal Places = 0
				Default Value = [no entry]
Assessment	Yes/No	Pre-assessment exam complete		Caption = Assessment Complete

16. Specify ContractID as the primary key, and then save the table using the name **Contract**.

17. Add a new field to the Contract table, between the TutorID and SessionType fields, with the field name **ContractDate**, the **Date/Time** data type, the description **Date contract is signed**, the **Short Date** format, and the caption **Contract Date**. Save and close the Contract table.

18. Use the Import Spreadsheet Wizard to add data to the Contract table. The data you need to import is contained in the Agreements workbook, which is an Excel file located in the Access1 > Case2 folder provided with your Data Files.

    a. Specify the Agreements workbook as the source of the data.

    b. Select the option for appending the data to the table.

    c. Select Contract as the table.

    d. In the Import Spreadsheet Wizard dialog boxes, choose the Agreements worksheet, make sure Access confirms that the first row contains column headings, and import to the Contract table. Do not save the import steps.

19. Open the **Contract** table, and add the records shown in Figure 2-54. (*Hint:* Use the New (blank) record button in the navigation buttons to add a new record.)

Figure 2-54   Records for the Contract table

Contract ID	Student ID	Tutor ID	Contract Date	Session Type	Length (Hrs)	Number of Sessions	Cost	Assessment Complete
6215	PER4055	1018	7/6/2017	Group	2	5	$400	Yes
6350	LOP4015	1010	10/12/2017	Private	3	4	$720	Yes

20. Resize columns in the datasheet to their best fit (as necessary), and then save and close the Contract table.

21. Define the one-to-many relationships between the database tables as follows: between the primary Student table and the related Contract table, and between the primary Tutor table and the related Contract table. Resize the table field lists so that all field names are visible. Select the referential integrity option and the cascade updates option for each relationship.

22. Save the changes to the Relationships window and close it, compact and repair the Programming database, and then close the database.

Case Problem 3

Data Files needed for this Case Problem: Center.accdb *(cont. from Module 1),* **Donations.xlsx, and Auctions.txt**

Diane's Community Center   Diane Coleman wants to use the Center database to maintain information about the patrons and donations for her not-for-profit community center. Diane asks you to help her maintain the database by updating one table and creating two new ones. Complete the following:

1. Open the **Center** database you created in the previous module, open the **Patron** table in Design view, and then change the following field properties:
   a. PatronID: Enter **Primary key** for the description, change the field size to **5**, and enter **Patron ID** for the caption.
   b. Title: Change the field size to **4**.
   c. FirstName: Change the field size to **20**, and enter **First Name** for the caption.
   d. LastName: Change the field size to **25**, and enter **Last Name** for the caption.
   e. Phone: Change the field size to **14**.
   f. Email: Change field size to **35**.

2. Save and close the Patron table. Click the Yes button when a message appears, indicating some data might be lost.

⊕ **Explore** 3. Use the Import Spreadsheet Wizard to create a table in the Center database. As the source of the data, specify the Donations workbook, which is located in the Access1 > Case3 folder provided with your Data Files. Select the option to import the source data into a new table in the database.

⊕ **Explore** 4. Complete the Import Spreadsheet Wizard dialog boxes as follows:
   a. Select Donation as the worksheet you want to import.
   b. Specify that the first row contains column headings.
   c. Accept the field options suggested by the wizard, and do not skip any fields.
   d. Choose DonationID as your own primary key.
   e. Import the data to a table named **Donation**, and do not save the import steps.

⊕ **Explore** 5. Open the Donation table in Datasheet view. Left-justify the DonationDescription field by clicking the column heading, and then on the Home tab, clicking the Align Left button in the Text Formatting group.

6. Open the Donation table in Design view, and then modify the table so it matches the design shown in Figure 2-55, including changes to data types, field name, and field position. For the Short Text fields, delete any formats specified in the Format property boxes.

Figure 2-55   Design for the Donation table

Field Name	Data Type	Description	Field Size	Other
DonationID	Short Text	Primary key	4	Caption = Donation ID
PatronID	Short Text	Foreign key	5	Caption = Patron ID
DonationDate	Date/Time			Format = mm/dd/yyyy
				Caption = Donation Date
Description	Short Text		30	
DonationValue	Currency	Dollar amount or estimated value		Format = Currency
				Decimal Places = 2
				Caption = Donation Value
				Default Value = [no entry]
CashDonation	Yes/No			Caption = Cash Donation?
AuctionItem	Yes/No			Caption = Possible Auction Item?

7. Save your changes to the table design, click Yes for the message about lost data, and then switch to Datasheet view.

8. Resize the columns in the Donation datasheet to their best fit.

✦ **Explore** 9. Diane decides that the values in the Donation Value column would look better without the two decimal places. Make this field the current field in the datasheet. Then, on the Table Tools Fields tab, in the Formatting group, use the Decrease Decimals button to remove the two decimal places and the period from these values. Switch back to Design view, and note that the Decimal Places property for the DonationValue field is now set to 0.

10. Save and close the Donation table.

11. Use Design view to create a table using the table design shown in Figure 2-56.

Figure 2-56   Design for the Auction table

Field Name	Data Type	Description	Field Size	Other
AuctionID	Short Text	Primary key	3	Caption = Auction ID
AuctionDate	Date/Time			Format = mm/dd/yyyy
				Caption = Date of Auction
DonationID	Short Text		4	Caption = Donation ID
MinPrice	Currency			Format = Currency
				Decimal Places = 0
				Caption = Minimum Sale Price
ItemSold	Yes/No			Caption = Item Sold at Auction?

12. Specify **AuctionID** as the primary key, save the table as **Auction**, and then close the table.

13. Use the Import Text File Wizard to add data to the Auction table. The data you need to import is contained in the Auctions text file, which is located in the Access1 > Case3 folder provided with your Data Files.

a. Specify the Auctions text file as the source of the data.

b. Select the option for appending the data.

c. Select Auction as the table.

d. In the Import Text File Wizard dialog boxes, choose the options to import delimited data, to use a comma delimiter, and to import the data into the Auction table. Do not save the import steps.

14. Open the Auction table in Datasheet view, and resize all columns to their best fit.

15. Display the Auction table in Design view. Move the DonationID field to make it the second field in the table, and enter the description **Foreign key** for the DonationID field. Save the modified Auction table design.

16. Switch to Datasheet view, and then add the records shown in Figure 2-57 to the Auction table. (*Hint:* Use the New (blank) record button in the navigation buttons to add a new record.) Close the table when finished.

Figure 2-57   Records for the Auction table

AuctionID	DonationID	AuctionDate	MinPrice	ItemSold
205	5132	8/12/2017	200	No
235	5217	10/14/2017	150	No

17. Define the one-to-many relationships between the database tables as follows: between the primary Patron table and the related Donation table, and between the primary Donation table and the related Auction table. Resize any field lists so that all field names are visible. Select the referential integrity option and the cascade updates option for each relationship.

18. Save the changes to the Relationships window and close it, compact and repair the Center database, and then close the database.

Case Problem 4

CHALLENGE

Data Files needed for this Case Problem: Appalachia.accdb *(cont. from Module 1)*, Travel.accdb, and Bookings.txt

Hike Appalachia   Molly and Bailey Johnson use the Appalachia database to track the data about the hikers and tours offered through their business. They ask you to help them maintain this database. Complete the following:

1. Open the **Appalachia** database you created in the previous module, open the **Hiker** table in Design view, and then change the following field properties:

   a. HikerID: Enter **Primary key** for the description, change the field size to **3**, and enter **Hiker ID** for the caption.

   b. HikerFirst: Change the field size to **20**, and enter **Hiker First Name** for the caption.

   c. HikerLast: Change the field size to **25**, and enter **Hiker Last Name** for the caption.

   d. Address: Change the field size to **35**.

   e. City: Change the field size to **25**.

   f. State: Change the field size to **2**.

   g. Zip: Change the field size to **10**.

   h. Phone: Change the field size to **14**.

2. Save the Hiker table, click the Yes button when a message appears, indicating some data might be lost, resize the Hiker First Name and Hiker Last Name columns in Datasheet view to their best fit, and then save and close the table.

   a. Import the **Trip** table structure and data from the **Travel** database into a new table in the **Appalachia** database. As the source of the data, specify the Travel database, which is located in the Access1 > Case4 folder provided with your Data Files; select the option button to import tables, queries, forms, reports, macros, and modules into the current database; and in the Import Objects dialog box, select the **Trip** table, click the **Options** button, and then make sure that the correct option is selected to import the table's data and structure (definition).

   b. Do not save your import steps.

⊕ **Explore** 3. Using a shortcut menu in the Navigation Pane, rename the Trip table as **Tour** to give this name to the new table in the Appalachia database.

4. Open the **Tour** table in Design view, and then delete the VIPDiscount field.

5. Change the following properties:

   a. TourID: Enter the description **Primary key**, change the field size to **3**, and enter **Tour ID** for the caption.

   b. TourName: Enter **Tour Name** for the caption, and change the field size to **35**.

   c. TourType: Enter **Tour Type** for the caption, and change the field size to **15**.

   d. PricePerPerson: Enter **Price Per Person** for the caption.

6. Save the modified table, click the Yes button when a message appears, indicating some data might be lost, and then display the table in Datasheet view. Resize all datasheet columns to their best fit, and then save and close the table.

7. In Design view, create a table using the table design shown in Figure 2-58.

Figure 2-58   **Design for the Reservation table**

Field Name	Data Type	Description	Field Size	Other
ReservationID	Short Text	Primary key	4	Caption = Reservation ID
HikerID	Short Text	Foreign key	3	Caption = Hiker ID
TourID	Short Text	Foreign key	3	Caption = Tour ID
TourDate	Date/Time			Caption = Tour Date
People	Number		Integer	Decimal Places = 0
				Default Value = [no entry]

8. Specify **ReservationID** as the primary key, and then save the table as **Reservation**.

⊕ **Explore** 9. Refer back to Figure 2-11 to review the custom date formats. Change the Format property of the TourDate field to a custom format that displays dates in a format similar to 02/15/17. Save and close the Reservation table.

10. Use the Import Text File Wizard to add data to the Reservation table. The data you need to import is contained in the Bookings text file, which is located in the Access1 > Case4 folder provided with your Data Files.

    a. Specify the Bookings text file as the source of the data.

    b. Select the option for appending the data.

    c. Select Reservation as the table.

    d. In the Import Text File Wizard dialog boxes, choose the options to import delimited data, to use a comma delimiter, and to import the data into the Reservation table. Do not save the import steps.

11. Open the **Reservation** table, and then resize columns in the table datasheet to their best fit (as necessary), verify that the date values in the StartDate field are displayed correctly according to the custom format, and then save and close the table.

12. Define the one-to-many relationships between the database tables as follows: between the primary Hiker table and the related Reservation table, and between the primary Tour table and the related Reservation table. (*Hint:* Place the Reservation table as the middle table in the Relationships window to make it easier to join the tables.) Resize the Hiker field list so that all field names are visible. Select the referential integrity option and the cascade updates option for each relationship.

13. Save the changes to the Relationships window and close it, compact and repair the Appalachia database, and then close the database.

OBJECTIVES

Session 3.1
- Find, modify, and delete records in a table
- Hide and unhide fields in a datasheet
- Work in the Query window in Design view
- Create, run, and save queries
- Update data using a query datasheet
- Create a query based on multiple tables
- Sort data in a query
- Filter data in a query

Session 3.2
- Specify an exact match condition in a query
- Use a comparison operator in a query to match a range of values
- Use the And and Or logical operators in queries
- Change the font size and alternate row color in a datasheet
- Create and format a calculated field in a query
- Perform calculations in a query using aggregate functions and record group calculations
- Change the display of database objects in the Navigation Pane

Maintaining and Querying a Database

Updating Tables and Retrieving Care Center Information

Case | *Riverview Veterinary Care Center*

At a recent meeting, Kimberly Johnson and her staff discussed the importance of maintaining accurate information about the animals seen by Riverview Veterinary Care Center, as well as the owners, visits, and invoices, and regularly monitoring the business activities of the care center. For example, Kelly Flannagan, Kimberly's assistant, needs to make sure she has up-to-date contact information, such as phone numbers and email addresses, for the owners of all the animals seen by the care center. The office staff also must monitor billing activity to ensure that invoices are paid on time and in full. In addition, the staff handles marketing efforts for the care center and tracks services provided to develop new strategies for promoting these services. Kimberly is also interested in analyzing other aspects of the business related to animal visits and finances. You can satisfy all these informational needs for Riverview Veterinary Care Center by updating data in the Riverview database and by creating and using queries that retrieve information from the database.

STARTING DATA FILES

Access1	→	Module	Review	Case1
		Riverview.accdb (*cont.*)	Vendor.accdb (*cont.*)	Beauty.accdb (*cont.*)

Case2	Case3	Case4
Programming.accdb (*cont.*)	Center.accdb (*cont.*)	Appalachia.accdb (*cont.*) HikeApp.accdb

Session 3.1 Visual Overview:

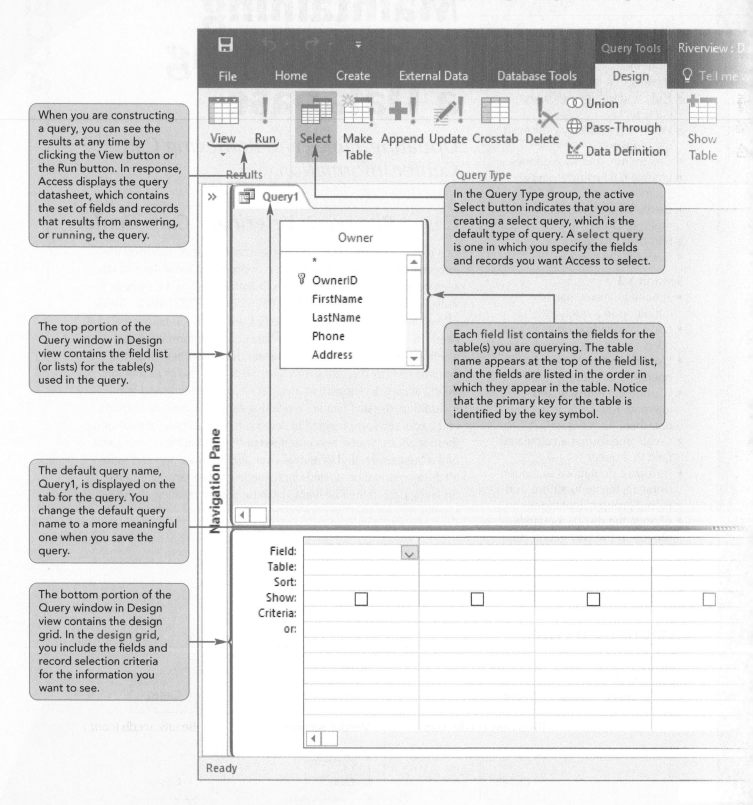

When you are constructing a query, you can see the results at any time by clicking the View button or the Run button. In response, Access displays the query datasheet, which contains the set of fields and records that results from answering, or running, the query.

The top portion of the Query window in Design view contains the field list (or lists) for the table(s) used in the query.

The default query name, Query1, is displayed on the tab for the query. You change the default query name to a more meaningful one when you save the query.

The bottom portion of the Query window in Design view contains the design grid. In the design grid, you include the fields and record selection criteria for the information you want to see.

In the Query Type group, the active Select button indicates that you are creating a select query, which is the default type of query. A select query is one in which you specify the fields and records you want Access to select.

Each field list contains the fields for the table(s) you are querying. The table name appears at the top of the field list, and the fields are listed in the order in which they appear in the table. Notice that the primary key for the table is identified by the key symbol.

Query Window in Design View

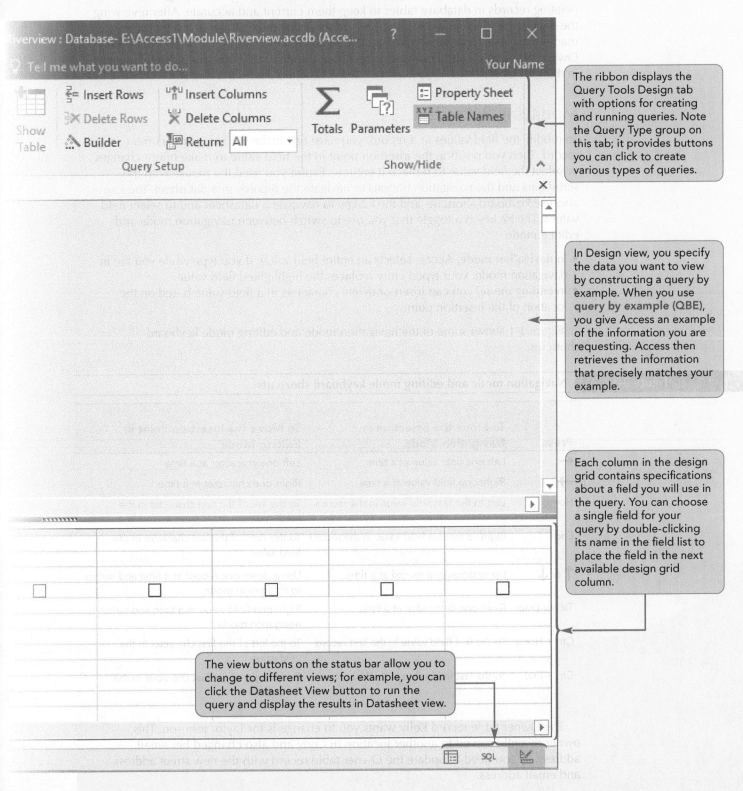

The ribbon displays the Query Tools Design tab with options for creating and running queries. Note the Query Type group on this tab; it provides buttons you can click to create various types of queries.

In Design view, you specify the data you want to view by constructing a query by example. When you use query by example (QBE), you give Access an example of the information you are requesting. Access then retrieves the information that precisely matches your example.

Each column in the design grid contains specifications about a field you will use in the query. You can choose a single field for your query by double-clicking its name in the field list to place the field in the next available design grid column.

The view buttons on the status bar allow you to change to different views; for example, you can click the Datasheet View button to run the query and display the results in Datasheet view.

Updating a Database

Updating, or **maintaining**, a database is the process of adding, modifying, and deleting records in database tables to keep them current and accurate. After reviewing the data in the Riverview database, Kelly identified some changes that need to be made to the data. She would like you to update the field values in one record in the Owner table, correct an error in one record in the Visit table, and then delete a record in the Visit table.

Modifying Records

To modify the field values in a record, you must first make the record the current record. Then you position the insertion point in the field value to make minor changes or select the field value to replace it entirely. Earlier you used the mouse with the scroll bars and the navigation buttons to navigate the records in a datasheet. You can also use keyboard shortcuts and the F2 key to navigate a datasheet and to select field values. The **F2 key** is a toggle that you use to switch between navigation mode and editing mode.

- In **navigation mode**, Access selects an entire field value. If you type while you are in navigation mode, your typed entry replaces the highlighted field value.
- In **editing mode**, you can insert or delete characters in a field value based on the location of the insertion point.

Figure 3-1 shows some of the navigation mode and editing mode keyboard shortcuts.

Figure 3-1 Navigation mode and editing mode keyboard shortcuts

Press	To Move the Selection in Navigation Mode	To Move the Insertion Point in Editing Mode
←	Left one field value at a time	Left one character at a time
→	Right one field value at a time	Right one character at a time
Home	Left to the first field value in the record	To the left of the first character in the field value
End	Right to the last field value in the record	To the right of the last character in the field value
↑ or ↓	Up or down one record at a time	Up or down one record at a time and switch to navigation mode
Tab or Enter	Right one field value at a time	Right one field value at a time and switch to navigation mode
Ctrl + Home	To the first field value in the first record	To the left of the first character in the field value
Ctrl + End	To the last field value in the last record	To the right of the last character in the field value

The Owner table record Kelly wants you to change is for Taylor Johnson. This owner recently moved to another location in Cody and also changed her email address, so you need to update the Owner table record with the new street address and email address.

To open the Owner table in the Riverview database:

▶ **1.** Start Access and open the **Riverview** database you created and worked with earlier.

Trouble? If the security warning is displayed below the ribbon, click the Enable Content button.

▶ **2.** Open the **Owner** table in Datasheet view.

The Owner table contains many fields. Sometimes, when updating data in a table, it can be helpful to remove the display of some fields on the screen.

Hiding and Unhiding Fields

When you are viewing a table or query datasheet in Datasheet view, you might want to temporarily remove certain fields from the displayed datasheet, making it easier to focus on the data you're interested in viewing. The **Hide Fields** command allows you to remove the display of one or more fields, and the **Unhide Fields** command allows you to redisplay any hidden fields.

To make it easier to modify the owner record, you'll first hide a couple of fields in the Owner table.

To hide fields in the Owner table and modify the owner record:

▶ **1.** Right-click the **State** field name to display the shortcut menu, and then click **Hide Fields**. The State column is removed from the datasheet display.

▶ **2.** Right-click the **Zip** field name, and then click **Hide Fields** on the shortcut menu. The Zip column is removed from the datasheet display.

With the fields hidden, you can now update the owner record. The record you need to modify is near the end of the table and has an OwnerID field value of 2412.

▶ **3.** Scroll the datasheet until you see the last record in the table.

▶ **4.** Click the OwnerID field value **2412**, for Taylor Johnson. The insertion point appears within the field value, indicating you are in editing mode.

▶ **5.** Press the **Tab** key to move to the First Name field value, Taylor. The field value is selected, indicating you are in navigation mode.

▶ **6.** Press the **Tab** key three times to move to the Address field and select its field value, type **458 Rose Ln**, and then press the **Tab** key twice to move to the Email field.

▶ **7.** Type **taylor.johnson@example.net**, and then press the **Tab** key to move to the insertion point to the OwnerID field in the blank record at the bottom of the table. The changes to the record are complete. See Figure 3-2.

| Figure 3-2 | Table after changing field values in a record |

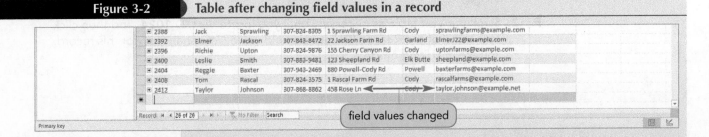

Access saves changes to field values when you move to a new field or another record, or when you close the table. You don't have to click the Save button to save changes to field values or records.

8. Press the **Ctrl+Home** keys to move to the first field value in the first record. With the changes to the record complete, you can unhide the hidden fields.

9. Right-click any field name to display the shortcut menu, and then click **Unhide Fields**. The Unhide Columns dialog box opens. See Figure 3-3.

| Figure 3-3 | Unhide Columns dialog box |

All currently displayed fields are checked in this dialog box, and all hidden fields are unchecked. To redisplay them, you simply click their check boxes to select them.

10. In the Unhide Columns dialog box, click the **State** check box to select it, click the **Zip** check box to select it, and then click the **Close** button to close the dialog box. The two hidden fields are now displayed in the datasheet.

11. Close the Owner table, and then click the **No** button in the dialog box that opens, asking if you want to save changes to the layout of the Owner table. This box appears because you hid fields and redisplayed them.

In this case, you can click either the Yes button or the No button, because no changes were actually made to the table layout or design.

Next you need to correct an error in the Visit table for a visit made by Molly, Animal ID 12312. A staff member incorrectly entered "Vaccinations" as the reason for the visit, when the animal actually came to the care center that day for a wellness exam. Ensuring the accuracy of the data in a database is an important maintenance task.

To correct the record in the Visit table:

1. Open the **Visit** table in Datasheet view. The record containing the error is for Visit ID 1024.

2. Scroll the Visit table as necessary until you locate Visit ID **1024**, and then click at the end of the **Reason/Diagnosis** field value "Vaccinations" for this record. You are in editing mode.

3. Delete **Vaccinations** from the Reason/Diagnosis field, type **Wellness exam**, and then press the **Enter** key twice. The record now contains the correct value in the Reason/Diagnosis field, and this change is automatically saved in the Visit table.

The next update Kelly asks you to make is to delete a record in the Visit table. The owner of Butch, one of the animals seen by the care center, recently notified Taylor that he received an invoice for a neutering visit, but that he had canceled this scheduled appointment. Because this visit did not take place, the record for this visit needs to be deleted from the Visit table. Rather than scrolling through the table to locate the record to delete, you can use the Find command.

Finding Data in a Table

Access provides options you can use to locate specific field values in a table. Instead of scrolling the Visit table datasheet to find the visit that you need to delete—the record for Visit ID 1128—you can use the Find command to find the record. The **Find command** allows you to search a table or query datasheet, or a form, to locate a specific field value or part of a field value. This feature is particularly useful when searching a table that contains a large number of records.

To search for the record in the Visit table:

TIP

You can click any value in the column containing the field you want to search to make the field current.

1. Make sure the VisitID field value **1028** is still selected, and the **Home** tab is selected on the ribbon. You need to search the VisitID field to find the record containing the value 1128, so the insertion point is already correctly positioned in the field you want to search.

2. In the Find group, click the **Find** button. The Find and Replace dialog box opens. See Figure 3-4.

Figure 3-4   **Find and Replace dialog box**

specifies that the current field will be searched

specifies that Access will search for a match to the entire field value

value selected in the table datasheet

specifies that all records in the table will be searched

The field value 1028 appears in the Find What box because this value is selected in the table datasheet. You also can choose to search for only part of a field value, such as when you need to find all Visit IDs that start with a certain value. The Search box indicates that all the records in the table will be searched for the value you want to find. You also can choose to search up or down from the currently selected record.

Trouble? Some of the settings in your dialog box might be different from those shown in Figure 3-4 depending on the last search performed on the computer you're using. If so, change the settings so that they match those in the figure.

> **3.** Make sure the value 1028 is selected in the Find What box, type **1128** to replace the selected value, and then click the **Find Next** button. Record 50 appears with the field value you specified selected.

> **4.** Click the **Cancel** button to close the Find and Replace dialog box.

Deleting Records

To delete a record, you need to select the record in Datasheet view and then delete it using the Delete button in the Records group on the Home tab or the Delete Record option on the shortcut menu.

REFERENCE

Deleting a Record

- With the table open in Datasheet view, click the row selector for the record you want to delete.
- In the Records group on the Home tab, click the Delete button (or right-click the row selector for the record, and then click Delete Record on the shortcut menu).
- In the dialog box asking you to confirm the deletion, click the Yes button.

Now that you have found the record with Visit ID 1128, you can delete it. To delete a record, you must first select the entire row for the record.

To delete the record:

> **1.** Click the row selector for the record containing the VisitID field value **1128**, which should still be highlighted. The entire row is selected.

> **2.** On the Home tab, in the Records group, click the **Delete** button. A dialog box opens indicating that you cannot delete the record because the Billing table contains records that are related to VisitID 1128. Recall that you defined a one-to-many relationship between the Visit and Billing tables and you enforced referential integrity. When you try to delete a record in the primary table (Visit), the enforced referential integrity prevents the deletion if matching records exist in the related table (Billing). This protection helps to maintain the integrity of the data in the database.

> To delete the record in the Visit table, you first must delete the related records in the Billing table.

> **3.** Click the **OK** button in the dialog box to close it. Notice the plus sign that appears at the beginning of each record in the Visit table. The plus sign, also called the **expand indicator**, indicates that the Visit table is the primary table related to another table—in this case, the Billing table. Clicking the expand indicator displays related records from other tables in the database in a **subdatasheet**.

> **4.** Scroll down the datasheet until the selected record is near the top of the datasheet, so that you have room to view the related records for the visit record.

5. Click the **expand indicator** next to VisitID 1128. Two related records from the Billing table for this visit are displayed in the subdatasheet. See Figure 3-5.

Figure 3-5   **Related records from the Billing table in the subdatasheet**

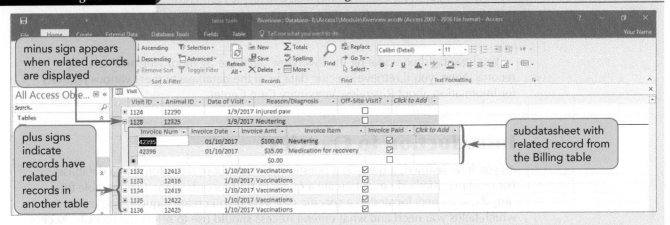

When the subdatasheet is open, you can navigate and update it, just as you can using a table datasheet. The expand indicator for an open subdatasheet is replaced by a minus sign. Clicking the minus sign, or **collapse indicator**, hides the subdatasheet.

You need to delete the records in the Billing table that are related to Visit ID 1128 before you can delete this visit record. The records are for the invoices that were mistakenly sent to the owner of Butch, who had canceled his dog's neutering visit at the care center. You could open the Billing table and find the related records. However, an easier way is to delete the records right in the subdatasheet. The records will be deleted from the Billing table automatically.

6. In the Billing table subdatasheet, click the row selector for invoice number **42395**, and then drag down one row. The rows are selected for both invoice number 42395 and invoice number 42396.

7. On the Home tab, in the Records group, click the **Delete** button. Because the deletion of records is permanent and cannot be undone, a dialog box opens asking you to confirm the deletion of two records.

8. Click the **Yes** button to confirm the deletion and close the dialog box. The records are removed from the Billing table, and the subdatasheet is now empty.

9. Click the **collapse indicator** next to VisitID 1128 to close the subdatasheet.

Now that you have deleted the related records in the Billing table, you can delete the record for Visit ID 1128. You'll use the shortcut menu to do so.

10. Right-click the row selector for the record for Visit ID **1128** to select the record and open the shortcut menu.

Be sure to select the correct record before deleting it.

11. Click **Delete Record** on the shortcut menu, and then click the **Yes** button in the dialog box to confirm the deletion. The record is deleted from the Visit table.

12. Close the Visit table.

Process for Deleting Records

When working with more complex databases that are managed by a database administrator, you typically need special permission to delete records from a table. Many companies also follow the practice of archiving records before deleting them so that the information is still available but not part of the active database.

You have finished updating the Riverview database by modifying and deleting records. Next, you'll retrieve specific data from the database to meet various requests for information about Riverview Veterinary Care Center.

Introduction to Queries

As you have learned, a query is a question you ask about data stored in a database. For example, Kimberly might create a query to find records in the Owner table for only those owners located in a specific city. When you create a query, you tell Access which fields you need and what criteria Access should use to select the records. Access provides powerful query capabilities that allow you to do the following:

- Display selected fields and records from a table
- Sort records
- Perform calculations
- Generate data for forms, reports, and other queries
- Update data in the tables in a database
- Find and display data from two or more tables

Most questions about data are generalized queries in which you specify the fields and records you want Access to select. These common requests for information, such as "Which owners are located in Ralston?" or "How many invoices have been paid?" are select queries. The answer to a select query is returned in the form of a datasheet. The result of a query is also referred to as a **recordset** because the query produces a set of records that answers your question.

Designing Queries vs. Using a Query Wizard

More specialized, technical queries, such as finding duplicate records in a table, are best formulated using a Query Wizard. A **Query Wizard** prompts you for information by asking a series of questions and then creates the appropriate query based on your answers. For example, earlier you used the Simple Query Wizard to display only some of the fields in the Visit table; Access provides other Query Wizards for more complex queries. For common, informational queries, designing your own query is more efficient than using a Query Wizard.

The care center staff is planning an email campaign advertising a microchipping service being offered to animals seen by Riverview Veterinary Care Center. You need to create a query to display the owner ID, last name, first name, city, and email address for each record in the Owner table. You'll open the Query window in Design view to create the query.

To open the Query window in Design view:

▶ 1. Close the Navigation Pane, and then, on the ribbon, click the **Create** tab.

▶ 2. In the Queries group, click the **Query Design** button to display the Query window in Design view, with the Show Table dialog box open and the Tables tab selected. See Figure 3-6.

Figure 3-6   Show Table dialog box

The Show Table dialog box lists all the tables in the Riverview database. You can choose to base a query on one or more tables, on other queries, or on a combination of tables and queries. The query you are creating will retrieve data from the Owner table, so you need to add this table to the Query window.

▶ 3. In the Tables list, click **Owner**, click the **Add** button, and then click the **Close** button to close the Show Table dialog box. The Owner table's field list appears in the Query window. Refer to the Session 3.1 Visual Overview to familiarize yourself with the Query window in Design view.

Trouble? If you add the wrong table to the Query window, right-click the bar at the top of the field list containing the table name, and then click Remove Table on the shortcut menu. To add the correct table to the Query window, repeat Steps 2 and 3.

Now you'll create and run the query to display selected fields from the Owner table.

Creating and Running a Query

The default table datasheet displays all the fields in the table in the same order as they appear in the table. In contrast, a query datasheet can display selected fields from a table, and the order of the fields can be different from that of the table, enabling those viewing the query results to see only the information they need and in the order they want.

You need the OwnerID, LastName, FirstName, City, and Email fields from the Owner table to appear in the query results. You'll add each of these fields to the design grid. First you'll resize the Owner table field list to display all of the fields.

To select the fields for the query, and then run the query:

1. Drag the bottom border of the Owner field list to resize the field list so that all the fields in the Owner table are visible.

2. In the Owner field list, double-click **OwnerID** to place the field in the design grid's first column Field box. See Figure 3-7.

Figure 3-7 **Field added to the design grid**

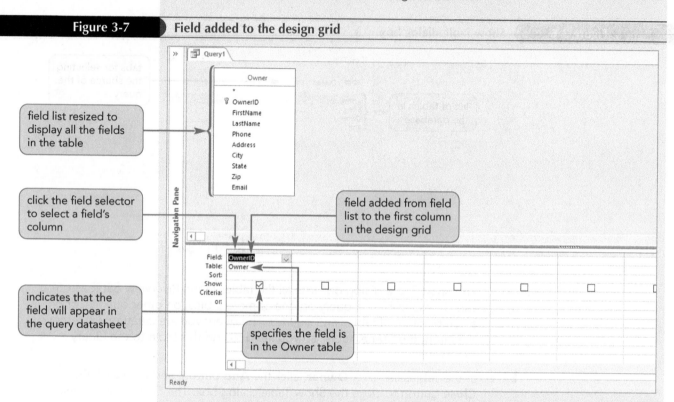

field list resized to display all the fields in the table

click the field selector to select a field's column

indicates that the field will appear in the query datasheet

field added from field list to the first column in the design grid

specifies the field is in the Owner table

In the design grid's first column, the field name OwnerID appears in the Field box, the table name Owner appears in the Table box, and the checkmark in the Show check box indicates that the field will be displayed in the datasheet when you run the query. Sometimes you might not want to display a field and its values in the query results. For example, if you are creating a query to list all owners located in Ralston, and you assign the name "RalstonOwners" to the query, you do not need to include the City field value for each record in the query results—the query design lists only owners with the City field value of "Ralston." Even if you choose not to display a field in the query results, you can still use the field as part of the query to select specific records or to specify a particular sequence for the records in the datasheet. You can also add a field to the design grid using the arrow on the Field box; this arrow appears when you click the Field box, and if you click the arrow or the right side of an empty Field box, a menu of available fields opens.

TIP

You can also use the mouse to drag a field from the field list to a column in the design grid.

3. In the design grid, click the right side of the second column's Field box to display a menu listing all the fields in the Owner table, and then click **LastName** to add this field to the second column in the design grid.

4. Add the **FirstName**, **City**, and **Email** fields to the design grid in that order.

   Trouble? If you accidentally add the wrong field to the design grid, select the field's column by clicking the pointer ↓ on the field selector, which is the thin bar above the Field box, for the field you want to delete, and then press the Delete key (or in the Query Setup group on the Query Tools Design tab, click the Delete Columns button).

   Now that the five fields for the query have been selected, you can run the query.

5. On the Query Tools Design tab, in the Results group, click the **Run** button. Access runs the query and displays the results in Datasheet view. See Figure 3-8.

Figure 3-8	Datasheet displayed after running the query

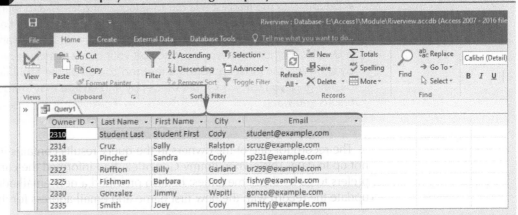

The five fields you added to the design grid appear in the datasheet in the same order as they appear in the design grid. The records are displayed in primary key sequence by OwnerID. The query selected all 25 records from the Owner table for display in the query datasheet. You will save the query as "OwnerEmail" so that you can easily retrieve the same data again.

6. On the Quick Access Toolbar, click the **Save** button. The Save As dialog box opens.

7. In the Query Name box, type **OwnerEmail** and then press the **Enter** key. The query is saved with the specified name in the Riverview database, and its name appears on the tab for the query.

PROSKILLS

Decision Making: Comparing Methods for Adding All Fields to the Design Grid

If the query you are creating includes every field from the specified table, you can use one of the following three methods to transfer all the fields from the field list to the design grid:

- Double-click (or click and drag) each field individually from the field list to the design grid. Use this method if you want the fields in your query to appear in an order that is different from the order in the field list.
- Double-click the asterisk at the top of the field list. The table name, followed by a period and an asterisk (as in "Owner.*"), appears in the Field box of the first column in the design grid, which signifies that the order of the fields is the same in the query as it is in the field list. Use this method if you don't need to sort the query or specify conditions based on the fields in the table you added in this way (for example, in a query based on more than one table). The advantage of using this method is that you do not need to change the query if you add or delete fields from the underlying table structure. Such changes are reflected automatically in the query.
- Double-click the field list title bar to select all the fields, and then click and drag one of the selected fields to the first column in the design grid. Each field appears in a separate column, and the fields are arranged in the order in which they appear in the field list. Use this method when you need to sort your query or include record selection criteria.

By choosing the most appropriate method to add all the table fields to the query design grid, you can work more efficiently and ensure that the query produces the results you want.

The record for one of the owners in the query results contains information that is not up to date. This owner, Jimmy Gonzalez, had informed the care center that he now prefers to go by the name James; he also provided a new email address. You need to update the record with the new first name and email address for this owner.

Updating Data Using a Query

A query datasheet is temporary, and its contents are based on the criteria in the query design grid; however, you can still update the data in a table using a query datasheet. In this case, you want to make changes to a record in the Owner table. Instead of making the changes in the table datasheet, you can make them in the OwnerEmail query datasheet because the query is based on the Owner table. The underlying Owner table will be updated with the changes you make.

To update data using the OwnerEmail query datasheet:

1. Locate the record with OwnerID 2330, Jimmy Gonzalez (record 6 in the query datasheet).

2. In the First Name column for this record, double-click **Jimmy** to select the name, and then type **James**.

3. Press the **Tab** key twice to move to the Email column, type **thewholething@example.com** and then press the **Tab** key.

4. Close the OwnerEmail query, and then open the Navigation Pane. Note that the OwnerEmail query is listed in the Queries section of the Navigation Pane.

Now you'll check the Owner table to verify that the changes you made in the query datasheet are reflected in the Owner table.

▶ **5.** Open the **Owner** table in Datasheet view, and then close the Navigation Pane.

▶ **6.** Locate the record for OwnerID 2330 (record 6). Notice that the changes you made in the query datasheet to the First Name and Email field values were made to the record in the Owner table.

▶ **7.** Close the Owner table.

Kelly also wants to view specific information in the Riverview database. She would like to review the visit data for animals while also viewing certain information about them. So, she needs to see data from both the Animal table and the Visit table at the same time.

Creating a Multitable Query

A multitable query is a query based on more than one table. If you want to create a query that retrieves data from multiple tables, the tables must have a common field. Earlier, you established a relationship between the Animal (primary) and Visit (related) tables based on the common AnimalID field that exists in both tables, so you can now create a query to display data from both tables at the same time. Specifically, Kelly wants to view the values in the AnimalType, AnimalBreed, and AnimalName fields from the Animal table and the VisitDate and Reason fields from the Visit table.

To create the query using the Animal and Visit tables:

▶ **1.** On the ribbon, click the **Create** tab.

▶ **2.** In the Queries group, click the **Query Design** button. The Show Table dialog box opens in the Query window. You need to add the Animal and Visit tables to the Query window.

▶ **3.** Click **Animal** in the Tables list, click the **Add** button, click **Visit**, click the **Add** button, and then click the **Close** button to close the Show Table dialog box. The Animal and Visit field lists appear in the Query window.

▶ **4.** Resize the Animal and Visit field lists if necessary so that all the fields in each list are displayed.

The one-to-many relationship between the two tables is shown in the Query window in the same way that a relationship between two tables is shown in the Relationships window. Note that the join line is thick at both ends; this signifies that you selected the option to enforce referential integrity. If you had not selected this option, the join line would be thin at both ends, and neither the "1" nor the infinity symbol would appear, even though the tables have a one-to-many relationship.

You need to place the AnimalType, AnimalBreed, and AnimalName fields (in that order) from the Animal field list into the design grid and then place the VisitDate and Reason fields from the Visit field list into the design grid. This is the order in which Taylor wants to view the fields in the query results.

▶ **5.** In the Animal field list, double-click **AnimalType** to place this field in the design grid's first column Field box.

6. Repeat Step 5 to add the **AnimalBreed** and **AnimalName** fields from the Animal table to the second and third columns of the design grid.

7. Repeat Step 5 to add the **VisitDate** and **Reason** fields (in that order) from the Visit table to the fourth and fifth columns of the design grid. The query specifications are complete, so you can now run the query.

8. In the Results group on the Query Tools Design tab, click the **Run** button. After the query runs, the results are displayed in Datasheet view. See Figure 3-9.

Figure 3-9   Datasheet for query based on the Animal and Visit tables

fields from the Animal table

fields from the Visit table

Animal Type	Animal Breed	Animal Name	Date of Visit	Reason/Diagnosis
Dog	Beagle	Bailey	12/2/2016	Vaccinations
Dog	Beagle	Bailey	1/20/2017	Spaying
Cat	Burmese	Whiskers	11/8/2016	Vaccinations
Cat	Burmese	Whiskers	12/14/2016	Grooming
Cat	Burmese	Whiskers	1/11/2017	Grooming
Dog	Border collie	Lady	12/1/2016	Vaccinations
Dog	Australian shepherd	Rustle	11/11/2016	Vaccinations
Dog	Australian shepherd	Rustle	12/16/2016	Vaccinations
Dog	Australian shepherd	Rustle	12/21/2016	Injured paw
Dog	Australian shepherd	Rustle	1/9/2017	Injured paw
Cat	Himalayan	Bushy	11/29/2016	Declawing
Cat	Himalayan	Bushy	1/18/2017	Grooming
Cat	Siberian	Patches	11/28/2016	Grooming
Cat	Siberian	Patches	1/3/2017	Declawing
Dog	Russell terrier	Buddy	11/28/2016	Grooming
Bird	Parakeet	Tweets	12/19/2016	Vaccinations
Bird	Parakeet	Tweets	1/9/2017	Not eating
Dog	Dalmatian	Rosie	11/15/2016	Nail clipping and grooming
Dog	Dalmatian	Rosie	1/13/2017	Injured paw
Dog	Labrador retriever	Molly	11/22/2016	Wellness exam
Dog	Labrador retriever	Molly	1/4/2017	Grooming
Dog	Chihuahua	Silly	12/9/2016	Injured paw
Dog	Chihuahua	Silly	1/23/2017	Not eating
Dog	Bloodhound	Tracker	12/2/2016	Injured paw
Dog	Bloodhound	Tracker	1/13/2017	Not eating

Record: 1 of 74   No Filter   Search

Ready

Only the five selected fields from the Animal and Visit tables appear in the datasheet. The records are displayed in order according to the values in the AnimalID field because it is the primary key field in the primary table, even though this field is not included in the query datasheet.

Kelly plans on frequently tracking the data retrieved by the query, so she asks you to save it as "AnimalVisits."

9. On the Quick Access Toolbar, click the **Save** button 🖫. The Save As dialog box opens.

10. In the Query Name box, type **AnimalVisits** and then press the **Enter** key. The query is saved, and its name appears on the object tab.

Kelly decides she wants the records displayed in alphabetical order by animal type. Because the query displays data in order by the field values in the AnimalID field, which is the primary key for the Animal table, you need to sort the records by the AnimalType field to display the data in the order Kelly wants.

Sorting Data in a Query

Sorting is the process of rearranging records in a specified order or sequence. Sometimes you might need to sort data before displaying or printing it to meet a specific request. For example, Kelly might want to review visit information arranged by the VisitDate field because she needs to know which months are the busiest for Riverview Veterinary Care Center in terms of animal visits. Kimberly might want to view billing information arranged by the InvoiceAmt field because she monitors the finances of the care center.

When you sort data in a query, you do not change the sequence of the records in the underlying tables. Only the records in the query datasheet are rearranged according to your specifications.

To sort records, you must select the **sort field**, which is the field used to determine the order of records in the datasheet. In this case, Kelly wants the data sorted alphabetically by animal type, so you need to specify AnimalType as the sort field. Sort fields can be Short Text, Number, Date/Time, Currency, AutoNumber, or Yes/No fields, but not Long Text, Hyperlink, or Attachment fields. You sort records in either ascending (increasing) or descending (decreasing) order. Figure 3-10 shows the results of each type of sort for these data types.

| Figure 3-10 | Sorting results for different data types |

Data Type	Ascending Sort Results	Descending Sort Results
Short Text	A to Z (alphabetical)	Z to A (reverse alphabetical)
Number	lowest to highest numeric value	highest to lowest numeric value
Date/Time	oldest to most recent date	most recent to oldest date
Currency	lowest to highest numeric value	highest to lowest numeric value
AutoNumber	lowest to highest numeric value	highest to lowest numeric value
Yes/No	yes (checkmark in check box) then no values	no then yes values

Access provides several methods for sorting data in a table or query datasheet and in a form. One of the easiest ways is to use the AutoFilter feature for a field.

Using an AutoFilter to Sort Data

TIP

You can also use the Ascending and Descending buttons in the Sort & Filter group on the Home tab to quickly sort records based on the currently selected field in a datasheet.

As you've probably noticed when working in Datasheet view for a table or query, each column heading has an arrow to the right of the field name. This arrow gives you access to the **AutoFilter** feature, which enables you to quickly sort and display field values in various ways. When you click this arrow, a menu opens with options for sorting and displaying field values. The first two options on the menu enable you to sort the values in the current field in ascending or descending order. Unless you save the datasheet or form after you've sorted the records, the rearrangement of records is temporary.

Next, you'll use an AutoFilter to sort the AnimalVisits query results by the AnimalType field.

To sort the records using an AutoFilter:

1. Click the **arrow** on the Animal Type column heading to display the AutoFilter menu. See Figure 3-11.

Figure 3-11

Figure 3-11   **Using AutoFilter to sort records in the datasheet**

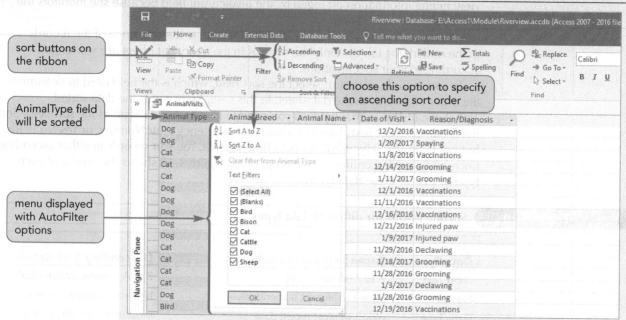

sort buttons on the ribbon

AnimalType field will be sorted

menu displayed with AutoFilter options

choose this option to specify an ascending sort order

Kelly wants the data sorted in ascending (alphabetical) order by the values in the AnimalType field, so you need to select the first option in the menu.

2. Click **Sort A to Z**. The records are rearranged in ascending alphabetical order by animal type. A small, upward-pointing arrow appears on the right side of the Animal Type column heading. This arrow indicates that the values in the field have been sorted in ascending order. If you used the same method to sort the field values in descending order, a small downward-pointing arrow would appear there instead.

After viewing the query results, Kelly decides that she would also like to see the records arranged by the values in the VisitDate field, so that the data is presented in chronological order. She still wants the records to be arranged by the AnimalType field values as well. To produce the results Kelly wants, you need to sort using two fields.

Sorting on Multiple Fields in Design View

Sort fields can be unique or nonunique. A sort field is **unique** if the value in the sort field for each record is different. The AnimalID field in the Animal table is an example of a unique sort field because each animal record has a different value in this primary key field. A sort field is **nonunique** if more than one record can have the same value for the sort field. For example, the AnimalType field in the Animal table is a nonunique sort field because more than one record can have the same AnimalType value.

When the sort field is nonunique, records with the same sort field value are grouped together, but they are not sorted in a specific order within the group. To arrange these grouped records in a specific order, you can specify a **secondary sort field**, which is a second field that determines the order of records that are already sorted by the **primary sort field** (the first sort field specified).

In Access, you can select up to 10 different sort fields. When you use the buttons on the ribbon to sort by more than one field, the sort fields must be in adjacent columns in the datasheet. (Note that you cannot use an AutoFilter to sort on more than one field. This method works for a single field only.) You can specify only one type of sort—either ascending or descending—for the selected columns in the datasheet. You select the adjacent columns, and Access sorts first by the first column and then by each remaining selected column in order from left to right.

Kelly wants the records sorted first by the AnimalType field values, as they currently are, and then by the VisitDate values. The two fields are in the correct left-to-right order in the query datasheet, but they are not adjacent, so you cannot use the Ascending and Descending buttons on the ribbon to sort them. You could move the AnimalType field to the left of the VisitDate field in the query datasheet, but both columns would have to be sorted with the same sort order. This is not what Kelly wants—she wants the AnimalType field values sorted in ascending order so that they are in the correct alphabetical order, for ease of reference; and she wants the VisitDate field values to be sorted in descending order, so that she can focus on the most recent animal visits first. To sort the AnimalType and VisitDate fields with different sort orders, you must specify the sort fields in Design view.

In the Query window in Design view, you must arrange the fields you want to sort from left to right in the design grid, with the primary sort field being the leftmost. In Design view, multiple sort fields do not have to be adjacent to each other, as they do in Datasheet view; however, they must be in the correct left-to-right order.

REFERENCE

Sorting a Query Datasheet

- In the query datasheet, click the arrow on the column heading for the field you want to sort.
- In the menu that opens, click Sort A to Z for an ascending sort, or click Sort Z to A for a descending sort.

or

- In the query datasheet, select the column or adjacent columns on which you want to sort.
- In the Sort & Filter group on the Home tab, click the Ascending button or the Descending button.

or

- In Design view, position the fields serving as sort fields from left to right.
- Click the right side of the Sort box for each field you want to sort, and then click Ascending or Descending for the sort order.

To achieve the results Kelly wants, you need to modify the query in Design view to specify the sort order for the two fields.

TIP

In Design view, the sort fields do not have to be adjacent, and fields that are not sorted can appear between the sort fields.

To select the two sort fields in Design view:

1. On the Home tab, in the Views group, click the **View** button to open the query in Design view. The fields are currently in the correct left-to-right order in the design grid, so you only need to specify the sort order for the two fields.

   First, you need to specify an ascending sort order for the AnimalType field. Even though the records are already sorted by the values in this field, you need to modify the query so that this sort order, and the sort order you will specify for the VisitDate field, are part of the query's design. Any time the query is run, the records will be sorted according to these specifications.

2. Click the right side of the **AnimalType Sort** box to display the arrow and the sort options, and then click **Ascending**. You've selected an ascending sort order for the AnimalType field, which will be the primary sort field. The AnimalType field is a Short Text field, and an ascending sort order will display the field values in alphabetical order.

3. Click the right side of the **VisitDate Sort** box, click **Descending**, and then click in one of the empty text boxes below the VisitDate field to deselect the setting. You've selected a descending sort order for the VisitDate field, which will be the secondary sort field because it appears to the right of the primary sort field (AnimalType) in the design grid. The VisitDate field is a Date/Time field, and a descending sort order will display the field values with the most recent dates first. See Figure 3-12.

Figure 3-12	Selecting two sort fields in Design view

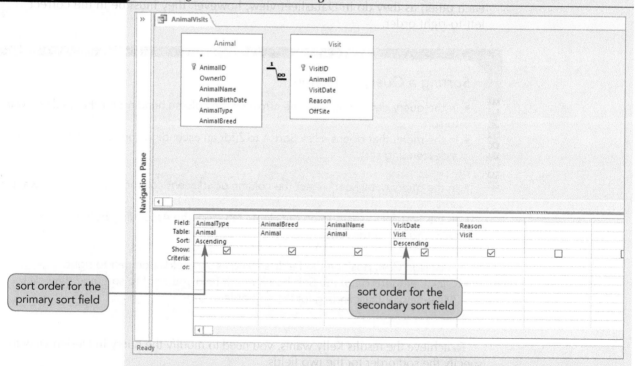

You have finished your query changes, so now you can run the query and then save the modified query with the same name.

4. On the Query Tools Design tab, in the Results group, click the **Run** button. After the query runs, the records appear in the query datasheet in ascending order based on the values in the AnimalType field. Within groups of records with the same AnimalType field value, the records appear in descending order by the values of the VisitDate field. See Figure 3-13.

| Figure 3-13 | **Datasheet sorted on two fields** |

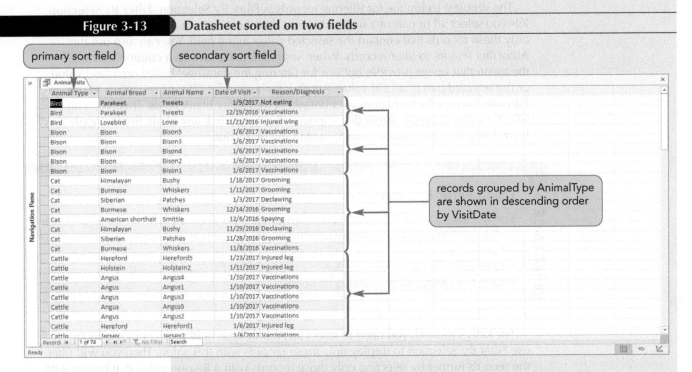

primary sort field

secondary sort field

records grouped by AnimalType are shown in descending order by VisitDate

When you save the query, all of your design changes—including the selection of the sort fields—are saved with the query. The next time Kelly runs the query, the records will appear sorted by the primary and secondary sort fields.

5. On the Quick Access Toolbar, click the **Save** button to save the revised AnimalVisits query.

Kelly knows that Riverview Veterinary Care Center has seen an increase in the number of dogs receiving care. She would like to focus briefly on the information for that animal type only. Also, she is interested in knowing how many dogs have had recent vaccinations. She is concerned that, although more dogs are being brought to the care center, not enough of them are receiving regular vaccinations. Selecting only the records with an AnimalType field value of "Dog" and a Reason field value beginning with "Vaccination" is a temporary change that Kelly wants in the query datasheet, so you do not need to switch to Design view and change the query. Instead, you can apply a filter.

Filtering Data

A **filter** is a set of restrictions you place on the records in an open datasheet or form to *temporarily* isolate a subset of the records. A filter lets you view different subsets of displayed records so that you can focus on only the data you need. Unless you save a query or form with a filter applied, an applied filter is not available the next time you run the query or open the form.

The simplest technique for filtering records is Filter By Selection. **Filter By Selection** lets you select all or part of a field value in a datasheet or form and then display only those records that contain the selected value in the field. You can also use the AutoFilter feature to filter records. When you click the arrow on a column heading, the menu that opens provides options for filtering the datasheet based on a field value or the selected part of a field value. Another technique for filtering records is to use **Filter By Form**, which changes your datasheet to display blank fields. Then you can select a value using the arrow that appears when you click any blank field to apply a filter that selects only those records containing that value.

REFERENCE

Using Filter By Selection

- In the datasheet or form, select the part of the field value that will be the basis for the filter; or, if the filter will be based on the entire field value, click anywhere within the field value.
- On the Home tab, in the Sort & Filter group, click the Selection button.
- Click the type of filter you want to apply.

For Kelly's request, you need to select an AnimalType field value of Dog and then use Filter By Selection to display only those records with this value. Then you will filter the records further by selecting only those records with a Reason value that begins with "Vaccination" (for visits that include a single vaccination or multiple vaccinations).

To display the records using Filter By Selection:

1. In the query datasheet, locate the first occurrence of an AnimalType field containing the value **Dog**, and then click anywhere within that field value.

2. On the Home tab, in the Sort & Filter group, click the **Selection** button. A menu opens with options for the type of filter to apply. See Figure 3-14.

Figure 3-14   **Using Filter By Selection**

options for the type of filter to apply

current field is the basis for the filter

The menu provides options for displaying only those records with an AnimalType field value that equals the selected value (in this case, Dog); does not equal the value; contains the value somewhere within the field; or does not contain the value somewhere within the field. You want to display all the records whose AnimalType field value equals Dog.

3. In the Selection menu, click **Equals "Dog"**. Only the 25 records that have an AnimalType field value of Dog appear in the datasheet. See Figure 3-15.

Figure 3-15   Datasheet after applying the filter

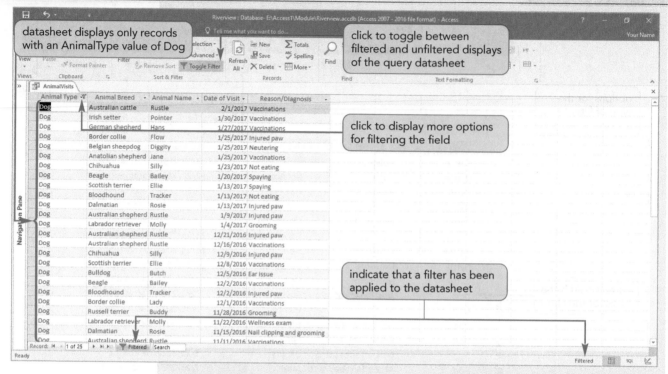

Next, Kelly wants to view only those records with a Reason field value beginning with the word "Vaccination" so she can view the records for visits that involved one or more vaccinations. You need to apply an additional filter to the datasheet.

4. In any Reason field value beginning with the word "Vaccination," select only the text **Vaccination**.

5. In the Sort & Filter group, click the **Selection** button. The same four filter types are available for this selection as when you filtered the AnimalType field.

6. On the Selection menu, click **Begins With "Vaccination"**. The first filter is applied to the query datasheet, which now shows only the nine records for dogs who have had one or more vaccinations at the care center.

   Trouble? If you do not see the Begins With "Vaccination" option, click anywhere in the datasheet to close the Selection menu, and then repeat Steps 4–6, being sure not to select the letter "s" at the end of the word "Vaccination."

   Now you can redisplay all the query records by clicking the Toggle Filter button, which you use to switch between the filtered and unfiltered displays.

TIP

The ScreenTip for this button is Remove Filter.

7. In the Sort & Filter group, click the **Toggle Filter** button. The filter is removed, and all 74 records appear in the query datasheet.

8. Close the AnimalVisits query. A dialog box opens, asking if you want to save your changes to the design of the query—in this case, the filtered display, which is still available through the Toggle Filter button. Kelly does not want the query saved with the filter because she doesn't need to view the filtered information on a regular basis.

9. Click the **No** button to close the query without saving the changes.

10. If you are not continuing to Session 3.2, click the **File** tab, and then click **Close** in the navigation bar to close the Riverview database.

Session 3.1 Quick Check

REVIEW

1. In Datasheet view, what is the difference between navigation mode and editing mode?
2. What command can you use in Datasheet view to remove the display of one or more fields from the datasheet?
3. What is a select query?
4. Describe the field list and the design grid in the Query window in Design view.
5. How are a table datasheet and a query datasheet similar? How are they different?
6. For a Date/Time field, how do the records appear when sorted in ascending order?
7. When you define multiple sort fields in Design view, describe how the sort fields must be positioned in the design grid.
8. A(n) _____ is a set of restrictions you place on the records in an open datasheet or form to isolate a subset of records temporarily.

Session 3.2 Visual Overview:

> When creating queries in Design view, you can enter criteria so that only selected records are displayed in the query results.

Field:	AnimalName	AnimalBirthDate	AnimalType	VisitDate	Reason
Table:	Animal	Animal	Animal	Visit	Visit
Sort:					
Show:	☑	☑	☑	☑	☑
Criteria:			"Bird" ←		
or:					

> To define a condition for a field, you place the condition in the field's Criteria box in the design grid.

> To indicate which records you want to select, you must specify a condition as part of the query. A condition is a criterion, or rule, that determines which records are selected.

Field:	InvoiceNum	InvoiceDate	InvoiceAmt	
Table:	Billing	Billing	Billing	
Sort:				
Show:	☑	☑	☑	☐
Criteria:			> 100	
or:				

> A condition usually consists of an operator, often a comparison operator, and a value. A comparison operator compares the value in a field to the condition value and selects all the records for which the condition is true.

Field:	VisitID	AnimalID	VisitDate	Reason
Table:	Visit	Visit	Visit	Visit
Sort:				
Show:	☑	☑	☑	☑
Criteria:			Between #1/1/2017# And #1/15/2017#	
or:				

> Most comparison operators (such as Between…And…) select records that match a range of values for the condition—in this case, all records with dates that fall within the range shown.

Selection Criteria in Queries

The results of a query containing selection criteria include only the records that meet the specified criteria.

BirdAnimalType

Animal Name	Animal Birth Date	Animal Type	Date of Visit
Tweets	11/12/2010	Bird	12/19/2016
Tweets	11/12/2010	Bird	1/9/2017
Lovie	02/03/2002	Bird	11/21/2016
*			

The results of this query show only birds because the condition "Bird" in the AnimalType field's Criteria box specifies that the query should select records only with AnimalType field values of bird. This type of condition is called an **exact match** because the value in the specified field must match the condition exactly in order for the record to be included in the query results.

LargeInvoiceAmts

Invoice Num	Invoice Date	Invoice Amt
42145	11/22/2016	$275.00
42182	11/30/2016	$225.00
42320	01/04/2017	$225.00
42435	01/16/2017	$125.00
42525	01/26/2017	$125.00
*		$0.00

The results of this query show only those invoices with amounts greater than $100 because the condition >100, which uses the greater than comparison operator, specifies that query should select records only with InvoiceAmt field values over $100.

EarlyJanuaryVisits

Visit ID	Animal ID	Date of Visit	Reason/Diagnosis
1098	12296	1/3/2017	Declawing
1101	12312	1/4/2017	Grooming
1120	12304	1/9/2017	Not eating
1124	12290	1/9/2017	Injured paw
1140	12282	1/11/2017	Grooming
1148	12308	1/13/2017	Injured paw
1152	12318	1/13/2017	Not eating
1156	12322	1/13/2017	Spaying
*			

The results of this query show only those visits that took place in the first half of January 2017 because the condition in the VisitDate Criteria box specifies that the query should select records only with a visit date between 1/1/2017 and 1/15/2017.

Defining Record Selection Criteria for Queries

Kimberly is considering offering a workshop on dog care at the care center, with a special emphasis on the needs of older dogs. To prepare for this, she is interested in knowing more about the level of care provided to the dogs that have visited the care center, as well as where these dogs live. For this request, you could create a query to select the correct fields and all records in the Owner, Animal, and Visit tables, select an AnimalType field value of Dog in the query datasheet, and then click the Selection button and choose the appropriate filter option to display the information for only those animals that are dogs. However, a faster way of accessing the data Kimberly needs is to create a query that displays the selected fields and only those records in the Owner, Animal, and Visit tables that satisfy a condition.

Just as you can display selected fields from a database in a query datasheet, you can display selected records. To identify which records you want to select, you must specify a condition as part of the query, as illustrated in the Session 3.2 Visual Overview. A condition usually includes one of the comparison operators shown in Figure 3-16.

| Figure 3-16 | Access comparison operators |

Operator	Meaning	Example
=	equal to (optional; default operator)	="Hall"
<>	not equal to	<>"Hall"
<	less than	<#1/1/99#
<=	less than or equal to	<=100
>	greater than	>"C400"
>=	greater than or equal to	>=18.75
Between ... And ...	between two values (inclusive)	Between 50 And 325
In ()	in a list of values	In ("Hall", "Seeger")
Like	matches a pattern that includes wildcards	Like "706*"

Specifying an Exact Match

For Kimberly's request, you need to first create a query that will display only those records in the Animal table with the value Dog in the AnimalType field. This type of condition is an exact match because the value in the specified field must match the condition exactly in order for the record to be included in the query results. You'll create the query in Design view.

To create the query in Design view:

1. If you took a break after the previous session, make sure that the Riverview database is open and the Navigation Pane is closed, and then on the ribbon, click the **Create** tab.

2. In the Queries group, click the **Query Design** button. The Show Table dialog box opens. You need to add the Owner, Animal, and Visit tables to the Query window.

3. Click **Owner** in the Tables list, click the **Add** button, click **Animal**, click the **Add** button, click **Visit**, click the **Add** button, and then click the **Close** button. The field lists for the Owner, Animal, and Visit tables appear in the top portion of the window, and join lines indicating one-to-many relationships connect the tables.

4. Resize all three field lists so that all the fields are displayed.

5. Add the following fields from the Animal table to the design grid in this order: **AnimalName**, **AnimalBirthDate**, and **AnimalType**.

   Kimberly also wants information from the Visit table and the Owner table included in the query results.

6. Add the following fields from the Visit table to the design grid in this order: **VisitDate** and **Reason**.

7. Add the following fields from the Owner table to the design grid in this order: **FirstName**, **LastName**, **Phone**, and **Email**. All the fields needed for the query appear in the design grid. See Figure 3-17.

Figure 3-17	Design grid after adding fields from both tables

enter condition here

To display the information Kimberly wants, you need to enter the condition for the AnimalType field in its Criteria box, as shown in Figure 3-17. Kimberly wants to display only those records with an AnimalType field value of Dog.

To enter the exact match condition, and then save and run the query:

1. Click the **AnimalType Criteria** box, type **Dog**, and then press the **Enter** key. The condition changes to "Dog".

   Access automatically enclosed the condition you typed in quotation marks. You must enclose text values in quotation marks when using them as selection criteria. If you omit the quotation marks, however, Access will include them automatically in most cases. Some words—including "in" and "select"—are special keywords in Access that are reserved for functions and commands. If you want to enter one of these keywords as the condition, you must type the quotation marks around the text or an error message will appear indicating the condition cannot be entered.

2. Save the query with the name **DogAnimalType**. The query is saved, and its name is displayed on the object tab.

3. Run the query. After the query runs, the selected field values for only those records with an AnimalType field value of Dog are shown. A total of 25 records is selected and displayed in the datasheet. See Figure 3-18.

Figure 3-18   Datasheet displaying selected fields and records

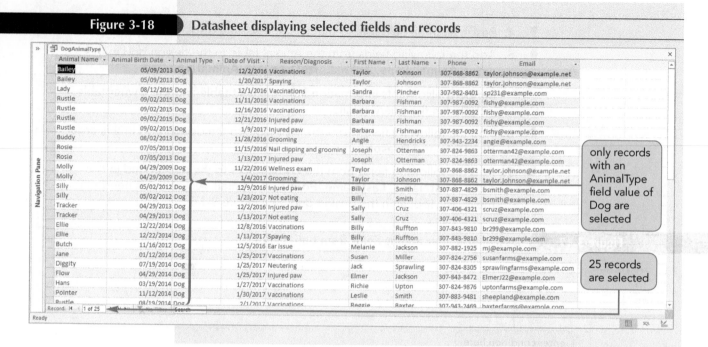

only records with an AnimalType field value of Dog are selected

25 records are selected

Kimberly realizes that it's not necessary to include the AnimalType field values in the query results. The name of the query, DogAnimalType, indicates that the query design includes all animals with an AnimalType of Dog, so the AnimalType field values are unnecessary and repetitive in the query results. Also, she decides that she would prefer the query datasheet to show the fields from the Owner table first, followed by the Animal table fields and then the Visit table fields. You need to modify the query to produce the results Kimberly wants.

Modifying a Query

After you create a query and view the results, you might need to make changes to the query if the results are not what you expected or require. First, Kimberly asks you to modify the DogAnimalType query so that it does not display the AnimalType field values in the query results.

To remove the display of the AnimalType field values:

1. On the Home tab, in the Views group, click the **View** button. The DogAnimalType query opens in Design view.

   You need to keep the AnimalType field as part of the query design because it contains the defined condition for the query. You only need to remove the display of the field's values from the query results.

2. Click the **AnimalType Show** check box to remove the checkmark. The query will still find only those records with the value Dog in the AnimalType field, but the query results will not display these field values.

Next, you need to change the order of the fields in the query so that the owner information is listed first.

To move the Owner table fields to precede the Animal and Visit table fields:

1. Position the pointer on the FirstName field selector until the pointer changes to ↓, and then click to select the field. See Figure 3-19.

Figure 3-19	Selected FirstName field

2. Position the pointer on the FirstName field selector, and then press and hold the mouse button; notice that the pointer changes to ↘, and a black vertical line appears to the left of the selected field. This line represents the selected field when you drag the mouse to move it.

3. Drag the pointer to the left until the vertical line representing the selected field is positioned to the left of the AnimalName field. See Figure 3-20.

Figure 3-20	Dragging the field in the design grid

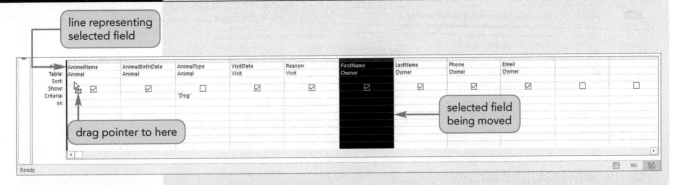

TIP

Instead of moving a field by dragging, you can also delete the field and then add it back to the design grid in the location you want.

4. Release the mouse button. The FirstName field moves to the left of the AnimalName field.

   You can also select and move multiple fields at once. You need to select and move the LastName, Phone, and Email fields so that they appear directly after the FirstName field in the query design. To select multiple fields, you click and drag the mouse over the field selectors for the fields you want.

5. Point to the LastName field selector. When the pointer changes to ↓, press and hold the mouse button, drag to the right to select the Phone and Email fields, and then release the mouse button. All three fields are now selected. See Figure 3-21.

Figure 3-21 Multiple fields selected to be moved

6. Position the pointer on the field selector for any of the three selected fields, press and hold the mouse button, and then drag to the left until the vertical line representing the selected fields is positioned to the left of the AnimalName field.

7. Release the mouse button. The four fields from the Owner table are now the first four fields in the query design.

You have finished making the modifications to the query Kimberly requested, so you can now run the query.

8. Run the query. The results of the modified query are displayed. See Figure 3-22.

Figure 3-22 Results of the modified query

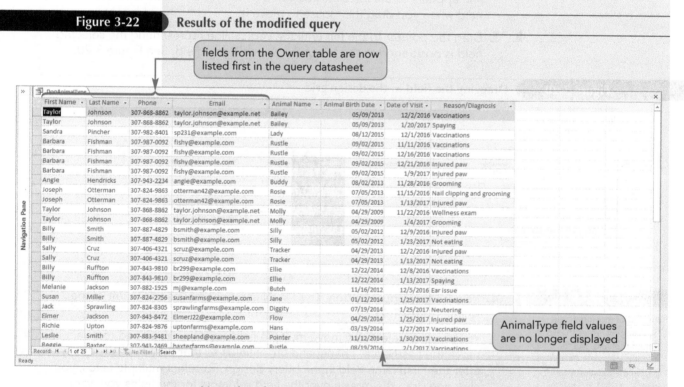

Note that the AnimalType field values are no longer displayed in the query results.

9. Save and close the DogAnimalType query.

Kimberly asks you to create a new query. She is interested to know which animals of all animal types that have not been to the care center recently, so that her staff can follow up with their owners by sending them reminder notes or emails. To create the query that will produce the results Kimberly wants, you need to use a comparison operator to match a range of values—in this case, any VisitDate value less than 1/1/2017. Because this new query will include information from several of the same fields as the DogAnimalType query, you can use that query as a starting point in designing this new query.

Using a Comparison Operator to Match a Range of Values

As you know, after you create and save a query, you can double-click the query name in the Navigation Pane to run the query again. You can then click the View button to change its design. You can also use an existing query as the basis for creating another query. Because the design of the query you need to create next is similar to the DogAnimalType query, you will copy, paste, and rename this query to create the new query. Using this approach keeps the DogAnimalType query intact.

To create the new query by copying the DogAnimalType query:

▶ 1. Open the Navigation Pane. Note that the DogAnimalType query is listed in the Queries section.

   You need to use the shortcut menu to copy the DogAnimalType query and paste it in the Navigation Pane; then you'll give the copied query a different name.

▶ 2. In the Queries section of the Navigation Pane, right-click **DogAnimalType** to select it and display the shortcut menu.

▶ 3. Click **Copy** on the shortcut menu.

▶ 4. Right-click the empty area near the bottom of the Navigation Pane, and then click **Paste** on the shortcut menu. The Paste As dialog box opens with the text "Copy Of DogAnimalType" in the Query Name box. Because Kimberly wants the new query to show data for animals that have not visited the care center recently, you'll name the new query "EarlierVisits."

▶ 5. In the Query Name box, type **EarlierVisits** and then press the **Enter** key. The new query appears in the Queries section of the Navigation Pane.

▶ 6. Double-click the **EarlierVisits** query to open, or run, the query. The design of this query is currently the same as the original DogAnimalType query.

▶ 7. Close the Navigation Pane.

Next, you need to open the query in Design view and modify its design to produce the results Kimberly wants—to display records for all animals and only those records with VisitDate field values that are earlier than, or less than, 1/1/2017.

To modify the design of the new query:

▶ **1.** Display the query in Design view.

▶ **2.** Click the **VisitDate Criteria** box, type **<1/1/2017** and then press the **Tab** key. Note that Access automatically encloses the date criteria with number signs. The condition specifies that a record will be selected only if its VisitDate field value is less than (earlier than) 1/1/2017. See Figure 3-23.

Figure 3-23 ▶ **Criteria entered for the VisitDate field**

new condition entered

original condition needs to be deleted

Before you run the query, you need to delete the condition for the AnimalType field. Recall that the AnimalType field is part of the query, but its values are not displayed in the query results. When you modified the query to remove the AnimalType field values from the query results, Access moved the field to the end of the design grid. You need to delete the AnimalType field's condition, specify that the AnimalType field values should be included in the query results, and then move the field back to its original position following the AnimalBirthDate field.

▶ **3.** Press the **Tab** key to select the condition for the AnimalType field, and then press the **Delete** key. The condition for the AnimalType field is removed.

▶ **4.** Click the **Show** check box for the AnimalType field to insert a checkmark so that the field values will be displayed in the query results.

▶ **5.** Use the pointer to select the AnimalType field, drag the selected field to position it to the left of the VisitDate field, and then click in an empty box to deselect the AnimalType field. See Figure 3-24.

Figure 3-24 ▶ **Design grid after moving the AnimalType field**

Show check box is selected

AnimalType field moved back to its original location

condition removed from AnimalType Criteria box

▶ **6.** Run the query. The query datasheet displays the selected fields for only those records with a VisitDate field value less than 1/1/2017, a total of 34 records. See Figure 3-25.

Figure 3-25	Running the modified query

query returns 34 records

only records with a VisitDate field value less than 1/1/2017 are displayed

7. Save and close the EarlierVisits query.

Kimberly continues to analyze animal visits to Riverview Veterinary Care Center. Although the care center offers payment plans and pet insurance options, she realizes that owners of younger animals seen off-site might not see the literature about these options that is available in the care center's waiting room. With this in mind, she would like to see a list of all animals that are less than a year old and that the care center has visited off-site. She wants to track these animals in particular so that her staff can contact their owners to review payment plans and pet insurance options. To produce this list, you need to create a query containing two conditions—one for the animal's date of birth and another for whether each visit was off-site.

Defining Multiple Selection Criteria for Queries

Multiple conditions require you to use **logical operators** to combine two or more conditions. When you want a record selected only if two or more conditions are met, you need to use the **And logical operator**. In this case, Kimberly wants to see only those records with an AnimalBirthDate field value greater than or equal to 7/1/2015 *and* an OffSite field value of "Yes" (indicating a checked box). If you place conditions in separate fields in the *same* Criteria row of the design grid, all conditions in that row must be met in order for a record to be included in the query results. However, if you place conditions in *different* Criteria rows, a record will be selected if at least one of the conditions is met. If none of the conditions are met, Access does not select the record. When you place conditions in different Criteria rows, you are using the **Or logical operator**. Figure 3-26 illustrates the difference between the And and Or logical operators.

Figure 3-26   **Logical operators And and Or for multiple selection criteria**

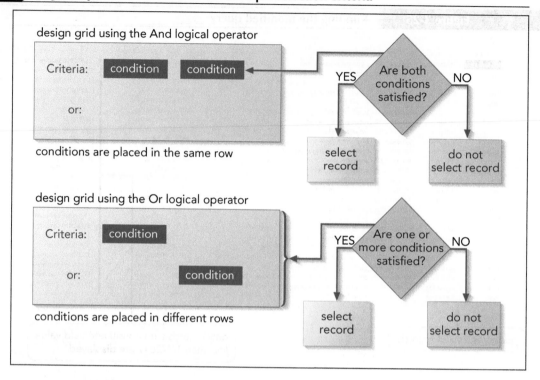

The And Logical Operator

To create the query for Kimberly, you need to use the And logical operator to show only the records for animals that were born on or after 7/1/2015 *and* who have had an off-site visit. You'll create a new query based on the Owner, Animal, and Visit tables to produce the necessary results. In the query design, both conditions you specify will appear in the same Criteria row; therefore, the query will select records only if both conditions are met.

To create a new query using the And logical operator:

▸ 1. On the ribbon, click the **Create** tab.

▸ 2. In the Queries group, click the **Query Design** button.

▸ 3. Add the **Owner**, **Animal**, and **Visit** tables to the Query window in that order, and then close the Show Table dialog box. Resize all three field lists to display all the field names.

▸ 4. Add the **AnimalName** and **AnimalBirthDate** fields from the Animal table to the design grid.

▸ 5. Add the **FirstName**, **LastName**, and **Phone** fields from the Owner field list to the design grid.

▸ 6. Add the **VisitDate** and **OffSite** fields from the Visit table to the design grid.

Now you need to enter the two conditions for the query.

▸ 7. Click the **AnimalBirthDate Criteria** box, and then type **>=7/1/2015**.

▸ 8. Press the **Tab** key five times to move to the **OffSite** box, type **Yes**, and then press the **Tab** key. Notice that for a Yes/No field such as OffSite, the criteria value is not automatically enclosed in quotes. See Figure 3-27.

Figure 3-27   **Query to find younger animals who have had off-site visits**

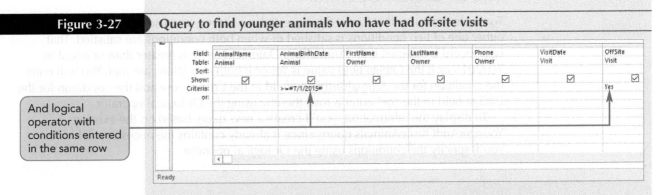

And logical operator with conditions entered in the same row

9. Run the query. The query displays only those records that meet both conditions: an AnimalBirthDate field value greater than or equal to 7/1/2015 *and* an OffSite field value of Yes. 14 records are displayed for 14 different animals. See Figure 3-28.

Figure 3-28   **Results of query using the And logical operator**

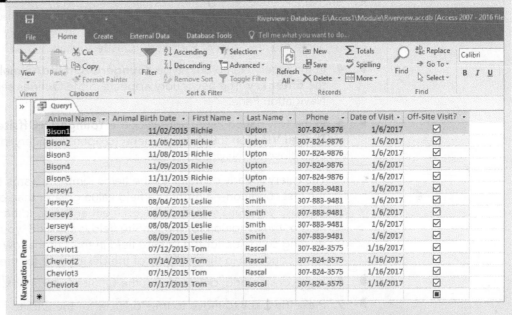

10. On the Quick Access Toolbar, click the **Save** button, and then save the query as **YoungerAndOffsiteAnimals**.

11. Close the query.

Kimberly meets with staff members to discuss the issue of owners with younger animals being informed of the care center's payment plans and insurance options. After viewing the results of the YoungerAndOffsiteAnimals query, the group agrees that the care center should reach out to the owners of all younger animals regarding these services, because first-time owners are more likely to be unaware of the care center's options. In addition, the care center should contact the owner of any animal that has received an off-site visit, because these owners are less likely to have seen the care center's waiting room literature on these payment options. To help with their planning, Kimberly asks you to produce a list of all animals that were born on or after 7/1/2015 or that received an off-site visit. To create this query, you need to use the Or logical operator.

The Or Logical Operator

To create the query that Kimberly requested, your query must select a record when either one of two conditions is satisfied or when both conditions are satisfied. That is, a record is selected if the AnimalBirthDate field value is greater than or equal to 7/1/2015 *or* if the OffSite field value is Yes *or* if both conditions are met. You will enter the condition for the AnimalBirthDate field in the Criteria row and the condition for the OffSite field in the "or" criteria row, thereby using the Or logical operator.

To display the information, you'll create a new query based on the existing YoungerAndOffsiteAnimals query, since it already contains the necessary fields. Then you'll specify the conditions using the Or logical operator.

To create a new query using the Or logical operator:

1. Open the Navigation Pane. You'll use the shortcut menu to copy and paste the YoungerAndOffsiteAnimals query to create the new query.

2. In the Queries section of the Navigation Pane, right-click **YoungerAndOffsiteAnimals**, and then click **Copy** on the shortcut menu.

3. Right-click the empty area near the bottom of the Navigation Pane, and then click **Paste** on the shortcut menu. The Paste As dialog box opens with the text "Copy Of YoungerAndOffsiteAnimals" in the Query Name box. You'll name the new query "YoungerOrOffsiteAnimals."

4. In the Query Name box, type **YoungerOrOffsiteAnimals** and then press the **Enter** key. The new query appears in the Queries section of the Navigation Pane.

5. In the Navigation Pane, right-click the **YoungerOrOffsiteAnimals** query, click **Design View** on the shortcut menu to open the query in Design view, and then close the Navigation Pane.

   The query already contains all the fields Kimberly wants to view, as well as the first condition—a BirthDate field value greater than or equal to 7/1/2015. Because you want records selected if either the condition for the BirthDate field or the condition for the OffSite field is satisfied, you must delete the existing condition for the OffSite field in the Criteria row and then enter this same condition in the "or" row of the design grid for the OffSite field.

6. In the design grid, delete **Yes** in the OffSite Criteria box.

7. Press the ↓ key to move to the "or" row for the OffSite field, type **Yes**, and then press the **Tab** key. See Figure 3-29.

Figure 3-29   Query window with the Or logical operator

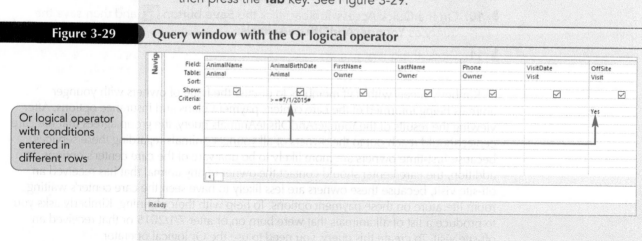

Or logical operator with conditions entered in different rows

To better analyze the data, Kimberly wants the list displayed in descending order by AnimalBirthDate.

▶ **8.** Click the right side of the **AnimalBirthDate Sort** box, and then click **Descending**.

▶ **9.** Run the query. The query datasheet displays only those records that meet either condition: a BirthDate field value greater than or equal to 7/1/2015 *or* an OffSite field value of Yes. The query also returns records that meet both conditions. The query displays a total of 43 records. The records in the query datasheet appear in descending order based on the values in the AnimalBirthDate field. See Figure 3-30.

Figure 3-30	Results of query using the Or logical operator

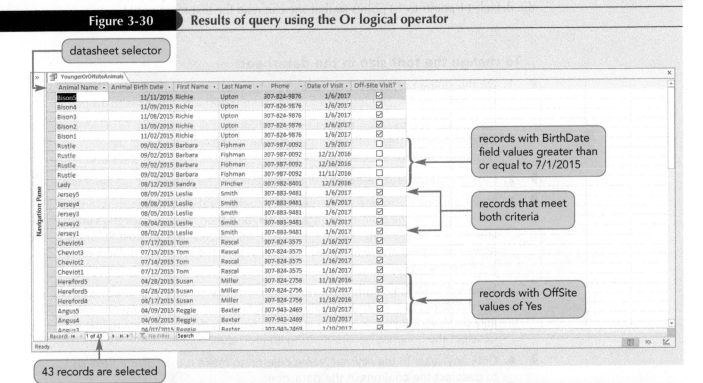

datasheet selector

records with BirthDate field values greater than or equal to 7/1/2015

records that meet both criteria

records with OffSite values of Yes

43 records are selected

Understanding the Results of Using And vs. Or

INSIGHT

When you use the And logical operator to define multiple selection criteria in a query, you *narrow* the results produced by the query because a record must meet more than one condition to be included in the results. For example, the YoungerAndOffsiteAnimals query you created resulted in only 14 records. When you use the Or logical operator, you *broaden* the results produced by the query because a record must meet only one of the conditions to be included in the results. For example, the YoungerOrOffsiteAnimals query you created resulted in 43 records. This is an important distinction to keep in mind when you include multiple selection criteria in queries, so that the queries you create will produce the results you want.

Kimberly would like to spend some time reviewing the results of the YoungerOrOffsiteAnimals query. To make this task easier, she asks you to change how the datasheet is displayed.

Changing a Datasheet's Appearance

You can make many formatting changes to a datasheet to improve its appearance or readability. Many of these modifications are familiar types of changes you can also make in Word documents or Excel spreadsheets, such as modifying the font type, size, color, and the alignment of text. You can also apply different colors to the rows and columns in a datasheet to enhance its appearance.

Modifying the Font Size

Depending on the size of the monitor you are using or the screen resolution, you might need to increase or decrease the size of the font in a datasheet to view more or fewer columns of data. Kimberly asks you to change the font size in the query datasheet from the default 11 points to 14 points so that she can read the text more easily.

To change the font size in the datasheet:

1. On the Home tab, in the Text Formatting group, click the **Font Size** arrow, and then click **14**. The font size for the entire datasheet increases to 14 points.

   Next, you need to resize the columns to their best fit, so that all field values are displayed. Instead of resizing each column individually, you'll use the datasheet selector to select all the columns and resize them at the same time.

2. Click the **datasheet selector**. All the columns in the datasheet are selected.

3. Move the pointer to one of the vertical lines separating two columns in the datasheet until the pointer changes to ↔, and then double-click the vertical line. All the columns visible on the screen are resized to their best fit. Scroll down and repeat the resizing, as necessary, to make sure that all field values are fully displayed.

   Trouble? If all the columns are not visible on your screen, you need to scroll the datasheet to the right to make sure all field values for all columns are fully displayed. If you need to resize any columns, click a field value first to deselect the columns before resizing an individual column.

4. Click any value in the Animal Name column to make it the current field and to deselect the columns in the datasheet.

Changing the Alternate Row Color in a Datasheet

Access uses themes to format the objects in a database. A **theme** is a predefined set of formats including colors, fonts, and other effects that enhance an object's appearance and usability. When you create a database, Access applies the Office theme to objects as you create them. By default, the Office theme formats every other row in a datasheet with a gray background color to distinguish one row from another, making it easier to view and read the contents of a datasheet. The gray alternate row color provides a subtle difference compared to the rows that have the default white color. You can change the alternate row color in a datasheet to something more noticeable using the Alternate Row Color button in the Text Formatting group on the Home tab. Kimberly suggests that you change the alternate row color in the datasheet to see the effect of using this feature.

To change the alternate row color in the datasheet:

1. On the Home tab, in the Text Formatting group, click the **Alternate Row Color button arrow** ▦ ▾ to display the gallery of color choices. See Figure 3-31.

Figure 3-31   Gallery of color choices for alternate row color

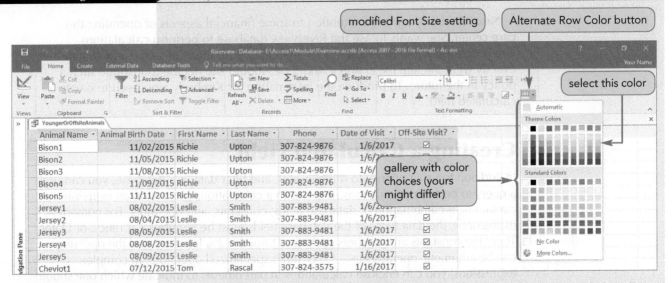

TIP

The name of the color appears in a ScreenTip when you point to a color in the gallery.

The Theme Colors section provides colors from the default Office theme, so that your datasheet's color scheme matches the one in use for the database. The Standard Colors section provides many standard color choices. You might also see a Recent Colors section, with colors that you have recently used in a datasheet. The No Color option, which appears at the bottom of the gallery, sets each row's background color to white. If you want to create a custom color, you can do so using the More Colors option. You'll use one of the theme colors.

2. In the Theme Colors section, click the **Green, Accent 6, Lighter 60%** color (third row, tenth color). The alternate row color is applied to the query datasheet. See Figure 3-32.

Figure 3-32   Datasheet formatted with alternate row color

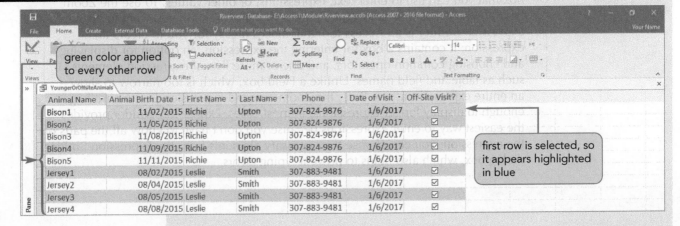

Every other row in the datasheet uses the selected theme color. Kimberly likes how the datasheet looks with this color scheme, so she asks you to save the query.

> **3.** Save and close the YoungerOrOffsiteAnimals query. The query is saved with both the increased font size and the green alternate row color.

Next, Kimberly turns her attention to some financial aspects of operating the care center. She wants to use the Riverview database to perform calculations. She is considering imposing a 2% late fee on unpaid invoices and wants to know exactly what the late fee charges would be, should she decide to institute such a policy in the future. To produce the information for Kimberly, you need to create a calculated field.

Creating a Calculated Field

In addition to using queries to retrieve, sort, and filter data in a database, you can use a query to perform calculations. To perform a calculation, you define an **expression** containing a combination of database fields, constants, and operators. For numeric expressions, the data types of the database fields must be Number, Currency, or Date/Time; the constants are numbers such as .02 (for the 2% late fee); and the operators can be arithmetic operators (+ − * /) or other specialized operators. In complex expressions, you can enclose calculations in parentheses to indicate which one should be performed first; any calculation within parentheses is completed before calculations outside the parentheses. In expressions without parentheses, Access performs basic calculations using the following order of precedence: multiplication and division before addition and subtraction. When operators have equal precedence, Access calculates them in order from left to right.

To perform a calculation in a query, you add a calculated field to the query. A **calculated field** is a field that displays the results of an expression. A calculated field that you create with an expression appears in a query datasheet or in a form or report; however, it does not exist in a database. When you run a query that contains a calculated field, Access evaluates the expression defined by the calculated field and displays the resulting value in the query datasheet, form, or report.

To enter an expression for a calculated field, you can type it directly in a Field box in the design grid. Alternately, you can open the Zoom box or Expression Builder and use either one to enter the expression. The **Zoom box** is a dialog box that you can use to enter text, expressions, or other values. To use the Zoom box, however, you must know all the parts of the expression you want to create. **Expression Builder** is an Access tool that makes it easy for you to create an expression; it contains a box for entering the expression, an option for displaying and choosing common operators, and one or more lists of expression elements, such as table and field names. Unlike a Field box, which is too narrow to show an entire expression at one time, the Zoom box and Expression Builder are large enough to display longer expressions. In most cases, Expression Builder provides the easiest way to enter expressions because you don't have to know all the parts of the expression; you can choose the necessary elements from the Expression Builder dialog box, which also helps to prevent typing errors.

REFERENCE

Creating a Calculated Field Using Expression Builder

- Create and save the query in which you want to include a calculated field.
- Open the query in Design view.
- In the design grid, click the Field box in which you want to create an expression.
- In the Query Setup group on the Query Tools Design tab, click the Builder button.
- Use the expression elements and common operators to build the expression, or type the expression directly in the expression box.
- Click the OK button.

To produce the information Kimberly wants, you need to create a new query based on the Billing and Visit tables and, in the query, create a calculated field that will multiply each InvoiceAmt field value by .02 to calculate the proposed 2% late fee.

To create the new query:

1. On the ribbon, click the **Create** tab.

2. In the Queries group, click the **Query Design** button. The Show Table dialog box opens.

   Kimberly wants to see data from both the Visit and Billing tables, so you need to add these two tables to the Query window.

3. Add the **Visit** and **Billing** tables to the Query window, and resize the field lists as necessary so that all the field names are visible. The field lists appear in the Query window, and the one-to-many relationship between the Visit (primary) and Billing (related) tables is displayed.

4. Add the following fields to the design grid in the order given: **VisitID**, **AnimalID**, and **VisitDate** from the Visit table; and **InvoiceItem**, **InvoicePaid**, and **InvoiceAmt** from the Billing table.

   Kimberly is interested in viewing data only for unpaid invoices because a late fee would apply only to them, so you need to enter the necessary condition for the InvoicePaid field. Recall that InvoicePaid is a Yes/No field. The condition you need to enter is the word "No" in the Criteria box for this field, so that Access will retrieve the records for unpaid invoices only.

5. In the **InvoicePaid Criteria box**, type **No**. As soon as you type the letter "N," a menu appears with options for entering various functions for the criteria. You don't need to enter a function, so you can close this menu.

6. Press the **Esc** key to close the menu.

> You must close the menu or you'll enter a function, which will cause an error.

7. Press the **Tab** key. The query name you'll use will indicate that the data is for unpaid invoices, so you don't need to include the InvoicePaid values in the query results.

8. Click the **InvoicePaid Show** check box to remove the checkmark.

9. Save the query with the name **UnpaidInvoiceLateFee**.

Now you can use Expression Builder to create the calculated field for the InvoiceAmt field.

To create the calculated field:

1. Click the blank Field box to the right of the InvoiceAmt field. This field will contain the expression.

2. On the Query Tools Design tab, in the Query Setup group, click the **Builder** button. The Expression Builder dialog box opens.

The insertion point is positioned in the large box at the top of the dialog box, ready for you to enter the expression. The Expression Categories section of the dialog box lists the fields from the query so you can include them in the expression. The Expression Elements section contains options for including other elements in the expression, including functions, constants, and operators. If the expression you're entering is a simple one, you can type it in the box; if it's more complex, you can use the options in the Expression Elements section to help you build the expression.

The expression for the calculated field will multiply the InvoiceAmt field values by the numeric constant .02 (which represents a 2% late fee).

3. In the Expression Categories section of the dialog box, double-click **InvoiceAmt**. The field name is added to the expression box, within brackets and with a space following it. In an expression, all field names must be enclosed in brackets.

Next you need to enter the multiplication operator, which is the asterisk (*), followed by the constant.

4. Type * (an asterisk) and then type **.02**. You have finished entering the expression. See Figure 3-33.

Figure 3-33	Completed expression for the calculated field

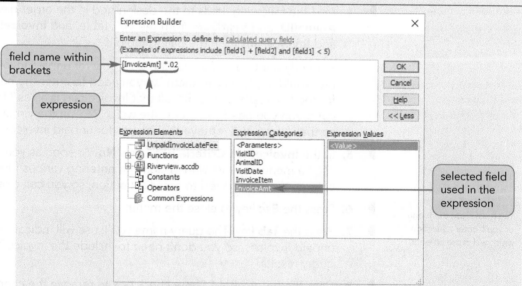

field name within brackets

expression

selected field used in the expression

If you're not sure which operator to use, you can click Operators in the Expression Elements section to display a list of available operators in the center section of the dialog box.

5. Click the **OK** button. The Expression Builder dialog box closes, and the expression is added to the design grid in the Field box for the calculated field.

When you create a calculated field, Access uses the default name "Expr1" for the field. You need to specify a more meaningful field name so it will appear in the query results. You'll enter the name "LateFee," which better describes the field's contents.

▶ **6.** Click to the left of the text "Expr1:" at the beginning of the expression, and then press the **Delete** key five times to delete the text **Expr1**. *Do not delete the colon*; it is needed to separate the calculated field name from the expression.

▶ **7.** Type **LateFee**. Next, you'll set this field's Caption property so that the field name will appear as "Late Fee" in the query datasheet.

▶ **8.** On the Query Tools Design tab, in the Show/Hide group, click the **Property Sheet** button. The Property Sheet for the current field, LateFee, opens on the right side of the window. See Figure 3-34.

Figure 3-34   **Property Sheet for the calculated field**

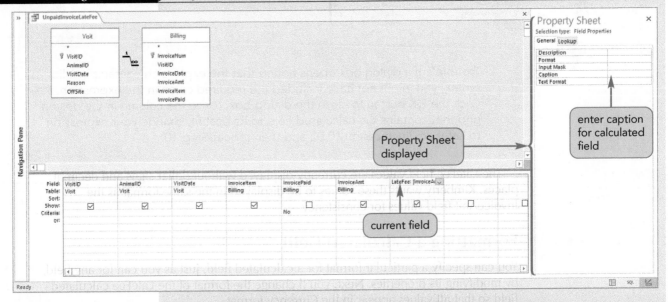

▶ **9.** In the Property sheet, click in the Caption box, type **Late Fee** and then close the Property Sheet.

▶ **10.** Run the query. The query datasheet is displayed and contains the specified fields and the calculated field with the caption "Late Fee." See Figure 3-35.

Figure 3-35   Datasheet displaying the calculated field

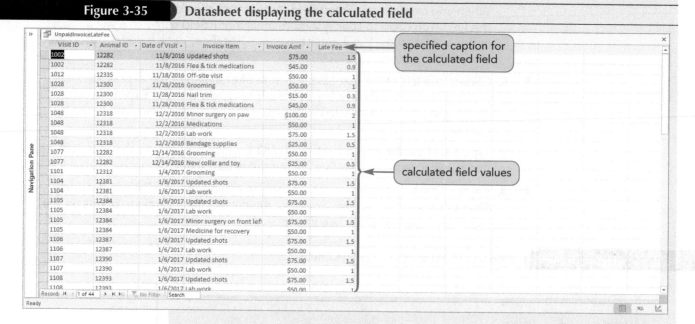

Trouble? If a dialog box opens noting that the expression contains invalid syntax, you might not have included the required colon in the expression. Click the OK button to close the dialog box, resize the column in the design grid that contains the calculated field to its best fit, change your expression to LateFee: [InvoiceAmt]*0.02 and then repeat Step 10.

The LateFee field values are currently displayed without dollar signs and decimal places. Kimberly wants these values to be displayed in the same format as the InvoiceAmt field values for consistency.

Formatting a Calculated Field

You can specify a particular format for a calculated field, just as you can for any field, by modifying its properties. Next, you'll change the format of the LateFee calculated field so that all values appear in the Currency format.

To format the calculated field:

1. Switch to Design view.

2. In the design grid, click in the **LateFee** calculated field to make it the current field, if necessary.

3. On the Query Tools Design tab, in the Show/Hide group, click the **Property Sheet** button to open the Property Sheet for the calculated field.

   You need to change the Format property to Currency, which displays values with a dollar sign and two decimal places.

4. In the Property Sheet, click the right side of the **Format** box to display the list of formats, and then click **Currency**.

5. Close the Property Sheet, and then run the query. The amounts in the LateFee calculated field are now displayed with dollar signs and two decimal places.

6. Save and close the UnpaidInvoiceLateFee query.

PROSKILLS

Problem Solving: Creating a Calculated Field vs. Using the Calculated Field Data Type

You can also create a calculated field using the Calculated Field data type, which lets you store the result of an expression as a field in a table. However, database experts caution users against storing calculations in a table for several reasons. First, storing calculated data in a table consumes valuable space and increases the size of the database. The preferred approach is to use a calculated field in a query; with this approach, the result of the calculation is not stored in the database—it is produced only when you run the query—and it is always current. Second, the Calculated Field data type provides limited options for creating a calculation, whereas a calculated field in a query provides more functions and options for creating expressions. Third, including a field in a table using the Calculated Field data type limits your options if you need to upgrade the database at some point to a more robust DBMS, such as Oracle or SQL Server, that doesn't support this data type; you would need to redesign your database to eliminate this data type. Finally, most database experts agree that including a field in a table whose value is dependent on other fields in the table violates database design principles. To avoid such problems, it's best to create a query that includes a calculated field to perform the calculation you want, instead of creating a field in a table that uses the Calculated Field data type.

To better analyze costs at Riverview Veterinary Care Center, Kimberly wants to view more detailed information about invoices for animal care. Specifically, she would like to know the minimum, average, and maximum invoice amounts. She asks you to determine these statistics from data in the Billing table.

Using Aggregate Functions

You can calculate statistical information, such as totals and averages, on the records displayed in a table datasheet or selected by a query. To do this, you use the Access aggregate functions. **Aggregate functions** perform arithmetic operations on selected records in a database. Figure 3-36 lists the most frequently used aggregate functions.

Figure 3-36	Frequently used aggregate functions

Aggregate Function	Determines	Data Types Supported
Average	Average of the field values for the selected records	AutoNumber, Currency, Date/Time, Number
Count	Number of records selected	AutoNumber, Currency, Date/Time, Long Text, Number, OLE Object, Short Text, Yes/No
Maximum	Highest field value for the selected records	AutoNumber, Currency, Date/Time, Number, Short Text
Minimum	Lowest field value for the selected records	AutoNumber, Currency, Date/Time, Number, Short Text
Sum	Total of the field values for the selected records	AutoNumber, Currency, Date/Time, Number

Working with Aggregate Functions Using the Total Row

If you want to quickly perform a calculation using an aggregate function in a table or query datasheet, you can use the Totals button in the Records group on the Home tab. When you click this button, a row labeled "Total" appears at the bottom of the datasheet. You can then choose one of the aggregate functions for a field in the datasheet, and the results of the calculation will be displayed in the Total row for that field.

Kimberly wants to know the total amount of all invoices for the care center. You can quickly display this amount using the Sum function in the Total row in the Billing table datasheet.

To display the total amount of all invoices in the Billing table:

1. Open the Navigation Pane, open the **Billing** table in Datasheet view, and then close the Navigation Pane.

2. Make sure the Home tab is displayed.

3. In the Records group, click the **Totals** button. A row with the label "Total" is added to the bottom of the datasheet.

4. Scroll to the bottom of the datasheet to view the Total row. You want to display the sum of all the values in the Invoice Amt column.

5. In the Total row, click the **Invoice Amt** field. An arrow appears on the left side of the field.

6. Click the **arrow** to display the menu of aggregate functions. The functions displayed depend on the data type of the current field; in this case, the menu provides functions for a Currency field. See Figure 3-37.

Figure 3-37	Using aggregate functions in the Total row

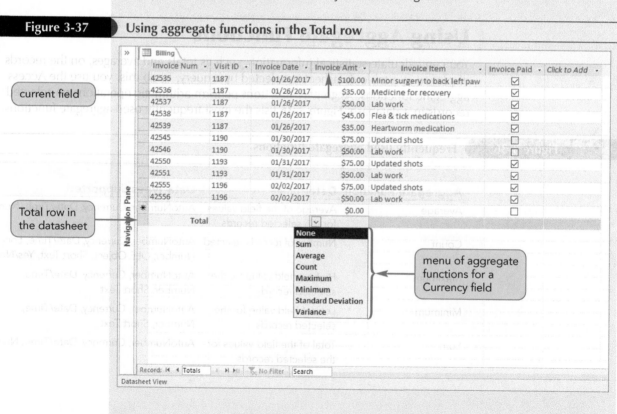

7. Click **Sum** in the menu. All the values in the Invoice Amt column are added, and the total $12,015.00 appears in the Total row for the column.

   Kimberly doesn't want to change the Billing table to always display this total. You can remove the Total row by clicking the Totals button again; this button works as a toggle to switch between the display of the Total row with the results of any calculations in the row, and the display of the datasheet without this row.

8. In the Records group, click the **Totals** button. The Total row is removed from the datasheet.

9. Close the Billing table without saving the changes.

Kimberly wants to know the minimum, average, and maximum invoice amounts for Riverview Veterinary Care Center. To produce this information for Kimberly, you need to use aggregate functions in a query.

Creating Queries with Aggregate Functions

Aggregate functions operate on the records that meet a query's selection criteria. You specify an aggregate function for a specific field, and the appropriate operation applies to that field's values for the selected records.

To display the minimum, average, and maximum of all the invoice amounts in the Billing table, you will use the Minimum, Average, and Maximum aggregate functions for the InvoiceAmt field.

To calculate the minimum of all invoice amounts:

1. Create a new query in Design view, add the **Billing** table to the Query window, and then resize the Billing field list to display all fields.

   To perform the three calculations on the InvoiceAmt field, you need to add the field to the design grid three times.

2. In the Billing field list, double-click **InvoiceAmt** three times to add three copies of the field to the design grid.

   You need to select an aggregate function for each InvoiceAmt field. When you click the Totals button in the Show/Hide group on the Design tab, a row labeled "Total" is added to the design grid. The Total row provides a list of the aggregate functions that you can select.

3. On the Query Tools Design tab, in the Show/Hide group, click the **Totals** button. A new row labeled "Total" appears between the Table and Sort rows in the design grid. The default entry for each field in the Total row is the Group By operator, which you will learn about later in this module. See Figure 3-38.

Figure 3-38

Figure 3-38 **Total row inserted in the design grid**

InvoiceAmt field included three times in the design grid

Total row

In the Total row, you specify the aggregate function you want to use for a field.

4. Click the right side of the first column's **Total** box, and then click **Min**. This field will calculate the minimum amount of all the InvoiceAmt field values.

   When you run the query, Access automatically will assign a datasheet column name of "MinOfInvoiceAmt" for this field. You can change the datasheet column name to a more descriptive or readable name by entering the name you want in the Field box. However, you must also keep the InvoiceAmt field name in the Field box because it identifies the field to use in the calculation. The Field box will contain the datasheet column name you specify followed by the field name (InvoiceAmt) with a colon separating the two names.

5. In the first column's Field box, click to the left of InvoiceAmt, and then type **MinimumInvoiceAmt:** (including the colon).

   Be sure to type the colon following the name or the query will not work correctly.

6. Resize the column so that you can see the complete field name, MinimumInvoiceAmt:InvoiceAmt.

   Next, you need to set the Caption property for this field so that the field name appears with spaces between words in the query datatsheet.

7. On the Query Tools Design tab, in the Show/Hide group, click the **Property Sheet** button to open the Property Sheet for the current field.

8. In the Caption box, type **Minimum Invoice Amt**, and then close the Property Sheet.

You'll follow the same process to complete the query by calculating the average and maximum invoice amounts.

To calculate the average and maximum of all invoice amounts:

1. Click the right side of the second column's **Total** box, and then click **Avg**. This field will calculate the average of all the InvoiceAmt field values.

2. In the second column's Field box, click to the left of InvoiceAmt, and then type **AverageInvoiceAmt:**.

3. Resize the second column to fully display the field name, AverageInvoiceAmt:InvoiceAmt.

4. Open the Property Sheet for the current field, and then set its Caption property to **Average Invoice Amt**.

5. Click the right side of the third column's **Total** box, and then click **Max**. This field will calculate the maximum amount of all the InvoiceAmt field values.

6. In the third column's Field box, click to the left of InvoiceAmt, and then type **MaximumInvoiceAmt:**.

7. Resize the third column to fully display the field name, MaximumInvoiceAmt:InvoiceAmt.

8. In the Property Sheet, set the Caption property to **Maximum Invoice Amt**, and then close the Property Sheet. See Figure 3-39.

Figure 3-39	Query with aggregate functions entered

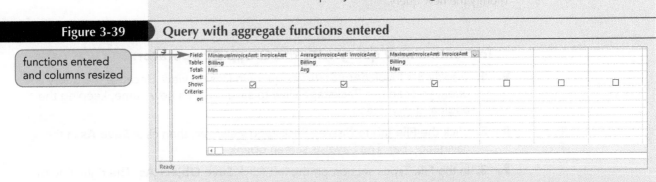

functions entered and columns resized

Trouble? Carefully compare your field names to those shown in the figure to make sure they match exactly; otherwise the query will not work correctly.

9. Run the query. One record displays containing the three aggregate function results. The single row of summary statistics represents calculations based on all the records selected for the query—in this case, all 202 records in the Billing table.

10. Resize all columns to their best fit so that the column names are fully displayed, and then click the field value in the first column to deselect the value and view the results. See Figure 3-40.

Figure 3-40	Result of the query using aggregate functions

11. Save the query as **InvoiceAmtStatistics**.

Kimberly would like to view the same invoice amount statistics (minimum, average, and maximum) as they relate to both appointments at the care center and off-site visits.

Using Record Group Calculations

In addition to calculating statistical information on all or selected records in selected tables, you can calculate statistics for groups of records. The **Group By operator** divides the selected records into groups based on the values in the specified field. Those records with the same value for the field are grouped together, and the datasheet displays one record for each group. Aggregate functions, which appear in the other columns of the design grid, provide statistical information for each group.

To create a query for Kimberly's latest request, you will modify the current query by adding the OffSite field and assigning the Group By operator to it. The Group By operator will display the statistical information grouped by the values of the OffSite field for all the records in the query datasheet. To create the new query, you will save the InvoiceAmtStatistics query with a new name, keeping the original query intact, and then modify the new query.

To create a new query with the Group By operator:

1. Display the InvoiceAmtStatistics query in Design view. Because the query is open, you can use Backstage view to save it with a new name, keeping the original query intact.

2. Click the **File** tab to display Backstage view, and then click **Save As** in the navigation bar. The Save As screen opens.

3. In the File Types section on the left, click **Save Object As**. The right side of the screen changes to display options for saving the current database object as a new object.

4. Click the **Save As** button. The Save As dialog box opens, indicating that you are saving a copy of the InvoiceAmtStatistics query.

5. Type **InvoiceAmtStatisticsByOffsite** to replace the selected name, and then press the **Enter** key. The new query is saved with the name you specified and appears in Design view.

   You need to add the OffSite field to the query. This field is in the Visit table. To include another table in an existing query, you open the Show Table dialog box.

TIP

You could also open the Navigation Pane and drag the Visit table from the pane to the Query window.

6. On the Query Tools Design tab, in the Query Setup group, click the **Show Table** button to open the Show Table dialog box.

7. Add the **Visit** table to the Query window, and then resize the Visit field list if necessary.

8. Drag the **OffSite** field from the Visit field list to the first column in the design grid. When you release the mouse button, the OffSite field appears in the design grid's first column, and the existing fields shift to the right. Group By, the default option in the Total row, appears for the OffSite field.

9. Run the query. The query displays two records—one for each OffSite group, Yes and No. Each record contains the OffSite field value for the group and the three aggregate function values. The summary statistics represent calculations based on the 202 records in the Billing table. See Figure 3-41.

Figure 3-41   **Aggregate functions grouped by OffSite**

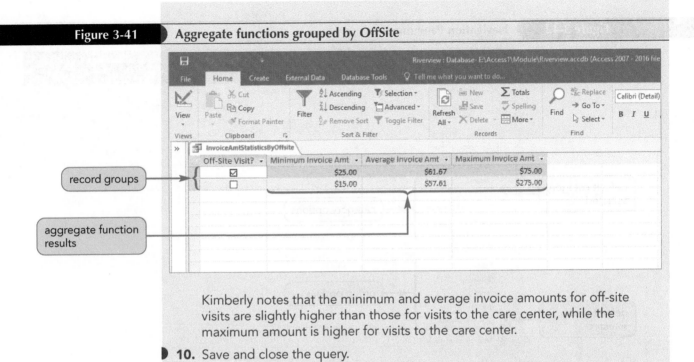

Kimberly notes that the minimum and average invoice amounts for off-site visits are slightly higher than those for visits to the care center, while the maximum amount is higher for visits to the care center.

▶ **10.** Save and close the query.

▶ **11.** Open the Navigation Pane.

You have created and saved many queries in the Riverview database. The Navigation Pane provides options for opening and managing the queries you've created, as well as the other objects in the database, such as tables, forms, and reports.

Working with the Navigation Pane

As noted earlier, the Navigation Pane is the main area for working with the objects in a database. As you continue to create objects in your database, you might want to display and work with them in different ways. The Navigation Pane provides options for grouping database objects in various ways to suit your needs. For example, you might want to view only the queries created for a certain table or all the query objects in the database.

As you know, the Navigation Pane divides database objects into categories. Each category contains groups, and each group contains one or more objects. The default category is **Object Type**, which arranges objects by type—tables, queries, forms, and reports. The default group is **All Access Objects**, which displays all objects in the database. You can also choose to display only one type of object, such as tables.

The default group name, All Access Objects, appears at the top of the Navigation Pane. Currently, each object type—Tables, Queries, Forms, and Reports—is displayed as a heading, and the objects related to each type are listed below the heading. To group objects differently, you can select another category by using the Navigation Pane menu. You'll try this next.

TIP

You can hide the display of a group's objects by clicking the button to the right of the group name; click the button again to expand the group and display its objects.

To group objects differently in the Navigation Pane:

▶ **1.** At the top of the Navigation Pane, click the **All Access Objects** button ⊙. A menu opens with options for choosing different categories and groups. See Figure 3-42.

Figure 3-42	Navigation Pane menu

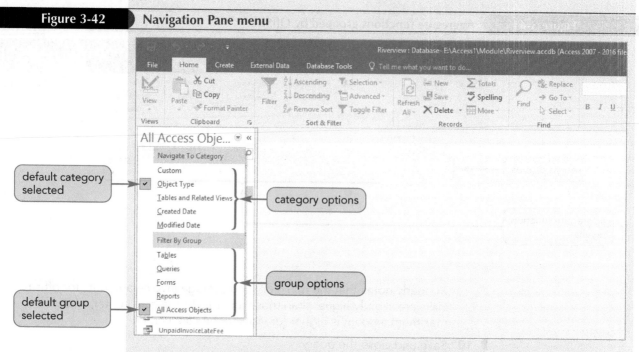

The top section of the menu provides the options for choosing a different category. The Object Type category has a checkmark next to it, signifying that it is the currently selected category. The lower section of the menu provides options for choosing a different group; these options might change depending on the selected category.

2. In the Navigate To Category section, click **Tables and Related Views**. The Navigation Pane is now grouped into categories of tables, and each table in the database—Visit, Billing, Owner, and Animal—is its own group. All database objects related to a table are listed below the table's name. Notice the UnpaidInvoiceLateFee query is based on both the Visit and Billing tables, so it is listed in the group for both tables. See Figure 3-43.

Figure 3-43   **Database objects grouped by table in the Navigation Pane**

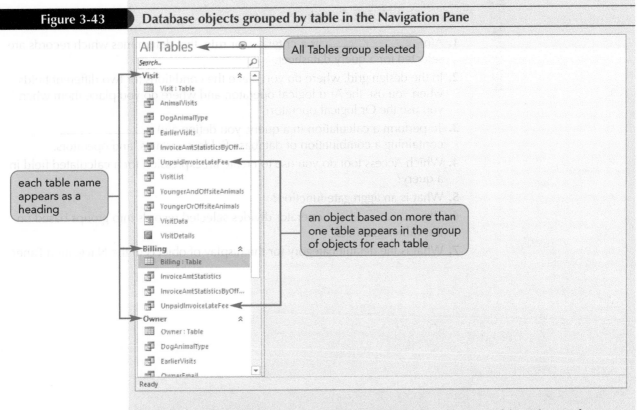

You can also choose to display the objects for only one table to better focus on that table.

3. At the top of the Navigation Pane, click the **All Tables** button ⊙ to display the Navigation Pane menu, and then click **Owner**. The Navigation Pane now shows only the objects related to the Owner table—the table itself plus the five queries you created that include fields from the Owner table.

4. At the top of the Navigation Pane, click the **Owner** button ⊙, and then click **Object Type** to return to the default display of the Navigation Pane.

5. Compact and repair the Riverview database, and then close the database.

   Trouble? If a dialog box opens and warns that this action will cause Microsoft Access to empty the Clipboard, click the Yes button to continue.

   The default All Access Objects category is a predefined category. You can also create custom categories to group objects in the way that best suits how you want to manage your database objects. As you continue to build a database and the list of objects grows, creating a custom category can help you to work more efficiently with the objects in the database.

   The queries you've created and saved will help Kimberly and her staff to monitor and analyze the business activity of Riverview Veterinary Care Center and its patients. Now any staff member can run the queries at any time, modify them as needed, or use them as the basis for designing new queries to meet additional information requirements.

REVIEW

Session 3.2 Quick Check

1. A(n) _____ is a criterion, or rule, that determines which records are selected for a query datasheet.
2. In the design grid, where do you place the conditions for two different fields when you use the And logical operator, and where do you place them when you use the Or logical operator?
3. To perform a calculation in a query, you define a(n) _____ containing a combination of database fields, constants, and operators.
4. Which Access tool do you use to create an expression for a calculated field in a query?
5. What is an aggregate function?
6. The _____ operator divides selected records into groups based on the values in a field.
7. What is the default category for the display of objects in the Navigation Pane?

Review Assignments

Data File needed for the Review Assignments: Vendor.accdb *(cont. from Module 2)*

Kimberly asks you to update some information in the Vendor database and also to retrieve specific information from the database. Complete the following:

1. Open the **Vendor** database you created and worked with in previous modules, and then click the Enable Content button next to the security warning, if necessary.

2. Open the **Supplier** table in Datasheet view, and then change the following field values for the record with the Supplier ID GGF099: Address to **738 26th St**, Contact Phone to **321-296-1958**, Contact First Name to **Carmela**, and Contact Last Name to **Montoya**. Close the table.

3. Create a query based on the Supplier table. Include the following fields in the query, in the order shown: Company, Category, ContactFirst, ContactLast, Phone, and City. Sort the query in ascending order based on the Category field values. Save the query as **ContactList**, and then run the query.

4. Use the ContactList query datasheet to update the Supplier table by changing the Phone field value for A+ Labs to **402-495-3957**.

5. Change the size of the font in the ContactList query datasheet to 12 points. Resize columns, as necessary, so that all field values and column headings are visible.

6. Change the alternate row color in the ContactList query datasheet to the Theme Color named Gold, Accent 4, Lighter 60%, and then save and close the query.

7. Create a query based on the Supplier and Product tables. Select the Company, Category, and State fields from the Supplier table, and the ProductName, Price, Units, and Weight fields from the Product table. Sort the query results in descending order based on price. Select only those records with a Category field value of Supplies, but do not display the Category field values in the query results. Save the query as **SupplyProducts**, run the query, and then close it.

8. Create a query that lists all products that cost more than $50 and are temperature controlled. Display the following fields from the Product table in the query results: ProductID, ProductName, Price, Units, and Sterile. (*Hint*: The TempControl field is a Yes/No field that should not appear in the query results.) Save the query as **HighPriceAndTempControl**, run the query, and then close it.

9. Create a query that lists information about suppliers who sell equipment or sterile products. Include the Company, Category, ContactFirst, and ContactLast fields from the Supplier table; and the ProductName, Price, TempControl, and Sterile fields from the Product table. Save the query as **EquipmentOrSterile**, run the query, and then close it.

10. Create a query that lists all resale products, along with a 10% markup amount based on the price of the product. Include the Company field from the Supplier table and the following fields from the Product table in the query: ProductID, ProductName, and Price. Save the query as **ResaleProductsWithMarkup**. Display the discount in a calculated field named **Markup** that determines a 10% markup based on the Price field values. Set the Caption property **Markup** for the calculated field. Display the query results in descending order by Price. Save and run the query.

11. Modify the format of the Markup field in the ResaleProductsWithMarkup query so that it uses the Standard format and two decimal places. Run the query, resize all columns in the datasheet to their best fit, and then save and close the query.

12. Create a query that calculates the lowest, highest, and average prices for all products using the field names **MinimumPrice**, **MaximumPrice**, and **AveragePrice**, respectively. Set the Caption property for each field to include a space between the two words in the field name. Run the query, resize all columns in the datasheet to their best fit, save the query as **PriceStatistics**, and then close it.

13. In the Navigation Pane, copy the PriceStatistics query, and then rename the copied query as **PriceStatisticsBySupplier**.

14. Modify the PriceStatisticsBySupplier query so that the records are grouped by the Company field in the Supplier table. The Company field should appear first in the query datasheet. Save and run the query, and then close it.

15. Compact and repair the Vendor database, and then close it.

Case Problem 1

Data File needed for this Case Problem: Beauty.accdb *(cont. from Module 2)*

Beauty To Go   Sue Miller needs to modify a few records in the Beauty database and analyze the data for customers that subscribe to her business. To help Sue, you'll update the Beauty database and create queries to answer her questions. Complete the following:

1. Open the **Beauty** database you created and worked with in previous modules, and then click the Enable Content button next to the security warning, if necessary.

2. In the **Member** table, find the record for MemberID 2163, and then change the Street value to **844 Sanford Ln** and the Zip to **32804**.

3. In the **Member** table, find the record for MemberID 2169, and then delete the record. Close the Member table.

4. Create a query that lists customers who did not have to pay a fee when they signed up for their current option. In the query results, display the FirstName, LastName, and OptionBegin fields from the Member table, and the OptionCost field from the Option table. Sort the records in ascending order by the option start date. Select records only for customers whose fees were waived. (*Hint*: The FeeWaived field is a Yes/No field that should not appear in the query results.) Save the query as **NoFees**, and then run the query.

5. Use the NoFees query datasheet to update the Member table by changing the Last Name value for Gilda Packson to **Washington**.

6. Use the NoFees query datasheet to display the total Option Cost for the selected members. Save and close the query.

7. Create a query that lists the MemberID, FirstName, LastName, OptionBegin, OptionDescription, and OptionCost fields for customers who signed up with Beauty To Go between January 1, 2017 and January 31, 2017. Save the query as **JanuaryOptions**, run the query, and then close it.

8. Create a query that lists all customers who live in Celebration and whose options end on or after 4/1/2017. Display the following fields from the Member table in the query results: MemberID, FirstName, LastName, Phone, and OptionEnd. (*Hint*: The City field values should not appear in the query results.) Sort the query results in ascending order by last name. Save the query as **CelebrationAndEndDate**, run the query, and then close it.

9. Copy and paste the CelebrationAndEndDate query to create a new query named **CelebrationOrEndDate**. Modify the new query so that it lists all members who live in Celebration or whose memberships expire on or after 4/1/2017. Display the City field values in the query results following the Phone field values, and sort the query results in ascending order by city (this should be the only sort in the query). Save and run the query.

10. Change the size of the font in the CelebrationOrEndDate query datasheet to 14 points. Resize columns, as necessary, so that all field values and column headings are visible.

11. Change the alternate row color in the CelebrationOrEndDate query datasheet to the Theme Color named Green, Accent 6, Lighter 80%, and then save and close the query.

12. Create a query that calculates the lowest, highest, and average cost for all options using the field names **LowestCost**, **HighestCost**, and **AverageCost**, respectively. Set the Caption property for each field to include a space between the two words in the field name. Run the query, resize all columns in the datasheet to their best fit, save the query as **CostStatistics**, and then close it.

13. Copy and paste the CostStatistics query to create a new query named **CostStatisticsByZip**.

14. Modify the CostStatisticsByZip query to display the same statistics grouped by Zip, with Zip appearing as the first field. (*Hint*: Add the Member table to the query.) Run the query, and then save and close it.

15. Compact and repair the Beauty database, and then close it.

Case Problem 2

Data File needed for this Case Problem: Programming.accdb *(cont. from Module 2)*

CREATE

Programming Pros   After reviewing the Programming database, Brent Hovis wants to modify some records and then view specific information about the students, tutors, and contracts for his tutoring services company. He asks you to update and query the Programming database to perform these tasks. Complete the following:

1. Open the **Programming** database you created and worked with in previous modules, and then click the Enable Content button next to the security warning, if necessary.

2. In the **Tutor** table, change the following information for the record with TutorID 1048: Major is **Computer Science** and Year In School is **Graduate**. Close the table.

3. In the **Student** table, find the record with the StudentID RAM4025, and then delete the related record in the subdatasheet for this student. Delete the record for StudentID RAM4025, and then close the Student table.

4. Create a query based on the Student table that includes the LastName, FirstName, and CellPhone fields, in that order. Save the query as **StudentCellList**, and then run the query.

5. In the results of the StudentCellList query, change the cell phone number for Hidalgo Hickman to **919-301-2209**. Close the query.

6. Create a query based on the Tutor and Contract tables. Display the LastName field from the Tutor table, and the StudentID, ContractDate, SessionType, Length, and Cost fields, in that order, from the Contract table. Sort first in ascending order by the tutor's last name, and then in ascending order by the StudentID. Save the query as **SessionsByTutor**, run the query, and then close it.

7. Copy and paste the SessionsByTutor query to create a new query named **GroupSessions**. Modify the new query so that it displays the same information for records with a Group session type only. Do not display the SessionType field values in the query results. Save and run the query, and then close it.

8. Create and save a query that produces the results shown in Figure 3-44. Close the query when you are finished.

Figure 3-44   **RaleighPrivate query results**

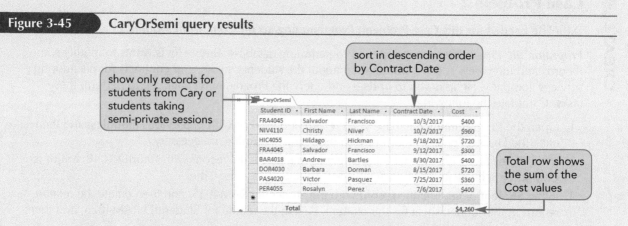

show only records for students from Raleigh who are taking private sessions

sort by Last Name

format with a font size of 12 and the Blue, Accent 5, Lighter 80% alternate row Theme Color

9. Create and save a query that produces the results shown in Figure 3-45. Close the query when you are finished.

Figure 3-45   **CaryOrSemi query results**

sort in descending order by Contract Date

show only records for students from Cary or students taking semi-private sessions

Total row shows the sum of the Cost values

10. Create and save a query to display statistics for the Cost field, as shown in Figure 3-46. Close the query when you are finished.

Figure 3-46   **CostStatistics query results**

set captions to include spaces between words

format values as Standard with two decimal places

11. Copy and paste the CostStatistics query to create a new query named **CostStatisticsByCity**.

12. Modify the CostStatisticsByCity query to display the same statistics grouped by City, with City appearing as the first field. (*Hint*: Add the Student table to the query.) Run the query, and then save and close it.

13. Compact and repair the Programming database, and then close it.

Case Problem 3

Data File needed for this Case Problem: Center.accdb *(cont. from Module 2)*

Diane's Community Center   Diane Coleman needs to modify some records in the Center database, and then she wants to find specific information about the patrons, donations, and auction items for her not-for-profit community center. Diane asks you to help her update the database and create queries to find the information she needs. Complete the following:

1. Open the **Center** database you created and worked with in previous modules, and then click the Enable Content button next to the security warning, if necessary.

2. In the **Patron** table, delete the record with PatronID 3024. (*Hint*: Delete the related records in the Donation subdatasheet first.) Close the Patron table without saving changes to the table layout.

3. Create a query based on the Auction and Donation tables that includes the AuctionID, DonationID, DonationDate, and Description fields, in that order. Save the query as **AuctionItemsByDate**, and then run it.

4. Modify the AuctionItemsByDate query design so that it sorts records in ascending order first by DonationDate and then by Description. Save and run the query.

5. In the AuctionItemsByDate query datasheet, find the record for the auction item with Auction ID 250, and then change the description for this item to **New scooter**. Close the query.

6. Create a query that displays the PatronID, FirstName, and LastName fields from the Patron table, and the Description and DonationValue fields from the Donation table for all donations over $150. Sort the query in ascending order by donation value. Save the query as **LargeDonations**, run the query, and then close it.

7. Copy and paste the LargeDonations query to create a new query named **LargeCashDonations**.

⊕ **Explore** 8. Modify the LargeCashDonations query to display only those records with donations valued at more than $150 in cash. Do not include the Description field values in the query results. Use the query datasheet to calculate the average cash donation. Save and close the query.

9. Create a query that displays the PatronID, FirstName, and LastName fields from the Patron table, and the AuctionID, AuctionDate, and MinPrice fields from the Auction table. Specify that the results show records for only those items with a minimum price greater than $150. Save the query as **ExpensiveAuctionItems**, and then run the query.

10. Filter the results of the ExpensiveAuctionItems query datasheet to display records with an auction date of 10/14/2017 only.

⊕ **Explore** 11. Format the datasheet of the ExpensiveAuctionItems query so that it does not display gridlines, uses an alternate row Standard Color of Maroon 2, and displays a font size of 12. (*Hint*: Use the Gridlines button in the Text Formatting group on the Home tab to select the appropriate gridlines option.) Resize the columns to display the complete field names and values, if necessary. Save and close the query.

⊕ **Explore** 12. Create a query that displays the PatronID, FirstName, and LastName fields from the Patron table, and the Description, DonationDate, and DonationValue fields from the Donation table. Specify that the query include records for noncash donations only or for donations made in the month of September 2017. Sort the records first in ascending order by the patron's last name, and then in descending order by the donation value. Save the query as **NonCashOrSeptemberDonations**, run the query, and then close it.

13. Copy and paste the NonCashOrSeptemberDonations query to create a new query named **DonationsAfterStorageCharge**.

⊕ **Explore** 14. Modify the DonationsAfterStorageCharge query so that it displays records for noncash donations made on all dates. Create a calculated field named **NetDonation** that displays the results of subtracting $3.50 from the DonationValue field values to account for the cost of storing each noncash donated item. Set the Caption property **Net Donation** for the calculated field. Display the results in ascending order by donation value and not sorted on any other field. Run the query, and then modify it to format both the DonationValue field and the calculated field as Currency with two decimal places. Run the query again, and resize the columns in the datasheet to their best fit, as necessary. Save and close the query.

⊕ **Explore** 15. Create a query based on the **Donation** table that displays the sum, average, and count of the DonationValue field for all donations. Then complete the following:

a. Specify field names of **TotalDonations**, **AverageDonation**, and **NumberOfDonations**. Then specify captions to include spaces between words.

b. Save the query as **DonationStatistics**, and then run it. Resize the query datasheet columns to their best fit.

c. Modify the field properties so that the values in the Total Donations and Average Donation columns display two decimal places and the Standard format. Run the query again, and then save and close the query.

d. Copy and paste the DonationStatistics query to create a new query named **DonationStatisticsByDescription**.

e. Modify the DonationStatisticsByDescription query to display the sum, average, and count of the DonationValue field for all donations grouped by Description, with Description appearing as the first field. Sort the records in descending order by Total Donations. Save, run, and then close the query.

16. Compact and repair the Center database, and then close it.

Case Problem 4

Data Files needed for this Case Problem: Appalachia.accdb *(cont. from Module 2)* **and HikeApp.accdb**

Hike Appalachia   Molly and Bailey Johnson need your help to maintain and analyze data about the hikers, reservations, and tours for their hiking tour business. Additionally, you'll troubleshoot some problems in another database containing tour information. Complete the following:

1. Open the **Appalachia** database you created and worked with in previous modules, and then click the Enable Content button next to the security warning, if necessary.

2. In the **Hiker** table, change the phone number for Wilbur Sanders to **828-910-2058**, and then close the table.

3. Create a query based on the Tour table that includes the TourName, Hours, PricePerPerson, and TourType fields, in that order. Sort in ascending order based on the PricePerPerson field values. Save the query as **ToursByPrice**, and then run the query.

TROUBLESHOOT

4. Use the ToursByPrice query datasheet to display the total Price Per Person for the tours. Save and close the query.

5. Create a query that displays the HikerLast, City, and State fields from the Hiker table, and the ReservationID, TourDate, and People fields from the Reservation table. Save the query as **HikerTourDates**, and then run the query. Change the alternate row color in the query datasheet to the Theme Color Blue, Accent 1, Lighter 80%. In Datasheet view, use an AutoFilter to sort the query results from oldest to newest Tour Date. Save and close the query.

6. Create a query that displays the HikerFirst, HikerLast, City, ReservationID, TourID, and TourDate fields for all guests from North Carolina (NC). Do not include the State field in the query results. Sort the query in ascending order by the guest's last name. Save the query as **NorthCarolinaHikers** and then run it. Close the query.

7. Create a query that displays data from all three tables in the database as follows: the HikerLast, City, and State fields from the Hiker table; the TourDate field from the Reservation table; and the TourName and TourType fields from the Tour table. Specify that the query select only those records for guests from West Virginia (WV) or guests who are taking climbing tours. Sort the query in ascending order by Tour Name. Save the query as **WestVirginiaOrClimbing** and then run the query. Resize datasheet columns to their best fit, as necessary, and then save and close the query.

8. Copy and paste the **WestVirginiaOrClimbing** query to create a new query named **SouthCarolinaAndSeptember**.

9. Modify the **SouthCarolinaAndSeptember** query to select all guests from South Carolina (SC) who are taking a tour starting sometime in the month of September 2017. Do not include the State field values in the query results. Run the query. Resize datasheet columns to their best fit, as necessary, and then save and close the query.

10. Create a query that displays the ReservationID, TourDate, and People fields from the Reservation table, and the TourName and PricePerPerson fields from the Tour table for all reservations with a People field value greater than 1. Save the query as **ReservationCosts**. Add a field to the query named **TotalCost** that displays the results of multiplying the People field values by the PricePerPerson field values. Set the Caption property **Total Cost** for the calculated field. Display the results in descending order by TotalCost. Run the query. Modify the query by formatting the TotalCost field to show 0 decimal places. Run the query, resize datasheet columns to their best fit, as necessary, and then save and close the query.

11. Create a query based on the Tour table that determines the minimum, average, and maximum price per person for all tours. Then complete the following:

a. Specify field names of **LowestPrice**, **AveragePrice**, and **HighestPrice**.

b. Set the Caption property for each field to include a space between the two words in the field name.

c. Save the query as **PriceStatistics**, and then run the query.

d. In Design view, specify the Standard format and two decimal places for each column.

e. Run the query, resize all the datasheet columns to their best fit, save your changes, and then close the query.

f. Create a copy of the PriceStatistics query named **PriceStatisticsByTourType**.

g. Modify the PriceStatisticsByTourType query to display the price statistics grouped by TourType, with TourType appearing as the first field. Save your changes, and then run and close the query.

h. Compact and repair the Appalachia database, and then close it.

⚙ **Troubleshoot** 12. Open the **HikeApp** database located in the Access1 > Case4 folder provided with your Data Files, and then click the Enable Content button next to the security warning, if necessary. Run the ReservationByDateAndState query in the HikeApp database. The query is not producing the desired results. Fix the query so that the data from the Reservation table is listed first and the data is sorted only by TourDate in ascending order. Save and close the corrected query.

⚙ **Troubleshoot** 13. Run the NCGuestsFewerPeople query, which displays no records in the results. This query is supposed to show data for guests from North Carolina (NC) with fewer than four people in their booking. Find and correct the errors in the query design, run the query, and then close it.

⚙ **Troubleshoot** 14. Run the GeorgiaOrOctStart query. This query should display the records for all guests who are from Georgia (GA) or whose tour date is on or after 10/1/2017. Find and correct the errors in the query design, run the query, and then close it.

15. Compact and repair the HikeApp database, and then close it.

OBJECTIVES

Session 4.1
- Create a form using the Form Wizard
- Apply a theme to a form
- Add a picture to a form
- Change the color of text on a form
- Find and maintain data using a form
- Preview and print selected form records
- Create a form with a main form and a subform

Session 4.2
- Create a report using the Report Wizard
- Apply a theme to a report
- Change the alignment of field values on a report
- Move and resize fields in a report
- Insert a picture in a report
- Change the color of text on a report
- Apply conditional formatting in a report
- Preview and print a report

Creating Forms and Reports

Using Forms and Reports to Display Owner, Animal, and Visit Data

Case | *Riverview Veterinary Care Center*

Kimberly Johnson wants to continue enhancing the Riverview database to make it easier for her staff to enter, locate, and maintain data. In particular, she wants the database to include a form based on the Owner table that staff can use to enter and change data about the owners of the animals that the care center sees. She also wants the database to include a form that shows data from both the Owner and Animal tables at the same time. This form will show the basic information for each owner along with the corresponding animal data, providing a complete picture of Riverview Veterinary Care Center clients and their animals.

In addition, she would like the database to include a report of owner and visit data so that she and other staff members will have printed output when completing analyses of the owners who are clients of the care center and planning strategies for making additional veterinary services available to them. She wants the report to be formatted professionally and easy to use.

In this module, you will create the forms and reports in the Riverview database for Kimberly and her staff.

ACCESS

STARTING DATA FILES

Access1 → Module
Animals.png
Riverview.accdb (*cont.*)

Review
Items.png
Vendor.accdb (*cont.*)

Case1
Beauty.accdb (*cont.*)
Salon.png

Case2
Coder.png
Programming.accdb (*cont.*)

Case3
Center.accdb (*cont.*)
Flower.png

Case4
Appalachia.accdb (*cont.*)
HikeApp.accdb (*cont.*)
Mountains.png

Session 4.1 Visual Overview:

The form object's name is displayed on the tab for the form.

The form title appears at the top of the form. By default, the form object name is used as the form title, but you can edit the title to display the text you want, as done here—a space was added between the two words for readability.

With the Columnar form layout, the field captions appear in a column on the left side of the form. If captions had not been specified for the fields, the field names would appear here instead.

The navigation buttons allow you to display the first, last, next, or previous record in the form, enter a specific record number and move to that record, and create a new record.

You can add graphic elements, such as a picture, to a form to improve its appearance or add visual appeal.

The Columnar form layout displays the corresponding field values in boxes to the right of the field captions (or field names).

You can use the Search box to find and display a record containing the text you enter.

Riverview : Database- E:\Access1\Module\Riverview.acc

File   Home   Create   External Data   Database Tools   Tell me what you wan

View   Paste   Cut   Copy   Format Painter   Filter   Ascending   Descending   Remove Sort   Selection   Advanced   Toggle Filter   Refresh All   New   Sav   Del

Views   Clipboard   Sort & Filter

OwnerData

Owner Data

Owner ID	2310
First Name	Student First
Last Name	Student Last
Address	12 Elm Ln
City	Cody
State	WY
Zip	82414
Email	student@example.com
Phone	307-824-1245

Navigation Pane

Record: 1 of 25   No Filter   Search

Form View

Form Displayed in Form View

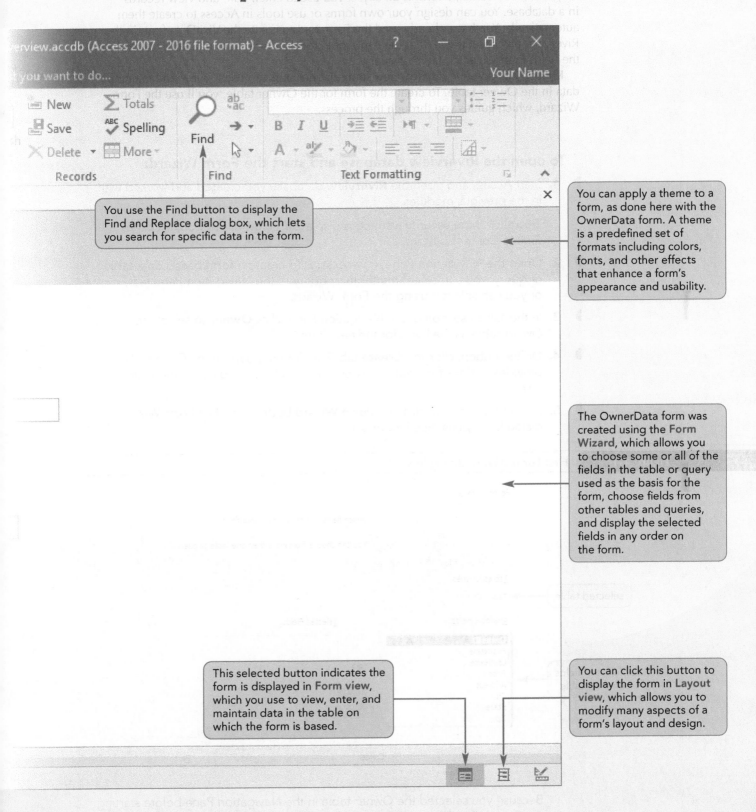

You use the Find button to display the Find and Replace dialog box, which lets you search for specific data in the form.

You can apply a theme to a form, as done here with the OwnerData form. A theme is a predefined set of formats including colors, fonts, and other effects that enhance a form's appearance and usability.

The OwnerData form was created using the Form Wizard, which allows you to choose some or all of the fields in the table or query used as the basis for the form, choose fields from other tables and queries, and display the selected fields in any order on the form.

This selected button indicates the form is displayed in Form view, which you use to view, enter, and maintain data in the table on which the form is based.

You can click this button to display the form in Layout view, which allows you to modify many aspects of a form's layout and design.

Creating a Form Using the Form Wizard

As you learned earlier, a form is an object you use to enter, edit, and view records in a database. You can design your own forms or use tools in Access to create them automatically. You have already used the Form tool to create the VisitData form in the Riverview database. Recall that the Form tool creates a form automatically, using all the fields in the selected table or query.

Kimberly asks you to create a new form that her staff can use to view and maintain data in the Owner table. To create the form for the Owner table, you'll use the Form Wizard, which guides you through the process.

To open the Riverview database and start the Form Wizard:

▶ **1.** Start Access and open the **Riverview** database you created and worked with in the previous modules.

   Trouble? If the security warning is displayed below the ribbon, click the Enable Content button.

▶ **2.** Open the Navigation Pane, if necessary. To create a form based on a table or query, you can select the table or query in the Navigation Pane first, or you can select it using the Form Wizard.

▶ **3.** In the Tables section of the Navigation Pane, click **Owner** to select the Owner table as the basis for the new form.

▶ **4.** On the ribbon, click the **Create** tab. The Forms group on the Create tab provides options for creating various types of forms and designing your own forms.

▶ **5.** In the Forms group, click the **Form Wizard** button. The first Form Wizard dialog box opens. See Figure 4-1.

Figure 4-1   **First Form Wizard dialog box**

Because you selected the Owner table in the Navigation Pane before starting the Form Wizard, this table is selected in the Tables/Queries box, and the fields for the Owner table are listed in the Available Fields box.

Kimberly wants the form to display all the fields in the Owner table, but in a different order. She would like the Phone field to appear at the bottom of the form so that it stands out, making it easier for someone who needs to call an animal's owner to use the form to quickly locate the phone number.

To create the form using the Form Wizard:

1. Click the >> button to move all the fields to the Selected Fields box. Next, you need to position the Phone field so it will appear as the bottom-most field on the form. To accomplish this, you will first remove the Phone field and then add it back as the last selected field.

2. In the Selected Fields box, click the **Phone** field, and then click the < button to move the field back to the Available Fields box.

   Because a new field is always added after the selected field in the Selected Fields box, you need to first select the last field in the list and then move the Phone field back to the Selected Fields box so it will be the last field on the form.

3. In the Selected Fields box, click the **Email** field.

4. With the Phone field selected in the Available Fields box, click the > button to move the Phone field to the end of the list in the Selected Fields box.

5. Click the **Next** button to display the second Form Wizard dialog box, in which you select a layout for the form. See Figure 4-2.

Figure 4-2	Choosing a layout for the form

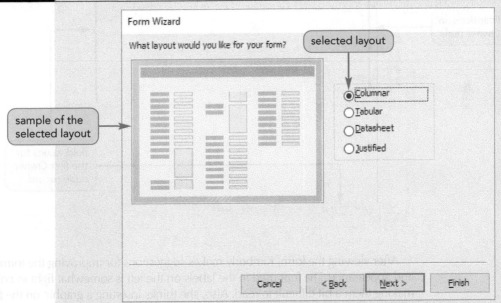

The layout choices are Columnar, Tabular, Datasheet, and Justified. A sample of the selected layout appears on the left side of the dialog box.

6. Click each of the option buttons and review the corresponding sample layout.

   The Tabular and Datasheet layouts display the fields from multiple records at one time, whereas the Columnar and Justified layouts display the fields from one record at a time. Kimberly thinks the Columnar layout is the appropriate arrangement for displaying and updating data in the table, so that anyone using the form can focus on just one owner record at a time.

▶ **7.** Click the **Columnar** option button (if necessary), and then click the **Next** button.

The third and final Form Wizard dialog box shows the Owner table's name as the default form name. "Owner" is also the default title that will appear on the tab for the form.

You'll use "OwnerData" as the form name, and, because you don't need to change the form's design at this point, you'll display the form.

▶ **8.** Click to position the insertion point to the right of Owner in the box, type **Data**, and then click the **Finish** button.

Close the Navigation Pane to display only the Form window. The completed form is displayed in Form view, displaying the values for the first record in the Owner table. The Columnar layout you selected places the field captions in labels on the left and the corresponding field values in boxes on the right, which vary in width depending on the size of the field. See Figure 4-3.

Figure 4-3	OwnerData form in Form view

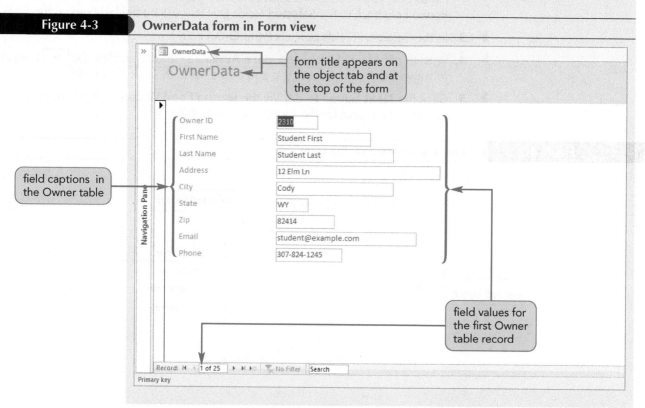

After viewing the form, Kimberly makes suggestions for improving the form's readability and appearance. The font used in the labels on the left is somewhat light in color and small, making them a bit difficult to read. Also, she thinks inserting a graphic on the form would add visual interest, and modifying other form elements—such as the color of the title text—would improve the look of the form. You can make all of these changes working with the form in Layout view.

Modifying a Form's Design in Layout View

TIP

Some form design changes require you to switch to Design view, which gives you a more detailed view of the form's structure.

After you create a form, you might need to modify its design to improve its appearance or to make the form easier to use. You cannot make any design changes in Form view. However, Layout view displays the form as it appears in Form view while allowing you to modify the form's design. Because you can see the form and its data while you are modifying the form, Layout view makes it easy for you to see the results of any design changes you make.

The first modification you'll make to the OwnerData form is to change its appearance by applying a theme.

Applying a Theme to a Database Object

By default, the objects you create in a database are formatted with the Office theme. A theme provides a design scheme for the colors and fonts used in the database objects. Access, like other Microsoft Office programs, provides many built-in themes, including the Office theme, making it easy for you to create objects with a unified look. You can also create a customized theme if none of the built-in themes suit your needs.

Sometimes a theme works well for one database object but is not as suitable for other objects in that database. Therefore, when applying a theme to an object, you can choose to apply the theme just to the open object or to objects of a particular type, or you can choose to apply the theme to all the existing objects in the database and set it as the default theme for any new objects that might be created.

To change a form's appearance, you can easily apply a new theme to it.

REFERENCE

Applying a Theme to Database Objects

- Display the object in Layout view.
- In the Themes group on the Form Layout Tools Design tab or Report Layout Tools Design tab, click the Themes button.
- In the Themes gallery, click the theme you want to apply to all objects; or, right-click the theme to display the shortcut menu, and then choose to apply the theme to the current object only or to all matching objects.

Kimberly would like to see if the OwnerData form's appearance can be improved with a different theme. To apply a theme, you first need to switch to Layout view.

To apply a theme to the OwnerData form:

▸ **1.** On the ribbon, make sure the Home tab is displayed.

▸ **2.** In the Views group, click the **View** button. The form is displayed in Layout view. See Figure 4-4.

Figure 4-4   Form displayed in Layout view

Themes button

Format Layout Tools Design tab displays options for changing the form's appearance

OwnerData

OwnerData

Owner ID	2310
First Name	Student First
Last Name	Student Last
Address	12 Elm Ln
City	Cody
State	WY
Zip	82414
Email	student@example.com
Phone	307-824-1245

orange border indicates the selected field value

Record: 14 ◄ 1 of 25 ► ►I ►□   No Filter   Search

Layout View

Trouble? If the Field List or Property Sheet opens on the right side of the program window, close it before continuing.

In Layout view, an orange border identifies the currently selected element on the form. In this case, the field value for the OwnerID field, 2310, is selected. You need to apply a theme to the OwnerData form.

3. On the Form Layout Tools Design tab, in the Themes group, click the **Themes** button. A gallery opens showing the available themes for the form. See Figure 4-5.

Figure 4-5   Themes gallery

TIP

Themes other than the
Office theme are listed
in alphabetical order in
the gallery.

The Office theme, the default theme currently applied in the database, is
listed in the "In this Database" section and is also the first theme listed in the
section containing other themes. You can point to each theme in the gallery
to see its name in a ScreenTip. Also, when you point to a theme, the Live
Preview feature shows the effect of applying the theme to the open object.

4. In the gallery, point to each of the themes to see how they would format
    the OwnerData form. Notice the changes in color and font type of the text,
    for example.

    Kimberly likes the Wisp theme because of its light gray color in the title area at
    the top and its larger font size, which makes the text in the form easier to read.

5. Right-click the **Wisp** theme. A shortcut menu opens with options for applying
    the theme. See Figure 4-6.

Figure 4-6   Shortcut menu for applying the theme

The menu provides options for applying the theme to all matching objects—for example, all the forms in the database—or to the current object only. You can also choose to make the theme the default theme in the database, which means any new objects you create will be formatted with the selected theme. Because Kimberly is not sure if all forms in the Riverview database will look better with the Wisp theme, she asks you to apply it only to the OwnerData form.

> Choose this option to avoid applying the theme to other forms in the database.

6. On the shortcut menu, click **Apply Theme to This Object Only**.

The gallery closes, and the Wisp theme's colors and fonts are applied to the form.

Trouble? If you choose the wrong option by mistake, you might have applied the selected theme to other forms and/or reports in the database. Repeat Steps 3 through 6 to apply the Wisp theme to the OwnerData form. You can also follow the same process to reapply the default Office theme to the other forms and reports in the Riverview database, as directed by your instructor.

INSIGHT

Working with Themes

Themes provide a quick and easy way for you to format the objects in a database with a consistent look, which is a good design principle to follow. In general, all objects of a type in a database—for example, all forms—should have a consistent design. However, keep in mind that when you select a theme in the Themes gallery and choose the option to apply the theme to all matching objects or to make the theme the default for the database, it might be applied to all the existing forms and reports in the database as well as to new forms and reports you create. Although this approach ensures a consistent design, it can cause problems. For example, if you have already created a form or report and its design is suitable, applying a theme that includes a larger font size could cause the text in labels and field value boxes to be cut off or to extend into other objects on the form or report. The colors applied by the theme could also interfere with elements on existing forms and reports. To handle these unintended results, you would have to spend time checking the existing forms and reports and fixing any problems introduced by applying the theme. A better approach is to select the option "Apply Theme to This Object Only," available on the shortcut menu for a theme in the Themes gallery, for each existing form and report. If the newly applied theme causes problems for any individual form or report, you can then reapply the original theme to return the object to its original design.

Next, you will add a picture to the form for visual interest. The picture, which is included on various flyers and other owner correspondence for Riverview Veterinary Care Center, is a small graphic of a dog and a cat.

Adding a Picture to a Form

A picture is one of many controls you can add and modify on a form. A **control** is an item on a form, report, or other database object that you can manipulate to modify the object's appearance. The controls you can add and modify in Layout view for a form are available in the Controls group and the Header/Footer group on the Form Layout Tools Design tab. The picture you need to add is contained in a file named Animals.png, which is located in the Access1 > Module folder provided with your Data Files.

To add the picture to the form:

1. Make sure the form is still displayed in Layout view and that the Form Layout Tools Design tab is active.

2. In the Header/Footer group, click the **Logo** button. The Insert Picture dialog box opens.

3. Navigate to the **Access1 > Module** folder provided with your Data Files, click the **Animals** file, and then click the **OK** button. The picture appears on top of the form's title. See Figure 4-7.

Figure 4-7   Form with picture added

picture selected

control layout containing the picture

A solid orange border surrounds the picture, indicating it is selected. The picture is placed in a **control layout**, which is a set of controls grouped together in a form or report so that you can manipulate the set as a single control. The dotted blue outline indicates the control layout. The easiest way to move the picture off the form title is to first remove it from the control layout. Doing so allows you to move the picture independently.

4. Right-click the picture to open the shortcut menu, point to **Layout**, and then click **Remove Layout**. The dotted blue outline no longer appears, and the picture is removed from the control layout. Now you can move the picture to the right of the form title.

5. Position the pointer ⊹ on the picture, and then drag to the right of the form title. Although the image may not be visible while dragging, you can use the position of the pointer as a guide to where the image will be placed.

TIP

You can resize a selected image by dragging a corner of the orange selection border.

6. When the pointer is roughly one-half inch to the right of the form's title, release the mouse button. The picture is positioned to the right of the form title.

7. Click in a blank area to the right of the field values in the form to deselect the picture. See Figure 4-8.

Trouble? Don't be concerned if the picture is not in the exact location as the one shown in Figure 4-8. Just make sure the picture is not blocking any part of the form title and that it appears to the right of the form title and within the gray shaded area at the top of the form.

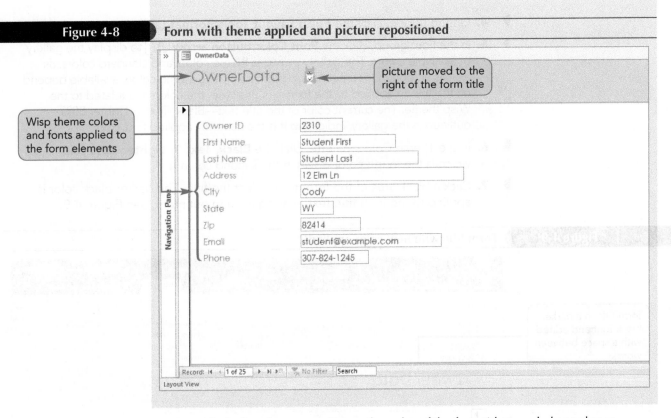

Figure 4-8   **Form with theme applied and picture repositioned**

Next, Kimberly asks you to change the color of the form title to a darker color so that it will stand out more on the form.

Changing the Color of Text on a Form

The Font group on the Form Layout Tools Format tab provides many options you can use to change the appearance of text on a form. For example, you can bold, italicize, and underline text; change the font, font color, and font size; and change the alignment of text. Before you change the color of the "OwnerData" title on the form, you'll change the title to two words so it is easier to read.

TIP

Changing the form's title does not affect the form object name; it is still OwnerData, as shown on the object tab.

To change the form title's text and color:

1. Click the **OwnerData** form title. An orange border surrounds the title, indicating it is selected.

2. Click between the letters "r" and "D" to position the insertion point, and then press the **spacebar**. The title on the form is now "Owner Data," but the added space caused the words to appear on two lines. You can fix this by resizing the box containing the title.

3. Position the pointer on the right edge of the box containing the form title until the pointer changes to ↔, and then drag to the right until the word "Data" appears on the same line as the word "Owner."

    Trouble? You might need to repeat Step 3 until the title appears on one line. Also, you might have to move the picture further to the right to make room for the title.

    Next you will change the title's font color.

4. On the ribbon, click the **Form Layout Tools Format** tab.

5. In the Font group, click the **Font Color button arrow** $\boxed{A}$ · to display the gallery of available colors. The gallery provides theme colors and standard colors, as well as an option for creating a custom color. The theme colors available depend on the theme applied to the form—in this case, the colors are related to the Wisp theme. The current color of the title text—Black, Text 1, Lighter 50%—is outlined in the gallery, indicating it is the currently applied font color.

6. In the Theme Colors palette, click the **Black, Text 1, Lighter 25%** color, which is the fourth color down in the second column.

7. Click a blank area of the form to deselect the title. The darker black color is applied to the form title text, making it stand out more. See Figure 4-9.

Figure 4-9	Form title with new color applied

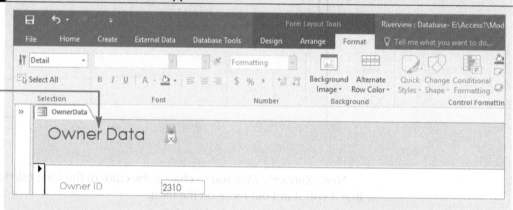

form title in a darker black font and edited with a space between words

8. On the Quick Access Toolbar, click the **Save** button $\boxed{}$ to save the modified form.

9. On the status bar, click the **Form View** button $\boxed{}$ to display the form in Form view.

Kimberly is pleased with the modified appearance of the form. Later, she plans to revise the existing VisitData form and make the same changes to it, so that it matches the appearance of the OwnerData form.

Written Communication: Understanding the Importance of Form Design

Similar to any document, a form must convey written information clearly and effectively. When you create a form, it's important to consider how the form will be used, so that its design will accommodate the needs of people using the form to view, enter, and maintain data. For example, if a form in a database is meant to mimic a paper form that users will enter data from, the form in the database should have the same fields in the same order as on the paper form. This will enable users to easily tab from one field to the next in the database form to enter the necessary information from the paper form. Also, it's important to include a meaningful title on the form to identify its purpose and to enhance the appearance of the form. A form that is visually appealing makes working with the database more user-friendly and can improve the readability of the form, thereby helping to prevent errors in data entry. Also, be sure to use a consistent design for the forms in your database whenever possible. Users will expect to see similar elements—titles, pictures, fonts, and so on—in each form contained in a database. A mix of form styles and elements among the forms in a database could lead to problems when working with the forms. Finally, make sure the text on your form does not contain any spelling or grammatical errors. By producing a well-designed and well-written form, you can help to ensure that users will be able to work with the form in a productive and efficient manner.

Navigating a Form

To view, navigate, and change data using a form, you need to display the form in Form view. As you learned earlier, you navigate a form in the same way that you navigate a table datasheet. Also, the same navigation mode and editing mode keyboard shortcuts you have used working with datasheets can also be used when working with a form.

Kimberly wants to view data in the Owner table. Before using the OwnerData form to display the specific information Kimberly wants to view, you will practice navigating between the fields in a record and navigating between records in the form. The OwnerData form is already displayed in Form view, so you can use it to navigate through the fields and records of the Owner table.

To navigate the OwnerData form:

1. If necessary, click in the **Owner ID** field value box to make it current.

2. Press the **Tab** key twice to move to the Last Name field value box, and then press the **End** key to move to the Phone field value box.

3. Press the **Home** key to move back to the Owner ID field value box. The first record in the Owner table still appears in the form.

4. Press the **Ctrl+End** keys to move to the Phone field value box for record 25, which is the last record in the table. The record number for the current record appears in the Current Record box between the navigation buttons at the bottom of the form.

5. Click the **Previous record** button ◀ to move to the Phone field value box in record 24.

6. Press the ↑ key twice to move to the Zip field value box in record 24.

7. Click to position the insertion point within the word "Rascal" in the Address field value to switch to editing mode, press the **Home** key to move the insertion point to the beginning of the field value, and then press the **End** key to move the insertion point to the end of the field value.

8. Click the **First record** button to move to the Address field value box in the first record. The entire field value is highlighted because you switched from editing mode to navigation mode.

9. Click the **Next record** button to move to the Address field value box in record 2, the next record.

Kimberly wants to find the record for an owner named Thomas. The paper form containing all the original contact information for this owner was damaged. Other than the owner's first name, Kimberly knows only the street the owner lives on. You will use the OwnerData form to locate and view the complete record for this owner.

Finding Data Using a Form

As you learned earlier, the Find command lets you search for data in a datasheet so you can display only those records you want to view. You can also use the Find command to search for data in a form. You first choose a field to serve as the basis for the search by making that field the current field, and then you enter the value you want Access to match in the Find and Replace dialog box.

REFERENCE

Finding Data in a Form or Datasheet

- Open the form or datasheet, and then make the field you want to search the current field.
- On the Home tab, in the Find group, click the Find button to open the Find and Replace dialog box.
- In the Find What box, type the field value you want to find.
- Complete the remaining options, as necessary, to specify the type of search to conduct.
- Click the Find Next button to begin the search.
- Click the Find Next button to continue searching for the next match.
- Click the Cancel button to stop the search operation.

You need to find the record for the owner Kimberly wants to contact. The owner whose record she needs to find is named Thomas and he lives on Bobcat Trail. You'll search for this record using the Address field.

To find the record using the OwnerData form:

1. Make sure the Address field value is still selected for the current record. This is the field you need to search.

    You can search for a record that contains part of the address anywhere in the Address field value. Performing a partial search such as this is often easier than matching the entire field value and is useful when you don't know or can't remember the entire field value.

2. On the Home tab, in the Find group, click the **Find** button. The Find and Replace dialog box opens. The Look In box indicates that the current field (in this case, Address) will be searched. You'll search for records that contain the word "bobcat" in the address.

3. In the Find What box, type **bobcat**. Note that you do not have to enter the word as "Bobcat" with a capital letter "B" because the Match Case check box is not selected in the Find and Replace dialog box. The search will find any record containing the word "bobcat" with any combination of uppercase and lowercase letters.

4. Click the **Match** arrow to display the list of matching options, and then click **Any Part of Field**. The search will find any record that contains the word "bobcat" in any part of the Address field. See Figure 4-10.

| Figure 4-10 | Completed Find and Replace dialog box |

5. Click the **Find Next** button. The Find and Replace dialog box remains open, and the OwnerData form now displays record 13, which is the record for Thomas Jones (OwnerID 2362). The word "Bobcat" is selected in the Address field value box because you searched for this word.

The search value you enter can be an exact value or it can include wildcard characters. A **wildcard character** is a placeholder you use when you know only part of a value or when you want to start or end with a specific character or match a certain pattern. Figure 4-11 shows the wildcard characters you can use when searching for data.

| Figure 4-11 | Wildcard characters |

Wildcard Character	Purpose	Example
*	Match any number of characters it can be used as the first and/or last character in the character string	th* *finds* the, that, this, therefore, *and so on*
?	Match any single alphabetic character	a?t *finds* act, aft, ant, apt, *and* art
[]	Match any single character within the brackets	a[fr]t *finds* aft *and* art *but not* act, ant, *or* apt
!	Match any character not within brackets	a[!fr]t *finds* act, ant, *and* apt *but not* aft *or* art
-	Match any one of a range of characters the range must be in ascending order (a to z, not z to a)	a[d-p]t *finds* aft, ant, *and* apt *but not* act *or* art
#	Match any single numeric character	#72 *finds* 072, 172, 272, 372, *and so on*

Next, to see how a wildcard works, you'll view the records for any owners with phone numbers that contain the exchange 824 as part of the phone number. The exchange consists of the three digits that follow the area code in the phone number. You could search for any record containing the digits 824 in any part of the Phone field, but this search would also find records with the digits 824 in any part of the phone number. To find only those records with the digits 824 as the exchange, you'll use the * wildcard character.

To find the records using the * wildcard character:

▶ **1.** Make sure the Find and Replace dialog box is still open.

▶ **2.** Click anywhere in the OwnerData form to make it active, and then press the **Tab** key until you reach the Phone field value box. This is the field you want to search.

▶ **3.** Click the title bar of the Find and Replace dialog box to make it active, and then drag the Find and Replace dialog box to the right so you can see the Phone field on the form, if necessary. "Current field" is still selected in the Look In box, meaning now the Phone field is the field that will be searched.

▶ **4.** Double-click **bobcat** in the Find What box to select the entire value, and then type **307-824***.

▶ **5.** Click the **Match** arrow, and then click **Whole Field**. Because you're using a wildcard character in the search value, you want the whole field to be searched.

With the settings you've entered, the search will find records in which any field value in the Phone field begins with the area code 307 followed by a hyphen and the exchange 824.

▶ **6.** Click the **Find Next** button. Record 15 displays in the form, which is the first record found for a customer with the exchange 824. Notice that the search process started from the point of the previously displayed record in the form, which was record 13.

▶ **7.** Click the **Find Next** button. Record 16 displays in the form, which is the next record found for a customer with the exchange 824.

▶ **8.** Click the **Find Next** button to display record 18, and then click the **Find Next** button again. Record 19 displays, the fourth record found.

▶ **9.** Click the **Find Next** button two more times to display records 21 and 24.

▶ **10.** Click the **Find Next** button again. Record 1 displays. Notice that the search process cycles back through the beginning of the records in the underlying table.

▶ **11.** Click the **Find Next** button. A dialog box opens, informing you that the search is finished.

▶ **12.** Click the **OK** button to close the dialog box, and then click the **Cancel** button to close the Find and Replace dialog box.

Kimberly has identified some owner updates she wants you to make. You'll use the OwnerData form to update the data in the Owner table.

Maintaining Table Data Using a Form

Maintaining data using a form is often easier than using a datasheet because you can focus on all the changes for a single record at one time. In Form view, you can edit the field values for a record, delete a record from the underlying table, or add a new record to the table.

Now you'll use the OwnerData form to make the changes Kimberly wants to the Owner table. First, you'll update the record for owner Sandra Pincher, who recently moved from Cody to Powell and provided a new mailing address. In addition to using the Find and Replace dialog box to locate a specific record, you can use the Search box to the right of the navigation buttons. You'll use the Search box to search for the owner's last name, Pincher, and display the owner record in the form.

To change the record using the OwnerData form:

1. To the right of the navigation buttons, click the **Search** box and then type **Pincher**. As soon as you start to type, Access begins searching through all fields in the records to match your entry. Record 3 (Sandra Pincher) is now current.

   You will first update the address in this record.

TIP

The pencil symbol appears in the upper-left corner of the form when the form is in editing mode.

2. Select the current entry in the Address field value box, and then type **53 Verde Ln** to replace it.

3. Press the **Tab** key to select the city in the City field value box, and then type **Powell**.

4. Press the **Tab** key twice to move to and select the Zip field value, and then type **82440**. The updates to the record are complete. See Figure 4-12.

Figure 4-12	Owner record after changing field values

pencil symbol indicates editing mode

Owner Data

Owner ID	2318
First Name	Sandra
Last Name	Pincher
Address	53 Verde Ln
City	Powell
State	WY
Zip	82440
Email	sp231@example.com
Phone	307-982-8401

field values changed

record 3 is the current record

Search box

Record: 14 ◄ 3 of 25 ► ►I ►☆ 🍸 No Filter   Pincher

Form View

Next, Kimberly asks you to add a record for a new owner. This person indicated plans to bring a pet to the care center at a recent adoption fair in which Riverview Veterinary Care Center participated, but the owner has not yet provided information about the animal or scheduled an appointment. You'll use the OwnerData form to add the new record.

To add the new record using the OwnerData form:

▶ **1.** On the Home tab, in the Records group, click the **New** button. Record 26, the next available new record, becomes the current record. All field value boxes are empty (except the State field, which displays the default value of WY), and the insertion point is positioned in the Owner ID field value box.

▶ **2.** Refer to Figure 4-13 and enter the value shown for each field, pressing the **Tab** key to move from field to field.

Figure 4-13 ▶ **Completed form for the new record**

Owner Data

Owner ID	2416
First Name	Mei
Last Name	Kostas
Address	812 Playa Hwy
City	Elk Butte
State	WY
Zip	82433
Email	meowmeow@example.com
Phone	307-824-5873

Record: H ◀ 26 of 26 ▶ H ▶* No Filter Search
Form View

▶ **3.** After entering the Phone field value, press the **Tab** key. Record 27, the next available new record, becomes the current record, and the record for OwnerID 2416 is saved in the Owner table.

Kimberly would like a printed copy of the OwnerData form to show to her staff members. She asks you to print one form record.

Previewing and Printing Selected Form Records

You can print as many form records as can fit on a printed page. If only part of a form record fits on the bottom of a page, the remainder of the record prints on the next page. You can print all pages or a range of pages. In addition, you can print just the currently selected form record.

Kimberly asks you to use the OwnerData form to print the first record in the Owner table. Before you do, you'll preview the form record to see how it will look when printed.

To preview the form and print the data for record 1:

1. Click the **First record** button ◄ to display record 1 in the form. This is the record in which you have entered your first and last names.

2. Click the **File** tab to open Backstage view, click **Print** in the navigation bar, and then click **Print Preview**. The Print Preview window opens, showing the form records for the Owner table. Notice that each record appears in its own form and that shading is used to distinguish one record from another. See Figure 4-14.

Figure 4-14	Form records displayed in Print Preview

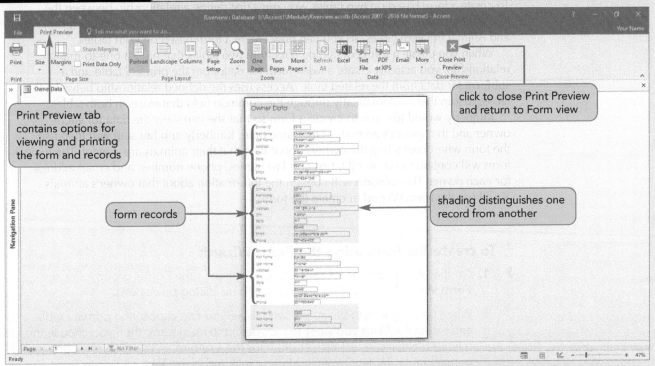

Print Preview tab contains options for viewing and printing the form and records

click to close Print Preview and return to Form view

form records

shading distinguishes one record from another

To print one selected record on a page by itself, you need to use the Print dialog box.

3. On the Print Preview tab, in the Close Preview group, click the **Close Print Preview** button. You return to Form view with the first record still displayed.

4. Click the **File** tab to open Backstage view again, click **Print** in the navigation bar, and then click **Print**. The **Print** dialog box opens.

5. Click the **Selected Record(s)** option button to print the current form record (record 1).

   Trouble? Check with your instructor to be sure you should print the form, then continue to the next step. If you should not print the form, click the Cancel button, and then skip to Step 7.

▶ **6.** Click the **OK** button to close the dialog box and print the selected record.

▶ **7.** Close the OwnerData form.

After reviewing the printed OwnerData form with her staff, Kimberly realizes that it would be helpful for staff members to also have a form showing information about both owners and their animals. Because this form will need to display information from two different tables, the type of form you need to create will include a main form and a subform.

Creating a Form with a Main Form and a Subform

To create a form based on two tables, you must first define a relationship between the two tables. Earlier, you defined a one-to-many relationship between the Owner (primary) and Animal (related) tables, so you can now create a form based on both tables.

When you create a form containing data from two tables that have a one-to-many relationship, you actually create a **main form** for data from the primary table and a **subform** for data from the related table. Access uses the defined relationship between the tables to join them automatically through the common field that exists in both tables.

Kimberly would like you to create a form so that she can view the data for each owner and that owner's animals at the same time. Kimberly and her staff will then use the form when contacting the owners about care that their animals are due for. The main form will contain the owner ID, first and last names, phone number, and email address for each owner. The subform will contain the information about that owner's animals. You'll use the Form Wizard to create the form.

To create the form using the Form Wizard:

▶ **1.** On the ribbon, click the **Create** tab, and then in the Forms group, click the **Form Wizard** button. The first Form Wizard dialog box opens.

When creating a form based on two tables, you first choose the primary table and select the fields you want to include in the main form; then you choose the related table and select fields from it for the subform. In this case, the correct primary table, Table: Owner, is already selected in the Tables/Queries box.

Trouble? If Table: Owner is not currently selected in the Tables/Queries box, click the Tables/Queries arrow, and then click Table: Owner.

The form needs to include only the OwnerID, FirstName, LastName, Phone, and Email fields from the Owner table.

▶ **2.** Click **OwnerID** in the Available Fields box if necessary, and then click the
 > button to move the field to the Selected Fields box.

▶ **3.** Repeat Step 2 for the **FirstName**, **LastName**, **Phone**, and **Email** fields.

The subform needs to include all the fields from the Animal table, with the exception of the OwnerID field, as that field has been added already for the main form.

▶ **4.** Click the **Tables/Queries** arrow, and then click **Table: Animal**. The fields from the Animal table appear in the Available Fields box. The quickest way to add the fields you want to include is to move all the fields to the Selected Fields box, and then remove the only field you don't want to include (OwnerID).

TIP

The table name (Animal) is included in the OwnerID field name to distinguish it from the same field in the Owner table.

5. Click the >> button to move all the fields in the Animal table to the Selected Fields box.

6. Click **Animal.OwnerID** in the Selected Fields box, and then click the < button to move the field back to the Available Fields box.

7. Click the **Next** button. The next Form Wizard dialog box opens. See Figure 4-15.

Figure 4-15	Choosing a format for the main form and subform

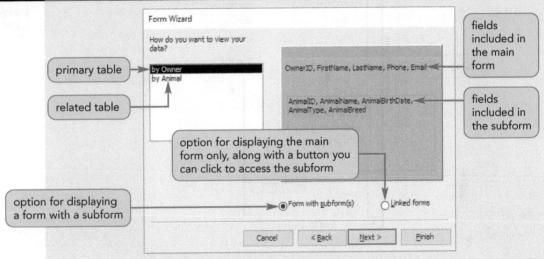

In this dialog box, the section on the left shows the order in which you will view the selected data: first by data from the primary Owner table, and then by data from the related Animal table. The form will be displayed as shown on the right side of the dialog box, with the fields from the Owner table at the top in the main form, and the fields from the Animal table at the bottom in the subform.

8. Click the **Next** button. The next Form Wizard dialog box opens, in which you choose the subform layout.

The Tabular layout displays subform fields as a table, whereas the Datasheet layout displays subform fields as a table datasheet. The layout choice is a matter of personal preference. You'll use the Datasheet layout.

9. Click the **Datasheet** option button to select it if necessary, and then click the **Next** button. The next Form Wizard dialog box opens, in which you specify titles for the main form and the subform. You'll use the title "OwnerAnimals" for the main form and the title "AnimalSubform" for the subform. These titles will also be the names for the form objects.

10. In the Form box, click to position the insertion point to the right of the last letter, and then type **Animals**. The main form name is now OwnerAnimals.

11. In the Subform box, delete the space between the two words so that the subform name appears as **AnimalSubform**, and then click the **Finish** button. The completed form opens in Form view. See Figure 4-16.

Figure 4-16) **Main form with subform in Form view**

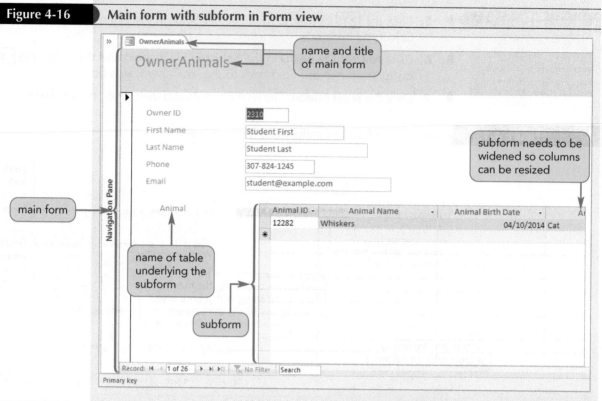

The main form displays the fields from the first record in the Owner table in a columnar format. The records in the main form appear in primary key order by OwnerID. OwnerID 2310 has one related record in the Animal table; this record, for AnimalID 12282, is shown in the subform, which uses the datasheet format. The main form name, "OwnerAnimals," appears on the object tab and as the form title. The name of the table "Animal" appears to the left of the subform indicating the underlying table for the subform. Note that only the word "Animal" and not the complete name "AnimalSubform" appears on the form. Only the table name is displayed for the subform itself, but the complete name of the object, "AnimalSubform," is displayed when you view and work with objects in the Navigation Pane. The subform designation is necessary in a list of database objects so that you can distinguish the Animal subform from other objects, such as the Animal table, but the subform designation is not needed in the OwnerAnimals form. Only the table name is required to identify the table containing the records in the subform.

TIP

The OwnerAnimals form is formatted with the default Office theme because you applied the Wisp theme only to the OwnerData form.

Next, you need to make some changes to the form. First, you'll edit the form title to add a space between the words so that it appears as "Owner Animals." Then, you'll resize the subform so that it is wide enough to allow for all the columns to be fully displayed. To make these changes, you need to switch to Layout view.

To modify the OwnerAnimals form in Layout view:

▸ **1.** Switch to Layout view.

▸ **2.** Click **OwnerAnimals** in the gray area at the top of the form. The form title is selected.

3. Click between the letters "r" and "A" to place the insertion point, and then press the **spacebar**. The title on the form is now "Owner Animals."

4. Click in a blank area of the form to the right of the field value boxes to deselect the title. Next, you'll increase the width of the subform.

5. Click the **subform**. An orange border surrounds the subform, indicating it is selected.

6. Position the pointer on the right border of the selected subform until the pointer changes to ↔, and then drag to the right approximately three inches. The wider subform makes all the columns visible. See Figure 4-17.

Figure 4-17	Modified form in Layout view

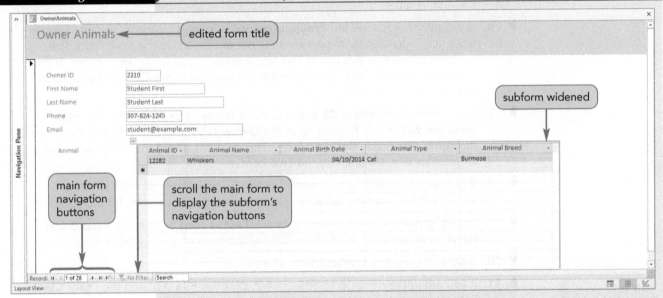

7. On the Quick Access Toolbar, click the **Save** button 🖫 to save both the main form and the subform.

8. Switch to Form view, and then if necessary, scroll up to view all the fields in the main form.

The form includes two sets of navigation buttons. You use the set of navigation buttons at the bottom of the Form window to select records from the primary table in the main form (see Figure 4-17). The second set of navigation buttons is currently not visible; you need to scroll down the main form to see these buttons, which appear at the bottom of the subform. You use the subform navigation buttons to select records from the related table in the subform.

You'll use the navigation buttons to view different records.

To navigate to different main form and subform records:

1. In the main form, click the **Next record** button ▶ six times. Record 7 of 26 total records in the Owner table (for Joey Smith) becomes the current record in the main form. The subform shows that this owner has one animal, a cat. Note that the Animal Name, Animal Birth Date, and Animal Type columns are much wider than necessary for the information displayed.

▶ **2.** Double-click the ↔ pointer on the right column divider of the Animal Name column in the subform to resize this field to its best fit.

▶ **3.** Repeat Step 2 to resize the Animal Birth Date and Animal Type columns in the subform.

▶ **4.** Use the main form navigation buttons to view each record, resizing any subform column to fully display any field values that are not completely visible.

▶ **5.** In the main form, click the **Last record** button ▶|. Record 26 in the Owner table (for Mei Kostas) becomes the current record in the main form. The subform shows that this owner currently has no animals; recall that you just entered this record using the OwnerData form. Kimberly could use the subform to enter the information on this owner's animal(s), and that information will be updated in the Animal table.

▶ **6.** In the main form, click the **Previous record** button ◀. Record 25 in the Owner table (for Taylor Johnson) becomes the current record in the main form. The subform shows that this owner has two animals. If you know the number of the record you want to view, you can enter the number in the Current Record box to move to that record.

▶ **7.** In the main form, select **25** in the Current Record box, type **18**, and then press the **Enter** key. Record 18 in the Owner table (for Susan Miller) becomes the current record in the main form. The subform shows that this owner has six animals that are seen by the care center.

▶ **8.** If necessary, use the vertical scroll bar for the main form to scroll down and view the bottom of the subform. Note the navigation buttons for the subform.

▶ **9.** At the bottom of the subform, click the **Last record** button ▶|. Record 6 in the Animal subform, for Animal ID 12440, becomes the current record.

▶ **10.** Save and close the OwnerAnimals form.

▶ **11.** If you are not continuing to Session 4.2, click the **File** tab, and then click **Close** in the navigation bar to close the Riverview database.

Both the OwnerData form and the OwnerAnimals form you created will enable Kimberly and her staff to view, enter, and maintain data easily in the Owner and Animal tables in the Riverview database.

Session 4.1 Quick Check

REVIEW

1. Describe the difference between creating a form using the Form tool and creating a form using the Form Wizard.

2. What is a theme, and how do you apply one to an existing form?

3. A(n) _____ is an item on a form, report, or other database object that you can manipulate to modify the object's appearance.

4. Which table record is displayed in a form when you press the Ctrl+End keys while you are in navigation mode?

5. Which wildcard character matches any single alphabetic character?

6. To print only the current record displayed in a form, you need to select the _____ option button in the Print dialog box.

7. In a form that contains a main form and a subform, what data is displayed in the main form and what data is displayed in the subform?

Session 4.2 Visual Overview:

The report object's name is displayed on the tab for the report.

The report title appears at the top of the report. By default, the report object name is used as the report title, but you can edit the title to display the text you want, as done here, with spaces added between words for readability.

Fields from the primary Owner table appear first in the report.

Fields from the related Visit Table appear below the fields from the primary table.

For a grouped report, the data from a record in the primary table (the Owner table in this report) appears as a group, followed on subsequent lines of the report by the joined records from the related table (the Visit table in this report).

The navigation buttons allow you to display the first, last, next, or previous page in the report, or to enter a specific page number and move to that page.

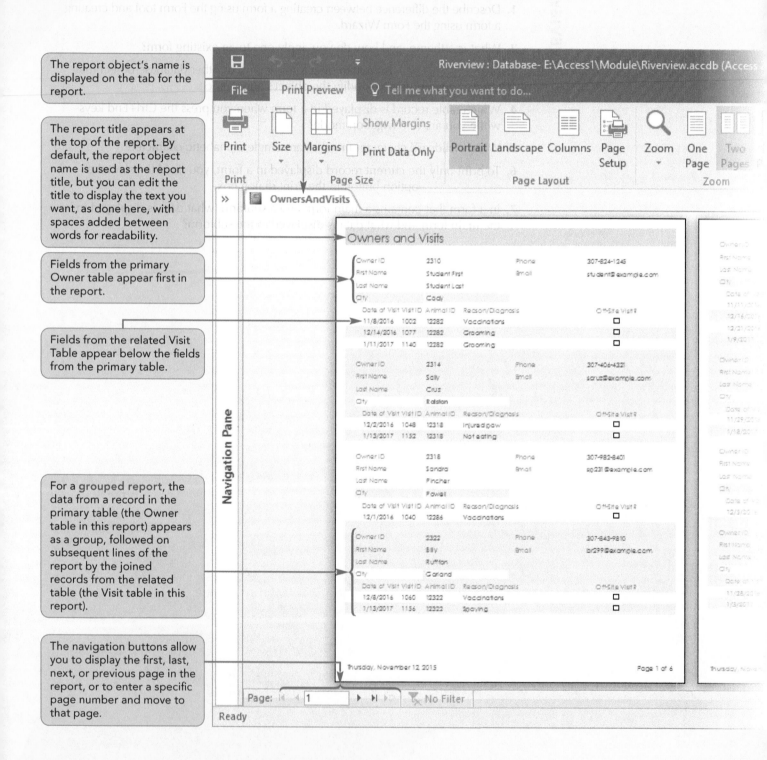

Report Displayed in Print Preview

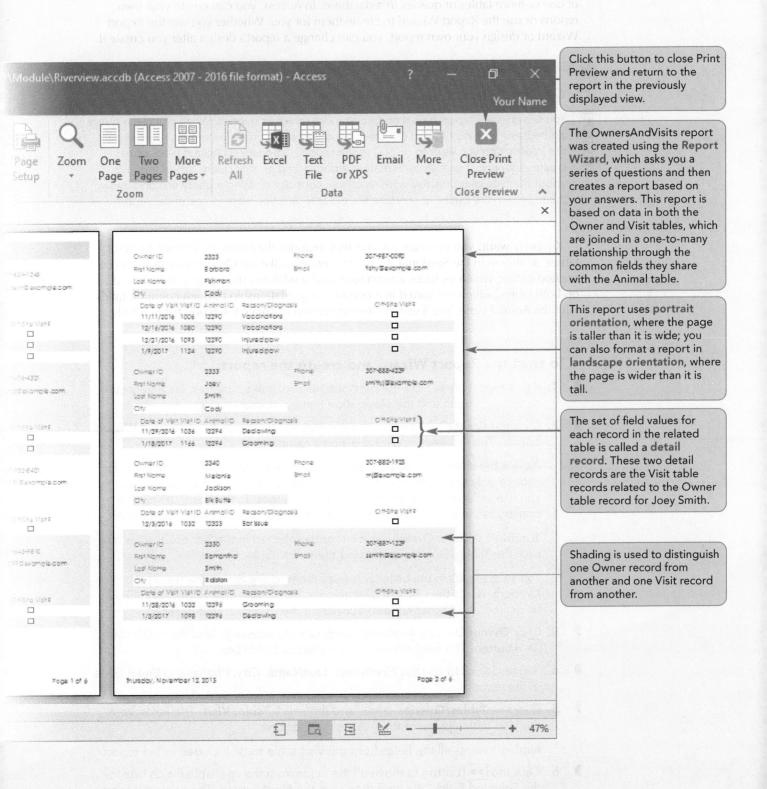

Click this button to close Print Preview and return to the report in the previously displayed view.

The OwnersAndVisits report was created using the **Report Wizard**, which asks you a series of questions and then creates a report based on your answers. This report is based on data in both the Owner and Visit tables, which are joined in a one-to-many relationship through the common fields they share with the Animal table.

This report uses **portrait orientation**, where the page is taller than it is wide; you can also format a report in **landscape orientation**, where the page is wider than it is tall.

The set of field values for each record in the related table is called a **detail record**. These two detail records are the Visit table records related to the Owner table record for Joey Smith.

Shading is used to distinguish one Owner record from another and one Visit record from another.

Creating a Report Using the Report Wizard

As you learned earlier, a report is a formatted printout or screen display of the contents of one or more tables or queries in a database. In Access, you can create your own reports or use the Report Wizard to create them for you. Whether you use the Report Wizard or design your own report, you can change a report's design after you create it.

INSIGHT

Creating a Report Based on a Query

You can create a report based on one or more tables or queries. When you use a query as the basis for a report, you can use criteria and other query features to retrieve only the information you want to display in the report. Experienced Access users often create a query just so they can create a report based on that query. When thinking about the type of report you want to create, consider creating a query first and basing the report on the query, to produce the exact results you want to see in the report.

Kimberly wants you to create a report that includes data from the Owner and Visit tables, as shown in the Session 4.2 Visual Overview. Like the OwnerAnimals form you created earlier, which includes a main form and a subform, the report will be based on both tables, which are joined in a one-to-many relationship through common fields with the Animal table. You'll use the Report Wizard to create the report for Kimberly.

To start the Report Wizard and create the report:

▶ 1. If you took a break after the previous session, make sure that the Riverview database is open and the Navigation Pane is closed.

▶ 2. Click the **Create** tab, and then in the Reports group, click the **Report Wizard** button. The first Report Wizard dialog box opens.

As was the case when you created the form with a subform, initially you can choose only one table or query to be the data source for the report. Then you can include data from other tables or queries. In this case, the correct primary table, Table: Owner, is already selected in the Tables/Queries box.

Trouble? If Table: Owner is not currently selected in the Tables/Queries box, click the Tables/Queries arrow, and then click Table: Owner.

You select fields in the order you want them to appear on the report. Kimberly wants the OwnerID, FirstName, LastName, City, Phone, and Email fields from the Owner table to appear on the report, in that order.

▶ 3. Click **OwnerID** in the Available Fields box (if necessary), and then click the > button. The field moves to the Selected Fields box.

▶ 4. Repeat Step 3 to add the **FirstName**, **LastName**, **City**, **Phone**, and **Email** fields to the report.

▶ 5. Click the **Tables/Queries** arrow, and then click **Table: Visit**. The fields from the Visit table appear in the Available Fields box.

Kimberly wants all the fields from the Visit table to be included in the report.

▶ 6. Click the >> button to move all the fields from the Available Fields box to the Selected Fields box, and then click the **Next** button. The second Report Wizard dialog box opens. See Figure 4-18.

Figure 4-18	Choosing a grouped or ungrouped report

data grouped by table

click to display tips, examples, and instructions for creating an ungrouped report

You can choose to arrange the selected data grouped by table, which is the default, or ungrouped. You're creating a grouped report; the data from each record in the Owner table will appear in a group, followed by the related records for that owner from the Visit table.

7. Click the **Next** button. The next Report Wizard dialog box opens, in which you choose additional grouping levels.

Currently the report contains only one grouping level, which is for the owner's data. Grouping levels are useful for reports with multiple levels, such as those containing monthly, quarterly, and annual totals, or for those containing city and country groups. The report requires no further grouping levels, so you can accept the default options.

8. Click the **Next** button. The next Report Wizard dialog box opens, in which you choose the sort order for the detail records. See Figure 4-19.

Figure 4-19	Choosing the sort order for detail records

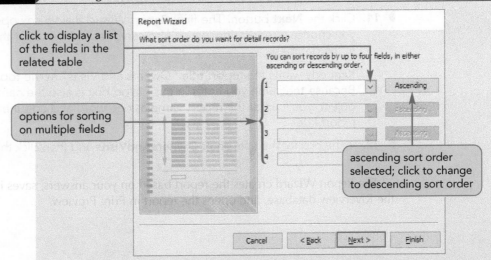

click to display a list of the fields in the related table

options for sorting on multiple fields

ascending sort order selected; click to change to descending sort order

The records from the Visit table for an owner represent the detail records for Kimberly's report. She wants these records to appear in ascending order by the value in the VisitDate field, so that the visits will be shown in chronological order. The Ascending option is already selected by default. To change to descending order, you click this same button, which acts as a toggle between the two sort orders. Also, you can sort on multiple fields, as you can with queries.

▶ **9.** Click the **arrow** on the first box, click **VisitDate**, and then click the **Next** button. The next Report Wizard dialog box opens, in which you choose a layout and page orientation for the report. See Figure 4-20.

Figure 4-20   Choosing the report layout

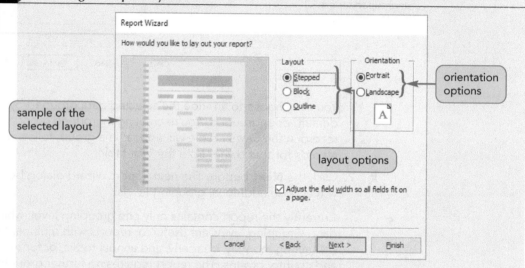

▶ **10.** Click each layout option to view each sample that appears, and then click the **Outline** option button to select that layout for the report.

Because most of the fields in both the Owner and Visit tables contain relatively short field values, the portrait page orientation should provide enough space across the page to display all the field values.

▶ **11.** Click the **Next** button. The final Report Wizard dialog box opens, in which you choose a report title, which also serves as the name for the report object in the database.

Kimberly wants the report title "Owners and Visits" at the top of the report. Because the name you enter in this dialog box is also the name of the report object, you'll enter the report name as one word and edit the title on the report later.

▶ **12.** In the box for the title, enter **OwnersAndVisits** and then click the **Finish** button.

The Report Wizard creates the report based on your answers, saves it as an object in the Riverview database, and opens the report in Print Preview.

After you create a report, you should view it in Print Preview to see if you need to make any formatting or design changes. To view the entire page, you need to change the Zoom setting.

To view the report in Print Preview:

▶ **1.** On the Print Preview tab, in the Zoom group, click the **Zoom button arrow**, and then click **Fit to Window**. The first page of the report is displayed in Print Preview.

▶ **2.** At the bottom of the window, click the **Next Page** button ▶ to display the second page of the report.

When a report is displayed in Print Preview, you can zoom in for a close-up view of a section of the report.

▶ **3.** Move the pointer to the center of the report, and then click the 🔍 pointer at the center of the report. The display changes to show a close-up view of the report. See Figure 4-21.

| Figure 4-21 | Close-up view of the report |

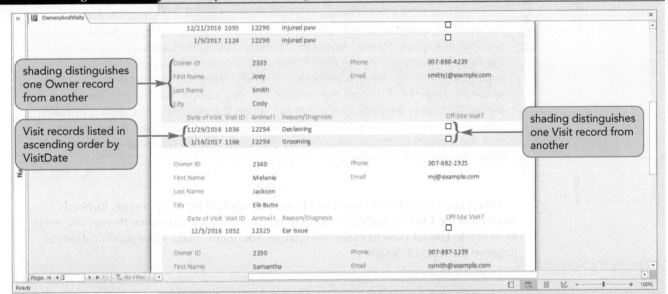

shading distinguishes one Owner record from another

Visit records listed in ascending order by VisitDate

shading distinguishes one Visit record from another

TIP

Clicking a report in Print Preview toggles between a full-page display and a close-up display of the report.

Shading is used to distinguish both one Owner record from another and, within a group of each owner's Visit records, one Visit record from another.

Trouble? Depending on your computer settings, the shading and colors used in your report might look different. This difference should not cause any problems.

The detail records for the Visit table fields appear in ascending order based on the values in the VisitDate field. Because the VisitDate field is used as the basis for sorting records, it appears as the first field in this section, even though you selected the fields in the order in which they appear in the Visit table.

▶ **4.** Scroll to the bottom of the second page, checking the text in the report as you scroll. Notice the current date and page number at the bottom of the page; the Report Wizard included these elements as part of the report's design.

▶ **5.** Move the pointer onto the report, click the 🔍 pointer to zoom back out, and then click the **Next Page** navigation button ▶ to move to page 3 of the report.

▶ **6.** Continue to move through the pages of the report, and then click the **First Page** button ◀ to return to the first page.

INSIGHT

Changing a Report's Page Orientation and Margins

When you display a report in Print Preview, you can easily change the report layout using options on the Print Preview tab (refer to the Session 4.2 Visual Overview). For example, sometimes fields with longer values cause the report content to overflow onto the next page. You can fix this problem by clicking the Landscape button in the Page Layout group on the Print Preview tab to switch the report orientation to landscape, where the page is wider than it is tall. Landscape orientation allows more space for content to fit across the width of the report page. You can also use the Margins button in the Page Size group to change the margins of the report, choosing from commonly used margin formats or creating your own custom margins. Simply click the Margins button arrow to display the menu of available margin options and select the one that works best for your report.

When you created the OwnerData form, you applied the Wisp theme. Kimberly would like the OwnersAndVisits report to be formatted with the same theme. You need to switch to Layout view to make this change. You'll also make other modifications to improve the report's design.

Modifying a Report's Design in Layout View

Similar to Layout view for forms, Layout view for reports enables you to make modifications to the report's design. Many of the same options—such as those for applying a theme and changing the color of text—are provided in Layout view for reports.

Applying a Theme to a Report

The same themes available for forms are also available for reports. You can choose to apply a theme to the current report object only, or to all reports in the database. In this case, you'll apply the Wisp theme only to the OwnersAndVisits report because Kimberly isn't certain if it is the appropriate theme for other reports in the Riverview database.

To apply the Wisp theme to the report and edit the report name:

1. On the status bar, click the **Layout View** button ▤. The report is displayed in Layout view and the Report Layout Tools Design tab is the active tab on the ribbon.

2. In the Themes group, click the **Themes** button. The "In this Database" section at the top of the gallery shows both the default Office theme and the Wisp theme. The Wisp theme is included here because you applied it earlier to the OwnerData form.

3. At the top of the gallery, right-click the **Wisp** theme to display the shortcut menu, and then click **Apply Theme to This Object Only**. The gallery closes and the theme is applied to the report.

   The larger font used by the Wisp theme has caused the report title text to be cut off on the right. You'll fix this problem and edit the title text as well.

   Trouble? After you apply the theme, some VisitDate values may be displayed as a series of # symbols rather than actual date values. You'll fix this later in the session.

4. Click the **OwnersAndVisits** title at the top of the report to select it.

5. Position the pointer on the right border of the title's selection box until it changes to ↔, and then drag to the right until the title is fully displayed.

6. Click between the letters "s" and "A" in the title, press the **spacebar**, change the capital letter "A" to **a**, place the insertion point between the letters "d" and "V," and then press the **spacebar**. The title is now "Owners and Visits."

7. Click to the right of the report title in the shaded area to deselect the title.

TIP

When you point to the Wisp theme, a ScreenTip displays the names of the database objects that use the theme—in this case, the OwnerData form.

Kimberly views the report and notices some other formatting changes she would like you to make. First, she doesn't like how the VisitDate field values are aligned compared to the other field values from the Visit table. You'll fix this next.

Changing the Alignment of Field Values

The Report Layout Tools Format tab provides options for you to easily modify the format of various report objects. For example, you can change the alignment of the text in a field value. Recall that Date/Time fields, like VisitDate, automatically right-align their field values, whereas Short Text fields, like VisitID, automatically left-align their field values. Kimberly asks you to change the alignment of the VisitDate field so its values appear left-aligned, which will improve the format of the report.

To change the alignment of the VisitDate field values:

1. On the ribbon, click the **Report Layout Tools Format** tab. The ribbon changes to display options for formatting the report. The options for modifying the format of a report are the same as those available for forms.

2. In the report, click the **first VisitDate** field value box, which contains the date 11/8/2016. The field value box has an orange border, indicating it is selected. Note that the other VisitDate field value boxes have a lighter orange border, indicating they are selected as well. Any changes you make will be applied to all VisitDate field values throughout the report.

3. On the Report Layout Tools Format tab, in the Font group, click the **Align Left** button. The text in the VisitDate field value boxes is now left-aligned. See Figure 4-22.

| Figure 4-22 | Report after applying a theme and changing field alignment |

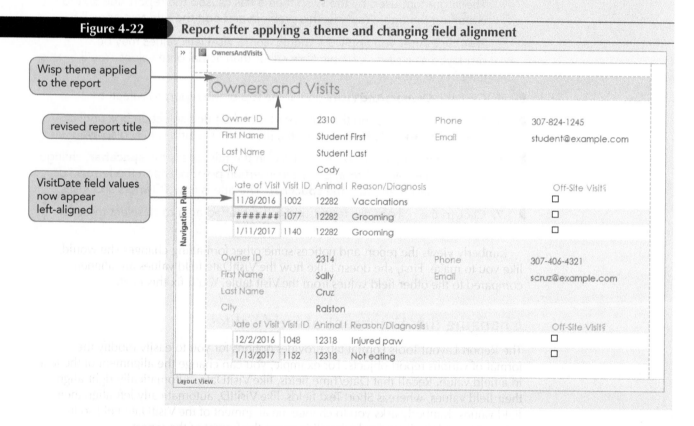

Wisp theme applied to the report

revised report title

VisitDate field values now appear left-aligned

Moving and Resizing Fields on a Report

Working in Layout view, you can resize and reposition fields and field value boxes to improve the appearance and readability of a report. You resize field value boxes by dragging their borders to the desired size. You can also move field labels and field value boxes by selecting one or more of them and then dragging them to a new location; or, for more precise control over the move, you can use the keyboard arrow keys to move selected objects.

In the OwnersAndVisits report, you need to move and resize the VisitDate, VisitID, and OffSite field labels so that the complete caption is displayed for each. Also, some of the VisitDate field values are not displayed on the report but are instead represented by a series of # symbols. This occurs when a field value box is not wide enough for its content. To fix this, you'll widen the VisitDate field value box. Before addressing these issues, you will move the OffSite field label so it appears centered over its check box.

To move and resize the OffSite field label:

1. In the report, click the first occurrence of the **Off-Site Visit?** field label. All instances of the label are selected throughout the report.

2. Press the ← key repeatedly until the label is centered (roughly) over its check box.

3. Position the pointer on the right border of the field label's selection box until the pointer changes to ↔, and then drag to the right until the label text is fully displayed.

Next, you need to move the field label and field value box for the Reason and OffSite fields to the right, to make room to widen the Animal ID field label. You also need to make adjustments to the field label and field value box for the VisitDate field.

To resize and move field labels and field value boxes in the report:

1. In the report, click the first occurrence of the **Reason/Diagnosis** field label, press and hold the **Shift** key, click the first occurrence of the **Reason** field value box, which contains the text "Vaccinations," click the first occurrence of the **Off-Site Visit?** field label, and then click the first occurrence of the **OffSite** field value box. Both field labels and their associated field value boxes are selected and can be moved. See Figure 4-23.

| Figure 4-23 | Report after selecting field labels and field value boxes |

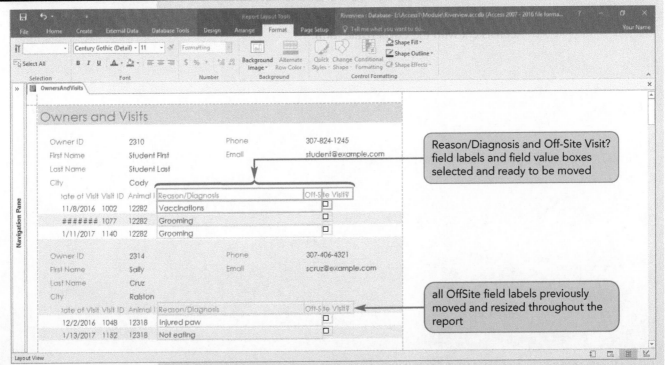

▶ **2.** Press the → key six times to move the field labels and field value boxes to the right.

   Trouble? Once you press the right arrow key, the report might jump to display the end of the report. Just continue to press the right arrow key to move the labels and values. Then scroll the window back up to display the beginning of the report.

▶ **3.** Click the **Animal ID** field label to select it and deselect the moved field labels and field value boxes.

▶ **4.** Position the pointer on the right border of the Animal ID field label's selection box until it changes to ↔, and then drag to the right until the Animal ID label is fully displayed.

   Now you need to modify the VisitDate field so that the # symbols that currently appear are replaced with the actual field values. You'll resize the VisitDate field value boxes to fix this problem.

▶ **5.** Scroll to the top of the report if necessary to display the first record in the report, and then click the ####### symbols that appear in the second VisitDate field value in the first record.

▶ **6.** Using the ↔ pointer, drag the left border of VisitDate field value's selection box to the left until the date value is fully displayed.

▶ **7.** Scroll through the report, resizing the VisitDate field values as necessary until all values are fully displayed, and then scroll back up to display the top of the report.

▶ **8.** Click the **Date of Visit** field label to select it, and then drag the left border of the selection box to the left until the label text is fully displayed.

▶ **9.** Click to the right of the report title in the shaded area to deselect the field label.

▶ **10.** On the Quick Access Toolbar, click the **Save** button 🖫 to save the modified report.

Next, Kimberly asks you to enhance the report's appearance to make it more consistent with the OwnerData form.

Changing the Font Color and Inserting a Picture in a Report

You can change the color of text on a report to enhance its appearance. You can also add a picture to a report for visual interest or to identify a particular section of the report.

Before you print the report for Kimberly, she asks you to change the report title color to the darker black you applied earlier to the OwnerData form and to include the Animals picture to the right of the report title.

Make sure the title is selected so the picture is inserted in the correct location.

To change the color of the report title and insert the picture:

▶ 1. At the top of the report, click the **Owners and Visits** title to select it.

▶ 2. Make sure the Report Layout Tools Format tab is still active on the ribbon.

▶ 3. In the Font group, click the **Font Color button arrow** $\boxed{A}$ ⋅, and then in the Theme Colors section, click the **Black, Text 1, Lighter 25%** color (fourth color in the second column). The color is applied to the report title.

   Now you'll insert the picture to the right of the report title text.

▶ 4. On the ribbon, click the **Report Layout Tools Design** tab. The options provided on this tab for reports are the same as those you worked with for forms.

▶ 5. In the Header/Footer group, click the **Logo** button.

▶ 6. Navigate to the **Access1 > Module** folder provided with your Data Files, and then double-click the **Animals** file. The picture is inserted in the top-left corner of the report, partially covering the report title.

▶ 7. Position the ⌖ pointer on the selected picture, and then drag it to the right of the report title.

▶ 8. Click in a blank area of the shaded bar to deselect the picture. See Figure 4-24.

| Figure 4-24 | Report after changing the title font color and inserting the picture |

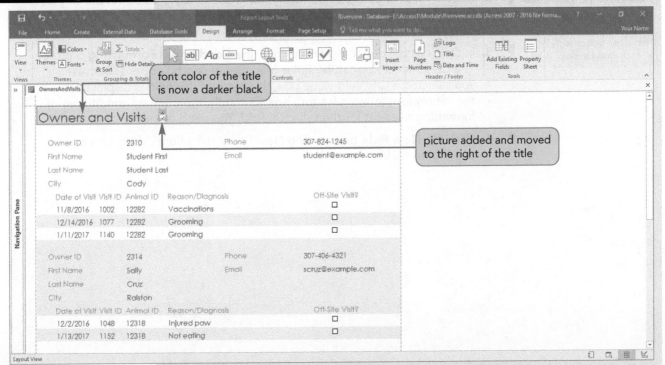

Trouble? Don't be concerned if the picture in your report is not in the exact same location as the one shown in the figure. Just make sure it is to the right of the title text and within the shaded area.

Riverview Veterinary Care Center is planning a mobile clinic day in Ralston. Kimberly would like to make it easier to locate the records in the report for owners who live in Ralston by applying unique formatting to their city names. Because you don't need to apply this formatting to the city names in all the records in the report, you will use conditional formatting.

Using Conditional Formatting in a Report

Conditional formatting in a report (or form) is special formatting applied to certain field values depending on one or more conditions—similar to criteria you establish for queries. If a field value meets the condition or conditions you specify, the formatting is applied to the value.

Kimberly would like the OwnersAndVisits report to show a city name of Ralston in a bold, dark red font. This formatting will help to highlight the owner records for owners who live in this location.

To apply conditional formatting to the City field in the report:

1. Make sure the report is still displayed in Layout view, and then click the **Report Layout Tools Format** tab on the ribbon.

   To apply conditional formatting to a field, you must first make it the active field by clicking any field value in the field's column.

TIP

You must select a field value box, and not the field label, before applying a conditional format.

2. Click the first City field value, **Cody**, for OwnerID 2310 to select the City field values in the report. The conditional formatting you specify will affect all the values for the field.

3. In the Control Formatting group, click the **Conditional Formatting** button. The Conditional Formatting Rules Manager dialog box opens. Because you selected a City field value box, the name of this field is displayed in the "Show formatting rules for" box. Currently, there are no conditional formatting rules set for the selected field. You need to create a new rule.

4. Click the **New Rule** button. The New Formatting Rule dialog box opens. See Figure 4-25.

Figure 4-25   **New Formatting Rule dialog box**

specify the condition in these boxes

a preview of the conditional format will appear here

use these options to specify the formatting

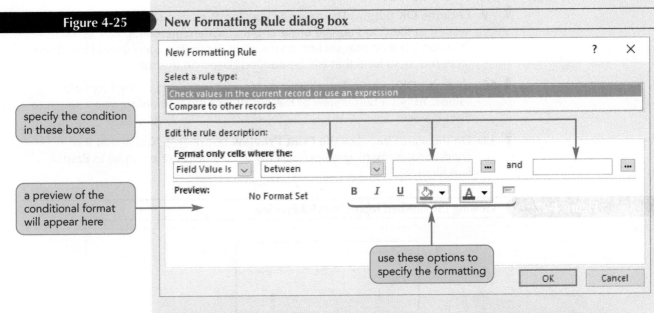

The default setting for "Select a rule type" specifies that Access will check field values and determine if they meet the condition. This is the setting you want. You need to enter the condition in the "Edit the rule description" section of the dialog box. The setting "Field Value Is" means that the conditional format you specify will be applied only when the value for the selected field, City, meets the condition.

5. Click the **arrow** for the box containing the word "between," and then click **equal to**. You want only the city name Ralston to be formatted.

6. Click in the next box, and then type **Ralston**.

7. In the Preview section, click the **Font color button arrow** [A ▾], and then click the **Dark Red** color (first color in the last row in the Standard Colors section).

8. In the Preview section, click the **Bold** button [B]. The specifications for the conditional formatting are complete. See Figure 4-26.

Figure 4-26   **Conditional formatting set for the City field**

condition specifies that the selected field value must be equal to Ralston

preview shows the bold, dark red font that will be applied to field values that meet the condition

Bold button selected

dark red font color selected

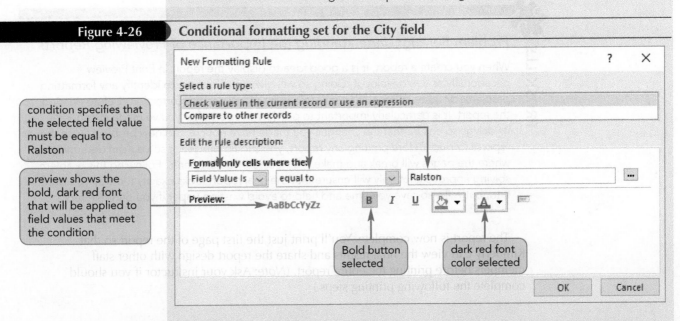

9. Click the **OK** button. The new rule you specified appears in the Rule section of the Conditional Formatting Rules Manager dialog box as Value = "Ralston"; the Format section on the right shows the conditional formatting (dark red, bold font) that will be applied based on this rule.

10. Click the **OK** button. The conditional format is applied to the City field values. To get a better view of the report and the formatting, you'll switch to Print Preview.

11. On the status bar, click the **Print Preview** button ⬚. Notice that the conditional formatting is applied only to City field values equal to Ralston. See Figure 4-27.

Figure 4-27   Viewing the finished report in Print Preview

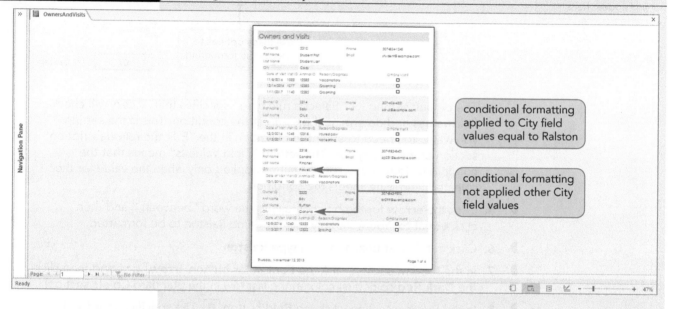

conditional formatting applied to City field values equal to Ralston

conditional formatting not applied other City field values

Problem Solving: Understanding the Importance of Previewing Reports

When you create a report, it is a good idea to display the report in Print Preview occasionally as you develop it. Doing so will give you a chance to identify any formatting problems or other issues so that you can make any necessary corrections before printing the report. It is particularly important to preview a report after you've made changes to its design to ensure that the changes you made have not created new problems with the report's format. Before printing any report, you should preview it so you can determine where the pages will break and make any necessary adjustments. Following this problem-solving approach not only will ensure that the final report looks exactly the way you want it to, but will also save you time and help to avoid wasting paper if you print the report.

The report is now complete. You'll print just the first page of the report so that Kimberly can view the final results and share the report design with other staff members before printing the entire report. (*Note:* Ask your instructor if you should complete the following printing steps.)

To print page 1 of the report:

▶ **1.** On the Print Preview tab, in the Print group, click the **Print** button. The Print dialog box opens.

▶ **2.** In the Print Range section, click the **Pages** option button. The insertion point now appears in the From box so that you can specify the range of pages to print.

▶ **3.** Type **1** in the From box, press the **Tab** key to move to the To box, and then type **1**. These settings specify that only page 1 of the report will be printed.

▶ **4.** Click the **OK** button. The Print dialog box closes, and the first page of the report is printed.

▶ **5.** Save and close the OwnersAndVisits report.

You've created many different objects in the Riverview database. Before you close it, you'll open the Navigation Pane to view all the objects in the database.

To view the Riverview database objects in the Navigation Pane:

▶ **1.** Open the **Navigation Pane** and scroll down, if necessary, to display the bottom of the pane.

The Navigation Pane now includes the OwnersAndVisits report in the Reports section of the pane. Also notice the OwnerAnimals form in the Forms section. This is the form you created containing a main form based on the Owner table and a subform based on the Animal table. The AnimalSubform object is also listed; you can open it separately from the main form. See Figure 4-28.

| Figure 4-28 | Riverview database objects in the Navigation Pane |

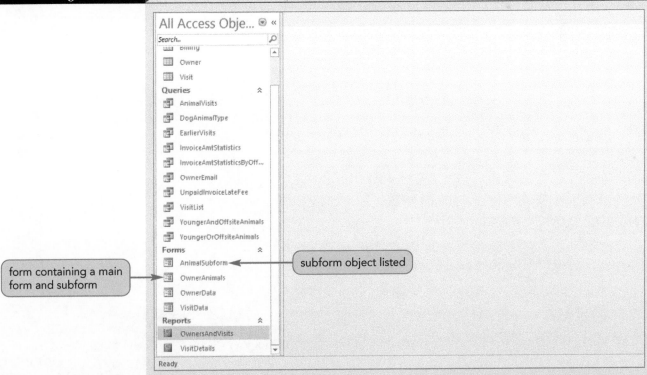

form containing a main form and subform

subform object listed

▶ **2.** Compact and repair the Riverview database, and then close the database.

Kimberly is satisfied that the forms you created—the OwnerData form and the OwnerAnimals form—will make it easier to enter, view, and update data in the Riverview database. The OwnersAndVisits report presents important information about the owners of the animals that the care center treats in an attractive and professional format, which will help Kimberly and other staff members in their work.

REVIEW

Session 4.2 Quick Check

1. In a(n) _____ report, the data from a record in the primary table appears together, followed on subsequent lines by the joined records from the related table.

2. When you create a report based on two tables that are joined in a one-to-many relationship, the field values for the records from the related table are called the _____ records.

3. Identify three types of modifications you can make to a report in Layout view.

4. Describe the process for moving a control to another location on a report in Layout view.

5. When working in Layout view for a report, which key do you press and hold down so that you can click to select multiple controls (field labels, field value boxes, and so on)?

6. _____ in a report (or form) is special formatting applied to certain field values depending on one or more conditions.

Review Assignments

Data Files needed for the Review Assignments: Items.png and Vendor.accdb *(cont. from Module 3)*

Kimberly asks you to enhance the Vendor database with forms and reports. Complete the following steps:

1. Open the **Vendor** database you created and worked with in previous modules, and then click the Enable Content button next to the security warning, if necessary.

2. Use the Form Wizard to create a form based on the Product table. Select all fields for the form and the Columnar layout; specify the title **ProductData** for the form.

3. Apply the Ion theme to the ProductData form *only*.

4. Insert the **Items** picture, which is located in the Access1 > Review folder provided with your Data Files, in the ProductData form. Remove the picture from the control layout, and then move the picture to the right of the form title.

5. Edit the form title so that it appears as "Product Data" (two words), resize the title box as necessary so the title appears on a single line, and then change the font color of the form title to the Gray-25%, Background 2, Darker 75% theme color.

6. Resize the Weight in Lbs field value box so it is the same width (approximately) as the Units/Case field value box above it.

7. Change the alignment of the Price, Units/Case, and Weight in Lbs fields so that their values appear left-aligned in the field value boxes.

8. Save your changes to the form design.

9. Use the ProductData form to update the Product table as follows:

   a. Use the Find command to search for the word "premium" anywhere in the ProductName field, and then display the record for the Premium puppy food (ProductID PF200). Change the Price in this record to **44.00**.

   b. Add a new record with the following field values:

      Product ID: **CT200**

      Supplier ID: **KLS321**

      Product Name: **Cloth tape roll**

      Price: **24.00**

      Units/Case: **10**

      Weight in Lbs: **4**

      Temp Controlled?: **no**

      Sterile?: **no**

   c. Use the form to view each record with a ProductID value that starts with "CT".

   d. Save and close the form.

10. Use the Form Wizard to create a form containing a main form and a subform. Select all fields from the Supplier table for the main form, and select ProductID, ProductName, Price, TempControl, and Sterile—in that order—from the Product table for the subform. Use the Datasheet layout. Specify the title **SuppliersAndProducts** for the main form and **ProductSubform** for the subform.

11. Change the form title text to **Suppliers and Products**.

12. Resize the subform by widening it from its right side, increasing its width by approximately one inch, and then resize all columns in the subform to their best fit, working left to right. Navigate through each record in the main form to make sure all the field values in the subform are completely displayed, resizing subform columns and the subform itself, as necessary. Save and close the SuppliersAndProducts form.

13. Use the Report Wizard to create a report based on the primary Supplier table and the related Product table. Select the SupplierID, Company, City, Category, ContactFirst, ContactLast, and Phone fields—in that order—from the Supplier table, and the ProductID, ProductName, Price, and Units fields from the Product table. Do not specify any additional grouping levels, and sort the detail records in ascending order by ProductID. Choose the Outline layout and Portrait orientation. Specify the title **ProductsBySupplier** for the report.

14. Change the report title text to **Products by Supplier**.

15. Apply the Ion theme to the ProductsBySupplier report *only*.

16. Resize and reposition the following objects in the report in Layout view, and then scroll through the report to make sure all field labels and field values are fully displayed:

    a. Resize the report title so that the text of the title, Products by Supplier, is fully displayed.

    b. Move the ProductName field label and field value box to the right a bit (be sure not to move them too far so that the longest product name will still be completely visible).

    c. Resize the Product ID field label from its right side, increasing its width slightly so the label is fully displayed.

    d. Move the Price field label to the left a bit so the right side of the field label aligns with the right side of the field value below it.

    e. Move the Units/Case field label and field value box to the right a bit; then resize the label on its left side, increasing its width slightly so the label is fully displayed.

    f. Select the field value boxes *only* (not the field labels) for the following four fields: SupplierID, Company, City, and Category. Then move the four field value boxes to the left until their left edges align (roughly) with the "S" in "Supplier" in the report title.

17. Change the color of the report title text to the Gray-25%, Background 2, Darker 75% theme color.

18. Insert the **Items** picture, which is located in the Access1 > Review folder provided with your Data Files, in the report. Move the picture to the right of the report title.

19. Apply conditional formatting so that the Category field values equal to Supplies appear as dark red and bold.

20. Preview each page of the report, verifying that all the fields fit on the page. If necessary, return to Layout view and make changes so the report prints within the margins of the page and so that all field names and values are completely displayed.

21. Save the report, print its first page (only if asked by your instructor to do so), and then close the report.

22. Compact and repair the Vendor database, and then close it.

Case Problem 1

APPLY

Data Files needed for this Case Problem: Beauty.accdb *(cont. from Module 3)* **and Salon.png**

Beauty To Go   Sue Miller uses the Beauty database to track and view information about the services her business offers. She asks you to create the necessary forms and a report to help her work with this data more efficiently. Complete the following:

1. Open the **Beauty** database you created and worked with in previous modules, and then click the Enable Content button next to the security warning, if necessary.

2. Use the Form Wizard to create a form based on the Member table. Select all the fields for the form and the Columnar layout. Specify the title **MemberData** for the form.

3. Apply the Slice theme to the MemberData form *only*.

4. Edit the form title so that it appears as "Member Data" (two words); resize the title so that both words fit on the same line; and then change the font color of the form title to the Orange, Accent 5, Darker 25% theme color.

5. Use the Find command to display the record for Maita Rios, and then change the OptionEnds field value for this record to **9/3/2017**.

6. Use the MemberData form to add a new record to the Member table with the following field values:

   Member ID: **2180**

   Option ID: **135**

   First Name: **Risa**

   Last Name: **Kaplan**

   Street: **122 Bolcher Ave**

   City: **Orlando**

   State: **FL**

   Zip: **32805**

   Phone: **212-858-4007**

   Option Begins: **11/11/2017**

   Option Ends: **5/11/2018**

7. Save and close the MemberData form.

8. Use the Form Wizard to create a form containing a main form and a subform. Select all the fields from the Option table for the main form, and select the MemberID, FirstName, LastName, OptionEnd, and Phone fields from the Member table for the subform. Use the Datasheet layout. Specify the title **MembersByOption** for the main form and the title **MemberSubform** for the subform.

9. Change the form title text for the main form to **Members by Option**.

10. Resize all columns in the subform to their best fit, working from left to right; then move through all the records in the main form and check to make sure that all subform field values are fully displayed, resizing the columns as necessary.

11. Save and close the MembersByOption form.

12. Use the Report Wizard to create a report based on the primary Option table and the related Member table. Select all the fields from the Option table, and then select the MemberID, FirstName, LastName, City, Phone, OptionBegin, and OptionEnd fields from the Member table. Do not select any additional grouping levels, and sort the detail records in ascending order by MemberID. Choose the Outline layout and Landscape orientation. Specify the title **MemberOptions** for the report.

13. Apply the Slice theme to the MemberOptions report *only*.

14. Resize the report title so that the text is fully displayed; edit the report title so that it appears as "Member Options" (two words); and change the font color of the title to the Orange, Accent 5, Darker 25% theme color.

15. Change the alignment of the Option Cost field so that its values appear left-aligned in the field value boxes.

16. Resize and reposition the following objects in the report in Layout view, and then scroll through the report to make sure all field labels and field values are fully displayed:

    a. Move the FirstName label and field value box to the right a bit (be sure not to move them too far so that the longest first name will still be completely visible).

    b. Resize the MemberID field label on its right side, increasing its width until the label is fully displayed.

    c. Move the Phone label and field value box to the left; then resize the Option Begins label on its left side, increasing its width until the label is fully displayed.

    d. Scroll to the bottom of the report; note that the page number might not be completely within the page border (the dotted vertical line). If necessary, select and move the box containing the text "Page 1 of 1" until the entire text is positioned to the left of the dotted vertical line marking the right page border.

17. Insert the **Salon** picture, which is located in the Access1 > Case1 folder provided with your Data Files, in the report. Move the picture to the right of the report title.

18. Apply conditional formatting so that any OptionEnds field value less than 3/15/2017 appears as bold and with the Red color applied.

19. Preview the entire report to confirm that it is formatted correctly. If necessary, return to Layout view and make changes so that all field labels and field values are completely displayed.

20. Save the report, print its first page (only if asked by your instructor to do so), and then close the report.

21. Compact and repair the Beauty database, and then close it.

Case Problem 2

Data Files needed for this Case Problem: Coder.png and Programming.accdb *(cont. from Module 3)*

CREATE

Programming Pros Brent Hovis is using the Programming database to track and analyze the business activity of his tutoring services company. To make his work easier, you'll create a form and a report in the Programming database. Complete the following:

1. Open the **Programming** database you created and worked with in previous modules, and then click the Enable Content button next to the security warning, if necessary.
2. Create the form shown in Figure 4-29.

Figure 4-29 | **Completed ContractsByTutor form**

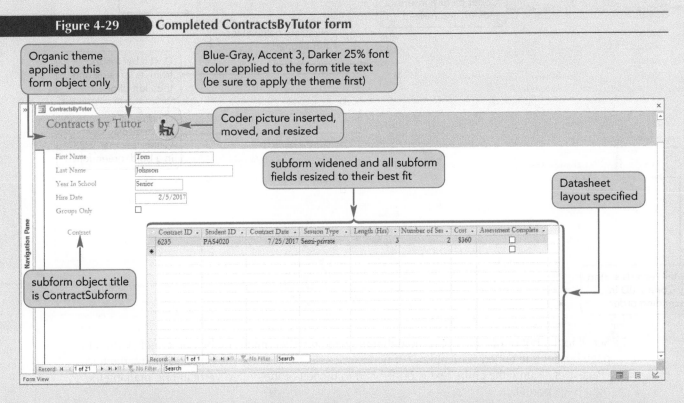

Organic theme applied to this form object only

Blue-Gray, Accent 3, Darker 25% font color applied to the form title text (be sure to apply the theme first)

Coder picture inserted, moved, and resized

subform widened and all subform fields resized to their best fit

Datasheet layout specified

subform object title is ContractSubform

3. Using the form you just created, navigate to the second record in the subform for the eighth main record, and then change the Assessment Complete field value to **yes**.
4. Use the Find command to move to the record for Gail Fordham, and then change the value in the Year In School field to **Senior**.

5. Use the appropriate wildcard character to find all records with a Hire Date field value that begins with the month of February (2). Change the Hire Date field value for Ian Rodriguez (Tutor ID 1020) to **1/17/2017**. Save and close the form.

6. Create the report shown in Figure 4-30.

Figure 4-30   **Completed TutorsAndContracts report**

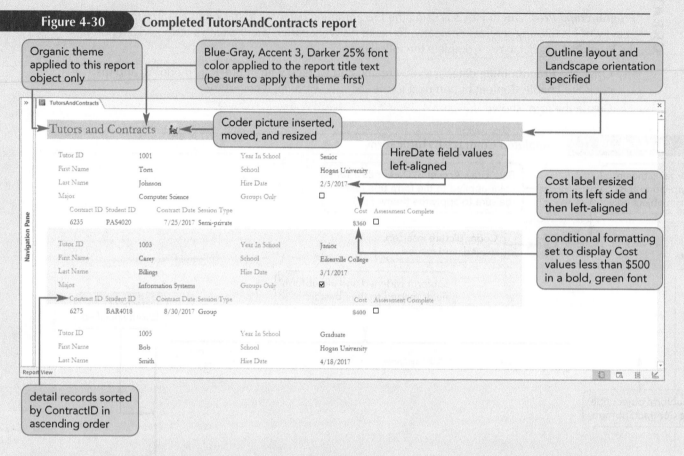

Organic theme applied to this report object only

Blue-Gray, Accent 3, Darker 25% font color applied to the report title text (be sure to apply the theme first)

Outline layout and Landscape orientation specified

Coder picture inserted, moved, and resized

HireDate field values left-aligned

Cost label resized from its left side and then left-aligned

conditional formatting set to display Cost values less than $500 in a bold, green font

detail records sorted by ContractID in ascending order

7. Scroll to the bottom of the report; note that the page number might not be completely within the page border (the dotted vertical line). If necessary, select and move the box containing the text "Page 1 of 1" until the entire text is positioned to the left of the dotted vertical line marking the right page border.

8. Preview each page of the report, verifying that all the fields fit on the page. If necessary, return to Layout view and make changes so the report prints within the margins of the page and all field names and values are completely displayed.

9. Save the report, print its first page (only if asked by your instructor to do so), and then close the report.

10. Compact and repair the Programming database, and then close it.

Case Problem 3

CHALLENGE

Data Files needed for this Case Problem: Center.accdb *(cont. from Module 3)* and Flower.png

Diane's Community Center   Diane Coleman uses the Center database to track, maintain, and analyze data about the patrons, donations, and auction items for her not-for-profit community center. You'll help Diane by creating a form and a report based on this data. Complete the following:

1. Open the **Center** database you created and worked with in previous modules, and then click the Enable Content button next to the security warning, if necessary.

2. Use the Form Wizard to create a form based on the Auction table. Select all the fields for the form and the Columnar layout. Specify the title **AuctionInfo** for the form.

3. Apply the Retrospect theme to the AuctionInfo form *only*.

4. Edit the form title so that it appears as "Auction Info" (two words), and change the font color of the form title to the Brown, Accent 3, Darker 25% theme color.

✤ **Explore** 5. Use the appropriate button in the Font group on the Form Layout Tools Format tab to italicize the form title. Save the form.

6. Use the AuctionInfo form to update the Auction table as follows:

   a. Use the Find command to search for the record that contains the value "240" for the AuctionID field, and then change the MinimumSalesPrice field value for this record to **275**.

   b. Add a new record with the following values:

   Auction ID: **260**

   Donation ID: **5265**

   Date of Auction: **11/11/2017**

   Minimum Sales Price: **125**

   Item Sold at Auction?: [leave blank]

   ✤ **Explore** c. Find the record with AuctionID 245, and then delete the record. (*Hint*: After displaying the record in the form, you need to select it by clicking the right-pointing triangle in the bar to the left of the field labels. Then use the appropriate button on the Home tab in the Records group to delete the record. When asked to confirm the deletion, click the Yes button.) Close the form.

7. Use the Form Wizard to create a form containing a main form and a subform. Select all the fields from the Patron table for the main form, and select all fields except PatronID from the Donation table for the subform. Use the Datasheet layout. Specify the name **PatronsAndDonations** for the main form and the title **DonationSubform** for the subform.

8. Apply the Retrospect theme to the PatronsAndDonations form *only*.

9. Edit the form title so that it appears as "Patrons and Donations." Resize the form title so that the text fits on one line. Change the font color of the title to the Brown, Accent 3, Darker 25% theme color.

10. Insert the **Flower** picture, which is located in the Access1 > Case3 folder provided with your Data Files, in the PatronsAndDonations form. Remove the picture from the control layout, and then move the picture to the right of the form title. Resize the picture so it is approximately double the original size.

⊕ **Explore** 11. Use the appropriate button in the Font group on the Form Layout Tools Format tab to apply the theme color Tan, Accent 5, Lighter 80% as a background color for all the field value boxes in the main form. Then use the appropriate button in the Control Formatting group to change the outline of all the main form field value boxes to have a line thickness of 1 pt. (*Hint*: Select all the field value boxes before making these changes.)

12. Resize the subform by extending it to the right, and then resize all columns in the subform to their best fit. Navigate through the records in the main form to make sure all the field values in the subform are completely displayed, resizing subform columns as necessary. Save and close the form.

13. Use the Report Wizard to create a report based on the primary Patron table and the related Donation table. Select all the fields from the Patron table, and select all fields except PatronID from the Donation table. Sort the detail records in *descending* order by DonationValue. Choose the Outline layout and Portrait orientation. Specify the name **PatronsAndDonations** for the report.

14. Apply the Retrospect theme to the PatronsAndDonations report *only*.

15. Resize the report title so that the text is fully displayed; edit the report title so that it appears as "Patrons and Donations"; and change the font color of the title to the Brown, Accent 3, Darker 25% theme color.

16. Move the Donation Value field label and its field value box to the left a bit. Then resize the Donation ID field label on the right to fully display the label. Move the Donation ID field label and its field value box to the left to provide space between the Donation ID and Donation Date fields, and then move the Description field label and its field value box to the right a bit, to provide more space between the Donation Date and Description fields. Widen the Cash Donation? field label so all the text is displayed, and then reposition the field label so it is centered over the CashDonation check boxes below it. Move the AuctionItem check boxes to the right so they are centered below the Possible Auction Item? field label. Finally, resize the Phone and Email field labels from their left sides to reduce the width of the label boxes, moving the words "Phone" and "Email" closer to the field value boxes. Save the report.

17. Insert the **Flower** picture, which is located in the Access1 > Case3 folder provided with your Data Files, in the PatronsAndDonations report. Move the picture to the right of the report title.

⊕ **Explore** 18. Use the appropriate button on the Report Layout Tools Format tab in the Background group to apply the theme color Tan, Accent 5, Lighter 60% as the alternate row color for the fields from the Patron table; then apply the theme color Tan, Accent 5, Lighter 80% as the alternate row color for the fields from the Donation table. (*Hint*: You must first select an entire row with no background color for the appropriate fields before applying each alternate row color.) Scroll through the report to find a patron record with multiple donations so you can verify the effect of applying the alternate row color to the Donation fields.

19. Apply conditional formatting so that any DonationValue greater than or equal to 250 is formatted as bold and with the Brown 5 font color.

⊕ **Explore** 20. Preview the report so you can see two pages at once. (*Hint*: Use a button on the Print Preview tab.) Check the report to confirm that it is formatted correctly and all field labels and field values are fully displayed. Save the report, print its first page (only if asked by your instructor to do so), and then close the report.

21. Compact and repair the Center database, and then close it.

TROUBLESHOOT

Case Problem 4

Data Files needed for this Case Problem: Appalachia.accdb *(cont. from Module 3)*, **HikeApp.accdb, and Mountains.png**

Hike Appalachia   Molly and Bailey Johnson use the Appalachia database to maintain and analyze data about the hikers, reservations, and tours for their hiking tour business. You'll help them by creating a form and a report in the Appalachia database. Additionally, you'll troubleshoot some problems in another database containing tour information. Complete the following:

1. Open the **Appalachia** database you created and worked with in previous modules, and then click the Enable Content button next to the security warning, if necessary.

2. Use the Form Wizard to create a form containing a main form and a subform. Select all the fields from the Hiker table for the main form, and select all the fields except HikerID from the Reservation table for the subform. Use the Datasheet layout. Specify the title **HikerReservations** for the main form and the title **ReservationSubform** for the subform.

3. Apply the Integral theme to the HikerReservations form *only*.

4. Edit the form title so that it appears with a space between the two words. Change the font color of the title to the Dark Teal, Text 2, Darker 25% theme color.

5. Insert the **Mountains** picture, which is located in the Access1 > Case4 folder provided with your Data Files, in the HikerReservations form. Remove the picture from the control layout, and then move the picture to the right of the form title. Resize the picture so it is approximately double the original size.

6. Resize all columns in the subform to their best fit so that the subform column titles are fully displayed. Save the form.

7. Use the Find command to search for records that contain "WV" in the State field. Display the record for Sarah Peeler (HikerID 509), and then change the Phone field value for this record to **703-599-2043**. Close the form.

8. Use the Report Wizard to create a report based on the primary Hiker table and the related Reservation table. Select all the fields from the Hiker table, and then select all the fields except HikerID from the Reservation table. Do not select any additional grouping levels, and sort the detail records in ascending order by ReservationID. Choose the Outline layout and Portrait orientation. Specify the title **HikersAndReservations** for the report.

9. Apply the Integral theme to the HikersAndReservations report *only*.

10. Edit the report title so that it appears as "Hikers and Reservations"; then change the font color of the title to the Dark Teal, Text 2, Darker 25% theme color.

11. Left-align the Tour Date field label and field value box, then move the People field label and field value box to the left, to reduce the space between the Tour Date and People columns.

12. Insert the **Mountains** picture, which is located in the Access1 > Case4 folder provided with your Data Files, in the HikersAndReservations report. Move the picture to the right of the report title.

13. Apply conditional formatting so that any People field value greater than or equal to 3 appears as bold and with the Red color applied.

14. Preview the entire report to confirm that it is formatted correctly. If necessary, return to Layout view and make changes so that all field labels and field values are completely displayed.

15. Save the report, print its first page (only if asked by your instructor to do so), and then close the report.

16. Compact and repair the Appalachia database, and then close it.

⚙ **Troubleshoot** 17. Open the **HikeApp** database located in the Access1 > Case4 folder provided with your Data Files. Open the HikerData form in the HikeApp database. The form is not formatted correctly; it should be formatted with the Ion Boardroom theme and the theme color Plum, Accent 1, Darker 50% applied to the title. There are other problems with the form title's format as well. Additionally, some of the field labels are not properly formatted with regard to spacing between words. Identify and fix the problems with the form's format. (*Hint*: To fix the spacing between words in the necessary field labels, use the same procedure you use to fix the spacing between words in the form title text.) Save and close the corrected form.

⚙ **Troubleshoot** 18. Open the **HikerReservations** form, which is also not formatted correctly. Modify the form so that it matches the corrected format of the HikerData form and has a consistent design, including the correctly placing the logo image and resizing it to approximately double its original size. Fix the formatting problems with the subform as well, and then save and close the corrected form with subform.

⚙ **Troubleshoot** 19. Open the **HikersAndReservations** report. This report should have a consistent format in terms of theme, color, and so on as the two forms. Additionally, some of the field labels are not properly formatted with regard to spacing between words. (*Hint*: To fix the spacing between words in the necessary field labels, use the same procedure you use to fix the spacing between words in the report title text.) Find and fix these formatting errors. The report also has several problems with field labels and field value boxes, where the labels and values are not fully displayed. Locate and correct all of these problems, being sure to scroll through the entire report. Also, the conditional formatting applied to the People field is supposed to use a bold Red font. Edit the rule to correct the conditional formatting. Save the corrected report, and then preview it to identify and correct any remaining formatting problems.

20. Compact and repair the HikeApp database, and then close it.

OBJECTIVES

Session 5.1
- Review object naming standards
- Use the Like, In, Not, and & operators in queries
- Filter data using an AutoFilter
- Use the IIf function to assign a conditional value to a calculated field in a query
- Create a parameter query

Session 5.2
- Use query wizards to create a crosstab query, a find duplicates query, and a find unmatched query
- Create a top values query

Session 5.3
- Modify table designs using lookup fields, input masks, and data validation rules
- Identify object dependencies
- Review a Long Text field's properties
- Designate a trusted folder

Creating Advanced Queries and Enhancing Table Design

Making the CareCenter Database Easier to Use

Case | *Riverview Veterinary Care Center*

Riverview Veterinary Care Center, a veterinary care center in Cody, Wyoming, provides a range of medical services for pets and livestock in the greater Cody area. In addition to caring for household pets, such as dogs and cats, the center specializes in serving the needs of livestock on ranches in the surrounding area. Kimberly Johnson, the office manager for Riverview Veterinary Care Center, oversees a small staff and is responsible for maintaining the medical records for all of the animals the care center serves.

Kimberly and her staff rely on Microsoft Access 2016 to manage electronic medical records for owner and animal information, billing, inventory control, purchasing, and accounts payable. The Riverview staff developed the CareCenter database, which contains tables, queries, forms, and reports that Kimberly and other staff members use to track animal, owner, visit, and billing information.

Kimberly is interested in taking better advantage of the power of Access to make the database easier to use and to create more sophisticated queries. For example, Kimberly wants to obtain lists of owners in certain cities. She also needs a summarized list of invoice amounts by city. In this module, you'll modify and customize the CareCenter database to satisfy these and other requirements.

STARTING DATA FILES

Access2 → Module	Review	Case1
CareCenter.accdb	Supplier.accdb	MoreBeauty.accdb
Case2	Case3	Case4
Tutoring.accdb	Community.accdb	AppTrail.accdb

Session 5.1 Visual Overview:

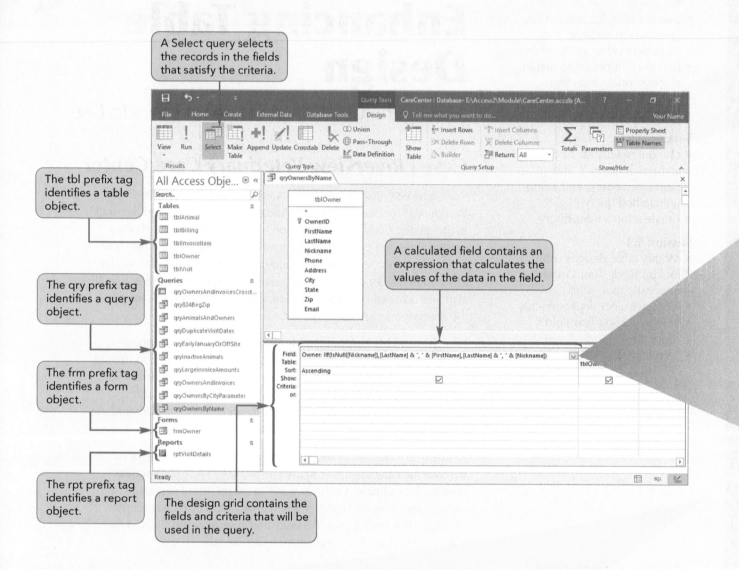

A Select query selects the records in the fields that satisfy the criteria.

The tbl prefix tag identifies a table object.

The qry prefix tag identifies a query object.

The frm prefix tag identifies a form object.

The rpt prefix tag identifies a report object.

A calculated field contains an expression that calculates the values of the data in the field.

The design grid contains the fields and criteria that will be used in the query.

Calculated Field

The name of the new calculated field is placed to the left of the expression, separated with a colon.

The **IIf function** tests a condition and returns one of two values. The function returns the first value if the condition is true and the second value if the condition is false.

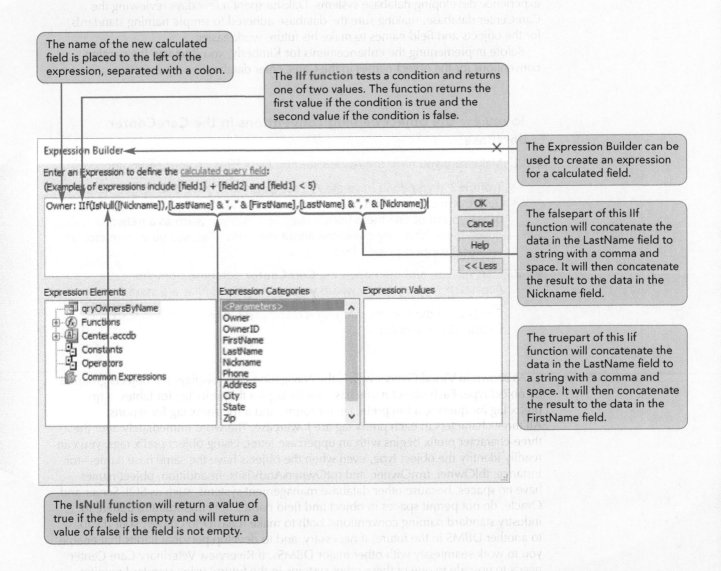

The Expression Builder can be used to create an expression for a calculated field.

Expression Builder

Enter an Expression to define the calculated query field:
(Examples of expressions include [field1] + [field2] and [field1] < 5)

Owner: IIf(IsNull([Nickname]),[LastName] & ", " & [FirstName],[LastName] & ", " & [Nickname])

OK
Cancel
Help
<< Less

Expression Elements

- qryOwnersByName
- Functions
- Center.accdb
- Constants
- Operators
- Common Expressions

Expression Categories

- <Parameters>
- Owner
- OwnerID
- FirstName
- LastName
- Nickname
- Phone
- Address
- City
- State
- Zip

Expression Values

The falsepart of this IIf function will concatenate the data in the LastName field to a string with a comma and space. It will then concatenate the result to the data in the Nickname field.

The truepart of this IIf function will concatenate the data in the LastName field to a string with a comma and space. It will then concatenate the result to the data in the FirstName field.

The **IsNull function** will return a value of true if the field is empty and will return a value of false if the field is not empty.

Reviewing the CareCenter Database

Kimberly and her staff had no previous database experience when they created the CareCenter database; they simply used the wizards and other easy-to-use Access tools. As business continued to grow at Riverview Veterinary Care Center, Kimberly realized she needed a database expert to further enhance the CareCenter database. She hired Daksha Yatawara, who has a business information systems degree and nine years of experience developing database systems. Daksha spent a few days reviewing the CareCenter database, making sure the database adhered to simple naming standards for the objects and field names to make his future work easier.

Before implementing the enhancements for Kimberly, you'll review the naming conventions for the object names in the CareCenter database.

To review the object naming conventions in the CareCenter database:

▶ **1.** Make sure you have the Access starting Data Files on your computer.

   Trouble? If you don't have the Access Data Files, you need to get them before you can proceed. Your instructor will either give you the Data Files or ask you to obtain them from a specified location (such as a network drive). If you have any questions about the Data Files, see your instructor or technical support person for assistance.

▶ **2.** Start Access, and then open the **CareCenter** database from the Access2 > Module folder where your starting Data Files are stored.

   Trouble? If the security warning is displayed below the ribbon, click the Enable Content button.

As shown in Visual Overview 5.1, the Navigation Pane displays the objects grouped by object type. Each object name has a prefix tag—a tbl prefix tag for tables, a qry prefix tag for queries, a frm prefix tag for forms, and a rpt prefix tag for reports. All three characters in each prefix tag are lowercase. The word immediately after the three-character prefix begins with an uppercase letter. Using object prefix tags, you can readily identify the object type, even when the objects have the same base name—for instance, tblOwner, frmOwner, and rptOwnersAndVisits. In addition, object names have no spaces, because other database management systems, such as SQL Server and Oracle, do not permit spaces in object and field names. It is important to adhere to industry standard naming conventions, both to make it easier to convert your database to another DBMS in the future, if necessary, and to develop personal habits that enable you to work seamlessly with other major DBMSs. If Riverview Veterinary Care Center needs to upscale to one of these other systems in the future, using standard naming conventions means that Daksha will have to do less work to make the transition.

Teamwork: Following Naming Conventions

Most Access databases have hundreds of fields, objects, and controls. You'll find it easier to identify the type and purpose of these database items when you use a naming convention or standard. Most companies adopt a standard naming convention, such as the one used for the CareCenter database, so that multiple people can develop a database, troubleshoot database problems, and enhance and improve existing databases. When working on a database, a team's tasks are difficult, if not impossible, to perform if a standard naming convention isn't used. In addition, most databases and database samples on websites and in training books use standard naming conventions that are similar to the ones used for the CareCenter database. By following the standard naming convention established by your company or organization, you'll help to ensure smooth collaboration among all team members.

Now you'll create the queries that Kimberly needs.

Using a Pattern Match in a Query

You are already familiar with queries that use an exact match or a range of values (for example, queries that use the > or < comparison operators) to select records. Many other operators are available for creating select queries. These operators let you build more complicated queries that are difficult or impossible to create with exact-match or range-of-values selection criteria.

Kimberly created a list of questions she wants to answer using the CareCenter database:

- Which owners have a zip code beginning with 824?
- What is the owner information for owners located in Cody, Ralston, or Powell?
- What is the owner information for all owners except those located in Cody, Ralston, or Powell?
- What is the owner and visit information for owners in Cody or Powell whose animals were seen offsite or visited during early January?
- What are the first and last names of Riverview Veterinary Care Center owners? Nicknames should be used where listed.
- What is the owner information for owners in a particular city? This query needs to be flexible to allow the user to specify the city.

Next, you will create the queries necessary to answer these questions. Kimberly wants to view the records for all owners whose zip code begins with 824. To answer Kimberly's question, you can create a query that uses a pattern match. A **pattern match** selects records with a value for the designated field that matches the pattern of a simple condition value—in this case, owners with a zip code beginning with 824. You do this using the Like comparison operator.

The **Like comparison operator** selects records by matching field values to a specific pattern that includes one or more of these wildcard characters: asterisk (*), question mark (?), and number symbol (#). The asterisk represents any string of characters, the question mark represents any single character, and the number symbol represents any single digit. Using a pattern match is similar to using an exact match, except that a pattern match includes wildcard characters.

To create the new query, you must first place the tblOwner table field list in the Query window in Design view.

To create the new query in Design view:

1. If necessary, click the **Shutter Bar Open/Close Button** ≪ at the top of the Navigation Pane to close it.

2. On the ribbon, click the **Create** tab.

3. In the Queries group, click the **Query Design** button. The Show Table dialog box opens in front of the Query window in Design view.

4. Click **tblOwner** in the Tables box, click the **Add** button, and then click the **Close** button. The tblOwner table field list is added to the Query window, and the Show Table dialog box closes.

5. Drag the bottom border of the tblOwner window down until you can see the full list of fields.

6. Double-click the **title bar** of the tblOwner field list to highlight all the fields, and then drag the highlighted fields to the first column's Field box in the design grid. Each field is placed in a separate column in the design grid, in the same order that the fields appear in the table. See Figure 5-1.

> **TIP**
>
> You can also double-click a table name to add the table's field list to the Query window.

Figure 5-1   Adding the fields for the pattern match query

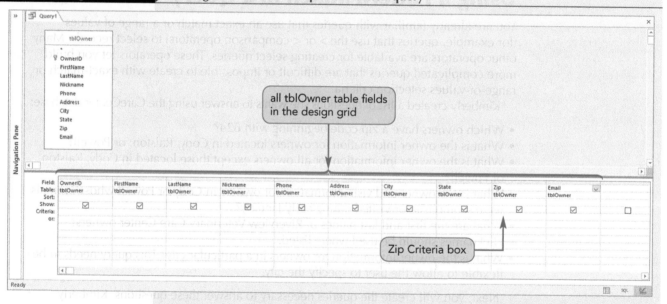

Trouble? If tblOwner.* appears in the first column's Field box, you dragged the * from the field list instead of the highlighted fields. Press the Delete key, and then repeat Step 6.

Now you will enter the pattern match condition Like "824*" for the Zip field. The query will select records with a Zip field value of 824 in positions one through three. The asterisk wildcard character specifies that any characters can appear in the remaining positions of the field value.

To specify records that match the indicated pattern:

TIP

If you omit the Like operator, it is automatically added when you run the query.

1. Click the **Zip Criteria** box, and then type **L**. The Formula AutoComplete menu displays a list of functions beginning with the letter L, but the Like operator is not one of the choices in the list. You'll finish typing the condition.

2. Type **ike "824*"**. See Figure 5-2.

| Figure 5-2 | Record selection based on matching a specific pattern |

pattern match selection criterion

3. Click the **Save** button 🖫 on the Quick Access Toolbar to open the Save As dialog box.

4. Type **qry824BegZip** in the Query Name box, and then press the **Enter** key. The query is saved, and the name is displayed on the object tab.

5. On the Query Tools Design tab, in the Results group, click the **Run** button. The query results are displayed in the query window. Twenty-three records have zip codes beginning with 824. See Figure 5-3.

| Figure 5-3 | tblOwner table records for zip codes starting with 824 |

Note that Daksha removed the hyphens from the Phone field values; for example, 3078241245 in the first record used to be 307-824-1245. You'll modify the Phone field later in this module to format its values with hyphens.

6. Change the first record in the table, with Owner ID 2310, so the Last Name and First Name columns contain your last and first names, respectively.

7. Close the qry824BegZip query.

Next, Kimberly asks you to create a query that displays information about owners who live in Cody, Ralston, or Powell. To produce the results Kimberly wants, you'll create a query using a list-of-values match.

Using a List-of-Values Match in a Query

A list-of-values match selects records whose value for the designated field matches one of two or more simple condition values. You could accomplish this by including several Or conditions in the design grid, but the In comparison operator provides an easier and clearer way to do this. The In comparison operator lets you define a condition with a list of two or more values for a field. If a record's field value matches one value from the list of defined values, then that record is selected and included in the query results.

To display the information Kimberly requested, you want to select records if their City field value equals Cody, Ralston, or Powell. These are the values you will use with the In comparison operator. Kimberly wants the query to contain the same fields as the qry824BegZip query, so you'll make a copy of that query and modify it.

To create the query using a list-of-values match:

1. Open the Navigation Pane.

2. In the Queries group on the Navigation Pane, right-click **qry824BegZip**, and then click **Copy** on the shortcut menu.

   Trouble? If you don't see the qry824BegZip query in the Queries group, press the F5 function key to refresh the object listings in the Navigation pane.

3. Right-click in the empty area in the Navigation Pane below the report and then click **Paste**.

4. In the Query Name box, type **qryCodyRalstonPowellOwners**, and then press the **Enter** key.

   To modify the copied query, you need to open it in Design view.

5. In the Queries group on the Navigation Pane, right-click **qryCodyRalstonPowellOwners** to select it and display the shortcut menu.

6. Click **Design View** on the shortcut menu to open the query in Design view, and then close the Navigation Pane.

   You need to delete the existing condition from the Phone field.

7. Click the **Zip Criteria** box, press the **F2** key to highlight the entire condition, and then press the **Delete** key to remove the condition.

   Now you can enter the criterion for the new query using the In comparison operator. When you use this operator, you must enclose the list of values you want to match within parentheses and separate the values with commas. In addition, for fields defined using the Short Text data type, you enclose each value in quotation marks, although the quotation marks are automatically added if you omit them. For fields defined using the Number or Currency data type, you don't enclose the values in quotation marks.

8. Right-click the **City Criteria** box to open the shortcut menu, click **Zoom** to open the Zoom dialog box, and then type **In ("Cody","Ralston","Powell")**, as shown in Figure 5-4.

| Figure 5-4 | Record selection based on matching field values to a list of values |

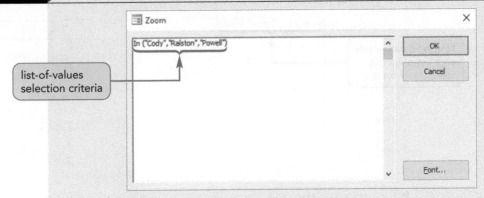

list-of-values
selection criteria

TIP

After clicking in a box, you can also open its Zoom dialog box by holding down the Shift key and pressing the F2 key.

9. Click the **OK** button to close the Zoom dialog box, and then save and run the query. The recordset is displayed, which shows the 17 records with Cody, Ralston, or Powell in the City field.

10. Close the query.

Kimberly would also like a list of owners who do not live in Cody, Ralston, or Powell. You can provide Kimberly with this information by creating a query with the Not logical operator.

Using the Not Logical Operator in a Query

The **Not logical operator** negates a criterion or selects records for which the designated field does not match the criterion. For example, if you enter *Not "Cody"* in the Criteria box for the City field, the query results show records that do not have the City field value Cody—that is, records of all owners not located in Cody.

To create Kimberly's query, you will combine the Not logical operator with the In comparison operator to select owners whose City field value is not in the list *("Cody","Ralston","Powell")*. The qryCodyRalstonPowellOwners query has the fields that Kimberly needs to see in the query results. Kimberly doesn't need to keep the qryCodyRalstonPowellOwners query, so you'll rename and then modify the query.

To create the query using the Not logical operator:

1. Open the Navigation Pane.

2. In the Queries group, right-click **qryCodyRalstonPowellOwners**, and then on the shortcut menu click **Rename**.

3. Position the insertion point after "qry," type **Non**, and then press the **Enter** key. The query name is now qryNonCodyRalstonPowellOwners.

4. Open the **qryNonCodyRalstonPowellOwners** query in Design view, and then close the Navigation Pane.

You need to change the existing condition in the City field to add the Not logical operator.

TIP

You can rename any type of object, including a table, in the Navigation Pane using the Rename command on the shortcut menu.

> 5. Click the **City Criteria** box, open the Zoom dialog box, click at the beginning of the expression, type **Not**, and then press the **spacebar**. See Figure 5-5.

Figure 5-5	Record selection based on not matching a list of values

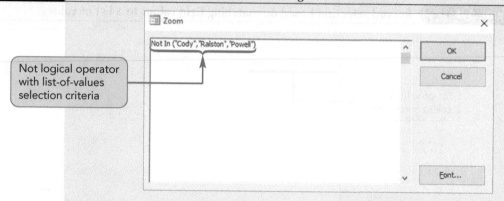

Not logical operator with list-of-values selection criteria

> 6. Click the **OK** button, and then save and run the query. The recordset displays only those records with a City field value that is not Cody, Ralston, or Powell. The recordset includes a total of nine owner records.

> 7. Scroll down the datasheet if necessary to make sure that no Cody, Ralston, or Powell owners appear in your results.
>
> Now you can close and delete the query, because Kimberly does not need to run this query again.

> 8. Close the query, and then open the Navigation Pane.

> 9. Right-click **qryNonCodyRalstonPowellOwners**, click **Delete** on the shortcut menu, and then click **Yes** in the dialog box warning that deleting this object will remove it from all groups.

TIP

You can delete any type of object, including a table, in the Navigation Pane using the Delete command on the shortcut menu.

You now are ready to answer Kimberly's question about owners in Cody or Powell who have invoice amounts for less than $75 or who visited during the first week of January.

Using an AutoFilter to Filter Data

Kimberly wants to view the owner first and last names, cities, animal names, visit dates, offsite statuses, and visit reasons for owners in Cody or Powell whose animals either were seen offsite or visited during the first week in January. The qryEarlyJanuaryOrOffSite query contains the same fields Kimberly wants to view. This query also uses the Or logical operator to select records if the OffSite field has a value of true or if the VisitDate field value is between 1/1/2017 and 1/7/2017. These are two of the conditions needed to answer Kimberly's question. You could modify the qryEarlyJanuaryOrOffSite query in Design view to further restrict the records selected to Owners located only in Cody or Powell. However, you can use the AutoFilter feature to choose the city restrictions faster and with more flexibility. You previously used the AutoFilter feature to sort records, and you previously used Filter By Selection to filter records. Now you'll use the AutoFilter feature to filter records.

To filter the records using an AutoFilter:

▶ 1. Open the **qryEarlyJanuaryOrOffSite** query in Design view, and then close the Navigation Pane.

The true condition for the OffSite field selects records for owners whose animals were seen offsite, and the Between #1/1/2017# And #1/7/2017# condition for the VisitDate field selects records for animals whose visit date was in the first week of January 2017. Although the OffSite field is a yes/no field, these values are represented by true (yes) and false (no). Because the conditions are in two different rows, the query uses the Or logical operator. If you wanted to answer Kimberly's question in Design view, you would add a condition for the City field, using either the Or logical operator—"Cody" Or "Powell"—or the In comparison operator—In ("Cody","Powell"). You'd place the condition for the City field in both the Criteria row and in the Or row. The query recordset would include a record only if both conditions in either row are satisfied. Instead of changing the conditions in Design view, though, you'll choose the information Kimberly wants using an AutoFilter.

▶ 2. Run the query, and then click the **arrow** on the City column heading to display the AutoFilter menu. See Figure 5-6.

Figure 5-6	Using an AutoFilter to filter records in the query recordset

The AutoFilter menu lists all City field values that appear in the recordset. A checkmark next to an entry indicates that records with that City field value appear in the recordset. To filter for selected City field values, you uncheck the cities you don't want selected and leave checked the cities you do want selected. You can click the "(Select All)" check box to select or deselect all field values. The "(Blanks)" option includes null values when checked and excludes null values when unchecked. (Recall that a null field value is the absence of a value for the field.)

3. Click the **(Select All)** check box to deselect all check boxes, click the **Cody** check box, and then click the **Powell** check box.

The two check boxes indicate that the AutoFilter will include only Cody and Powell City field values.

4. Click the **OK** button. The AutoFilter displays the 28 records for owners in Cody and Powell whose animals were seen offsite or who had a visit in the first week in January. See Figure 5-7.

| Figure 5-7 | Recordset showing results of an AutoFilter |

You click the Toggle Filter button in the Sort & Filter group on the Home tab to remove the current filter and display all records in the query. If you click the Toggle Filter button a second time, you reapply the filter.

5. On the Home tab, in the Sort & Filter group, click the **Toggle Filter** button. The filter is removed, and all 40 records appear in the recordset.

6. Click the **Toggle Filter** button. The City filter is applied, displaying the 28 records for owners in Cody and Powell.

7. Save the query and close it.

Next, Kimberly wants to view all fields from the tblOwner table, along with the owner name. If a nickname is available, she would like it to be used in place of the proper first name of the owner.

Assigning a Conditional Value to a Calculated Field

If a field in a record does not contain any information at all, it has a null value. Such a field is also referred to as a null field. A field in a record that contains any data at all—even a single space—is nonnull. Records for owners have nonnull FirstName and LastName field values in the tblOwner table. If an owner does not have a requested nickname, the owner has a null Nickname field value. Kimberly wants to view records from the tblOwner table in order by last name. She wants the owner's nickname to be shown in place of the first name if the Nickname field is nonnull; otherwise, if the Nickname field is null, she wants the FirstName field value to be shown. To produce this information for Kimberly, you need to create a query that includes all fields from the tblOwner table and then add a calculated field that will display the owner name, including either the Nickname field value, if present, or the FirstName field value. The LastName field and either the Nickname or FirstName fields will be separated by a comma and a space.

To combine the LastName and FirstName fields, you'll use the expression *LastName & ", " & FirstName*. The **& (ampersand) operator** is a concatenation operator that joins text expressions. **Concatenation** refers to joining two or more text fields or characters encapsulated in quotes. When you join the LastName field value to the string that contains the comma and space, you are concatenating these two strings. If the LastName field value is Vasquez and the FirstName field value is Katrina, for example, the result of the expression *LastName & ", " & FirstName* is *Vasquez & ", " & Katrina* which results in *Vasquez, Katrina*.

Using Concatenation

IT professionals generally refer to a piece of text data as a string. Most programming languages include the ability to join two or more strings using concatenation.

Imagine you're working with a database table that contains Title, FirstName, and LastName values for people who have made donations, and you've been asked to add their names to a report. You could add each individual field separately, but the data would look awkward, with each field in a separate column. Alternatively, you could create a calculated field with an expression that combines the fields with spaces into a more readable format, such as "Mr. Jim Sullivan". To do this, you would concatenate the fields with a space separator. The expression to perform this task might look like *=Title & " " & FirstName & " " & LastName*.

To display the correct owner value, you'll use the IIf function. The IIf (Immediate If) function assigns one value to a calculated field or control if a condition is true and a second value if the condition is false. The IIf function has three parts: a condition that is true or false, the result when the condition is true, and the result when the condition is false. Each part of the IIf function is separated by a comma. The condition you'll use is *IsNull(Nickname)*. The IsNull function tests a field value or an expression for a null value; if the field value or expression is null, the result is true; otherwise, the result is false. The expression *IsNull(Nickname)* is true when the Nickname field value is null and is false when the Nickname field value is not null.

For the calculated field, you'll enter *IIf(IsNull(Nickname),LastName & ", " & FirstName,LastName & ", " & Nickname)*. You interpret this expression as follows: If the Nickname field value is null, then set the calculated field value to the concatenation of the LastName field value and the text string ", " and the FirstName field value. If the Nickname field value is not null, then set the calculated field value to the concatenation of the LastName field value and the text string ", " and the Nickname field value.

Now you're ready to create Kimberly's query to display the owner name.

To create the query to display the owner name:

1. Click the **Create** tab, and then in the Queries group, click the **Query Design** button. The Show Table dialog box opens on top of the Query window in Design View.

2. Click **tblOwner** in the Tables box, click the **Add** button, and then click the **Close** button. The tblOwner table field list is placed in the Query window, and the Show Table dialog box closes.

   Kimberly wants all fields from the tblOwner table to appear in the query recordset, with the new calculated field in the first column.

3. Drag the bottom border of the tblOwner field list down until all fields are visible, double-click the title bar of the tblOwner field list to highlight all the fields, and then drag the highlighted fields to the second column's Field box in the design grid. Each field is placed in a separate column in the design grid starting with the second column, in the same order that the fields appear in the table.

   Trouble? If you accidentally drag the highlighted fields to the first column in the design grid, click the OwnerID Field box, and then in the Query Setup group, click the Insert Columns button. Continue with Step 4.

4. Right-click the blank Field box to the left of the OwnerID field, and then click **Build** on the shortcut menu. The Expression Builder dialog box opens.

   Kimberly wants to use "Owner" as the name of the calculated field, so you'll type that name, followed by a colon, and then you'll choose the IIf function.

5. Type **Owner:** and then press the **spacebar**.

6. Double-click **Functions** in the Expression Elements (left) column, and then click **Built-In Functions**.

7. Scroll down the Expression Categories (middle) column, click **Program Flow**, and then in the Expression Values (right) column, double-click **IIf**. The IIf function is added with four placeholders to the right of the calculated field name in the expression box. See Figure 5-8.

Figure 5-8	IIf function inserted for the calculated field

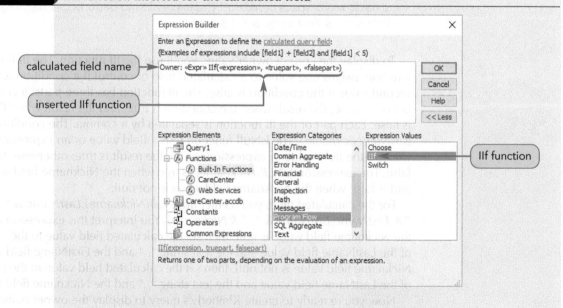

The expression you will create does not need the leftmost placeholder (<<Expr>>), so you'll delete it. You'll replace the second placeholder (<<expression>>) with the condition using the IsNull function, the third placeholder (<<truepart>>) with the expression using the & operator and the FirstName and LastName fields, and the fourth placeholder (<<falsepart>>) with the expression using the & operator and the Nickname and LastName fields.

▶ 8. Click **<<Expr>>** in the expression box, and then press the **Delete** key. The first placeholder is deleted.

▶ 9. Click **<<expression>>** in the expression box, and then click **Inspection** in the Expression Categories (middle) column.

▶ 10. Double-click **IsNull** in the Expression Values (right) column, click **<<expression>>** in the expression box, and then type **Nickname**. You've completed the entry of the condition in the IIf function. See Figure 5-9.

Figure 5-9   **After entering the condition for the calculated field's IIf function**

condition for the IIf function

ScreenTip for the IsNull function

you may see a second ScreenTip for the Nickname expression value

IsNull function

After you typed the first letter of "Nickname," the Formula AutoComplete box displayed a list of functions beginning with the letter N, and a ScreenTip for the IsNull function was displayed above the box. The box closed after you typed the third letter, but the ScreenTip remains on the screen.

Instead of typing the field name of Nickname in the previous step, you could have double-clicked CareCenter.accdb in the Expression Elements column, double-clicked Tables in the Expression Elements column, clicked tblOwner in the Expression Elements column, and then double-clicked Nickname in the Expression Categories column.

Now you'll replace the third placeholder and then the fourth placeholder.

▶ 11. Click **<<truepart>>**, and then type **LastName & ", " & FirstName**. Be sure you type a space after the comma within the quotation marks.

▶ 12. Click **<<falsepart>>**, and then type **LastName & ", " & Nickname**. Be sure you type a space after the comma within the quotation marks. See Figure 5-10.

Figure 5-10	Completed calculated field

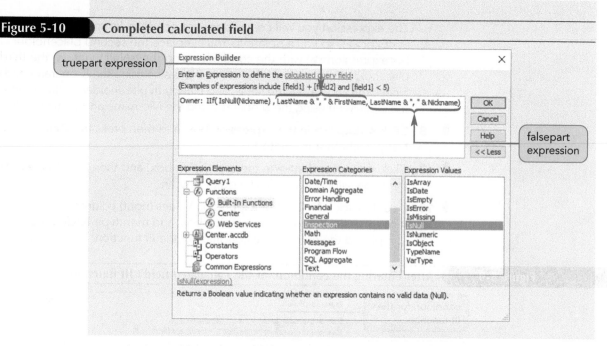

Kimberly wants the query to sort records in ascending order by the Owner calculated field.

To sort, save, and run the query:

1. Click the **OK** button in the Expression Builder dialog box to close it.

2. Click the right side of the Owner Sort box to display the sort order options, and then click **Ascending**. The query will display the records in alphabetical order based on the Owner field values.

   The calculated field name of Owner consists of a single word, so you do not need to set the Caption property for it. However, you'll review the properties for the calculated field by opening its property sheet.

3. On the Query Tools Design tab, in the Show/Hide group, click the **Property Sheet** button. The property sheet opens and displays the properties for the Owner calculated field. See Figure 5-11.

Figure 5-11	Property sheet for the Owner calculated field

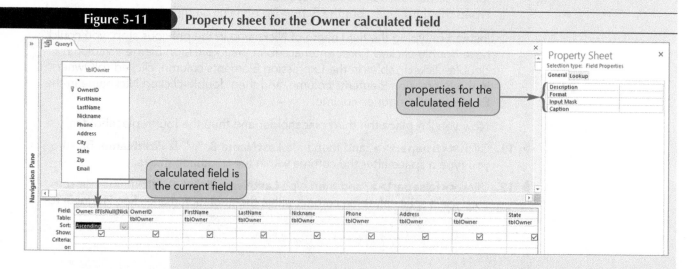

Among the properties for the calculated field, which is the current field, is the Caption property. Leaving the Caption property set to null means that the column name for the calculated field in the query recordset will be Owner, which is the calculated field name. The Property Sheet button is a toggle, so you'll click it again to close the property sheet.

▶ **4.** Click the **Property Sheet** button again to close the property sheet.

▶ **5.** Save the query as **qryOwnersByName**, run the query, and then resize the Owner column to its best fit. All records from the tblOwner table are displayed in alphabetical order by the Owner field. See Figure 5-12.

Figure 5-12	Completed query displaying the Owner calculated field

owner names are the concatenation for LastName, FirstName for null Nickname values

owner names are the concatenation for LastName, Nickname for nonnull Nickname values

Owner	Owner ID	First Name	Last Name	Nickname	Phone	Address
Baxter, Reg	2404	Reggie	Baxter	Reg	3079432469	880 Powell-Cody Rd
Billings, Curt	2370	Curt	Billings		4066124711	10 Ridgewood Ln
Blacksmith, Wilbur	2354	Randy	Blacksmith	Wilbur	3078829987	245 18th Ave
Cruz, Sally	2314	Sally	Cruz		3074064321	199 18th Ave
Fishman, Barbara	2325	Barbara	Fishman		4067921410	21 Mountain Ln
Gonzalez, James	2330	James	Gonzalez		3079870334	16 Rockway Rd
Hendricks, Angie	2358	Angie	Hendricks		3079432234	27 Locklear Ln
Jackson, Aaron	2366	Aaron	Jackson		4068172392	417 Rocky Rd
Jackson, Elmer	2392	Elmer	Jackson		3078438472	22 Jackson Farm Rd
Jackson, Melanie	2340	Melanie	Jackson		3078821925	42 Blackwater Way
Johnson, Taylor	2412	Taylor	Johnson		3078688862	458 Rose Ln
Jones, Thomas	2362	Thomas	Jones		3079859981	622 Bobcat Tr
Kostas, Mei	2416	Mei	Kostas		3078245873	812 Playa Hwy
Miller, Susan	2384	Susan	Miller		3078242756	1283 Old Roundabout Rd
Otterman, Zack	2375	Joseph	Otterman	Zack	3078249863	42 Rock Ln
Pincher, Sandra	2318	Sandra	Pincher		3079828401	53 Verde Ln
Poleman, Dan	2345	Dan	Poleman		3078878873	75 Stream Rd
Rascal, Tom	2408	Tom	Rascal		3078243575	1 Rascal Farm Rd

▶ **6.** Save and close the query.

You're now ready to create the query to satisfy Kimberly's request for information about owners in a particular city.

Creating a Parameter Query

Kimberly's next request is for records in the qryOwnersByName query for owners in a particular city. For this query, she wants to specify a city, such as Cody or Garland, each time she runs the query.

To create this query, you will copy, rename, and modify the qryOwnersByName query. You could create a simple condition using an exact match for the City field, but you would need to change it in Design view every time you run the query. Alternatively, Kimberly or a member of her staff could filter the qryOwnersByName query for the city records they want to view. Instead, you will create a parameter query. A **parameter query** displays a dialog box that prompts the user to enter one or more criteria values when the query is run. In this case, you want to create a query that prompts for the city and selects only those owner records with that City field value from the table. You will enter the prompt in the Criteria box for the City field. When the query runs, it will open a dialog box and prompt you to enter the city. The query results will then be created, just as if you had changed the criteria in Design view.

Creating a Parameter Query

- Create a select query that includes all fields to appear in the query results.
- Choose the sort fields, and set the criteria that do not change when you run the query.
- Decide which fields to use as prompts when the query runs. In the Criteria box for each of these fields, type the prompt you want to appear in a dialog box when you run the query, and enclose the prompt in brackets.

You'll copy and rename the qryOwnersByName query now, and then you'll change its design to create the parameter query.

To create the parameter query based on an existing query:

1. Open the Navigation Pane, copy and paste the qryOwnersByName query, and then name the new copy **qryOwnersByCityParameter**.

2. Open the **qryOwnersByCityParameter** query in Design view, and then close the Navigation Pane.

   Next, you must enter the criterion for the parameter query. In this case, Kimberly wants the query to prompt users to enter the city for the owner records they want to view. You need to enter the prompt in the Criteria box for the City field. Brackets must enclose the text of the prompt.

3. Click the **City Criteria** box, type **[Type the city:]** and then press the **Enter** key. See Figure 5-13.

Figure 5-13   **Specifying the prompt for the parameter query**

prompt text enclosed in brackets

4. Save and run the query. A dialog box is displayed, prompting you for the name of the city. See Figure 5-14.

Figure 5-14   **Enter Parameter Value dialog box**

type value here

prompt

The bracketed text you specified in the Criteria box of the City field appears above a box, in which you must type a City field value. Kimberly wants to see all owners in Cody.

5. Type **Cody**, press the **Enter** key, and then scroll the datasheet to the right, if necessary, to display the City field values. The recordset displays the data for the 10 owners in Cody. See Figure 5-15.

Figure 5-15   **Results of the parameter query**

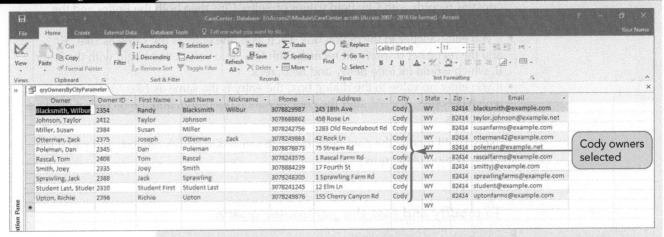

Kimberly asks what happens if she doesn't enter a value in the dialog box when she runs the qryOwnersByCityParameter query. You can run the query again to show Kimberly the answer to her question.

6. Switch to Design view, and then run the query. The Enter Parameter Value dialog box opens.

If you click the OK button or press the Enter key, you'll run the parameter query without entering a value for the City field criterion.

7. Click the **OK** button. No records are displayed in the query results.

When you run the parameter query and enter "Cody" in the dialog box, the query runs just as if you had entered "Cody" in the City Criteria box in the design grid and displays all Cody owner records. When you do not enter a value in the dialog box, the query runs as if you had entered "null" in the City Criteria box. Because none of the records has a null City field value, no records are displayed. Kimberly asks if there's a way to display records for a selected City field value when she enters its value in the dialog box and to display all records when she doesn't enter a value.

Creating a More Flexible Parameter Query

Most users want a parameter query to display the records that match the parameter value the user enters or to display all records when the user doesn't enter a parameter value. To provide this functionality, you can change the value in the Criteria box in the design grid for the specified column. For example, you could change an entry for a City field from *[Type the city:]* to *Like [Type the city:] & "*".* That is, you can prefix the Like operator to the original criterion and concatenate the criterion to a wildcard character. When you run the parameter query with this new entry, one of the following recordsets will be displayed:

- If you enter a specific City field value in the dialog box, such as *Belfry*, the entry is the same as *Like "Belfry" & "*"*, which becomes *Like "Belfry*"* after the concatenation operation. That is, all records are selected whose City field values have Belfry in the first six positions and any characters in the remaining positions. If the table on which the query is based contains records with City field values of Belfry, only those records are displayed. However, if the table on which the query is based also contains records with City field values of Belfry City, then both the Belfry and the Belfry City records would be displayed.
- If you enter a letter in the dialog box, such as *B*, the entry is the same as *Like "B*"*, and the recordset displays all records with City field values that begin with the letter B, which would include Belfry and Bearcreek.
- If you enter no value in the dialog box, the entry is the same as *Like Null & "*"*, which becomes *Like "*"* after the concatenation operation, and the recordset displays all records.

Now you'll modify the parameter query to satisfy Kimberly's request, and you'll test the new version of the query.

To modify and test the parameter query:

1. Switch to Design view.

2. Click the **City Criteria** box, and then open the **Zoom** dialog box.

   You'll use the Zoom dialog box to modify the value in the City Criteria box.

3. Click to the left of the expression in the Zoom dialog box, type **Like**, press the **spacebar**, and then press the **End** key.

4. Press the **spacebar**, type **&**, press the **spacebar**, and then type **"*"** as shown in Figure 5-16.

   Be sure you type "*" at the end of the expression.

Figure 5-16	Modified City Criteria value in the Zoom dialog box

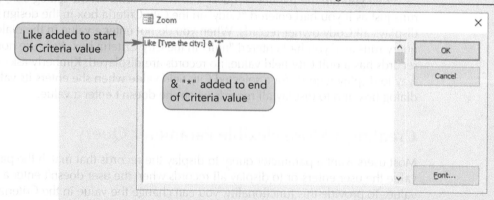

Like added to start of Criteria value

& "*" added to end of Criteria value

Now you can test the modified parameter query.

▶ 5. Click the **OK** button to close the Zoom dialog box, save your query design changes, and then run the query.

First, you'll test the query to display owners in Powell.

▶ 6. Type **Powell**, and then press the **Enter** key. The recordset displays the data for the three owners in Powell.

Now you'll test the query without entering a value when prompted.

▶ 7. Switch to Design view, run the query, and then click the **OK** button. The recordset displays all 26 original records from the tblOwner table.

Finally, you'll test how the query performs when you enter B in the dialog box.

▶ 8. On the Home tab, in the Records group, click the **Refresh All** button to open the Enter Parameter Value dialog box.

▶ 9. Type **B**, press the **Enter** key, and then scroll to the right, if necessary, to display the City field values. The recordset displays the two records for owners in Belfry and Bearcreek.

▶ 10. Close the query.

▶ 11. If you are not continuing on to the next session, close the CareCenter database, and then click the **Yes** button if necessary to empty the Clipboard.

The queries you created will make the CareCenter database easier to use. In the next session, you'll use query wizards to create three different types of queries, and you'll use Design view to create a top values query.

REVIEW

Session 5.1 Quick Check

1. According to the naming conventions used in this session, you use the _____ prefix tag to identify queries.
2. Which comparison operator selects records based on a specific pattern?
3. What is the purpose of the asterisk (*) in a pattern match query?
4. When do you use the In comparison operator?
5. How do you negate a selection criterion?
6. The _____ function returns one of two values based on whether the condition being tested is true or false.
7. When do you use a parameter query?

Session 5.2 Visual Overview:

A crosstab query uses aggregate functions such as Sum and Count to perform arithmetic operations on selected records.

A simple query selects records from one or more tables that satisfy criteria.

A find duplicates query is a select query that finds duplicate records in a table or query.

A find unmatched query is a select query that finds all records in a table or query that have no related records in a second table or query.

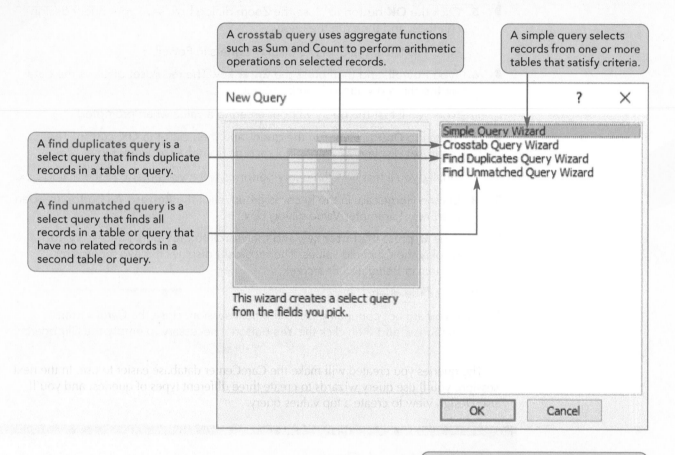

Each column and row intersection will display the sum of the InvoiceAmt values.

The selected field (InvoiceAmt) is used in the calculations for each column and row intersection.

This option determines whether to display an overall totals column in the crosstab query.

The crosstab query will display one column for the paid invoices and a second column for the unpaid invoices.

The crosstab query will display one row for each unique City field value.

Advanced Query Wizards

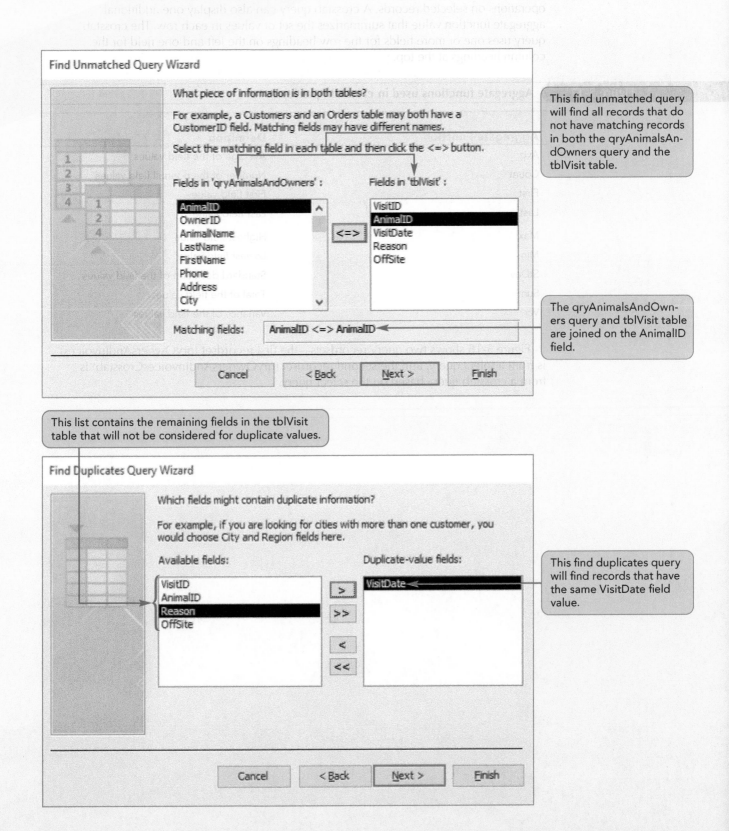

Find Unmatched Query Wizard

What piece of information is in both tables?

For example, a Customers and an Orders table may both have a CustomerID field. Matching fields may have different names.

Select the matching field in each table and then click the <=> button.

Fields in 'qryAnimalsAndOwners' :

AnimalID
OwnerID
AnimalName
LastName
FirstName
Phone
Address
City

Fields in 'tblVisit' :

VisitID
AnimalID
VisitDate
Reason
OffSite

<=>

Matching fields: AnimalID <=> AnimalID

Cancel   < Back   Next >   Finish

> This find unmatched query will find all records that do not have matching records in both the qryAnimalsAndOwners query and the tblVisit table.

> The qryAnimalsAndOwners query and tblVisit table are joined on the AnimalID field.

> This list contains the remaining fields in the tblVisit table that will not be considered for duplicate values.

Find Duplicates Query Wizard

Which fields might contain duplicate information?

For example, if you are looking for cities with more than one customer, you would choose City and Region fields here.

Available fields:

VisitID
AnimalID
Reason
OffSite

>
>>
<
<<

Duplicate-value fields:

VisitDate

Cancel   < Back   Next >   Finish

> This find duplicates query will find records that have the same VisitDate field value.

Creating a Crosstab Query

Kimberly wants to analyze the Riverview Veterinary Care Center invoices by city, so she can view the paid and unpaid invoice amounts for all owners located in each city. Crosstab queries use the aggregate functions shown in Figure 5-17 to perform arithmetic operations on selected records. A crosstab query can also display one additional aggregate function value that summarizes the set of values in each row. The crosstab query uses one or more fields for the row headings on the left and one field for the column headings at the top.

Figure 5-17   Aggregate functions used in crosstab queries

Aggregate Function	Definition
Avg	Average of the field values
Count	Number of the nonnull field values
First	First field value
Last	Last field value
Max	Highest field value
Min	Lowest field value
StDev	Standard deviation of the field values
Sum	Total of the field values
Var	Variance of the field values

Figure 5-18 shows two query recordsets—the first recordset (qryOwnersAndInvoices) is from a select query, and the second recordset (qryOwnersAndInvoicesCrosstab) is from a crosstab query based on the select query.

| Figure 5-18 | Comparing a select query to a crosstab query |

The qryOwnersAndInvoices query, a select query, joins the tblOwner, tblVisit, and tblBilling tables to display selected data from those tables for all invoices. The qryOwnersAndInvoicesCrosstab query, a crosstab query, uses the qryOwnersAndInvoices query as its source query and displays one row for each unique City field value. The City column in the crosstab query identifies each row. The crosstab query uses the Sum aggregate function on the InvoiceAmt field to produce the displayed values in the Paid and Unpaid columns for each City row. An entry in the Total Of InvoiceAmt column represents the sum of the Paid and Unpaid values for the City field value in that row.

Decision Making: Using Both Select Queries and Crosstab Queries

Companies use both select queries and crosstab queries in their decision making. A select query displays several records—one for each row selected by the select query—while a crosstab query displays only one summarized record for each unique field value. When managers want to analyze data at a high level to see the big picture, they might start with a crosstab query, identify which field values to analyze further, and then look in detail at specific field values using select queries. Both select and crosstab queries serve as valuable tools in tracking and analyzing a company's business, and companies use both types of queries in the appropriate situations. By understanding how managers and other employees use the information in a database to make decisions, you can create the correct type of query to provide the information they need.

The quickest way to create a crosstab query is to use the **Crosstab Query Wizard**, which guides you through the steps for creating one. You could also change a select query to a crosstab query in Design view using the Crosstab button in the Query Type group on the Query Tools Design tab.

Using the Crosstab Query Wizard

- On the Create tab, in the Queries group, click the Query Wizard button.
- In the New Query dialog box, click Crosstab Query Wizard, and then click the OK button.
- Complete the Wizard dialog boxes to select the table or query on which to base the crosstab query, select the row heading field (or fields), select the column heading field, select the calculation field and its aggregate function, and enter a name for the crosstab query.

The crosstab query you will create, which is similar to the one shown in Figure 5-18, has the following characteristics:

- The qryOwnersAndInvoices query in the CareCenter database is the basis for the new crosstab query. The base query includes the LastName, FirstName, City, InvoiceAmt, and InvoicePaid fields.
- The City field is the leftmost column in the crosstab query and identifies each crosstab query row.
- The values from the InvoicePaid field, which is a Yes/No field, identify the rightmost columns of the crosstab query.
- The crosstab query applies the Sum aggregate function to the InvoiceAmt field values and displays the resulting total values in the Paid and Unpaid columns of the query results.
- The grand total of the InvoiceAmt field values appears for each row in a column with the heading Total Of InvoiceAmt.

Next you will create the crosstab query based on the qryOwnersAndInvoices query.

To start the Crosstab Query Wizard:

▶ 1. If you took a break after the previous session, make sure that the CareCenter database is open and the Navigation Pane is closed.

   Trouble? If the security warning is displayed below the ribbon, click the Enable Content button next to the security warning.

▶ 2. Click the **Create** tab on the ribbon.

▶ 3. In the Queries group, click the **Query Wizard** button. The New Query dialog box opens.

▶ 4. Click **Crosstab Query Wizard**, and then click the **OK** button. The first Crosstab Query Wizard dialog box opens.

You'll now use the Crosstab Query Wizard to create the crosstab query for Kimberly.

To finish the Crosstab Query Wizard:

▶ 1. In the View section, click the **Queries** option button to display the list of queries in the CareCenter database, and then click **Query: qryOwnersAndInvoices**. See Figure 5-19.

Figure 5-19	Choosing the query for the crosstab query

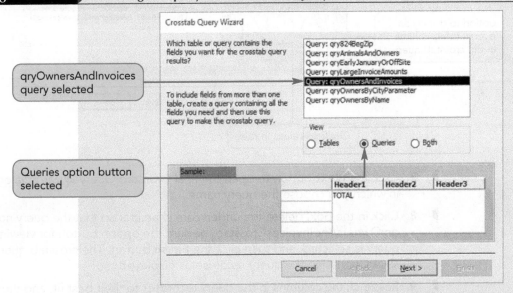

▶ 2. Click the **Next** button to open the next Crosstab Query Wizard dialog box. This is the dialog box where you choose the field (or fields) for the *row* headings. Because Kimberly wants the crosstab query to display one row for each unique City field value, you will select that field for the row headings.

TIP

When you select a field, the sample crosstab query in the dialog box changes to illustrate your choice.

▶ 3. In the Available Fields box, click **City**, and then click the > button to move the City field to the Selected Fields box.

▶ 4. Click the **Next** button to open the next Crosstab Query Wizard dialog box, in which you select the field values that will serve as column headings. Kimberly wants to see the paid and unpaid total invoice amounts, so you need to select the InvoicePaid field for the column headings.

▶ **5.** Click **InvoicePaid** in the box, and then click the **Next** button.

In the next Crosstab Query Wizard dialog box, you choose the field that will be calculated for each row and column intersection and the function to use for the calculation. The results of the calculation will appear in the row and column intersections in the query results. Kimberly needs to calculate the sum of the InvoiceAmt field value for each row and column intersection.

▶ **6.** Click **InvoiceAmt** in the Fields box, click **Sum** in the Functions box, and then make sure that the "Yes, include row sums" check box is checked. The "Yes, include row sums" option creates a column showing the overall totals for the values in each row of the query recordset. See Figure 5-20.

Figure 5-20	**Completed crosstab query design**

selected field for crosstab calculation

Sum aggregate function selected

InvoicePaid field values in columns

option to display an overall totals column in the crosstab query

City field values in rows

▶ **7.** Click the **Next** button to open the final Crosstab Query Wizard dialog box, in which you choose the query name.

▶ **8.** Click in the box, delete the underscore character so that the query name is qryOwnersAndInvoicesCrosstab, be sure the option button for viewing the query is selected, and then click the **Finish** button. The crosstab query is saved, and then the query recordset is displayed.

▶ **9.** Resize all the columns in the query recordset to their best fit, and then click the City field value in the first row (**Bearcreek**). See Figure 5-21.

| Figure 5-21 | Crosstab query recordset |

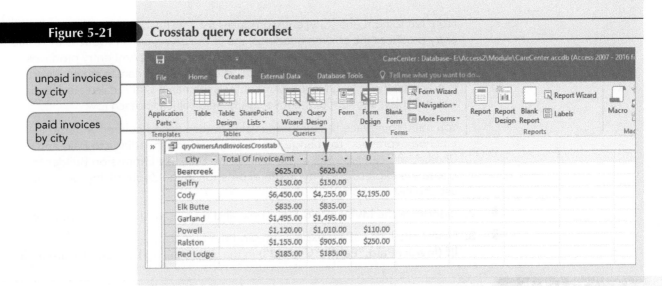

The query recordset contains only one row for each City field value. The Total Of InvoiceAmt column shows the total invoice amount for the owners in each city. The columns labeled -1 and 0 show the sum total paid (-1 column) and sum total unpaid (0 column) invoice amounts for owners in each city. Because the InvoicePaid field is a Yes/No field, by default, field values in datasheets, forms, and reports are displayed in a check box (either checked or unchecked), but a checked value is stored in the database as a -1 and an unchecked value as a 0. Instead of displaying check boxes, the crosstab query displays the stored values as column headings.

Kimberly wants you to change the column headings of -1 to Paid and 0 to Unpaid. You'll use the IIf function to change the column headings, using the expression *IIf (InvoicePaid,"Paid","Unpaid")*—if the InvoicePaid field value is true (because it's a Yes/No field or a True/False field), or is checked, use "Paid" as the column heading; otherwise, use "Unpaid" as the column heading. Because the InvoicePaid field is a Yes/No field, the condition *InvoicePaid* is the same as the condition *InvoicePaid = -1*, which uses a comparison operator and a value. For all data types except Yes/No fields, you must use a comparison operator in a condition.

To change the crosstab query column headings:

1. Click the **Home** tab on the ribbon, and then switch to Design view. The design grid has four entries. See Figure 5-22.

| Figure 5-22 | Crosstab query in the design grid |

From left to right, the [City] entry produces the row headings, the [InvoicePaid] entry produces the column headings, the [InvoiceAmt] entry produces the totals in each row/column intersection, and the Total Of InvoiceAmt entry produces the row total column heading and total values. The field names are enclosed in brackets; the Total Of InvoiceAmt entry is the name of this calculated field, which displays the sum of the InvoiceAmt field values for each row.

You need to replace the Field box value in the second column with the IIf function expression to change the -1 and 0 column headings to Paid and Unpaid. You can type the expression in the box, use Expression Builder to create the expression, or type the expression in the Zoom dialog box. You'll use the last method.

▶ **2.** Right-click the **InvoicePaid Field** box, and then open the Zoom dialog box.

▶ **3.** Delete the InvoicePaid expression, and then type **IIf (InvoicePaid,"Paid","Unpaid")** in the Zoom dialog box. See Figure 5-23.

Figure 5-23 ▶ **IIf function for the crosstab query column headings**

heading text for InvoicePaid values of Yes (or -1)

heading text for InvoicePaid values of No (or 0)

IIf (InvoicePaid, "Paid", "Unpaid")

▶ **4.** Click the **OK** button, and then save and run the query. The completed crosstab query is displayed with Paid and Unpaid as the last two column headings, in alphabetical order, as shown in Figure 5-18.

▶ **5.** Close the query, and then open the Navigation Pane.

TIP

Point to an object in the Navigation Pane to display the full object name in a ScreenTip.

In the Navigation Pane, unique icons represent different types of queries. The crosstab query icon appears in the Queries list to the left of the qryOwnersAndInvoicesCrosstab query. This icon looks different from the icon that appears to the left of the other queries, which are all select queries.

Using Special Database Features Cautiously

When you create a query in Design view or with a wizard, an equivalent SQL statement is constructed, and only the SQL statement version of the query is saved. **SQL (Structured Query Language)** is a standard language used in querying, updating, and managing relational databases. If you learn SQL for one relational DBMS, it's a relatively easy task to begin using SQL for other relational DBMSs. However, differences exist between DBMSs in their versions of SQL—somewhat like having different dialects in English—and in what additions they make to SQL. The SQL-equivalent statement created for a crosstab query in Access is one such SQL-language addition. If you need to convert an Access database to SQL Server, Oracle, or another DBMS, crosstab queries created in Access will not work in these other DBMSs. You'd have to construct a set of SQL statements in the other DBMS to replace the SQL statement automatically created by Access. Constructing this replacement set of statements is a highly technical process that only an experienced programmer can complete, so you should use special features of a DBMS judiciously.

Next, Kimberly wants to identify any visit dates that have the same visit dates as other owners because these are the ones that might have potential scheduling difficulties. To find the information Kimberly needs, you'll create a find duplicates query.

Creating a Find Duplicates Query

A find duplicates query is a select query that finds duplicate records in a table or query. You can create this type of query using the **Find Duplicates Query Wizard**. A find duplicates query searches for duplicate values based on the fields you select when answering the Wizard's questions. For example, you might want to display all employers that have the same name, all students who have the same phone number, or all products that have the same description. Using this type of query, you can locate duplicates to avert potential problems (for example, you might have inadvertently assigned two different numbers to the same product), or you can eliminate duplicates that cost money (for example, you could send just one advertising brochure to all owners having the same address).

Using the Find Duplicates Query Wizard

- On the Create tab, in the Queries group, click the Query Wizard button.
- In the New Query dialog box, click Find Duplicates Query Wizard, and then click the OK button.
- Complete the Wizard dialog boxes to select the table or query on which to base the query, select the field (or fields) to check for duplicate values, select the additional fields to include in the query results, enter a name for the query, and then click the Finish button.

You'll use the Find Duplicates Query Wizard to create and run a new query to display duplicate visit dates in the tblVisit table.

To create the query using the Find Duplicates Query Wizard:

▶ **1.** Close the Navigation Pane, click the **Create** tab on the ribbon, and then, in the Queries group, click the **Query Wizard** button to open the New Query dialog box.

▶ **2.** Click **Find Duplicates Query Wizard**, and then click the **OK** button. The first Find Duplicates Query Wizard dialog box opens. In this dialog box, you select the table or query on which to base the new query. You'll use the tblVisit table.

▶ **3.** Click **Table: tblVisit** (if necessary), and then click the **Next** button. The next Find Duplicates Query Wizard dialog box opens, in which you choose the fields you want to check for duplicate values.

▶ **4.** In the Available fields box, click **VisitDate**, click the ▢ > ▢ button to select the VisitDate field as the field to check for duplicate values, and then click the **Next** button. In the next Find Duplicates Query Wizard dialog box, you select the additional fields you want displayed in the query results.

Kimberly wants all remaining fields to be included in the query results.

▶ **5.** Click the ▢ >> ▢ button to move all fields from the Available fields box to the Additional query fields box, and then click the **Next** button. The final Find Duplicates Query Wizard dialog box opens, in which you enter a name for the query. You'll use qryDuplicateVisitDates as the query name.

▶ **6.** Type **qryDuplicateVisitDates** in the box, be sure the option button for viewing the results is selected, and then click the **Finish** button. The query is saved, and then the 51 records for visits with duplicate visit dates are displayed. See Figure 5-24.

Figure 5-24	Query recordset for duplicate visit dates

all records returned by the query share a visit date with other records

Date of Visit	Visit ID	Animal ID	Reason/Diagnosis	Off-Site Visit?
11/18/2016	1013	12337	Vaccinations	☑
11/18/2016	1014	12340	Vaccinations	☑
11/18/2016	1015	12343	Vaccinations	☑
11/18/2016	1016	12345	Vaccinations	☑
11/18/2016	1012	12335	Vaccinations	☑
11/28/2016	1028	12300	Grooming	☐
11/28/2016	1032	12296	Grooming	☐
12/2/2016	1044	12278	Vaccinations	☐
12/2/2016	1048	12318	Injured paw	☐
12/12/2016	1072	12356	Vaccinations	☑
12/12/2016	1073	12359	Vaccinations	☑
12/12/2016	1071	12353	Vaccinations	☑
12/12/2016	1070	12350	Vaccinations	☑
12/12/2016	1074	12362	Vaccinations	☑
12/20/2016	1087	12365	Vaccinations	☑
12/20/2016	1088	12368	Vaccinations	☑
12/20/2016	1089	12372	Vaccinations	☑
12/20/2016	1090	12375	Vaccinations	☑
12/20/2016	1091	12378	Vaccinations	☑
1/6/2017	1114	12404	Vaccinations	☑
1/6/2017	1104	12381	Vaccinations	☑
1/6/2017	1105	12384	Vaccinations	☑
1/6/2017	1106	12387	Vaccinations	☑
1/6/2017	1107	12390	Vaccinations	☑
1/6/2017	1108	12393	Vaccinations	☑

Record: ◄ ◄ 1 of 51 ► ►I ►✱   No Filter   Search

Datasheet View

▶ **7.** Close the query.

Kimberly now asks you to find the records for animals with no visits. These are animals whose owners have contacted the center and have given the center information about themselves and their animals; however, the animals have not had a first visit. Kimberly wants to contact the owners of these animals to see if they would like to book initial appointments. To provide Kimberly with this information, you need to create a find unmatched query.

Creating a Find Unmatched Query

A find unmatched query is a select query that finds all records in a table or query that have no related records in a second table or query. For example, you could display all owners who have had an appointment but have never been invoiced or all students who are not currently enrolled in classes. Such a query provides information for a veterinary care center to ensure all owners who have received services have also been billed for those services and for a school administrator to contact the students to find out their future educational plans. You can use the **Find Unmatched Query Wizard** to create this type of query.

REFERENCE

Using the Find Unmatched Query Wizard

- On the Create tab, in the Queries group, click the Query Wizard button.
- In the New Query dialog box, click Find Unmatched Query Wizard, and then click the OK button.
- Complete the Wizard dialog boxes to select the table or query on which to base the new query, select the table or query that contains the related records, specify the common field in each table or query, select the additional fields to include in the query results, enter a name for the query, and then click the Finish button.

Kimberly wants to know which animals have no visits. She will contact their owners to determine if they will be visiting Riverview Veterinary Care Center or whether they are receiving their veterinary care elsewhere. To create a list of animals who have not had a visit to the Center, you'll use the Find Unmatched Query Wizard to display only those records from the tblAnimal table with no matching AnimalID field value in the related tblVisit table.

To create the query using the Find Unmatched Query Wizard:

▶ 1. On the Create tab, in the Queries group, click the **Query Wizard** button to open the New Query dialog box.

▶ 2. Click **Find Unmatched Query Wizard**, and then click the **OK** button. The first Find Unmatched Query Wizard dialog box opens. In this dialog box, you select the table or query on which to base the new query. You'll use the qryAnimalsAndOwners query.

▶ 3. In the View section, click the **Queries** option button to display the list of queries, click **Query: qryAnimalsAndOwners** in the box to select this query, and then click the **Next** button. The next Find Unmatched Query Wizard dialog box opens, in which you choose the table that contains the related records. You'll select the tblVisit table.

▶ 4. Click **Table: tblVisit** in the box (if necessary), and then click the **Next** button. The next dialog box opens, in which you choose the common field for both tables. See Figure 5-25.

Figure 5-25 Selecting the common field

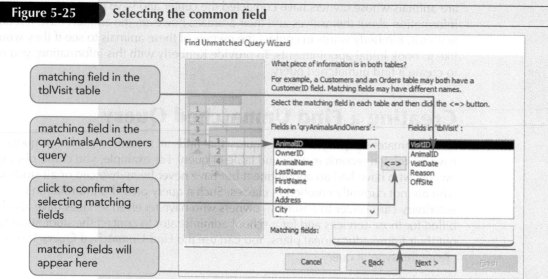

matching field in the tblVisit table

matching field in the qryAnimalsAndOwners query

click to confirm after selecting matching fields

matching fields will appear here

The common field between the query and the table is the AnimalID field. You need to click the common field in each box and then click the <=> button between the two boxes to join the two objects. The Matching fields box then will display AnimalID <=> AnimalID to indicate the joining of the two matching fields. If the two selected objects already have a one-to-many relationship defined in the Relationships window, the Matching fields box will join the correct fields automatically.

5. In the Fields in 'qryAnimalsAndOwners' box click **AnimalID**, in the Fields in 'tblVisit' box click **AnimalID**, click the <=> button to connect the two selected fields, and then click the **Next** button. The next Find Unmatched Query Wizard dialog box opens, in which you choose the fields you want to see in the query recordset. Kimberly wants the query recordset to display all available fields.

> Be sure you click the AnimalID field in both boxes.

6. Click the >> button to move all fields from the Available fields box to the Selected fields box, and then click the **Next** button. The final dialog box opens, in which you enter the query name.

7. Type **qryInactiveAnimals**, be sure the option button for viewing the results is selected, and then click the **Finish** button. The query is saved, and then two records are displayed in the query recordset. See Figure 5-26.

Figure 5-26 Query recordset displaying two animals without visits

records for animals without visits

8. Close the query.

Next, Kimberly wants to contact those owners who have the highest invoice amounts to make sure that Riverview Veterinary Care Center is providing satisfactory service. To display the information Kimberly needs, you will create a top values query.

Creating a Top Values Query

Whenever a query displays a large group of records, you might want to limit the number to a more manageable size by displaying, for example, just the first 10 records. The **Top Values property** for a query lets you limit the number of records in the query results. To find a limited number of records using the Top Values property, you can click one of the preset values from a list or enter either an integer (such as 15, to display the first 15 records) or a percentage (such as 20%, to display the first fifth of the records).

For instance, suppose you have a select query that displays 45 records. If you want the query recordset to show only the first five records, you can change the query by entering a Top Values property value of either 5 or 10%. If the query contains a sort, and the last record that can be displayed is one of two or more records with the same value for the primary sort field, all records with that matching key value are displayed.

Kimberly wants to view the same data that appears in the qryLargeInvoiceAmounts query for owners with the highest 25 percent invoice amounts. Based on the number or percentage you enter, a top values query selects that number or percentage of records starting from the top of the recordset. Thus, you usually include a sort in a top values query to display the records with the highest or lowest values for the sorted field. You will modify the query and then use the Top Values property to produce this information for Kimberly.

To set the Top Values property for the query:

▶ **1.** Open the Navigation Pane, open the **qryLargeInvoiceAmounts** query in Datasheet view, and then close the Navigation Pane. Ten records are displayed, all with InvoiceAmt field values greater than $75, in descending order by InvoiceAmt.

▶ **2.** Switch to Design view.

▶ **3.** On the Query Tools Design tab, in the Query Setup group, click the **Return** arrow (with the ScreenTip "Top Values"), and then click **25%**. See Figure 5-27.

Figure 5-27) **Creating the top values query**

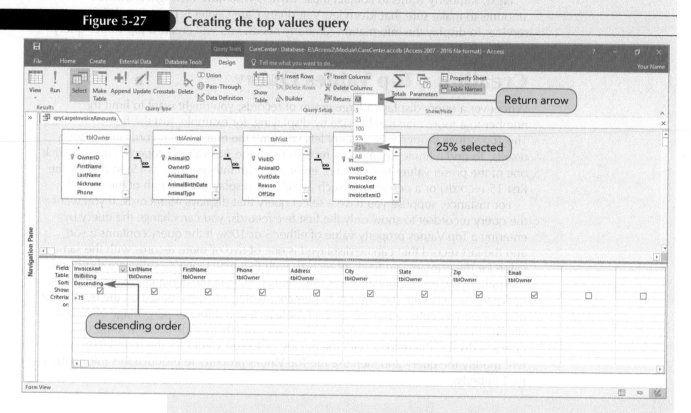

If the number or percentage of records you want to select, such as 15 or 20%, doesn't appear in the Top Values list, you can type the number or percentage in the Return box.

4. Run the query. Three records are displayed in the query recordset; these records represent the owners with the highest 25 percent of the invoice amounts (25 percent of the original 10 records). See Figure 5-28.

| Figure 5-28 | Top values query recordset |

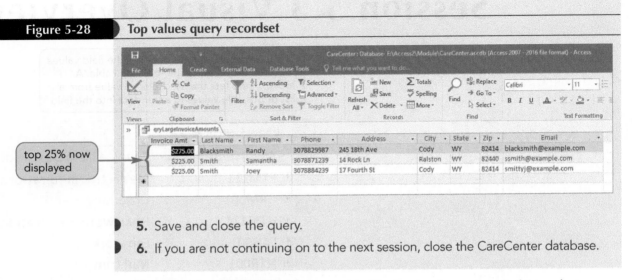

5. Save and close the query.

6. If you are not continuing on to the next session, close the CareCenter database.

Kimberly will use the information provided by the queries you created to analyze the Riverview Veterinary Care Center business and to contact owners. In the next session, you will enhance the tblOwner and tblVisit tables.

REVIEW

Session 5.2 Quick Check

1. What is the purpose of a crosstab query?
2. What are the four query wizards you can use to create a new query?
3. What is a find duplicates query?
4. What does a find unmatched query do?
5. What happens when you set a query's Top Values property?
6. What happens if you set a query's Top Values property to 2, and the first five records have the same value for the primary sort field?

Session 5.3 Visual Overview:

The tblInvoiceItem table supplies the field values for the lookup field in the tblBilling table. A lookup field lets the user select a value from a list of possible values to enter data into the field.

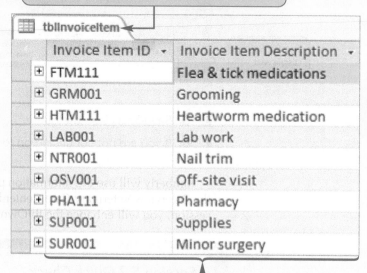

The InvoiceItemID and InvoiceItemDesc fields from the tblInvoiceItem table are used to look up InvoiceItemID values in the tblBilling table.

The tblBilling table contains the lookup field.

tblInvoiceItem

Invoice Item ID	Invoice Item Description
⊞ FTM111	Flea & tick medications
⊞ GRM001	Grooming
⊞ HTM111	Heartworm medication
⊞ LAB001	Lab work
⊞ NTR001	Nail trim
⊞ OSV001	Off-site visit
⊞ PHA111	Pharmacy
⊞ SUP001	Supplies
⊞ SUR001	Minor surgery

tblBilling

Invoice Num	Visit ID	Invoice Date	Invoice Amt	Invoice Item ID	Invoice Paid
42098	1002	11/09/2016	$50.00	Lab work	☑
42099	1002	11/09/2016	$75.00		
42100	1002	11/09/2016	$45.00		
42110	1006	11/14/2016	$35.00		
42111	1006	11/14/2016	$65.00		
42112	1006	11/14/2016	$50.00		
42118	1009	11/16/2016	$50.00		
42119	1009	11/16/2016	$15.00		
42125	1012	11/21/2016	$50.00		
42126	1012	11/21/2016	$75.00		
42127	1012	11/21/2016	$75.00		
42128	1013	11/21/2016	$75.00		
42129	1013	11/21/2016	$75.00		
42130	1014	11/21/2016	$75.00		
42131	1014	11/21/2016	$75.00	Lab work	☑
42132	1015	11/21/2016	$75.00	Vaccinations	☑

Lookup list:

Description	ID
Flea & tick medicati	FTM111
Grooming	GRM001
Heartworm medicat	HTM111
Lab work	LAB001
Nail trim	NTR001
Off-site visit	OSV001
Pharmacy	PHA111
Supplies	SUP001
Minor surgery	SUR001
Major surgery	SUR002
Spaying - surgery	SUR111
Neutering - surgery	SUR222
Declawing - surgery	SUR333
Vaccinations	VAC111

Values in the lookup field appear in alphabetical order, sorted by Invoice Item ID.

Only the InvoiceItemID values are stored in the InvoiceItemID field in the tblBilling table even though the user also sees the InvoiceItemDesc values in the datasheet.

Lookup Fields and Input Masks

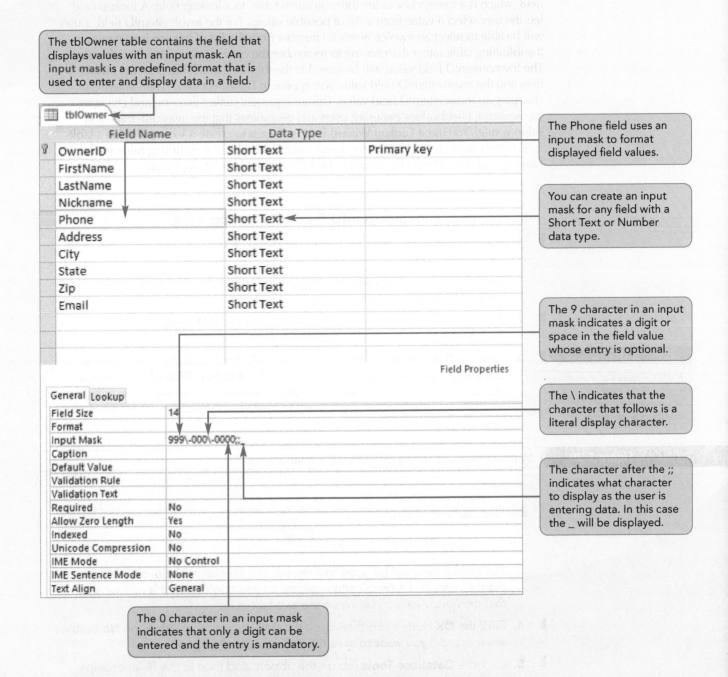

The tblOwner table contains the field that displays values with an input mask. An input mask is a predefined format that is used to enter and display data in a field.

The Phone field uses an input mask to format displayed field values.

You can create an input mask for any field with a Short Text or Number data type.

The 9 character in an input mask indicates a digit or space in the field value whose entry is optional.

The \ indicates that the character that follows is a literal display character.

The character after the ;; indicates what character to display as the user is entering data. In this case the _ will be displayed.

The 0 character in an input mask indicates that only a digit can be entered and the entry is mandatory.

tblOwner

Field Name	Data Type	
OwnerID	Short Text	Primary key
FirstName	Short Text	
LastName	Short Text	
Nickname	Short Text	
Phone	Short Text	
Address	Short Text	
City	Short Text	
State	Short Text	
Zip	Short Text	
Email	Short Text	

Field Properties

General Lookup

Field Size	14
Format	
Input Mask	999\-000\-0000;;
Caption	
Default Value	
Validation Rule	
Validation Text	
Required	No
Allow Zero Length	Yes
Indexed	No
Unicode Compression	No
IME Mode	No Control
IME Sentence Mode	None
Text Align	General

Creating a Lookup Field

The tblBilling table in the CareCenter database contains information about owner invoices. Kimberly wants to make entering data in the table easier for her staff. In particular, data entry is easier if they do not need to remember the correct InvoiceItemID field value for each treatment. Because the tblInvoiceItem and tblBilling tables have a one-to-many relationship, Kimberly asks you to change the tblBilling table's InvoiceItemID field, which is a foreign key to the tblInvoiceItem table, to a lookup field. A lookup field lets the user select a value from a list of possible values. For the InvoiceItemID field, a user will be able to select an invoice item's ID number from the list of invoice item names in the tblBilling table rather than having to remember the correct InvoiceItemID field value. The InvoiceItemID field value will be stored in the tblBilling table, but both the invoice item and the InvoiceItemID field value will appear in Datasheet view when entering or changing an InvoiceItemID field value. This arrangement makes entering and changing InvoiceItemID field values easier for users and guarantees that the InvoiceItemID field value is valid. You use a **Lookup Wizard field** in Access to create a lookup field in a table.

Kimberly asks you to change the InvoiceItemID field in the tblBilling table to a lookup field. You'll begin by opening the tblBilling table in Design view.

To change the InvoiceItemID field to a lookup field:

1. If you took a break after the previous session, make sure that the CareCenter database is open.

   Trouble? If the security warning is displayed below the ribbon, click the Enable Content button next to the warning.

2. If necessary, open the Navigation Pane, open the **tblBilling** table in Design view, and then close the Navigation Pane.

TIP

You can display the arrow and the menu simultaneously if you click the box near its right side.

3. Click the **Data Type** box for the InvoiceItemID field, click the drop-down arrow to display the list of data types, and then click **Lookup Wizard**. A message box appears, instructing you to delete the relationship between the tblBilling and tblInvoiceItem tables if you want to make the InvoiceItemID field a lookup field. See Figure 5-29.

Figure 5-29   Warning message for an existing table relationship

The lookup field will be used to form the one-to-many relationship between the tblBilling and tblInvoiceItem tables, so you don't need the relationship that previously existed between the two tables.

4. Click the **OK** button and then close the tblBilling table, clicking the **No** button when asked if you want to save the table design changes.

5. Click the **Database Tools** tab on the ribbon, and then in the Relationships group, click the **Relationships** button to open the Relationships window.

6. Right-click the join line between the tblBilling and tblInvoiceItem tables, click **Delete**, and then click the **Yes** button to confirm the deletion.

   Trouble? If the Delete command does not appear on the shortcut menu, click a blank area in the Relationships window to close the shortcut menu, and then repeat Step 6, ensuring you right-click on the relationship line.

7. Close the Relationships window.

Now you can resume changing the InvoiceItemID field to a lookup field.

To finish changing the InvoiceItemID field to a lookup field:

1. Open the **tblBilling** table in Design view, and then close the Navigation Pane.

2. Click the right side of the **Data Type** box for the InvoiceItemID field, if necessary click the drop-down arrow, and then click **Lookup Wizard**. The first Lookup Wizard dialog box opens.

This dialog box lets you specify a list of allowed values for the InvoiceItemID field in a record in the tblBilling table. You can specify a table or query from which users select the value, or you can enter a new list of values. You want the InvoiceItemID values to come from the tblInvoiceItem table.

3. Make sure the option for "I want the lookup field to get the values from another table or query" is selected, and then click the **Next** button to display the next Lookup Wizard dialog box.

4. In the View section, click the **Tables** option button, if necessary, to display the list of tables, click **Table: tblInvoiceItem**, and then click the **Next** button to display the next Lookup Wizard dialog box. See Figure 5-30.

Figure 5-30   Selecting the lookup fields

This dialog box lets you select the lookup fields from the tblInvoiceItem table. You need to select the InvoiceItemID field because it's the common field that links the tblInvoiceItem table and the tblBilling table. You must also select the InvoiceItemDesc field because Kimberly wants the user to be able to select from a list of invoice item names when entering a new contract record or changing an existing InvoiceItemID field value.

5. Click the >> button to move the InvoiceItemID and InvoiceItemDesc fields to the Selected Fields box, and then click the **Next** button to display the next Lookup Wizard dialog box. This dialog box lets you choose a sort order for the box entries. Kimberly wants the entries to appear in ascending Invoice Item Description order. Note that ascending is the default sort order.

6. Click the **arrow** for the first box, click **InvoiceItemDesc**, and then click the **Next** button to open the next dialog box.

   In this dialog box, you can adjust the widths of the lookup columns. Note that when you resize a column to its best fit, the column is resized so that the widest column heading and the visible field values fit the column width. However, some field values that aren't visible in this dialog box might be wider than the column width, so you must scroll down the column to make sure you don't have to repeat the column resizing.

7. Click the **Hide key column** check box to remove the checkmark and display the InvoiceItemID field.

8. Click the Invoice Item ID column heading to select it. With the mouse pointer on the Invoice Item ID heading, drag it to the right of the Invoice Item Description column to reposition it.

9. Place the pointer on the right edge of the Invoice Item Description field column heading, and then when the pointer changes to **↔**, double-click to resize the column to its best fit.

10. Scroll down the columns, and repeat Step 9 as necessary until the Invoice Item Description column accommodates all contents, and then press **Ctrl + Home** to scroll back to the top of the columns. See Figure 5-31.

Figure 5-31   **Adjusting the width of the lookup column**

11. Click the **Next** button.

   In the next dialog box, you select the field you want to store in the table. You'll store the InvoiceItemID field in the tblBilling table because it's the foreign key to the tblInvoiceItem table.

12. Click **InvoiceItemID** in the Available Fields box if it's not already selected, and then click the **Next** button.

   In the next dialog box, you specify the field name for the lookup field. Because you'll be storing the InvoiceItemID field in the table, you'll accept the default field name, InvoiceItemID.

13. Click the **Finish** button, and then click **Yes** to save the table.

The Data Type value for the InvoiceItemID field is still Short Text because this field contains text data. However, when you update the field, the InvoiceItemID field value will be used to look up and display in the tblBilling table datasheet both the InvoiceItemDesc and InvoiceItemID field values from the tblInvoiceItem table.

In reviewing animal visits recently, Kimberly noticed that the InvoiceItemID field value stored in the tblBilling table for visit number 42112 is incorrect. She asks you to test the new lookup field to select the correct field value. To do so, you need to switch to Datasheet view.

To change the InvoiceItemID field value:

▶ **1.** Switch to Datasheet view, and then resize the Invoice Item ID column to its best fit.

Notice that the Invoice Item ID column displays InvoiceItem field values, even though the InvoiceItemID field values are stored in the table.

▶ **2.** For Invoice Num 42112, click **Lab work** in the Invoice Item ID column, and then click the **arrow** to display the list of InvoiceItemDesc and InvoiceItemID field values from the tblInvoiceItems table. See Figure 5-32.

| Figure 5-32 | List of InvoiceItemDesc and InvoiceItemID field values |

scrollable list of values for the lookup table

Note that the column displaying InvoiceItemDesc values in your list may be narrower than the values themselves, even though you resized the column. This bug should be fixed in a future version of Access.

The invoice item for visit 42112 should be Pharmacy, so you need to select this entry in the list to change the InvoiceItemID field value.

▶ **3.** Scroll through the list if necessary, and then click **Pharmacy** to select that value to display in the datasheet and to store the InvoiceItemID field value of PHA111 in the table. The list closes, and "Pharmacy" appears in the Invoice Item ID column.

▶ **4.** Save and close the tblBilling table.

Next, Kimberly asks you to change the appearance of the Phone field in the tblOwner table to a standard telephone number format.

Using the Input Mask Wizard

The Phone field in the tblOwner table is a 10-digit number that's difficult to read because it appears with none of the special formatting characters usually associated with a telephone number. For example, the Phone field value for Sally Cruz, which appears as 3074064321, would be more readable in any of the following formats: 307-406-4321, 307.406.4321, 307/406/4321, or (307) 406-4321. Kimberly asks you to use the (307) 406-4321 style for the Phone field.

Kimberly wants the parentheses and hyphens to appear as literal display characters whenever users enter Phone field values. A literal display character is a special character that automatically appears in specific positions of a field value; users don't need to type literal display characters. To include these characters, you need to create an input mask, which is a predefined format used to enter and display data in a field. An easy way to create an input mask is to use the **Input Mask Wizard**, an Access tool that guides you in creating a predefined format for a field. You must be in Design view to use the Input Mask Wizard.

To use the Input Mask Wizard for the Phone field:

1. Open the **tblOwner** table, close the Navigation Pane, and then, if necessary, switch to Design view.

2. Click the **Phone Field Name** box to make that row the current row and to display its Field Properties options.

3. Click the **Input Mask** box in the Field Properties pane. The Build button ⋯ appears at the right edge of the Input Mask box.

4. Click the **Build** button ⋯ in the Input Mask box. The first Input Mask Wizard dialog box opens. See Figure 5-33.

| Figure 5-33 | Input Mask Wizard dialog box |

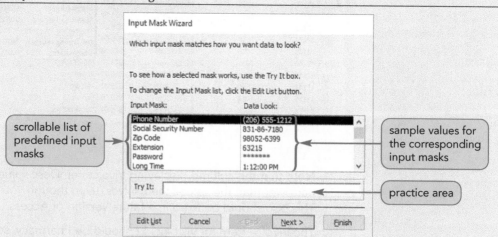

scrollable list of predefined input masks

sample values for the corresponding input masks

practice area

You can scroll the Input Mask box, select the input mask you want, and then enter representative values to practice using the input mask.

5. If necessary, click **Phone Number** in the Input Mask box to select it.

6. Click the far left side of the **Try It** box. (__) ___-____ appears in the Try It box. As you type a phone number, the underscores, which are placeholder characters, are replaced.

   Trouble? If your insertion point is not immediately to the right of the left parenthesis, press the ← key until it is.

7. Type **3074064321** to practice entering a sample phone number. The input mask formats the typed value as (307) 406-4321.

8. Click the **Next** button. The next Input Mask Wizard dialog box opens. In it, you can change the input mask and the placeholder character. Because you can change an input mask easily after the Input Mask Wizard finishes, you'll accept all wizard defaults.

9. Click the **Finish** button, and then click to the right of the value in the Input Mask box to deselect the characters. The Input Mask Wizard creates the phone number input mask, placing it in the Input Mask box for the Phone field. See Figure 5-34.

| Figure 5-34 | Phone number input mask created by the Input Mask Wizard |

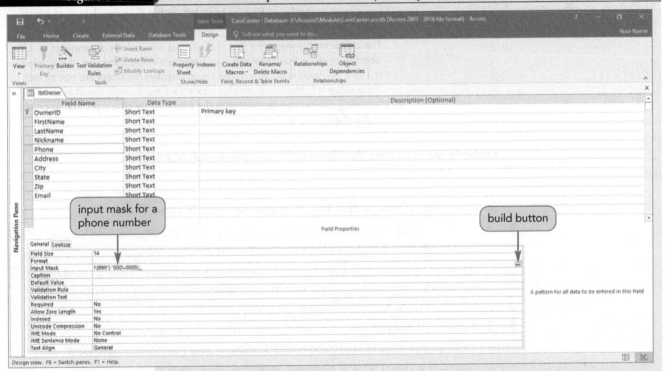

The characters used in a field's input mask restrict the data you can enter in the field, as shown in Figure 5-35. Other characters that appear in an input mask, such as the left and right parentheses in the phone number input mask, are literal display characters.

Figure 5-35	Input mask characters

Input Mask Character	Description
0	Digit only must be entered. Entry is required.
9	Digit or space can be entered. Entry is optional.
#	Digit, space, or a plus or minus sign can be entered. Entry is optional.
L	Letter only must be entered. Entry is required.
?	Letter only can be entered. Entry is optional.
A	Letter or digit must be entered. Entry is required.
a	Letter or digit can be entered. Entry is optional.
&	Any character or a space must be entered. Entry is required.
C	Any character or a space can be entered. Entry is optional.
>	All characters that follow are displayed in uppercase.
<	All characters that follow are displayed in lowercase.
"	Enclosed characters treated as literal display characters.
\	Following character treated as a literal display character. This is the same as enclosing a single character in quotation marks.
!	Input mask is displayed from right to left, rather than the default of left to right. Characters typed into the mask always fill in from left to right.
;;	The character between the first and second semicolons determines whether to store the literal display characters in the database. If the value is 1 or if no value is provided, the literal display characters are not stored. If the value is 0, the literal display characters are stored. The character following the second semicolon is the placeholder character that appears in the displayed input mask.

Kimberly wants to view the Phone field with the default input mask.

To view and change the input mask for the Phone field:

1. Save the table, and then switch to Datasheet view. The Phone field values now have the format specified by the input mask.

   Kimberly decides that she would prefer to omit the parentheses around the area codes and use only hyphens as separators in the displayed Phone field values, so you'll change the input mask in Design view.

2. Switch to Design view.

   The input mask is set to !\(999") "000\-0000;;_. The backslash character (\) causes the character that follows it to appear as a literal display character. Characters enclosed in quotation marks also appear as literal display characters. (See Figure 5-35.) The exclamation mark (!) forces the existing data to fill the input mask from right to left instead of left to right. This does not affect new data. This applies only to the situation when data already exists in the table and a new input mask is applied. For instance, if the existing data is 5551234 and the input mask fills from left to right, the data with the input mask would look like (555) 123-4. If the input mask fills from right to left, the data with the input mask applied would look like ( ) 555-1234.

   If you omit the backslashes preceding the hyphens, they will automatically be inserted when you press the Tab key. However, backslashes are not added automatically for other literal display characters, such as periods and slashes, so it's best to always type the backslashes. Since all of the existing data includes the area code, it will not make a difference whether the input mask applied to the data fills the data from left to right or from right to left, so you'll omit the ! symbol.

▶ **3.** In the Input Mask box for the Phone field, change the input mask to **999\-000\-0000;;_** and then press the **Tab** key.

Because you've modified a field property, the Property Update Options button 🗲 appears to the left of the Input Mask property.

▶ **4.** Click the **Property Update Options** button 🗲. A menu opens below the button, as shown in Figure 5-36.

| Figure 5-36 | Property Update Options button menu |

Property Update Options button

▶ **5.** Click **Update Input Mask everywhere Phone is used**. The Update Properties dialog box opens. See Figure 5-37.

| Figure 5-37 | Update Properties dialog box |

object dependent on Phone field

Because the frmOwner form displays the Phone field values from the tblOwner table, the Phone field's Input Mask property in this object will automatically be changed to your new input mask. If other form objects included the Phone field from the tblOwner table, they would be included in this dialog box as well. This capability to update field properties in objects automatically when you modify a table field property is called **property propagation**. Although the Update Properties dialog box displays no queries, property propagation also occurs with queries automatically. Property propagation is limited to field properties such as the Decimal Places, Description, Format, and Input Mask properties.

6. Click the **Yes** button, save the table, switch to Datasheet view, and then resize the Phone column to its best fit. The Phone field values now have the format Kimberly requested. See Figure 5-38.

| Figure 5-38 | After changing the Phone field input mask |

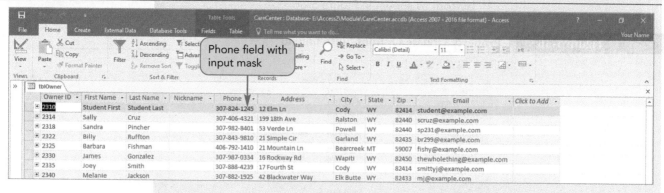

Because Kimberly wants her staff to store only standard 10-digit U.S. phone numbers for owners, the input mask you've created will enforce the standard entry and display format that Kimberly desires.

Understanding When to Use Input Masks

An input mask is appropriate for a field only if all field values have a consistent format. For example, you can use an input mask with hyphens as literal display characters to store U.S. phone numbers in a consistent format of 987-654-3210. However, a multinational company would not be able to use an input mask to store phone numbers from all countries because international phone numbers do not have a consistent format. In the same way, U.S. zip codes have a consistent format, and you could use an input mask of 00000#9999 to enter and display U.S. zip codes such as 98765 and 98765-4321, but you could not use an input mask if you need to store and display foreign postal codes in the same field. If you need to store and display phone numbers, zip/postal codes, and other fields in a variety of formats, it's best to define them as Short Text fields without an input mask so users can enter the correct literal display characters.

After you changed the Phone field's input mask, you had the option to update, selectively and automatically, the Phone field's Input Mask property in other objects in the database. Kimberly is thinking about making significant changes to the way data is stored in the tblOwner table and wants to understand which other elements those changes might impact. To determine the dependencies among objects in an Access database, you'll open the Object Dependencies pane.

Identifying Object Dependencies

An **object dependency** exists between two objects when a change to the properties of data in one object affects the properties of data in the other object. Dependencies between Access objects, such as tables, queries, and forms, can occur in various ways. For example, the tblVisit and tblBilling tables are dependent on each other because they have a one-to-many relationship. In the same way, the tblOwner table uses the qryOwnersByName query to obtain the Owner field to display along with the OwnerID field, and this creates a dependency between these two objects. Any query, form, or other object that uses fields from a given table is dependent on that table. Any form or report that uses fields from a query is directly dependent on the query and is indirectly dependent on the tables that provide the data to the query. Large databases contain hundreds of objects, so it is useful to have a way to easily view the dependencies among objects before you attempt to delete or modify an object. The **Object Dependencies pane** displays a collapsible list of the dependencies among the objects in an Access database; you click the list's expand indicators to show or hide different levels of dependencies. Next, you'll open the Object Dependencies pane to examine the object dependencies in the CareCenter database.

To open and use the Object Dependencies pane:

1. Click the **Database Tools** tab on the ribbon.

2. In the Relationships group, click the **Object Dependencies** button to open the Object Dependencies pane, and then drag the left edge of the pane to the left until none of the items in the list are cut off.

3. If necessary, click the **Objects that depend on me** option button to select it, then click the **Refresh** link to display the list of objects. See Figure 5-39.

Figure 5-39   After opening the Object Dependencies pane

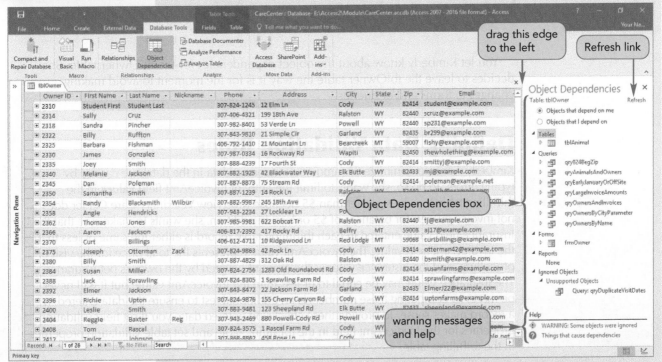

The Object Dependencies pane displays the objects that depend on the tblOwner table, the object name that appears at the top of the pane. If you change the design of the tblOwner table, the change might affect objects in the pane. Changing a property for a field in the tblOwner table that's also used by a listed object affects that listed object. If a listed object does not use the field you are changing, that listed object is not affected.

Objects listed in the Ignored Objects section of the box might have an object dependency with the tblOwner table, and you'd have to review them individually to determine if a dependency exists. The Help section at the bottom of the pane displays links for further information about object dependencies.

4. Click the **frmOwner** link in the Object Dependencies pane. The frmOwner form opens in Design view. All the fields in the form are fields from the tblOwner table, which is why the form has an object dependency with the table.

5. Switch to Form view for the frmOwner form. Note that the Phone field value is displayed using the input mask you applied to the field in the tblOwner table. This change was propagated from the table to the form.

6. Close the frmOwner form, open the Navigation Pane, open the **tblAnimal** table in Datasheet view, and then click the **Refresh** link near the top of the Object Dependencies pane. The Object Dependencies box now displays the objects that depend on the tblAnimal table.

7. Click the **Objects that I depend on** option button near the top of the pane to view the objects that affect the tblAnimal table.

8. Click the **Objects that depend on me** option button, and then click the **expand indicator** ▷ for the qryAnimalsAndOwners query in the Object Dependencies pane. The list expands to display the qryInactiveAnimals query, which is another query that the qryAnimalsAndOwners query depends upon.

9. Close the tblAnimal table, close the Object Dependencies pane, and then save and close the tblOwner table.

You let Kimberly know about the object dependencies for the tblOwner table. She decides to leave the tblOwner table the way it is for the moment to avoid making changes to forms and/or queries.

Defining Data Validation Rules

Kimberly wants to minimize the amount of incorrect data in the database caused by typing errors. To do so, she wants to limit the entry of InvoiceAmt field values in the tblBilling table to values greater than $5 because Riverview Veterinary Care Center does not invoice owners for balances of $5 or less. In addition, she wants to make sure that the Insurance field value entered in each tblBilling table record is either the same or less than the InvoiceAmt field value. The InvoiceAmt value represents the total price for the visit or procedure, and the Insurance value is the amount covered by the owner's pet insurance. The Insurance value may be equal to or less than the InvoiceAmt value, but it will never be more, so comparing these numbers is an additional test to ensure the data entered in a record makes sense. To provide these checks on entered data, you'll set field validation properties for the InvoiceAmt field in the tblBilling table and set table validation properties in the tblBilling table.

Defining Field Validation Rules

To prevent a user from entering an unacceptable value in the InvoiceAmt field, you can create a **field validation rule** that verifies a field value by comparing it to a constant or to a set of constants. You create a field validation rule by setting the Validation Rule and the Validation Text field properties. The **Validation Rule property** value specifies the valid values that users can enter in a field. The **Validation Text property** value will be displayed in a dialog box if a user enters an invalid value (in this case, an InvoiceAmt field value of $5 or less). After you set these two InvoiceAmt field properties in the tblBilling table, users will be prevented from entering an invalid InvoiceAmt field value in the tblBilling table and in all current and future queries and future forms that include the InvoiceAmt field.

You'll now set the Validation Rule and Validation Text properties for the InvoiceAmt field in the tblBilling table.

To create and test a field validation rule for the InvoiceAmt field:

1. Open the **tblBilling** table in Design view, close the Navigation Pane, and then click the **InvoiceAmt Field Name** box to make that row the current row.

   To make sure that all values entered in the InvoiceAmt field are greater than 5, you'll use the > comparison operator in the Validation Rule box.

2. In the Field Properties pane, click the **Validation Rule** box, type **>5**, and then press the **Tab** key.

   You can set the Validation Text property to a value that appears in a dialog box that opens if a user enters a value not listed in the Validation Rule box.

3. In the Validation Text box, type **Invoice amounts must be greater than 5.** See Figure 5-40.

Figure 5-40	Validation properties for the InvoiceAmt field

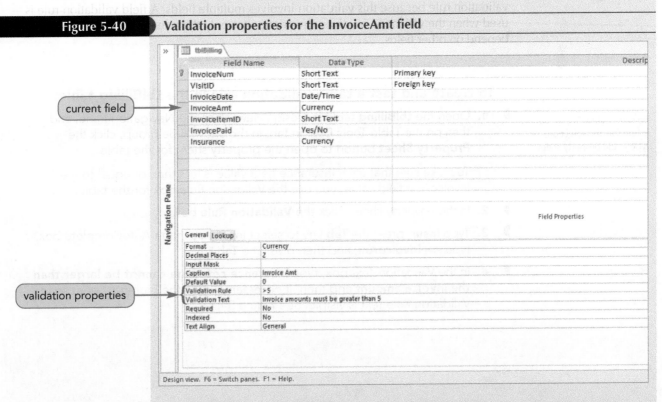

You can now save the table design changes and then test the validation properties.

▶ 4. Save the table, and then click the **Yes** button when asked if you want to test the existing InvoiceAmt field values in the tblBilling table against the new validation rule.

The existing records in the tblBilling table are tested against the validation rule. If any existing record violated the rule, you would be prompted to continue testing or to revert to the previous Validation Rule property setting. Next, you'll test the validation rule.

▶ 5. Switch to Datasheet view, select **$50.00** in the first row's InvoiceAmt field box, type **3**, and then press the **Tab** key. A dialog box opens containing the message "Invoice amounts must be greater than 5," which is the Validation Text property setting you created in Step 3.

▶ 6. Click the **OK** button, and then press the **Esc** key. The first row's InvoiceAmt field reverts to its original value, $50.00.

▶ 7. Close the tblBilling table.

Now that you've finished entering the field validation rule for the InvoiceAmt field in the tblBilling table, you'll enter the table validation rule for the date fields in the tblVisit table.

Defining Table Validation Rules

To make sure that the Insurance field value that a user enters in the tblBilling table is not larger than the InvoiceAmt field value, you can create a **table validation rule**. Once again, you'll use the Validation Rule and Validation Text properties, but this time you'll set these properties for the table instead of for an individual field. You'll use a table validation rule because this validation involves multiple fields. A field validation rule is used when the validation involves a restriction for only the selected field and does not depend on other fields.

To create and test a table validation rule in the tblBilling table:

▶ 1. Open the **tblBilling** table in Design view, close the Navigation Pane, and then on the Table Tools Design tab, in the Show/Hide group, click the **Property Sheet** button to open the property sheet for the table.

To make sure that each Insurance field value is less than or equal to the InvoiceAmt field value, you use the Validation Rule box for the table.

Be sure "Table Properties" is listed as the selection type in the property sheet.

▶ 2. In the property sheet, click the **Validation Rule** box.

▶ 3. Type **Insur**, press the **Tab** key to select Insurance in the AutoComplete box, type **<= InvoiceAm**, and then press the **Tab** key.

▶ 4. In the Validation Text box, type **Insurance coverage cannot be larger than the invoice amount** and then, if necessary, widen the Property Sheet so the Validation Rule text is visible. See Figure 5-41.

Figure 5-41   Setting table validation properties

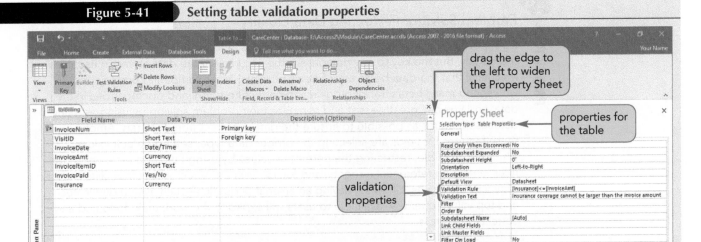

You can now test the validation properties.

5. Close the property sheet, save the table, and then click the **Yes** button when asked if you want to test the existing dates in the tblBilling table against the new validation rule.

6. Switch to Datasheet view, and then click the Insurance column value in the first record.

7. Edit the Insurance value to change it to $150.00, and then press the **Tab** key to complete your changes to the record. A dialog box opens containing the message "Insurance coverage cannot be larger than the invoice amount," which is the Validation Text property setting you entered in Step 4.

Unlike field validation rule violations, which are detected immediately after you finish a field entry and advance to another field, table validation rule violations are detected only when you finish all changes to the current record and advance to another record.

8. Click the **OK** button, and then press the **Esc** key to undo your change to the Insurance column value.

9. Close the tblBilling table.

Problem Solving: Perfecting Data Quality

It's important that you design useful queries, forms, and reports and that you test them thoroughly. But the key to any database is the accuracy of the data stored in its tables. It's critical that the data be as error-free as possible. Most companies employ people who spend many hours tracking down and correcting errors and discrepancies in their data, and you can greatly assist and minimize their problem solving by using as many database features as possible to ensure the data is correct from the start. Among these features for fields are selecting the proper data type, setting default values whenever possible, restricting the permitted values by using field and table validation rules, enforcing referential integrity, and forcing users to select values from lists instead of typing the values. Likewise, having an arsenal of queries—such as find duplicates and top values queries—available to users will expedite the work they do to find and correct data errors.

Based on a request from Kimberly, Daksha added a Long Text field to the tblVisit table. Next you'll review Daksha's work.

Working with Long Text Fields

You use a Long Text field to store long comments and explanations. Short Text fields are limited to 255 characters, but Long Text fields can hold up to 65,535 characters. In addition, Short Text fields limit you to plain text with no special formatting, but you can define Long Text fields to store plain text similar to Short Text fields or to store rich text, which you can selectively format with options such as bold, italic, and different fonts and colors.

You'll review the Long Text field, named Comments, that Daksha added to the tblVisit table.

To review the Long Text field in the tblVisit table:

1. Open the Navigation Pane, open the **tblVisit** table in Datasheet view, and then close the Navigation Pane.

2. Increase the width of the Comments field so most of the comments fit in the column.

   Although everything fits on the screen when using a screen of average size and resolution, on some computer systems freezing panes is necessary to be able to view everything at once. On a smaller screen, if you scroll to the right to view the Comments field, you'll no longer be able to identify which animal applies to a row because the Animal ID column will be hidden. You may also see this effect if you shrink the size of the Access window. You'll freeze the Visit ID, Animal ID, and Date of Visit columns so they remain visible in the datasheet as you scroll to the right.

3. Click the **Visit ID column** selector, press and hold down the **Shift** key, click the **Date of Visit** column selector, and then release the **Shift** key. The Visit ID, Animal ID, and Date of Visit columns are selected.

4. On the Home tab, in the Records group, click the **More** button, and then click **Freeze Fields**.

5. If necessary, reduce the size of the Access window so not all columns are visible, and then scroll to the right until you see the Comments column. Notice that the Visit ID, Animal ID, and Date of Visit columns, the three leftmost columns, remain visible when you scroll. See Figure 5-42.

| Figure 5-42 | Freezing three datasheet columns |

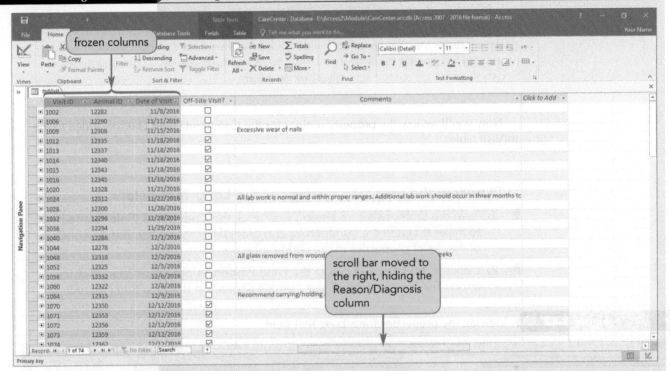

The Comments column is a Long Text field that Riverview Veterinary Care Center clinicians use to store observations and other commentary about each animal visit. Note that the Comment for Visit ID 1048 displays rich text using a bold and red font. Comments field values are partially hidden because the datasheet column is not wide enough. You'll view a record's Comments field value in the Zoom dialog box.

6. Click the **Comments** box for the record for Visit ID 1024, hold down the **Shift** key, press the **F2** key, and then release the **Shift** key. The Zoom dialog box displays the entire Comments field value.

7. Click the **OK** button to close the Zoom dialog box.

INSIGHT

Viewing Long Text Fields with Large Contents in Datasheet View

For a Long Text field that contains many characters, you can widen the field's column to view more of its contents by dragging the right edge of the field's column selector to the right or by using the Field Width command when you click the More button in the Records group on the Home tab. However, increasing the column width reduces the number of other columns you can view at the same time. Further, for Long Text fields containing thousands of characters, you can't widen the column enough to be able to view the entire contents of the field at one time across the width of the screen. Therefore, increasing the column width of a Long Text field isn't necessarily the best strategy for viewing table contents. Instead, you should use the Zoom dialog box in a datasheet or use a large scrollable box on a form.

Now you'll review the property settings for the Comments field Daksha added to the tblVisit table.

To review the property settings of the Long Text field:

1. Save the table, switch to Design view, click the **Comments Field Name** box to make that row the current row, and then, if necessary, scroll to the bottom of the list of properties in the Field Properties pane.

2. Click the **Text Format** box in the Field Properties pane, and then click its arrow. The list of available text formats appears in the box. See Figure 5-43.

Figure 5-43	Viewing the properties for a Long Text field

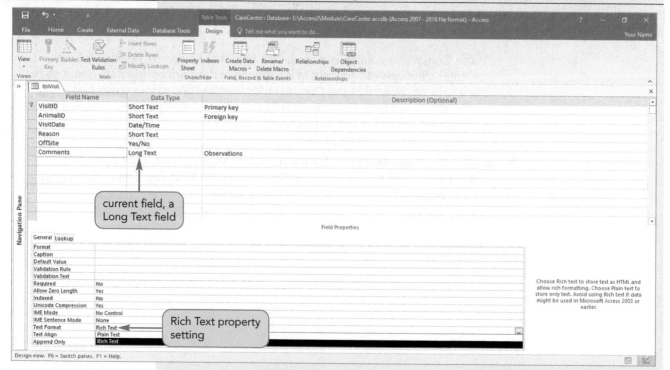

Daksha set the **Text Format property** for the Comments field to Rich Text, which lets you format the field contents using the options in the Font group on the Home tab. The default Text Format property setting for a Long Text field is Plain Text, which doesn't allow text formatting.

3. Click the **arrow** on the Text Format box to close the list, and then click the **Append Only** box.

   The **Append Only property**, which appears at the bottom of the list of properties, enables you to track the changes that you make to a Long Text field. Setting this property to Yes causes a historical record of all versions of the Long Text field value to be maintained. You can view each version of the field value, along with a date and time stamp of when each version change occurred.

   You've finished your review of the Long Text field, so you can close the table.

4. Close the tblVisit table.

When employees at Riverview Veterinary Care Center open the CareCenter database, a security warning might appear below the ribbon, and they must enable the content of the database before beginning their work. Kimberly asks if you can eliminate this extra step when employees open the database.

Designating a Trusted Folder

A database is a file, and files can contain malicious instructions that can damage other files on your computer or files on other computers on your network. Unless you take special steps, every database is treated as a potential threat to your computer. One special step that you can take is to designate a folder as a trusted folder. A **trusted folder** is a folder on a drive or network that you designate as trusted and where you place databases you know are safe. When you open a database located in a trusted folder, it is treated as a safe file, and a security warning is no longer displayed. You can also place files used with other Microsoft Office programs, such as Word documents and Excel workbooks, in a trusted folder to eliminate warnings when you open them.

Because the CareCenter database is from a trusted source, you'll specify its location as a trusted folder to eliminate the security warning when a user opens the database.

To designate a trusted folder:

1. Click the **File** tab, and then click **Options** in the navigation bar. The Access Options dialog box opens.

2. In the left section of the dialog box, click **Trust Center**. The Trust Center options are displayed in the dialog box.

3. In the right section of the dialog box, click the **Trust Center Settings** button to open the Trust Center dialog box.

4. In the left section of the Trust Center dialog box, click **Trusted Locations**. The trusted locations for your installation of Access and other trust options are displayed on the right. See Figure 5-44.

Figure 5-44 Designating a trusted folder

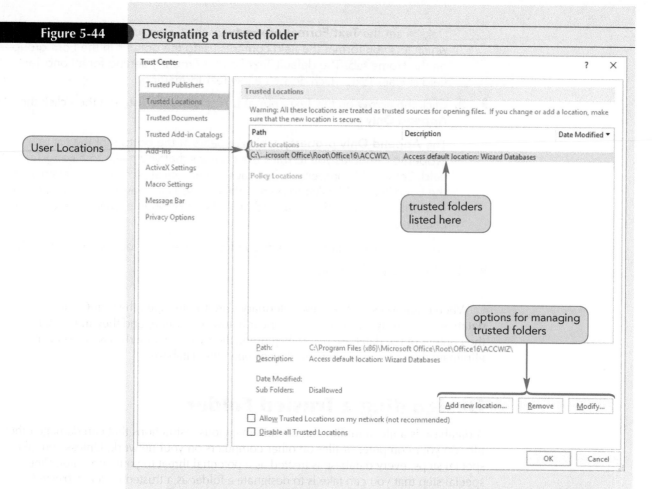

Existing trusted locations appear in the list at the top, and options to add, remove, and modify trusted locations appear at the bottom.

Trouble? Check with your instructor before adding a new trusted location. If your instructor tells you not to create a new trusted location, skip to Step 8.

5. Click the **Add new location** button to open the Microsoft Office Trusted Location dialog box.

6. In the Microsoft Office Trusted Location dialog box, click the **Browse** button, navigate to the Access2 > Module folder where your Data Files are stored, and then click the **OK** button.

You can also choose to designate subfolders of the selected location as trusted locations, but you won't select this option. By default, files in subfolders are not trusted.

7. Click the **OK** button. The Access2 > Module folder is added to the list of trusted locations.

8. Click the **OK** button to close the Trust Center dialog box, and then click the **OK** button to close the Access Options dialog box.

You've created several queries and completed several table design changes, so you should compact and repair the CareCenter database. Daksha doesn't use the Compact on Close option with the CareCenter database because it's possible to lose the database if there's a computer malfunction when the Compact on Close operation runs.

As a precaution, you'll make a backup copy of the database before you compact and repair it. Making frequent backup copies of your critical files safeguards your data from hardware and software malfunctions, which can occur at any time.

To back up, compact, and repair the CareCenter database:

▶ **1.** Click the **File** tab on the ribbon, and then click the **Save As** menu item.

▶ **2.** Click the **Back Up Database** option, and then click the **Save As** button. The Save As dialog box opens with a suggested filename of CareCenter_date in the File name box, where date is the current date in the format year-month-day. For instance, if you made a backup on February 15, 2017, the suggested filename would be CareCenter_2017-02-15.

▶ **3.** Navigate to the location of a USB drive or other external medium, if available, and then click the **Save** button to save the backup file.

Next, you'll verify that the trusted location is working.

▶ **4.** Click the **File** tab on the ribbon, and then click the **Close** command to close the CareCenter database.

▶ **5.** Click the **File** tab on the ribbon, click **Open** on the navigation bar, and then click **CareCenter.accdb** in the Recent list. The database opens, and no security warning appears below the ribbon because the database is located in the trusted location you designated.

Next, you'll compact and repair the database.

▶ **6.** Click the **File** tab on the ribbon, and then click the **Compact & Repair Database** button.

▶ **7.** Close the CareCenter database.

You've completed the table design changes to the CareCenter database, which will make working with it easier and more accurate.

Session 5.3 Quick Check

REVIEW

1. What is a lookup field?

2. A(n) _____ is a predefined format you use to enter and display data in a field.

3. What is property propagation?

4. Define the Validation Rule property, and give an example of when you would use it.

5. Define the Validation Text property, and give an example of when you would use it.

6. Setting a Long Text field's Text Format property to _____ lets you format its contents.

7. A(n) _____ folder is a location where you can place databases that you know are safe.

Review Assignments

PRACTICE

Data File needed for the Review Assignments: Supplier.accdb

Kimberly asks you to create several new queries and enhance the table design for the Vendor database. This database contains information about the vendors that Riverview Veterinary Care Center works with to obtain medical supplies and equipment for the center, as well as the vendors who service and maintain the equipment. Complete the following steps:

1. Open the **Supplier** database located in the Access2 > Review folder provided with your Data Files.

2. Modify the first record in the **tblSupplier** table datasheet by changing the Contact First Name and Contact Last Name field values to your first and last names. Close the table.

3. Create a query called **qrySupplierNameAndAddress** that lists the following fields from the tblSupplier table: SupplierID, Company, City, State, and Zip. After you have created the query, use the Autofilter feature of Access to list on the suppliers in NC, SC, and VA only. Use the Toggle Filter button to remove and reapply the filter. Save and close the query.

4. Create a query to find all records in the tblSupplier table in which the City field value starts with the letter A. Display all fields in the query recordset, and sort in ascending order by the Company Name. Save the query as **qryASelectedCities**, run the query, and then close it.

5. Make a copy of the qryASelectedCities query using the new name **qryOtherSelectedCities**. Modify the new query to find all records in the tblSupplier table in which the City field values are not Boston, Charlotte, or Billings. Save and run the query, and then close it.

6. Create a query to find all records from the tblSupplier table in which the State value is GA, MA, or NC. Use a list-of-values match for the selection criteria. Display all fields in the query recordset, and sort in descending order by the company name. Save the query as **qrySelectedStates**, run the query, and then close it.

7. Create a query to display all records from the tblSupplier table, selecting the Company, City, and Phone fields, and sorting in ascending order by Company. Add a calculated field named **ContactName** as the last column that concatenates the ContactFirst value, a space, and the ContactLast value. If the contact has a nickname, use the nickname in place of the first name in the calculated field. Set the Caption property for the ContactName field to **Contact Name**. Save the query as **qryCompanyContacts**, run the query, resize the Contact Name column to its best fit, and then save and close the query.

8. Create a parameter query to select the tblSupplier table records for a State field value that the user specifies. If the user doesn't enter a State field value, select all records from the table. Display the Company, Category, City, State, ContactFirst, ContactLast, and Phone fields in the query recordset, sorting in ascending order by City. Save the query as **qryStateParameter**. Run the query and enter no value as the State field value, and then run the query again and enter **NC** as the State field value. Close the query.

9. Create a find duplicates query based on the tblProduct table. Select ProductName as the field that might contain duplicates, and select the ProductID, SupplierID, Price, and Units fields as additional fields in the query recordset. Save the query as **qryDuplicateProductTypes**, run the query, and then close it. Because the tblProduct table does not have any duplicate ProductName values, running this query should show that no duplicate records are found.

10. Create a find unmatched query that finds all records in the tblSupplier table for which there is no matching record in the tblProduct table. Display the SupplierID, Company, City, State, Phone, ContactFirst, and ContactLast fields from the tblSupplier table in the query recordset. Save the query as **qrySuppliersWithoutMatchingProducts**, run the query, and then close it. Because the tblSupplier and tblProduct tables do not have unmatched records, running this query should show that no unmatched records are found.

11. Create a query to display all records from the tblProduct table, selecting the ProductID, SupplierID, ProductName, and Price fields, and sorting in descending order by Price. Use the Top Values property to select the top 25 percent of records. Save the query as **qryTop25Price**, run the query, and then close it.

12. In the tblProduct table, change the SupplierID field to a lookup field. Select the Company field and then the SupplierID field from the tblSupplier table. Sort in ascending order by the Company field, do not hide the key column, make sure the Company Name column is the leftmost column, resize the lookup columns to their best fit, select SupplierID as the field to store in the table, and accept the default label for the lookup column. View the tblProduct table datasheet, resize the Supplier ID column to its best fit, test the lookup field without changing a value permanently, and then save and close the table.

13. Use the Input Mask Wizard to add an input mask to the Phone field in the tblSupplier table. The ending input mask should use periods as separators, as in 987.654.3210 with only the last seven digits required; do not store the literal display characters, if you are asked to do so. Update the Input Mask property everywhere the Phone field is used. Resize all columns in the datasheet to their best fit, and then test the input mask by typing over an existing Phone field value, being sure not to change the value by pressing the Esc key after you type the last digit in the Phone field.

14. Create a crosstab query based on the tblSupplier table. Use the Category field values for the row headings, the SupplierID field values for the column headings, and the count of the Company field values as the summarized value, and include row sums. Save the query as **qrySupplierCategoryCrosstab**. Change the column heading for the total of each category to **Total of Companies**. Resize the Total of Companies column in the query recordset to its best fit, and then save and close the query.

15. Open the tblProduct table, and then open the Object Dependencies pane for the tblProduct object. Click on the Objects that depend on me option button, then click the Refresh link if necessary to see the list of objects that depend upon the tblProduct table. Verify that the following objects depend upon the tblProduct table: tblSupplier table, qrySuppliersWithoutMatchingProducts query, and qryTop25Price query. Close the Object Dependencies pane.

16. Set a field validation rule on the Price field in the tblProduct table. Ensure that each product entered will have a price greater than zero. Should a user attempt to enter a value of zero, or less than zero, the following message should be displayed: "All prices must be greater than zero." Test the field validation rule by modifying the price of the first item in the recordset to 0, and verify that the error message is displayed. Reset the value of the record to its original value. Save and close the tblProduct table.

17. Open the tblSupplier table, and then set a table validation rule on the tblSupplier table to ensure the initial contact date is prior to, or equal to, the latest contact date. If an invalid value is entered, the following message should be displayed: "Latest contact date cannot be prior to the initial contact date." Test the table validation rule by changing the latest contact date prior to the initial contact date in the first record. Advance to the next record, then verify that the error message is displayed. Reset the values of the first record to their original values. Save your changes to the tblSupplier table.

18. In the tblSupplier table, examine the field properties pane for the Notes field. Verify that the Text Format property is set to Rich Text, and that the Append Only property is set to Yes. Close the tblSupplier table without saving changes.

19. Designate the Access2 > Review folder as a trusted folder. (*Note:* Check with your instructor before adding a new trusted location.)

20. Make a backup copy of the database, compact and repair the database, and then close it.

Case Problem 1

Data File needed for this Case Problem: MoreBeauty.accdb

Beauty To Go   Sue Miller, an owner of a nail and hair salon in Orlando, Florida, regularly checks in on her grandmother, who resides in a retirement community. On some of her visits, Sue does her grandmother's hair and nails. Her grandmother told Sue that some of her friends would be glad to pay her and have regularly scheduled services if she could do their hair and nails also. Sue expanded her business to include the services to friends of her grandmother in local retirement communities to meet the needs of these ladies. Sue created an Access database named MoreBeauty to store data about members, plans, and contracts. She wants to create several new queries and make design changes to the tables. Complete the following steps:

1. Open the **MoreBeauty** database located in the Access2 > Case1 folder provided with your Data Files.

2. Modify the first record in the tblMember table datasheet by changing the First Name and Last Name column values to your first and last names. Close the table.

3. Create a query to find all records in the tblOption table in which the OptionCost field is 70, 125, 140, or 250. Use a list-of-values match for the selection criterion, and include all fields from the table in the query recordset. Sort the query in descending order by the OptionID field. Save the query as **qryLowVolumePlans**, run the query, and then close it.

4. Make a copy of the qryLowVolumePlans query using the new name **qryHighVolumePlans**. Modify the new query to find all records in the tblPlan table in which the PlanCost field is not 70, 125, 140, or 250. Save and run the query, and then close it.

5. Create a query to display all records from the tblMember table, selecting the LastName, FirstName, Street, and Phone fields, and sorting in ascending order by LastName and then in ascending order by FirstName. Add a calculated field named **MemberName** as the first column that concatenates FirstName, a space, and LastName. Set the Caption property for the MemberName field to **Member Name**. Do not display the LastName and FirstName fields in the query recordset. Create a second calculated field named **CityLine**, inserting it between the Street and Phone fields. The CityLine field concatenates City, a space, State, two spaces, and Zip. Set the Caption property for the CityLine field to **City Line**. Save the query as **qryMemberNames**, run the query, resize all columns to their best fit, and then save and close the query.

6. Create a query to display all matching records from the tblOption and tblMember tables, selecting the LastName and FirstName fields from the tblMember table and the OptionDescription and OptionCost fields from the tblOption table. Add a calculated field named **FeeStatus** as the last column that equals *Fee Waived* if the FeeWaived field is equal to *yes*, and that equals *Fee Not Waived* otherwise. Set the Caption property for the calculated field to **Fee Status**. Sort the list in ascending order on the LastName field. Save the query as **qryFeeStatus**, run the query, resize all columns to their best fit, and then save and close the query.

7. Create a query based on the tblOption and tblMember tables, selecting the LastName, FirstName, and City fields from the tblMember table and the FeeWaived, OptionDescription, and OptionCost fields from the tblOption table. The query should find the records in which the City field value is Orlando or Celebration and the FeeWaived field value is *Yes*. Save the query as **qryOrlandoAndCelebrationFeeWaived**. Save and run the query, and then close the query.

8. Create a parameter query to select the tblMember table records for a City field value that the user specifies. If the user doesn't enter a City field value, select all records from the table. Display all fields from the tblMember table in the query recordset. Save the query as **qryMemberCityParameter**. Run the query and enter no value as the City field value, and then run the query again and enter **Celebration** as the City field value. Close the query.

9. Create a find duplicates query based on the tblMember table. Select OptionEnd as the field that might contain duplicates, and select all other fields in the table as additional fields in the query recordset. Save the query as **qryDuplicateMemberExpirationDates**, run the query, and then close it.

10. Create a find unmatched query that finds all records in the tblMember table for which there is no matching record in the tblOption table. Select FirstName, LastName, and Phone fields from the tblMembers table. Save the query as **qryMembersWithoutPlans**, run the query, and then close it. Because the tblMember and tblOption tables do not have unmatched records, running this query should show that no unmatched records are found.

11. Create a new query based on the tblMember table. Display the FirstName, LastName, Phone, OptionEnd, and OptionID fields, in this order, in the query recordset. Sort in ascending order by the OptionEnd field, and then use the Top Values property to select the top 25 percent of records. Save the query as **qryUpcomingExpirations**, run the query, and then close it.

12. Use the Input Mask Wizard to add an input mask to the Phone field in the tblMember table. Create the input mask such that the phone number is displayed with a dot separating each part of the phone number. For instance, if the phone number is (303) 123-4567 it should be displayed as 303.123.4567 for new entries. Test the input mask by typing over an existing Phone column value, being certain not to change the value by pressing the Esc key after you type the last digit in the Phone column, and then save and close the table.

13. Define a field validation rule for the OptionCost field in the tblOption table. Acceptable field values for the OptionCost field are values greater than or equal to 70. Enter the message **Value must be greater than or equal to 70** so it appears if a user enters an invalid OptionCost field value. Save your table changes, and then test the field validation rule for the OptionCost field; be certain the field values are the same as they were before your testing, and then close the table.

14. Define a table validation rule for the tblMember table to verify that OptionBegin field values precede OptionEnd field values in time. Use an appropriate validation message. Save your table changes, and then test the table validation rule, making sure any tested field values are the same as they were before your testing.

15. Add a Long Text field named **MemberComments** as the last field in the tblMember table. Set the Caption property to **Member Comments** and the Text Format property to Rich Text. In the table datasheet, resize the new column to its best fit, and then add a comment in the Member Comments column in the first record about special instructions for this member, formatting part of the text with blue, italic font. Save your table changes, and then close the table.

16. Designate the Access2 > Case1 folder as a trusted folder. (*Note:* Check with your instructor before adding a new trusted location.)

17. Make a backup copy of the database, compact and repair the database, and then close it.

APPLY

Case Problem 2

Data File needed for this Case Problem: Tutoring.accdb

Programming Pros   While in college obtaining his bachelor's degree in Raleigh, North Carolina, Brent Hovis majored in computer science. Prior to graduating, Brent began tutoring freshman and sophomore students in programming to make some extra money. When Brent entered graduate school, he started Programming Pros, a company offering expanded tutoring services for high school and college students through group, private, and semiprivate tutoring sessions. Brent created an Access database to maintain information about the tutors who work for him, the students who sign up for tutoring, and the contracts they sign. To make the database easier to use, Brent wants you to create several queries and modify its table design. Complete the following steps:

1. Open the **Tutoring** database located in the Access2 > Case2 folder provided with your Data Files.
2. Change the last record in the tblTutor table datasheet so the FirstName and LastName field values contain your first and last names. Close the table.
3. Create a query to find all records in the tblStudent table in which the LastName field value begins with L. Display the FirstName, LastName, City, and HomePhone fields in the query recordset, and sort in ascending order by LastName. Save the query as **qryLastNameL**, run the query, and then close it.
4. Create a query that finds all records in the tblTutor table in which the YearInSchool field value is either Senior or Graduate. Use a list-of-values criterion, and include the fields First Name, Last Name, and YearInSchool in the recordset, sorted in ascending order on the LastName field. Save the query using the name **qrySelectedYearInSchool**. Run the query, and then close it.
5. Create a query to find all records in the tblStudent table in which the City field value is not equal to Raleigh. Display the FirstName, LastName, City, and HomePhone fields in the query recordset, and sort in ascending order by City. Save the query as **qryNonRaleigh**, run the query, and then close it.
6. Create a query to display all records from the tblTutor table, selecting all fields, and sorting in ascending order by LastName and then in ascending order by FirstName. Add a calculated field named **TutorName** as the second column that concatenates FirstName, a space, and LastName for each teacher. Set the Caption property for the TutorName field to **Tutor Name**. Do not display the FirstName and LastName fields in the query recordset. Save the query as **qryTutorNames**, run the query, resize the Tutor Name column to its best fit, and then save and close the query.
7. Create a parameter query to select the tblContract table records for a SessionType field value that the user specifies. If the user doesn't enter a SessionType field value, select all records from the table. Include all fields from the tblContract table in the query recordset. Save the query as **qrySessionTypeParameter**. Run the query and enter no value as the SessionType field value, and then run the query again and enter **Group** as the SessionType field value. Close the query.
8. Create a crosstab query based on the tblContract table. Use the SessionType field values for the row headings, the Length field values for the column headings, and the count of the ContractID field values as the summarized value, and include row sums. Save the query as **qrySessionTypeCrosstab**. Change the column heading for the row sum column, which represents the total of each type of session, to **Total Number of Sessions**. Resize the columns in the query recordset to their best fit, and then save and close the query.
9. Create a find duplicates query based on the tblContract table. Select StudentID and SessionType as the fields that might contain duplicates, and select all other fields in the table as additional fields in the query recordset. Save the query as **qryMultipleSessionsForStudents**, run the query, and then close it.

10. Create a find unmatched query that finds all records in the tblStudent table for which there is no matching record in the tblContract table. Display all fields from the tblStudent table in the query recordset. Save the query as **qryStudentsWithoutContracts**, run the query, and then close it.

11. In the tblContract table, change the TutorID field data type to Lookup Wizard. Select the FirstName, LastName, and TutorID fields from the tblTutor table, sort in ascending order by LastName, resize the lookup columns to their best fit, select TutorID as the field to store in the table, and accept the default label for the lookup column. In datasheet view, change the TutorID value for the first record to verify that the lookup functions correctly, then restore the original TutorID value for the first record. Save and close the table.

12. Use the Input Mask Wizard to add an input mask to the HomePhone and CellPhone fields in the tblStudent table. The ending input mask should use periods as separators, as in 987.654.3210, with only the last seven digits required; do not store the literal display characters, if you are asked to do so. Resize the Home Phone and Cell Phone columns to their best fit, and then test the input mask by typing over an existing Phone field value, being sure not to change the value permanently by pressing the Esc key after you type the last digit in the Phone field.

13. Define a field validation rule for the Gender field in the tblStudent table. Acceptable field values for the Gender field are F or M. Use the message "Gender value must be F or M" to notify a user who enters an invalid Gender field value. Save your table changes, test the field validation rule for the Gender field, making sure any tested field values are the same as they were before your testing, and then close the table.

14. Designate the Access2 > Case2 folder as a trusted folder. (*Note:* Check with your instructor before adding a new trusted location.)

15. Make a backup copy of the database, compact and repair the database, and then close it.

Case Problem 3

CHALLENGE

Data File needed for this Case Problem: Community.accdb

Diane's Community Center   Diane Coleman is a successful businesswoman in Dallas, Georgia, but things were not always that way. Diane experienced trying times and fortunately had people in the community come into her life to assist her and her children when times were difficult. To give back to her community and support those in need, Diane has created a community center in Dallas where those in need can come in for goods and services. She has also opened a thrift store to sell and auction donated items to support the center. Diane has created an Access database to manage information about the center's patrons and donations. Diane now wants to create several queries and to make changes to the table design of the database. You'll help Diane by completing the following steps:

1. Open the **Community** database located in the Access2 > Case3 folder provided with your Data Files.

2. Modify the first record in the tblPatron table datasheet by changing the Title, FirstName, and LastName column values to your title and name. Close the table.

3. Create a query to find all records in the tblDonation table that were cash donations. Display the DonationID, PatronID, DonationDate, and DonationValue fields in the query recordset. Sort by descending order by DonationValue. Save the query as **qryCashDonations**, run the query, and then close it.

4. Create a query to find all records in the tblDonation table in which the item donated is a potential auction item. Display the DonationID, PatronID, DonationDate, Description, and DonationValue fields from the tblDonation table. Sort in ascending order by DonationDate. Save the query as **qryPotentialAuctionItems**, run the query, and then close it.

5. Create a query called **qryDonationsSeptemberOrLater** that will contain all fields from the tblDonation and tblPatron tables except for PatronID and DonationID, for all donations that are on or after September 1, 2017. Sort this query by DonationValue in descending order. Save and run the query, and then close it.

6. Create a query to display all records from the tblPatron table, selecting the Title and Phone fields. Add a calculated field named **PatronName** that concatenates FirstName, a space, and LastName. Position this column as the second column, and sort the recordset in ascending order by LastName. Set the Caption property for the PatronName field to **Patron Name**. Save the query as **qryPatronNames**, run the query, resize the new column to its best fit, and then save and close the query.

7. Create a parameter query to select the tblDonation table records for a Description field value that contains a phrase the user specifies. If the user doesn't enter a Description field phrase value, select all records from the table. Display all fields from the tblDonation table in the query recordset, and sort in ascending order by Description. Save the query as **qryDonationParameter**. Run the query and enter no value as the Description phrase field value, and then run the query again and enter **clothes** as the Description field phrase value. Close the query.

✪ **Explore** 8. Create a crosstab query based on the qryDonationsSeptemberOrLater query. Use the DonationDate field values for the row headings, the CashDonation field values for the column headings, and the sum of the DonationValue field values as the summarized value, and include row sums. Save the query as **qryDonationsSeptemberOrLaterCrosstab**. Change the format of the displayed values to Fixed. Change the column headings to Cash and NonCash. Resize the columns in the query recordset to their best fit, and then save and close the query.

✪ **Explore** 9. Create a find duplicates query based on the qryDonationsSeptemberOrLater query. Select FirstName and LastName as the fields that might contain duplicates, and select the CashDonation and DonationValue fields in the query as additional fields in the query recordset. Save the query as **qryMultipleDonorDonations**, run the query, and then close it.

10. Create a find unmatched query that finds all records in the tblPatron table for which there is no matching record in the tblDonation table. Include all fields from the tblPatron table, except for PatronID, in the query recordset. Save the query as **qryPatronsWithoutDonations**, run the query, and then close it.

✪ **Explore** 11. Make a copy of the qryDonationsSeptemberOrLater query using the new name **qryTopDonations**. (*Hint:* Be sure to copy the correct query and not the qryDonationsSeptemberOrLaterCrosstab query.) Modify the new query by using the Top Values property to select the top 40 percent of the records. Save and run the query, and then close the query.

12. Use the Input Mask Wizard to add an input mask to the Phone field in the tblPatron table. The ending input mask should use hyphens as separators, as in 987-654-3210, with only the last seven digits required; do not store the literal display characters, if you are asked to do so. Test the input mask by typing over an existing Phone field value, being sure not to change the value permanently by pressing the Esc key after you type the last digit in the Phone field. Close the table.

13. Designate the Access2 > Case3 folder as a trusted folder. (*Note:* Check with your instructor before adding a new trusted location.)

14. Make a backup copy of the database, compact and repair the database, and then close it.

Case Problem 4

Data File needed for this Case Problem: AppTrail.accdb

Hike Appalachia   Molly and Bailey Johnson own Hike Appalachia, a business in which they guide clients on hikes in the Blue Ridge Mountains of North Carolina. They advertise in local and regional outdoor magazines and field requests from people all around the region. Molly and Bailey have created an Access database for their business and now want you to create several queries and modify the table design. To do so, you'll complete the following steps:

1. Open the **AppTrail** database located in the Access2 > Case4 folder provided with your Data Files.

2. Modify the first record in the tblHiker table datasheet by changing the Hiker First Name and Hiker Last Name column values to your first and last names, and then close the table.

3. Create a query to find all records in the tbHiker table in which the HikerLast field value starts with the letter S, sorted in ascending order by HikerLast. Display all fields except the HikerID field in the query recordset. Save the query as **qryHikerLastNameS**, run the query, and then close it.

4. Create a query to find all records in the tblTour table where the tour type is not hiking. Name this query **qryNonHikingTours**. Display all fields, sorting by TourName. Save and run the query, and then close it.

5. Create a query to find all records in the tblHiker table in which the State field value is NC, SC, or GA and display all fields from the tblHiker table in the query recordset, sorted by HikerLast in ascending order. Save the query as **qrySelectedStates**, run the query, and then close it.

6. Create a query to select all records from the tblTour table with a price per person of $100 or less, where the TourType is Hiking. Display all fields in the query recordset, sorted by PricePerPerson in descending order. Save the query as **qryInexpensiveHikingTours**, run the query, and then close it.

7. Create a parameter query to select the tblTour table records for a TourType field phrase value that the user specifies. If the user doesn't enter a phrase field value, select all records from the table. Display all fields from the tblTour table in the query recordset, and sort in ascending order by TourName. Save the query as **qryTourParameter**. Run the query and enter no value as the phrase field value, and then run the query again and enter **Van** as the TourType phrase field value. Close the query.

8. Create a query that contains all records from the tblHiker table and all matching records from the tblReservation table. Display all fields from the tblHiker table and all fields except HikerID from the tblReservation table. Save the query as **qryHikersAndReservations**, run the query, and then close it.

⊕ **Explore** 9. Create a crosstab query based on the qryHikersAndReservations query. Use the TourID field values for the row headings, the HikerID field values for the column headings, and the sum of the People field as the summarized value, and include row sums. Save the query as **qryReservationsCrosstab**, resize the columns in the query recordset to their best fit, and then save and close the query.

⊕ **Explore** 10. Create a find duplicates query based on the qryHikersAndReservations query. Select HikerID as the field that might contain duplicates, and select the fields HikerFirst, HikerLast, TourID, TourDate, and People in the table as additional fields in the query recordset. Save the query as **qryMultipleReservations**, run the query, and then close it.

11. Create a find unmatched query that finds all records in the tblHiker table for which there is no matching record in the tblReservation table. Display the HikerFirst, HikerLast, City, State, and Phone fields from the tblHiker table in the query recordset. Save the query as **qryHikersWithoutReservations**, run the query, and then close it.

12. Copy the qryInexpensiveHikingTours query, and save it as **qryTopInexpensiveHikingTours**. Use the Top Values property to select the top 50 percent of the records. Save and run the query, and then close it.

13. In the tblReservation table, change the TourID field data type to Lookup Wizard. Select all of the fields from the tblTour table, sort in ascending order by TourName, do not show the key column, resize the lookup columns to their best fit, select TourID as the field to store in the table, and accept the default label for the lookup column. View the tblReservation datasheet, resize the TourID column to its best fit, test the lookup field without changing a field value permanently, and then close the table.

14. Define a field validation rule for the People field in the tblReservation table. Acceptable field values for the People field are values less than or equal to 6. Display the message **Please book a custom tour for large groups.** when a user enters an invalid People field value. Save your table changes, and then test the field validation rule for the People field; be certain the field values are the same as they were before your testing.

15. Designate the Access2 > Case4 folder as a trusted folder. (*Note:* Check with your instructor before adding a new trusted location.)

16. Make a backup copy of the database, compact and repair the database, and then close it.

Using Form Tools and Creating Custom Forms

Creating Forms for Riverview Veterinary Care Center

OBJECTIVES

Session 6.1
- Change a lookup field to a Short Text field
- View and print database documentation
- Create datasheet, multiple item, and split forms
- Modify a form and anchor form controls in Layout view

Session 6.2
- Plan, design, and create a custom form in Design view and in Layout view
- Select, move, align, resize, delete, and rename controls in a form
- Add a combo box to a form
- Add headers and footers to a form

Session 6.3
- Use a combo box in a form to find records
- Add a subform to a form
- Add calculated controls to a form and a subform
- Change the tab order in a form
- Improve the appearance of a form

Case | *Riverview Veterinary Care Center*

Kimberly Johnson hired Daksha Yatawara to enhance the CareCenter database, and he initially concentrated on standardizing the table design and creating queries for Riverview Veterinary Care Center. Kimberly and her staff created a few forms before Daksha came onboard, and Daksha's next priority is to work with Kimberly to create new forms that will be more functional and easier to use.

In this module, you will create new forms for Riverview Veterinary Care Center. In creating the forms, you will use many Access form customization features, such as adding controls and a subform to a form, using combo boxes and calculated controls, and adding color and special effects. These features make it easier for database users like Kimberly and her staff to interact with a database.

STARTING DATA FILES

Access2 → **Module**
CareCenter.accdb (cont.)

Review
Supplier.accdb (cont.)

Case1
MoreBeauty.accdb (cont.)

Case2
Tutoring.accdb (cont.)

Case3
Community.accdb (cont.)

Case4
AppTrail.accdb (cont.)

Session 6.1 Visual Overview:

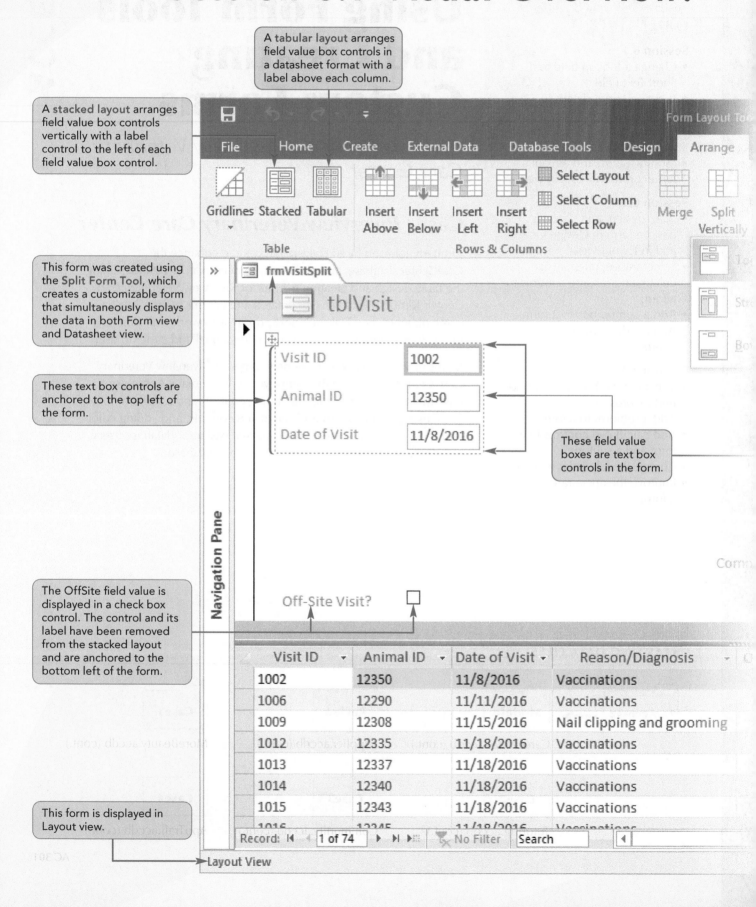

A tabular layout arranges field value box controls in a datasheet format with a label above each column.

A stacked layout arranges field value box controls vertically with a label control to the left of each field value box control.

This form was created using the Split Form Tool, which creates a customizable form that simultaneously displays the data in both Form view and Datasheet view.

These text box controls are anchored to the top left of the form.

These field value boxes are text box controls in the form.

The OffSite field value is displayed in a check box control. The control and its label have been removed from the stacked layout and are anchored to the bottom left of the form.

This form is displayed in Layout view.

Anchoring Controls

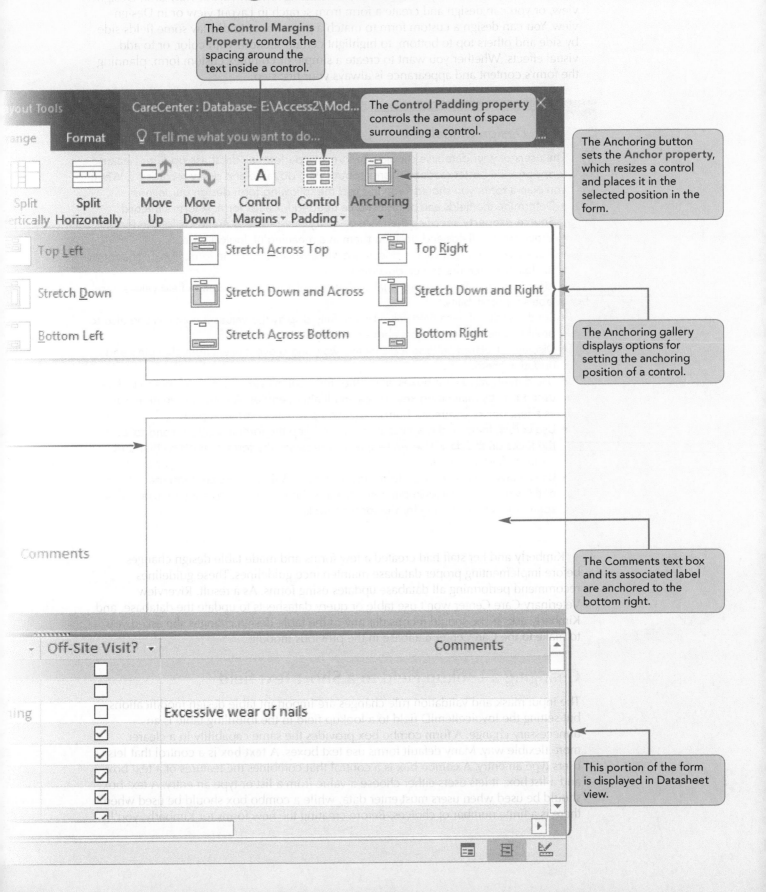

The **Control Margins Property** controls the spacing around the text inside a control.

The **Control Padding** property controls the amount of space surrounding a control.

The Anchoring button sets the **Anchor** property, which resizes a control and places it in the selected position in the form.

The Anchoring gallery displays options for setting the anchoring position of a control.

The Comments text box and its associated label are anchored to the bottom right.

This portion of the form is displayed in Datasheet view.

Designing Forms

To create a **custom form**, you can modify an existing form in Layout view or in Design view, or you can design and create a form from scratch in Layout view or in Design view. You can design a custom form to match a paper form, to display some fields side by side and others top to bottom, to highlight certain sections with color, or to add visual effects. Whether you want to create a simple or complex custom form, planning the form's content and appearance is always your first step.

Form Design Guidelines

The users of your database should use forms to perform all database updates because forms provide better readability and control than do table and query recordsets. When you plan a form, you should keep in mind the following form design guidelines:

- Determine the fields and record source needed for each form. A form's **Record Source property** specifies the table or query that provides the fields for the form.
- Group related fields and position them in a meaningful, logical order.
- If users will refer to a source document while working with the form, design the form to closely match the source document.
- Identify each field value with a label that names the field, and align field values and labels for readability.
- Set the width of each field value box to fully display the values it contains and also to provide a visual cue to users about the length of those values.
- Display calculated fields in a distinctive way, and prevent users from changing and updating them.
- Use default values, list boxes, and other form controls whenever possible to reduce user errors by minimizing keystrokes and limiting entries. A control is an item, such as a text box or command button, that you place in a form or report.
- Use colors, fonts, and graphics sparingly to keep the form uncluttered and to keep the focus on the data. Use white space to separate the form controls so that they are easier to find and read.
- Use a consistent style for all forms in a database. When forms are formatted differently, with form controls in different locations from one form to another, users must spend extra time looking for the form controls.

Kimberly and her staff had created a few forms and made table design changes before implementing proper database maintenance guidelines. These guidelines recommend performing all database updates using forms. As a result, Riverview Veterinary Care Center won't use table or query datasheets to update the database, and Kimberly asks if she should reconsider any of the table design changes she asked you to make to the CareCenter database in the previous module.

Changing a Lookup Field to a Short Text field

The input mask and validation rule changes are important table design modifications, but setting the InvoiceItemID field to a lookup field in the tblBilling table is an unnecessary change. A form combo box provides the same capability in a clearer, more flexible way. Many default forms use text boxes. A **text box** is a control that lets users type an entry. A **combo box** is a control that combines the features of a text box and a list box; it lets users either choose a value from a list or type an entry. A text box should be used when users must enter data, while a combo box should be used when there is a finite number of choices. Before creating the new forms for Kimberly, you'll change the data type of the InvoiceItemID field in the tblBilling table from a Lookup Wizard field to a Short Text field, so that you can create the relationship with referential integrity between the tblBilling and tblInvoiceItems tables.

To change the data type of the InvoiceItemID field:

1. Start Access, and then open the **CareCenter** database you worked with in the previous module.

   Trouble? If the security warning is displayed below the ribbon, click the Enable Content button.

TIP

You can press the F11 key to open or close the Navigation Pane.

2. Open the Navigation Pane, if necessary, open the **tblBilling table** in Design view, and then close the Navigation Pane.

3. Click the **InvoiceItemID** Field Name box, and then in the Field Properties pane, click the **Lookup** tab. The Field Properties pane displays the lookup properties for the InvoiceItemID field. See Figure 6-1.

Figure 6-1	Lookup properties for the InvoiceItemID field

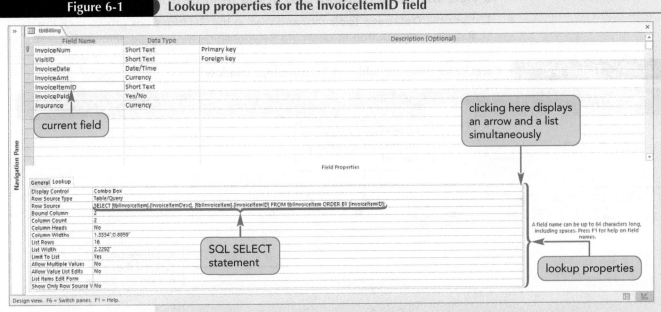

Notice the **Row Source property**, which specifies the data source for a control in a form or report or for a field in a table or query. The Row Source property is usually set to a table name, a query name, or an SQL statement. For the InvoiceItemID field, the Row Source property is set to an SQL SELECT statement. You'll learn more about SQL later in this text.

To remove the lookup feature for the InvoiceItemID field, you need to change the **Display Control property**, which specifies the default control used to display a field, from Combo Box to Text Box.

4. Click the right end of the **Display Control** box, and then click **Text Box** in the list. All the lookup properties in the Field Properties pane disappear, and the InvoiceItemID field changes back to a standard Short Text field without lookup properties.

5. Click the **General** tab in the Field Properties pane, and notice that the properties for a Short Text field still apply to the InvoiceItemID field.

6. Save the table, switch to Datasheet view, resize the Invoice Item ID column to its best fit, and then click one of the Invoice Item ID boxes. An arrow does not appear in the Invoice Item ID box because the InvoiceItemID field is no longer a lookup field.

7. Save the table, and then close the tblBilling table.

Before you could change the InvoiceItemID field in the tblBilling table to a lookup field in the previous module, you had to delete the one-to-many relationship between the tblInvoiceItem and tblBilling tables. Now that you've changed the data type of the InvoiceItemID field back to a Short Text field, you'll view the table relationships to make sure that the tables in the CareCenter database are related correctly.

To view the table relationships in the Relationships window:

1. Click the **Database Tools** tab, and then in the Relationships group, click the **Relationships** button to open the Relationships window. See Figure 6-2.

Figure 6-2	CareCenter database tables in Relationships window

Trouble? If the order of the table field lists in your Relationships window do not match Figure 6-2, simply drag the table field lists to rearrange them so that they appear in the same left to right order shown in the figure.

The tblVisit table and the related tblBilling table have a one-to-many relationship with referential integrity enforced. You need to establish a similar one-to-many relationship between the tblInvoiceItem and tblBilling tables.

2. Double-click the **relationship line** between the tblBilling and tblInvoiceItem tables to open the Edit Relationships dialog box.

3. Click the **Enforce Referential Integrity** check box, click the **Cascade Update Related Fields** check box, and then click the **OK** button to close the dialog box. The join line connecting the tblInvoiceItem and tblBilling tables now indicates a one-to-many relationship with referential integrity enforced.

Kimberly is interested in documenting information on the objects and relationships between objects in the database she and her staff can use as a reference. In Access, you can create a report of the database relationships. You can also give Kimberly information on all the objects in the database using the Documenter.

Creating a Relationship Report and Using the Documenter

From the Relationships window, you can create a Relationship report to document the fields, tables, and relationships in a database. You can also use the **Documenter**, another Access tool, to create detailed documentation of all, or selected, objects in a database. For each selected object, the Documenter lets you print documentation, such as the object's properties and relationships, and the names and properties of fields used by the object. You can use the documentation on an object, referred to as an Object Definition Report, to help you understand an object and to help you plan changes to that object.

PROSKILLS

Written Communication: Satisfying User Documentation Requirements

The Documenter produces object documentation that is useful to the technical designers, analysts, and programmers who develop and maintain Access databases and who need to understand the intricate details of a database's design. However, users who interact with databases generally have little interest in the documentation produced by the Documenter. Users need to know how to enter and maintain data using forms and how to obtain information using forms and reports, so they require special documentation that matches these needs; this documentation isn't produced by the Documenter, though. Many companies assign one or more users the task of creating the documentation needed by users based on the idea that users themselves are the most familiar with their company's procedures and understand most clearly the specific documentation that they and other users require. Databases with dozens of tables and with hundreds of other objects are complicated structures, so be sure you provide documentation that satisfies the needs of users separate from the documentation for database developers.

Next, you will create a Relationship report and use the Documenter to create documentation for the tblVisit table.

To create the Relationship report:

▶ **1.** On the Relationship Tools Design tab, in the Tools group, click the **Relationship Report** button to open the Relationships for CareCenter report in Print Preview.

▶ **2.** In the Page Layout group, click the **Landscape** button to change the report to landscape orientation and display the entire relationship structure. See Figure 6-3.

Figure 6-3   **Relationships for CareCenter report**

relationships for CareCenter

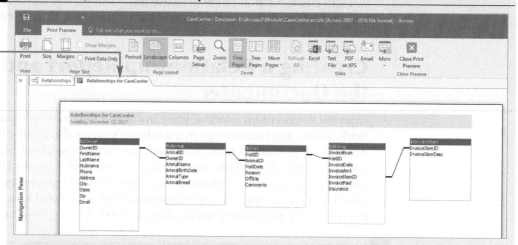

Trouble? If the order of the table field lists in your Relationships window do not match Figure 6-3, simply drag the table field lists to rearrange them so that they appear in the same left-to-right order shown in the figure.

3. Right-click the **Relationships for CareCenter** tab, and then click **Close** to close the tab. A dialog box opens and asks if you want to save the design of the report.

4. Click the **Yes** button to save the report, click the **OK** button to use the default report name Relationships for CareCenter, and then close the Relationships window.

Kimberly wants to show her staff a sample of the information the Documenter provides.

REFERENCE

Using the Documenter

- In the Analyze group on the Database Tools tab, click the Database Documenter button.
- In the Documenter dialog box, select the object(s) you want to document.
- If necessary, click the Options button to open the Print Table Definition dialog box, select specific documentation options for the selected object(s), and then click the OK button.
- Click the OK button to close the Documenter dialog box and open the Object Definition window in Print Preview.
- Print the documentation if desired, and then close the Object Definition window.

You will use the Documenter to create an Object Definition Report on the tblVisit table.

To use the Documenter to create, save, and print an Object Definition report:

1. On the ribbon, click the **Database Tools** tab.

2. In the Analyze group, click the **Database Documenter** button to open the Documenter dialog box, and then click the **Tables** tab (if necessary). See Figure 6-4.

Figure 6-4   Documenter dialog box

click to display all database objects

click to select all objects

click to display more options for the selected object type

> **3.** Click the **tblVisit** check box, and then click the **Options** button. The Print Table Definition dialog box opens. In this dialog box, you select which documentation you want the Documenter to include for the selected table, its fields, and its indexes.

> **4.** Make sure the **Properties**, **Relationships**, and **Permissions by User and Group** check boxes are all checked in the Include for Table section.

> **5.** In the Include for Fields section, click the **Names, Data Types, and Sizes** option button (if necessary), then click the **Names and Fields** option button in the Include for Indexes section (if necessary). See Figure 6-5.

Figure 6-5   Print Table Definition dialog box

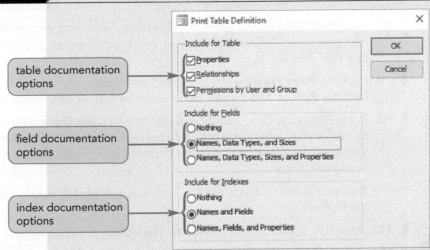

table documentation options

field documentation options

index documentation options

TIP

The Print Preview tab in the Print Preview window provides options for setting various printing options, such as page margins, page orientation, and number of columns to print for a form or report.

> **6.** Click the **OK** button to close the Print Table Definition dialog box, and then click the **OK** button to close the Documenter dialog box. The Object Definition report opens in Print Preview.

> **7.** On the Print Preview tab, in the Zoom group, click the **Zoom button arrow**, and then click **Zoom 100%**. To display more of the report, you will collapse the ribbon.

8. On the right end of the ribbon, click the **Collapse the Ribbon** button ⌃, and then scroll down the report and examine its contents. See Figure 6-6.

| Figure 6-6 | Print Preview of the Object Definition report |

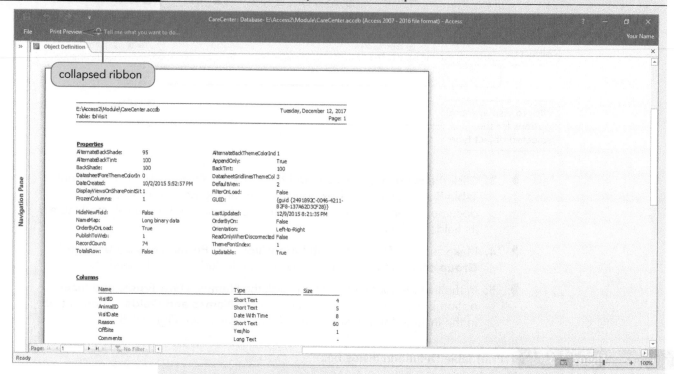

The Object Definition report displays table, field, and relationship documentation for the tblVisit table. Next, you'll export the report and save it as a PDF document.

9. Click the **Print Preview** tab to expand the ribbon, and then in the Data group, click the **PDF or XPS** button. The Publish as PDF or XPS dialog box opens.

10. In the File name box, change the filename to **ClinicDocumenter**, navigate to the location where you are saving your files, click the **Publish** button, and then click the **Close** button in the Export – PDF dialog box to close without saving the steps.

    Trouble? If the PDF you created opens automatically during Step 10, close the PDF viewer.

11. Close the Object Definition report. The ribbon is still collapsed.

12. On the ribbon, click the **Home** tab, and then, on the right end of the ribbon, click the **Pin the ribbon** button ⊣ to expand and pin the ribbon again.

TIP

You can also collapse the ribbon by double-clicking any ribbon tab or by right-clicking a blank area of the ribbon and clicking Collapse the Ribbon on the shortcut menu.

The CareCenter database currently contains the frmOwner form. The frmOwner form was created using the Form Wizard with some design changes that were made in Layout view including changing the theme, changing the form title color and line type, adding a picture, and moving a field. Next Kimberly would like you to create a form that allows her and her staff to see and modify the relevant data for animal visits. You will create this form using other form tools.

Creating Forms Using Form Tools

In earlier modules you created forms with and without subforms using the Form Wizard. You can create other types of forms using different form tools, namely the Datasheet tool, the Multiple Items tool, and the Split Form tool.

Decision Making: Creating Multiple Forms and Reports

When developing a larger database application, it's not uncommon for the users of the database to be unsure as to what they want with respect to forms and reports. You may obtain some sample data and sample reports during the requirements-gathering phase that give you some ideas, but in the end, it is a good idea to have the users approve the final versions.

While you are actively developing the application, you might design different versions of forms and reports that you think will meet users' needs; later in the process, you might narrow the selection to a few forms and reports. Ultimately, you should ask the users to make the final choices of which forms and reports to incorporate into the database. By involving the users in the planning phase for forms and reports, the database is more likely to meet everyone's needs.

Kimberly has requested a form that her staff can use to work with information from the tblVisit table. Because her requirements at this point are vague, you'll create a selection of form designs for Kimberly to choose from. You'll create two simple forms that show the contents of the tblVisit in a layout that resembles a table, and you'll create a custom form that Kimberly's staff may find a bit more user-friendly. First, you'll create the simple forms for Kimberly and her staff.

Creating a Form Using the Datasheet Tool

You can create a simple form using the Datasheet Tool. The **Datasheet tool** creates a form in a datasheet format that contains all the fields in the source table or query. Kimberly might prefer this if she and her staff are very comfortable entering data in an Access table in Datasheet view. You'll use the Datasheet tool to create a form based on the tblVisit table. When you use the Datasheet tool, the record source (either a table or query) for the form must either be open or selected in the Navigation Pane.

To create the form using the Datasheet tool:

▶ **1.** Open the Navigation Pane, and then click **tblVisit**.

▶ **2.** On the ribbon, click the **Create** tab.

▶ **3.** In the Forms group, click the **More Forms** button, click **Datasheet**, and then, if necessary, close the Property Sheet. The Datasheet tool creates a form showing every field in the tblVisit table in a datasheet format. See Figure 6-7.

Figure 6-7 Form created with the Datasheet tool

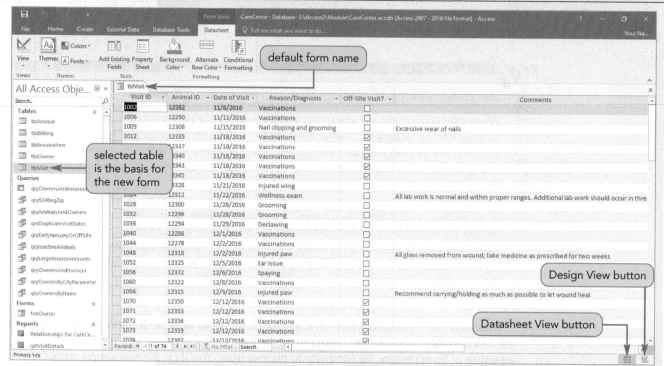

The form resembles the Datasheet view for the table except that it does not include the expand buttons at the beginning of each row. The form name, tblVisit, is the same name as the table used as the basis for the form. Recall that each table and query in a database must have a unique name. Although you could give a form or report the same name as a table or query, doing so would likely cause confusion. Fortunately, using object name prefixes prevents this confusing practice, and you will change the name when you save the form.

As you know, when working with forms, you view and update data in Form view, you view and make simple design changes in Layout view, and you make simple and complex design changes in Design view. However, not all of these views are available for every type of form. For the form created with the Datasheet tool, you'll check the available view options.

▶ **4.** On the Form Tools Datasheet tab, in the Views group, click the **View button arrow**. See Figure 6-8.

Figure 6-8 View options for a form created with the Datasheet tool

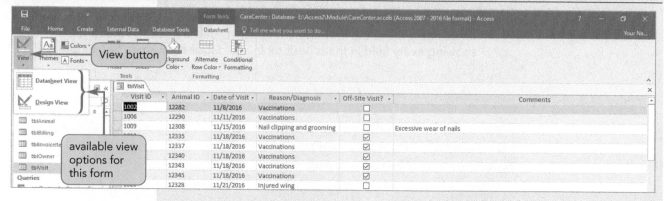

Notice Form view and Layout view are not options on the menu, which means that they are unavailable for this form type. Datasheet view allows you to view and update data, and Design view allows you to modify the form's layout and design. The buttons for accessing these two available views are also on the status bar.

You'll save this form to show Kimberly as one of the options for the forms for animal visits.

▶ **5.** Save the form as **frmVisitDatasheet**, and close the form.

Kimberly might prefer a form created using the Multiple Items tool because it will provide a form with larger text boxes for displaying a record's field values.

Creating a Form Using the Multiple Items Tool

The **Multiple Items tool** creates a customizable form that displays multiple records from a source table or query in a datasheet format. You'll use the Multiple Items tool to create a form based on the tblVisit table.

To create the form using the Multiple Items tool:

▶ **1.** Make sure that the tblVisit table is selected in the Navigation Pane, and then click the **Create** tab.

▶ **2.** In the Forms group, click the **More Forms** button, and then click **Multiple Items**. The Multiple Items tool creates a form showing every field in the tblVisit table and opens the form in Layout view. See Figure 6-9.

Figure 6-9	Form created with the Multiple Items tool

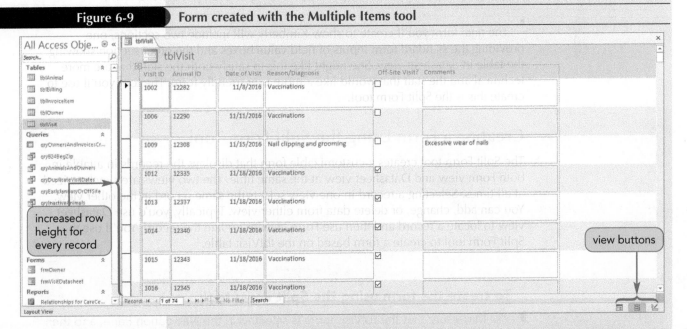

The new form displays all the records and fields from the tblVisit table in a format similar to a datasheet, but the row height for every record is increased compared to a standard datasheet. Unlike a form created with the Datasheet tool, which has only Datasheet view and Design view available, a Multiple Items form is a standard form that can be displayed in Form view, Layout view, and Design view, as indicated by the buttons on the right end of the status bar. You can also access these views for the forms created with the Multiple Items tool from the ribbon.

3. On the Form Layout Tools Design tab, in the Views group, click the **View button arrow**. See Figure 6-10.

Figure 6-10   **Views available for a form created with Multiple Items tool**

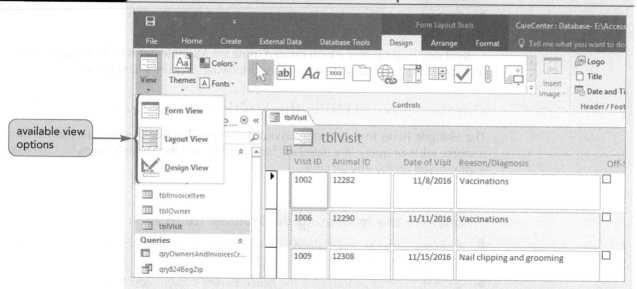

You'll want to show this form to Kimberly as one of the options, so you'll save it.

4. Save the form as **frmVisitMultipleItems**, and then close the form.

The final form you'll create to show Kimberly will include two sections, one providing the standard form inputs of field value boxes and the other section showing the table in datasheet view. She might like this to satisfy both the staff that are more technical and the staff that would like a more user-friendly form. The tool you'll use to create this is the Split Form tool.

Creating a Form Using the Split Form Tool

The Split Form tool creates a customizable form that displays the records in a table in both Form view and Datasheet view at the same time. The two views are synchronized at all times. Selecting a record in one view selects the same record in the other view. You can add, change, or delete data from either view. Typically, you'd use Datasheet view to locate a record and then use Form view to update the record. You'll use the Split Form tool to create a form based on the tblVisit table.

To create the form using the Split Form tool:

1. Make sure that the tblVisit table is selected in the Navigation Pane, and then click the **Create** tab.

2. In the Forms group, click the **More Forms** button, click **Split Form**, and then close the Navigation Pane. The Split Form tool creates a split form that opens in Layout view and displays a form with the contents of the first record in the tblVisit table in the top section and a datasheet showing the first several records in the tblVisit table in the bottom section. In Layout view, the form on top will present a record's fields either in either a single column or in two columns, depending on the size of the Access window when the form was created. If you have a two-column layout, that won't affect your ability to complete the steps that follow. Figure 6-11 shows the single-column layout.

Figure 6-11	Form created with the Split Form tool

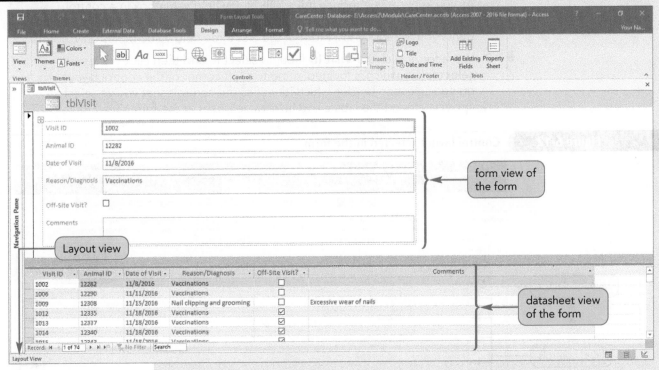

In Layout view, you can make layout and design changes to the form section and layout changes to the datasheet section of the split form.

Modifying a Split Form in Layout View

In previous modules, you've modified forms using options on the Form Layout Tools Format tab. Additional options for modifying forms are available on the Form Layout Tools Arrange tab. When working with a split form, you use the options on the Form Layout Tools Design tab to add controls and make other modifications to the form section but not to the datasheet section. Also in this case, the options on the Arrange tab apply only to the form section and do not apply to the datasheet section.

Kimberly notices that first three field value boxes in the form, Visit ID, Animal ID, and Date of Visit, are much wider than necessary. You will resize these field value boxes, and you will also move and resize the Reason/Diagnosis field label and field value box.

To resize field value boxes in the split form in Layout view:

▶ **1.** On the ribbon, click the **Form Layout Tools Arrange** tab.

The form's field label and field value boxes from the tblVisit table are grouped in a control layout. Recall that a control layout is a set of controls grouped together in a form or report so that you can manipulate the set as a single control. The control layout is a stacked layout, which arranges field value box controls vertically with a label control to the left of each field value box control in one or more vertical columns. You can also choose a tabular layout, which arranges field value box controls in a datasheet format with labels above each column.

As you know, if you reduce the width of any field value box in a control layout, all the value boxes in the control layout are also resized. Kimberly wants you to reduce the width of the first three field value boxes only.

▶ **2.** In the form, click the **Visit ID** label to select it, and then click the **layout selector** ⊞, which is located in the top-left corner of the control layout. An orange selection border, which identifies the controls that you've selected, appears around the labels and field value boxes in the form. See Figure 6-12.

Figure 6-12	Control layout selected in the form

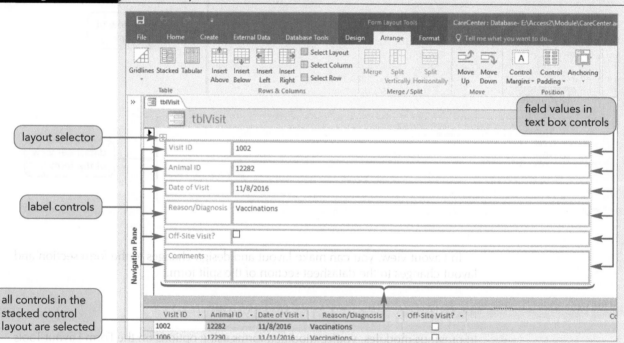

Next, you'll resize the field value boxes in the control layout.

▶ **3.** Click the **VisitDate** field value box (containing the value 11/8/2016) to deselect the control layout and select just the **VisitDate** field value box.

▶ **4.** Position the pointer on the right border of the VisitDate field value box until the pointer changes to ↔, click and drag to the left until the right edge is just to the right of the VisitDate field value, and then release the mouse button. If you have a one-column layout, you've resized all five field value boxes. If you have a two-column layout, you've resized the three field value boxes on the left. Figure 6-13 shows the single-column layout.

| Figure 6-13 | Resizing field value boxes in the control layout |

options for creating a control layout

resized field value boxes

Trouble? If you resize the field value boxes too far to the left, number signs appear inside the field value boxes, indicating the boxes are too small to display the full values. Repeat Step 4, this time dragging the right border of the field value box to the right until the date values are visible inside the boxes.

With the one-column layout shown in Figure 6-13, the form has too much white space. To better balance the elements in the form, Kimberly suggests you move and resize the Reason/Diagnosis, Off-Site Visit?, and Comments labels and field value boxes to a second column so that they fill this available space. To do this, you first need to remove these items from the stacked layout control.

To remove field value labels and boxes from the layout control, and move, and resize them on the form:

1. Click the **Reason/Diagnosis** label, press and hold the **Ctrl** key, click the **Reason** field value box, click the **Off-Site Visit?** label, click the **OffSite** check box, click the **Comments** label, and then click the **Comments** field value box to select all six controls, and then release the **Ctrl** key.

2. Right-click the **Reason** field value box, point to **Layout** on the shortcut menu, and then click **Remove Layout**. You've removed the six selected controls from the stacked layout.

3. If your form has the single-column layout shown in Figure 6-13, make sure that the six controls are still selected, and then use the ⬚ to drag them up and to the right until the tops of the Reason label and field value box align with the tops of the VisitID label and field value box.

   Trouble? If your form already has a two-column layout, skip Step 3.

4. Click the **Off-Site Visit?** label, press and hold the **Ctrl** key, click the **OffSite** check box, and then release the **Ctrl** key. The Off-Site Visit? label and the OffSite check box are selected.

5. Drag the **Off-Site Visit?** label and **OffSite** check box to the left and position them below the Date of Visit label and VisitDate field value box.

6. Select the **Comments** label and the **Comments** field value box, and then drag the selected controls up until they are top-aligned with the Date of Visit label and VisitDate field value box.

7. Click the **Comments** field value box to select it, and then drag the right border of the control to the right until the field value box is about four inches wide.

8. Click the **Reason** field value box so that it's the only selected control, and then drag the right border of the control to the right until it is the same width as the Comments field value box. Compare your screen with Figure 6-14, making any necessary adjustments.

| Figure 6-14 | Moved and resized controls in the form |

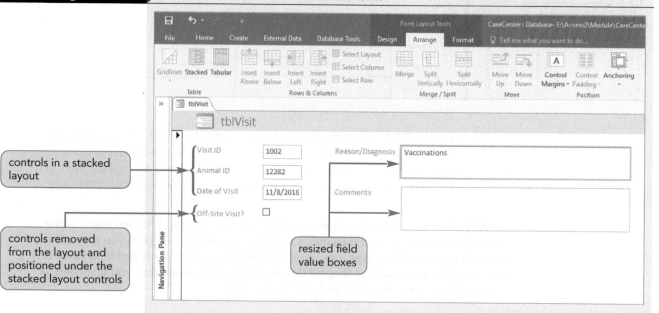

controls in a stacked layout

controls removed from the layout and positioned under the stacked layout controls

resized field value boxes

Trouble? It won't cause any problems if the controls on your screen are in slightly different positions than the ones shown in the figure.

You do not usually need to change the default settings for the Control Margins property, which controls the spacing around the text inside a control, or the Control Padding property, which controls the spacing around the outside of a control. However, you'll explore the effects of changing these properties.

9. In the form, click the **Visit ID** label to select it, and then click the **layout selector** to select the six controls that are still grouped in the stacked layout.

10. On the Arrange tab, in the Position group, click the **Control Margins** button, and then click **Medium**. The text inside the stacked layout controls moves down slightly.

11. Click the **Control Margins** button, click **Wide**, and observe the effect of this setting on the text inside the controls.

12. Click the **Control Margins** button again, and then click **Narrow**. Narrow is the default setting for the Control Margins property. Narrow is also the default setting for the Control Padding property.

Now that the form is complete and the controls are sized appropriately, you will save the form.

▶ **13.** Save the form as **frmVisitSplit**.

Next, you'll anchor the controls on the form.

Anchoring Controls in a Form

You can design forms that use the screen dimensions effectively when all the users of a database have the same-sized monitors and use the same screen resolution. How do you design forms when users have a variety of monitor sizes and screen resolutions? If you design a form to fit on large monitors using high screen resolutions, then only a portion of the controls in the form fit on smaller monitors with lower resolutions, forcing users to scroll the form. If you design a form to fit on smaller monitors with low screen resolutions, then the form displays on larger monitors in a small area in the upper-left corner of the screen, making the form look unattractively cramped. As a compromise, you can anchor the controls in the form. As shown in the Visual Overview for this session, as the screen size and resolution change, the Anchor property for a control automatically resizes the control and places it in the same relative position on the screen. Unfortunately, when you use the Anchor property, the control's font size is not scaled to match the screen size and resolution. Sometimes the results of anchoring controls work well, but sometimes the controls are spaced across a large screen, and the form may seem unorganized with controls moved to the corners of the screen.

Next, you'll anchor controls in the frmVisitSplit form. You can't anchor individual controls in a control layout; you can only anchor the entire control layout as a group. You've already removed the Reason/Diagnosis, Off-Site Visit?, and Comments controls from the stacked layout so that you can anchor them separately from the stacked layout. Therefore, you'll have four sets of controls to anchor—the stacked layout is one set, the Reason/Diagnosis controls are the second set, the Comments controls are the third set, and the Off-Site Visit? controls make up the fourth set.

To anchor controls in the form:

▶ **1.** Click the **Off-Site Visit?** label, press and hold the **Ctrl** key, and then click the **OffSite** check box.

▶ **2.** On the Arrange tab, in the Position group, click the **Anchoring** button to open the Anchoring gallery. See Figure 6-15.

| Figure 6-15 | The Anchoring gallery |

Four of the nine options in the Anchoring gallery fix the position of the selected controls in the top-left (the default setting), bottom-left, top right, or bottom-right positions in the form. If other controls block the corner positions for controls you're anchoring for the first time, the new controls are positioned in relation to the blocking controls. The other five anchoring options resize (or stretch) and position the selected controls.

You'll anchor the Off-Site Visit? controls in the bottom left, the Reason/Diagnosis controls in the top right, and the Comments controls in the bottom right.

▶ 3. Click **Bottom Left** in the Anchoring gallery. The gallery closes, and the Off-Site Visit? label and field value box move to the bottom-left corner of the form.

▶ 4. Click the **Reason** field value box, in the Position group, click the **Anchoring** button, and then click **Top Right**. The Reason label and field value box move to the upper-right corner of the form.

▶ 5. Anchor the Comments label and field value box to the Bottom Right.

Next, you'll increase the height of the form to simulate the effect of a larger screen for the form.

▶ 6. Open the Navigation Pane. The four sets of controls on the left shift to the right because the horizontal dimensions of the form decreased from the left, and these four sets of controls are anchored to the left in the form. The Reason and Comments controls remain in the same position in the form.

▶ 7. Position the pointer on the border between the form and the datasheet until the pointer changes to ⟷, and then drag down until only the column headings and the first row in the datasheet are visible. The bottom sets of controls shift down, because they are anchored to the bottom of the form, and the two sets of controls at the top remain in the same positions in the form. See Figure 6-16.

Figure 6-16	Anchored controls in a resized form

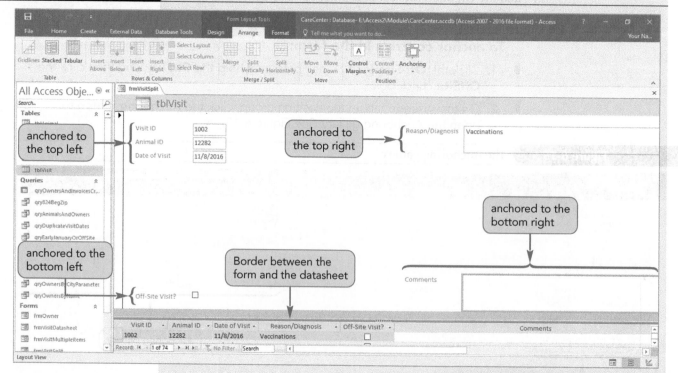

Finally, you'll use another anchoring option to resize the Comments text box as the form dimensions change.

▶ **8.** Click the **Comments** field value box (if necessary), in the Position group, click the **Anchoring** button, and then click **Stretch Down and Right**. Because the Comments field value box is already anchored to the bottom right, it can't stretch any more to the right, but it does stretch up while leaving the label in place, to increase the height of the box.

▶ **9.** Position the pointer on the border between the form and the datasheet until the pointer changes to ✚, and then drag up to display several rows in the datasheet. The bottom set of controls shifts up, and the bottom edge of the Comments field value box shifts up, and its height is reduced.

Kimberly and her staff have the same computer monitors and screen resolutions, so the controls do not need to be anchored. Therefore, you can close the form without saving the anchoring changes.

▶ **10.** Close the form without saving the anchoring changes you've made to the form's design, and then, if you are not continuing on to the next session, close the CareCenter database.

You've used form tools to create forms, and you've modified forms in Layout view. In the next session, you will continue your work with forms.

REVIEW

Session 6.1 Quick Check

1. Which object(s) should you use to perform all database updates?
2. The _____ property specifies the data source for a control in a form or report or for a field in a table or query.
3. What is the Documenter?
4. What is the Multiple Items tool?
5. What is a split form?
6. As the screen's size and resolution change, the _____ property for a control automatically resizes the control.

Session 6.2 Visual Overview:

To move selected controls to the next nearest grid dot, press and hold the Ctrl key, and then press the appropriate arrow key.

Form Design Too

| File | Home | Create | External Data | Database Tools | Design | Arrange |

Auto_Header0 ▾   Calibri Light (Header) ▾ 18 ▾   Formatting ▾   Backgrou Image

Select All   **B** *I* U   A ▾ ◇ ▾   ≡ ≡ ≡ $ % ,   .0 .00   Ba

Selection   Font   Number

The larger handle in a control's upper-left corner is its move handle, which you use to move the control.

» ⊑⊒ **frmVisitsAndInvoices**

· · · I · · · I · · · **1** · · · I · · · I · · · **2** · · · I · · · I · · · **3** · · · I · · · I · · · **4** · · · I · · ·

The AnimalID field value box is a combo box control.

◆ **Form Header**

Visits and Invoices

You can click the Detail section bar to select the entire Detail section.

◆ **Detail**

Animal ID   AnimalID ▾

Visit ID   VisitID   ☑ Off-Site Visit?

Date of Visit   VisitDate

Reason/Diagnosis   Reason

Comments   Comments

The grid is the area with dotted and solid lines that helps you position controls precisely in a form.

Navigation Pane

◆ **Form Footer**

The Comments field value box is a text box, and a bound control, which is a control that is connected, or bound, to a field in the database.

◀

Design View

Custom Form in Design View

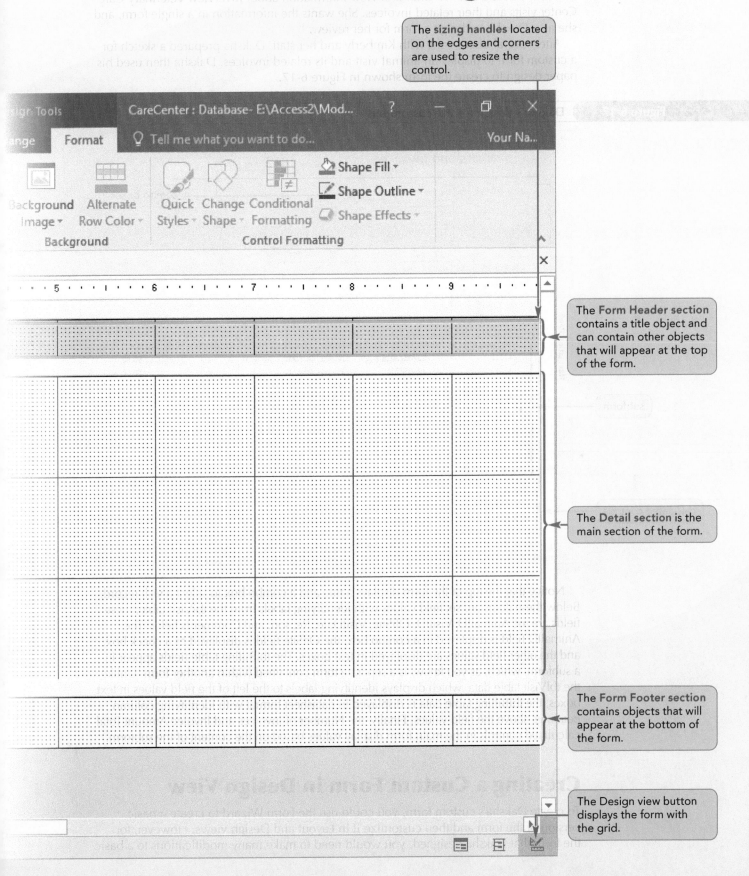

The sizing handles located on the edges and corners are used to resize the control.

The Form Header section contains a title object and can contain other objects that will appear at the top of the form.

The Detail section is the main section of the form.

The Form Footer section contains objects that will appear at the bottom of the form.

The Design view button displays the form with the grid.

Planning and Designing a Custom Form

Kimberly needs a form to enter and view information about Riverview Veterinary Care Center visits and their related invoices. She wants the information in a single form, and she asks Daksha to design a form for her review.

After several discussions with Kimberly and her staff, Daksha prepared a sketch for a custom form to display an animal visit and its related invoices. Daksha then used his paper design to create the form shown in Figure 6-17.

Figure 6-17   **Daksha's design for the custom form**

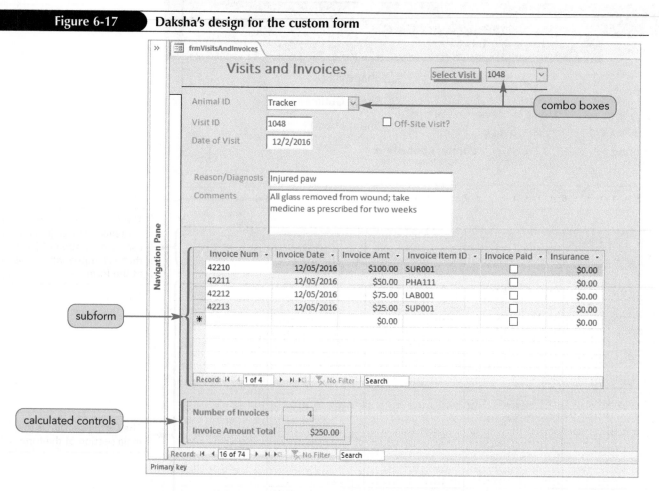

Notice that the top of the form displays a title and a combo box to select a visit record. Below these items are six field values with identifying labels from the tblVisit table; these fields are the AnimalID, VisitID, OffSite, VisitDate, Reason, and Comments fields. The AnimalID field is displayed in a combo box, the OffSite field is displayed as a check box, and the other field values are displayed in text boxes. The tblBilling table fields appear in a subform, which, as you know, is a separate form contained within another form. Unlike the tblVisit table data, which displays identifying labels to the left of the field values in text boxes, the tblBilling table data is displayed in datasheet format with identifying column headings above the field values. Finally, the Number of Invoices and Invoice Amount Total calculated controls in the main form display values based on the content of the subform.

Creating a Custom Form in Design View

To create Daksha's custom form, you could use the Form Wizard to create a basic version of the form and then customize it in Layout and Design views. However, for the form that Daksha designed, you would need to make many modifications to a basic form created by a wizard. You can instead build the form in a more straightforward manner by creating it directly in Design view. Creating forms in Design view allows you more control and precision and provides more options than creating forms in Layout view. You'll also find that you'll create forms more productively if you switch between Design view and Layout view because some design modifications are easier to make in one of the two views than in the other view.

Working in the Form Window in Design View

You can use the Form window in Design view to create and modify forms. To create the custom form based on Daksha's design, you'll create a blank form, add the fields from the tblVisit and tblBilling tables, and then add other controls and make other modifications to the form.

The form you'll create will be a bound form. A **bound form** is a form that has a table or query as its record source. You use bound forms for maintaining and displaying table data. **Unbound forms** are forms that do not have a record source and are usually forms that help users navigate among the objects in a database.

REFERENCE

Creating a Form in Design View

- On the ribbon, click the Create tab.
- In the Forms group, click the Blank Form button to open the Form window in Layout view.
- Click the Design View button on the status bar to switch to Design view.
- Make sure the Field List pane is open, and then add the required fields to the form.
- Add other required controls to the form.
- Modify the size, position, and other properties as necessary for the fields and other controls in the form.
- Save the form.

Now you'll create a blank bound form based on the tblVisit table.

To create a blank bound form in Design view:

1. If you took a break after the previous session, make sure that the CareCenter database is open and the Navigation Pane is open.

2. On the ribbon, click the **Create** tab, and then, in the Forms group, click the **Blank Form** button. The Form window opens in Layout view.

3. Click the **Design View** button 🔲 on the status bar to switch to Design view, and then close the Navigation Pane. See Figure 6-18.

Figure 6-18 **Blank form in Design view**

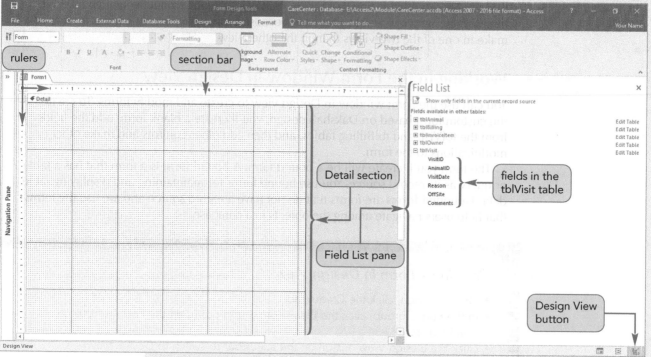

Trouble? If the Field List pane displays the "No fields available to be added to the current view" message, click the "Show all tables" link to display the tables in the CareCenter database, and then click the plus sign next to tblVisit in the Field List pane to display the fields in the tblVisit table.

Trouble? If the tblVisit table in the Field List pane is not expanded to show the fields in the table, click the plus sign next to tblVisit to display the fields.

Design view contains the tools necessary to create a custom form. You create the form by placing controls in the blank form. You can place three kinds of controls in a form:

- A **bound control** is connected, or bound, to a field in the database. The field could be selected from the fields in a table or query that are used as the record source. You use bound controls to display and maintain table field values.
- An **unbound control** is not connected to a field in the database. You use unbound controls to display text, such as a form title or instructions; to display lines, rectangles, and other objects; or to display graphics and pictures created using other software programs. An unbound control that displays text is called a **label**.
- A **calculated control** displays a value that is the result of an expression. The expression usually contains one or more fields, and the calculated control is recalculated each time any value in the expression changes.

To create a bound control, you add fields from the Field List pane to the Form window, and then position the bound controls where you want them to appear in the form. To place other controls in a form or a report, you use the tools in the Controls and Header/Footer groups on the Form Design Tools Design tab. The tools in the Controls group let you add controls such as lines, rectangles, images, buttons, check boxes, and list boxes to a form.

Design view for a form contains a Detail section, which is a rectangular area consisting of a grid with a section bar above the grid. You click the section bar to select the section in preparation for setting properties for the entire section. Some forms use Header, Detail, and Footer sections, but a simple form might have only a Detail section. The grid consists of dotted and solid lines that you use to position controls precisely in a form. In the Detail section, you place bound controls, unbound controls, and calculated controls in your form. You can change the size of the Detail section by dragging its borders. Rulers at the top and left edges of the Detail section define the horizontal and vertical dimensions of the form and serve as guides for placing controls in a form.

Your first task is to add bound controls to the Detail section for the six fields from the tblVisit table.

Adding Fields to a Form

When you add a bound control to a form, Access adds a field value box and, to its left, an attached label. The field value box displays a field value from the record source. The attached label displays either the Caption property value for the field, if the Caption property value has been set, or the field name. To create a bound control, you first display the Field List pane by clicking the Add Existing Fields button in the Tools group on the Form Design Tools Design tab. Then you double-click a field in the Field List pane to add the bound control to the Detail section. You can also drag a field from the Field List pane to the Detail section.

The Field List pane displays the five tables in the CareCenter database and the six fields in the tblVisit table. Next, you'll add bound controls to the Detail section for the tblVisit table's six fields.

To add bound controls from the tblVisit table to the Detail section:

▶ 1. Double-click **VisitID** in the Field List pane. A bound text box control appears in the Detail section of the form, and the Field List pane lists the tblVisit table in the "Fields available for this view" section and lists the tblAnimal and tblBilling and tables in the "Fields available in related tables" section.

▶ 2. Repeat Step 1 for the **VisitDate**, **AnimalID**, **Reason**, **Comments**, and **OffSite** fields, in this order, in the Field List pane. Six bound controls—one for each of the six fields in the Field List pane—are added in the Detail section of the form. See Figure 6-19.

Figure 6-19   Bound controls added to the form

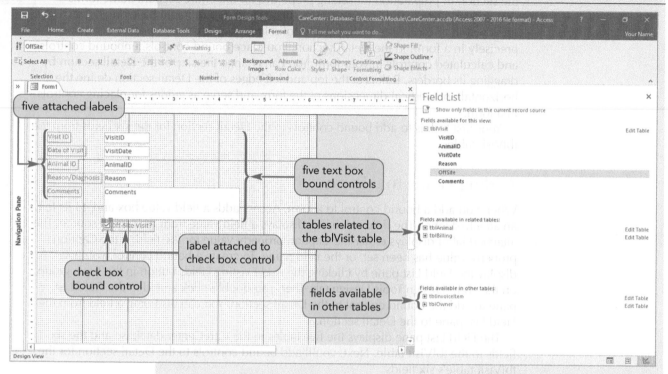

You should periodically save your work as you create a form, so you'll save the form now.

3. Click the **Save** button 🖫 on the Quick Access Toolbar. The Save As dialog box opens.

4. With the default name selected in the Form Name box, type **frmVisitsAndInvoices**, and then press the **Enter** key. The tab for the form now displays the form name, and the form design is saved in the CareCenter database.

You've added the fields you need to the grid, so you can close the Field List pane.

5. Click the **Form Design Tools Design** tab, and then, in the Tools group, click the **Add Existing Fields** button to close the Field List pane.

INSIGHT

Strategies for Building Forms

To help prevent common problems and more easily recover from errors while building forms, you should keep in mind the following suggestions:

- You can click the Undo button one or more times immediately after you make one or more errors or make form adjustments you don't wish to keep.

- You should back up your database frequently, especially before you create new objects or customize existing objects. If you run into difficulty, you can revert to your most recent backup copy of the database.

- You should save your form after you've completed a portion of your work successfully and before you need to perform steps you've never done before. If you're not satisfied with subsequent steps, close the form without saving the changes you made since your last save, and then open the form and perform the steps again.

- You can always close the form, make a copy of the form in the Navigation Pane, and practice with the copy.

- Adding controls, setting properties, and performing other tasks correctly in Access should work all the time with consistent results, but in rare instances, you might find a feature doesn't work properly. If a feature you've previously used successfully suddenly doesn't work, you should save your work, close the database, make a backup copy of the database, open the database, and then compact and repair the database. Performing a compact and repair resolves most of these types of problems.

To make your form's Detail section match Daksha's design (Figure 6-17), you need to move the OffSite bound control up and to the right. To do so, you must start by selecting the bound control.

Selecting, Moving, and Aligning Form Controls

Six field value boxes now appear in the form's Detail section, one below the other. Each field value box is a bound control connected to a field in the underlying table, with an attached label to its left. Each field value box and each label is a control in the form; in addition, each pairing of a field value box and its associated label is itself a control. When you select a control, an orange selection border appears around the control, and eight squares, called handles, appear on the selection border's four corners and at the midpoints of its four edges. The larger handle in a control's upper-left corner is its move handle, which you use to move the control. You use the other seven handles, called sizing handles, to resize the control. When you work in Design view, controls you place in the form do not become part of a control layout, so you can individually select, move, resize, and otherwise manipulate one control without also changing the other controls. However, at any time you can select a group of controls and place them in a control layout—either a stacked layout or a tabular layout.

Based on Daksha's design for the custom form, shown in Figure 6-17, you need to move the OffSite bound control up and to the right in the Detail section. The OffSite bound control consists of a check box and an attached label, displaying the text "Off-Site Visit?" to its right.

You can move a field value box and its attached label together. To move them, you place the pointer anywhere on the selection border of the field value box, but not on a move handle or a sizing handle. When the pointer changes to ⁺⟨, you drag the field value box and its attached label to the new location. As you move a control, an outline of the control moves on the rulers to indicate the current position of the control as you drag it. To move a group of selected controls, point to any selected control until the pointer changes to ✛, and then drag the group of selected controls to the new position. As you know, you can move controls with more precision by pressing the appropriate arrow key on the keyboard to move the selected control in small increments. To move selected controls to the next nearest grid dot, press and hold the Ctrl key and then press the appropriate arrow key on the keyboard.

You can also move either a field value box or its label individually. If you want to move the field value box but not its label, for example, place the pointer on the field value box's move handle. When the pointer changes to ✛, drag the field value box to the new location. You use the label's move handle in a similar way to move only the label.

You'll now arrange the controls in the form to match Daksha's design.

To move the OffSite bound control:

1. If necessary, click the **Off-Site Visit?** label box to select it. Move handles, which are the larger handles, appear on the upper-left corners of the selected label box and its associated bound control. Sizing handles also appear but only on the label box. See Figure 6-20.

Figure 6-20   Selected OffSite bound control and label

Be sure to position the pointer on one of the edges but not on a move handle or a sizing handle.

2. Position the pointer on the Off-Site Visit? label box's orange selection border, but not on a move handle or a sizing handle, until the pointer changes to a ✛, drag the control up and to the right of the VisitID field value box, as shown in Figure 6-21, and then release the mouse button.

Figure 6-21   **Repositioned Off-Site Visit? label and associated bound control**

selected label and associated bound control moved here

Trouble? If you need to make major adjustments to the placement of the OffSite bound control, click the Undo button 🔄 on the Quick Access Toolbar one or more times until the bound control is back to its starting position, and then repeat Step 2. If you need to make minor adjustments to the placement of the OffSite bound control, use the arrow keys on the keyboard.

Now you need to top-align the OffSite and VisitID bound controls (meaning their top borders are aligned with one another). When you select a column of controls, you can align the controls along their left or their right borders (left-align or right-align). When you select a row of controls, you can top-align or bottom-align the controls. You can also align To Grid, which aligns the selected controls with the dots in the grid. You access these five alignment options on the Form Design Tools Arrange tab or on the shortcut menu for the selected controls.

You'll use the shortcut menu to align the two bound controls. Then you'll save the modified form and review your work in Form view.

To align the OffSite and VisitID bound controls:

1. Make sure the Off-Site Visit? label box is selected.

2. Press and hold the **Shift** key, click the **OffSite** check box, click the **VisitID** field value box, click the **Visit ID** label, and then release the **Shift** key. The four controls are selected, and each selected control has an orange selection border.

3. Right-click one of the selected controls, point to **Align** on the shortcut menu, and then click **Top**. The four selected controls are top-aligned. See Figure 6-22.

Figure 6-22   Aligned controls in the Detail section

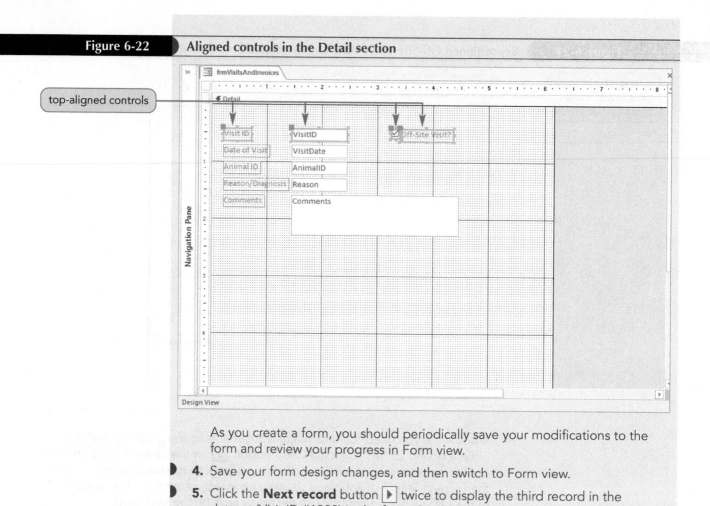

top-aligned controls

As you create a form, you should periodically save your modifications to the form and review your progress in Form view.

4. Save your form design changes, and then switch to Form view.

5. Click the **Next record** button ▶ twice to display the third record in the dataset (Visit ID #1009) in the form. See Figure 6-23.

Figure 6-23   Form displayed in Form view

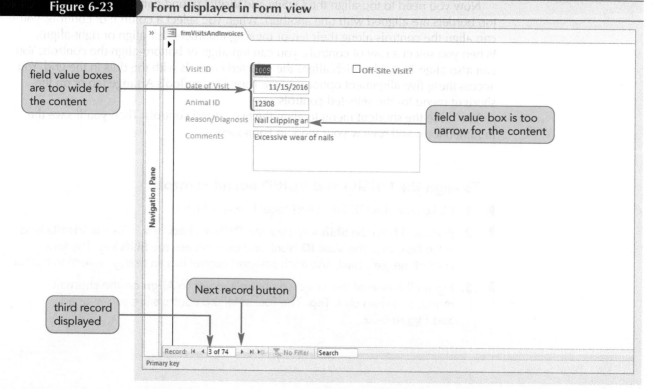

field value boxes are too wide for the content

field value box is too narrow for the content

third record displayed

Next record button

The value in the Reason field value box is not fully displayed, so you need to increase the width of the text box control. The widths of the VisitID and VisitDate text boxes are wider than necessary, so you'll reduce their widths. Also, the AnimalID bound control consists of a label and a text box, but the plan for the form shows a combo box for the AnimalID positioned below the OffSite bound control. You'll delete the AnimalID bound control, and then add it to the form, this time as a combo box.

Resizing and Deleting Controls

As you have seen, a selected control displays seven sizing handles: four at the midpoints on each edge of the control and one at each corner except the upper-left corner. Recall that the upper-left corner displays the move handle. Positioning the pointer over a sizing handle changes the pointer to a two-headed arrow; the directions in which the arrows point indicate in which direction you can resize the selected control. When you drag a sizing handle, you resize the control. As you resize the control, a thin line appears alongside the sizing handle to guide you in completing the task accurately, along with outlines that appear on the horizontal and vertical rulers.

You'll begin by deleting the AnimalID bound control. Then you'll resize the Reason text box, which is too narrow and too short to display Reason field values. Next you'll resize the VisitID and VisitDate text boxes to reduce their widths.

To delete a bound control and resize field value boxes:

1. Switch to Design view, click a blank area of the screen to deselect all controls, and then click the **AnimalID** text box control to select it.

2. Right-click the **AnimalID** text box to open the shortcut menu, and then click **Delete**. The label and the bound text box control for the AnimalID field are deleted.

3. Click the **Reason** text box to select it.

4. Place the pointer on the middle-right handle of the Reason text box until it changes to ↔, drag the right border to the right until it is approximately the same width as the Comments text box. See Figure 6-24.

Figure 6-24 | Resized Reason text box

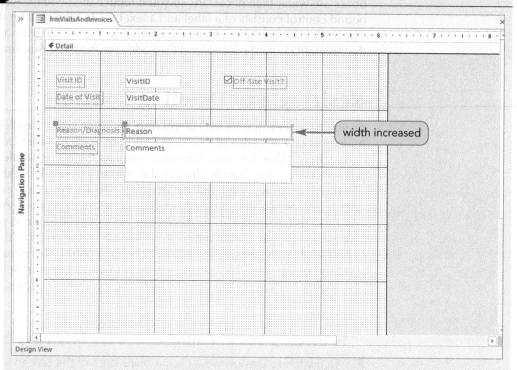

Design View

Resizing controls in Design view is a trial-and-error process, in which you resize a control in Design view, switch to Form view to observe the effect of the resizing, switch back to Design view to make further refinements to the control's size, and continue until the control is sized correctly. It's easier to resize controls in Layout view because you can see actual field values while you resize the controls. You'll resize the other two text box controls in Layout view. The sizes of the VisitID and VisitDate controls will look fine if you reduce them to have the same widths, so you'll select both boxes and resize them with one action.

5. Switch to Layout view, and then click the **VisitID** field value box (if necessary) to select it.

6. Press and hold the **Shift** key, click the **VisitDate** field value box (next to the label "Date of Visit") to select it, and then release the mouse button.

7. Position the pointer on the right border of the **VisitID** field value box until the pointer changes to ↔, drag the border to the left until the field box is slightly wider than the field value it contains, and the date in the VisitID field is also visible, and then release the mouse button. See Figure 6-25.

Figure 6-25	Resized field value boxes in Layout view

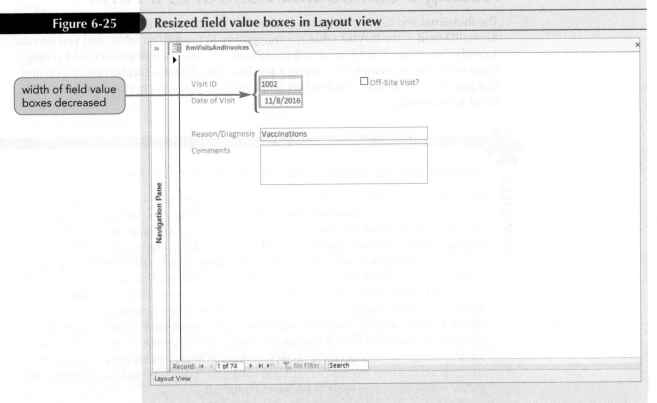

width of field value boxes decreased

Trouble? If you resized the field value boxes too far to the left, number signs will be displayed inside the VisitDate field value box. Drag the right border to the right slightly until the date value is visible.

8. Navigate through the first several records to make sure the three field value boxes are sized properly and display the full field values. If any field value box is too small, select it, and then resize it as appropriate.

9. Save your form design changes, switch to Design view, and then deselect all controls by clicking a blank area of the screen.

Making Form Design Modifications

INSIGHT

When you design forms and other objects, you'll find it helpful to switch frequently between Design view and Layout view. Some form modifications are easier to make in Layout view, other form modifications are easier to make in Design view, and still other form modifications can be made only in Design view. You should check your progress frequently in either Layout view or Form view, and you should save your modifications after completing a set of changes successfully.

Recall that you removed the lookup feature from the AnimalID field because a combo box provides the same lookup capability in a form. Next, you'll add a combo box control for the AnimalID field to the custom form.

Adding a Combo Box Control to a Form

The tblAnimal and tblVisit tables are related in a one-to-many relationship. The AnimalID field in the tblVisit table is a foreign key to the tblVisit table, and you can use a combo box control in the custom form to view and maintain AnimalID field values more easily and accurately than using a text box. Recall that a combo box is a control that provides the features of a text box and a list box; you can choose a value from the list or type an entry.

PROSKILLS

Problem Solving: Using Combo Boxes for Foreign Keys

When you design forms, combo box controls are a natural choice for foreign keys because foreign key values must match one of the primary key values in the related primary table. If you do not use a combo box control for a foreign key, you force users to type values in the text box control. When they make typing mistakes, Access rejects the values and displays nonmatching error messages, which can be frustrating and make the form less efficient for users. Combo box controls allow users to select only from a list of valid foreign key values so that nonmatching situations are eliminated. At the same time, combo boxes allow users who are skilled at data entry to more rapidly type the values, instead of using the more time-consuming technique of choosing a value from the list the combo box control provides. Whenever you use an Access feature such as combo boxes for foreign keys, it takes extra time during development to add the feature, but you save users time and improve their accuracy for the many months or years they use the database.

You use the **Combo Box tool** in Design view to add a combo box control to a form. If you want help when adding the combo box, you can select one of the Control Wizards. A **Control Wizard** asks a series of questions and then, based on your answers, creates a control in a form or report. Access offers Control Wizards for the Combo Box, List Box, Option Group, Command Button, Subform/Subreport, and other control tools.

You will use the Combo Box Wizard to add a combo box control to the form for the AnimalID field.

To add a combo box control to the form:

1. Click the **Form Design Tools Design** tab, and then in the Controls group, click the **More** button to open the Controls gallery. See Figure 6-26.

Figure 6-26   Controls gallery

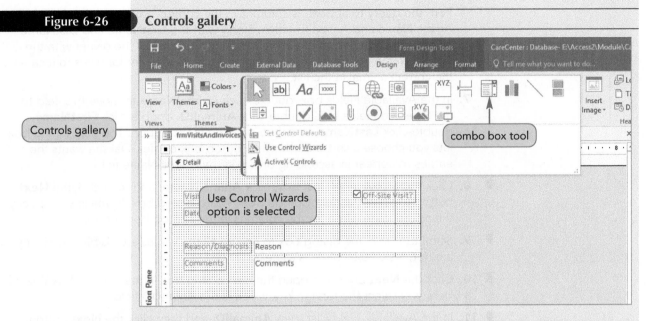

The Controls gallery contains tools that allow you to add controls (such as text boxes, lines, charts, and labels) to a form. You drag a control from the Controls gallery and place it in position in the grid. If you want to use the Combo Box Wizard to add a control, you need to select that option below the gallery.

2. In the gallery, make sure the Use Control Wizards option is selected (its icon should appear with an orange background) at the bottom of the Controls gallery, and if it is not selected, click **Use Control Wizards** to select it, and then click the **More** button again to open the Controls gallery.

3. In the Controls gallery, click the **Combo Box** tool ▦. The Controls gallery closes.

Once you select the Combo Box tool (or most other tools in the Controls gallery) and move the mouse pointer into the Detail section of the form, the pointer changes to a shape that is unique for the control with a plus symbol in its upper-left corner. You position the plus symbol in the location where you want to place the upper-left corner of the control.

You'll place the combo box near the top of the form, below the OffSite bound control, and then position it more precisely after you've completed the steps in the wizard.

4. Position the plus symbol of the pointer shape below the OffSite bound control and at the 3.5 inch mark on the horizontal ruler, and then click the mouse button. A combo box control appears in the form, and the first Combo Box Wizard dialog box opens.

You can use an existing table or query as the source for a new combo box or type the values for the combo box. In this case, you'll use the qryAnimalsAndOwners query as the basis for the new combo box.

5. Click the **I want the combo box to get the values from another table or query** option button (if necessary), then click the **Next** button to open the next Combo Box Wizard dialog box, in which you will specify the source of information for the combo box.

6. In the View section of the dialog box, click the **Queries** option button, click **Query: qryAnimalsAndOwners** in the list, and then click the **Next** button. The next dialog box in the Combo Box Wizard lets you select the fields

from the query to appear as columns in the combo box. You will select the AnimalName and AnimalID fields, along with the FirstName and LastName fields corresponding to the owner. Having the name of the owner with the Animal Name and Animal ID values might make it easier for users to locate the correct animal in the list.

▶ **7.** In the Available Fields box, double-click **AnimalName** to move this field to the Selected Fields box, double-click **AnimalID**, double-click **FirstName**, double-click **LastName**, and then click the **Next** button. The next dialog box lets you choose a sort order for the combo box entries. Daksha wants the entries to appear in ascending order on the AnimalName field.

▶ **8.** Click the **arrow** in the first box, click **AnimalName**, and then click the **Next** button to open the next Combo Box Wizard dialog box, in which you specify the appropriate width for the columns in the combo box control.

▶ **9.** Scroll the list in the dialog box to ensure all the values are visible, and if any are not, resize the columns as necessary.

▶ **10.** Click the **Next** button to open the next dialog box in the Combo Box Wizard. Here you select the foreign key, which is the AnimalID field.

▶ **11.** In the Available Fields list, click **AnimalID**, and then click the **Next** button.

In this dialog box, you specify the field in the tblVisit table where to store the selected AnimalID value from the combo box. You'll store the value in the AnimalID field in the tblVisit table.

▶ **12.** Click the **Store that value in this field** option button, click the arrow to display a list of fields, click **AnimalID**, and then click the **Next** button.

Trouble? If AnimalID doesn't appear in the list, click the Cancel button, press the Delete key to delete the combo box, click the Add Existing Fields button in the Tools group on the Form Design Tools Design tab, double-click AnimalID in the Field List pane, press the Delete key to delete AnimalID, close the Field List pane, and then repeat Steps 1–12.

In the final Combo Box Wizard dialog box, you specify the name for the combo box control. You'll use the field name of AnimalID.

▶ **13.** With the current text selected in the "What label would you like for your combo box?" box, type **AnimalID** and then click the **Finish** button. The completed AnimalID combo box control appears in the form.

You need to position and resize the combo box control, but first you will change the caption property for the AnimalID combo box label control so that it matches the format used by the other label controls in the form.

REFERENCE

Changing a Label's Caption

- Right-click the label to select it and to display the shortcut menu, and then click Properties to display the Property Sheet.
- If necessary, click the All tab to display the All page in the Property Sheet.
- Edit the existing text in the Caption box; or click the Caption box, press the F2 key to select the current value, and then type a new caption.

You want the label control attached to the combo box control to display "Animal ID" instead of "AnimalID". You will change the Caption property for the label control next.

To set the Caption property for the AnimalID combo box's label control:

1. Right-click the **AnimalID** label, which is the control to the left of the AnimalID combo box control, and then click **Properties** on the shortcut menu. The Property Sheet for the AnimalID label control opens.

   Trouble? If the Selection type entry below the Property Sheet title bar is not "Label," then you selected the wrong control in Step 1. Click the AnimalID label in the form to change to the Property Sheet for this control.

2. If necessary, in the Property Sheet, click the **All** tab to display all properties for the selected AnimalID label control.

   The Selection type entry, which appears below the Property Sheet title bar, displays the control type (Label in this case) for the selected control. Below the Selection type entry in the Property Sheet is the Control box, which you can use to select another control in the form and list its properties in the Property Sheet. Alternately, you can simply click a control in the form and modify its properties in the Property Sheet. The first property in the Property Sheet, the **Name property**, specifies the name of a control, section, or object (AnimalID_Label in this case). The Name property value is the same as the value displayed in the Control box, unless the Caption property has been set. For bound controls, the Name property value matches the field name. For unbound controls, an underscore and a suffix of the control type (for example, Label) is added to the Name property setting. For unbound controls, you can set the Name property to another, more meaningful value at any time.

3. In the Caption box, click before "ID", press the **spacebar**, and then press the **Tab** key to move to the next property in the Property Sheet. The Caption property value changes to Animal ID, and the label for the AnimalID bound label control displays Animal ID. See Figure 6-27.

| Figure 6-27 | AnimalID combo box and updated label added to the form |

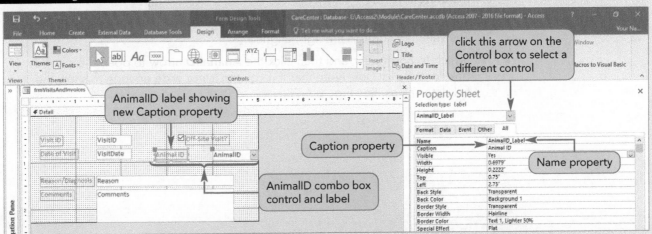

Trouble? Some property values in your Property Sheet, such as the Width and Top property values, might differ if your label's position slightly differs from the label position used as the basis for Figure 6-27. These differences cause no problems.

TIP

You won't see the effects of the new property setting until you select another property, select another control, or close the Property Sheet.

4. Close the Property Sheet, and then save your design changes to the form.

Now that you've added the combo box control to the form, you can position and resize it appropriately. You'll need to view the form in Form view to determine any fine-tuning necessary for the width of the combo box.

To modify the combo box in Design and Layout views:

1. Click the **AnimalID** combo box control, press and hold the **Shift** key, click the **Animal ID** label control, and then release the **Shift** key to select both controls.

   First, you'll move the selected controls above the VisitID controls. Then you'll left-align the AnimalID, VisitID, VisitDate, Reason, and Comments labels; left-align the AnimalID combo box control with the VisitID, VisitDate, Reason, and Comments text box controls; and then right-align the OffSite label and check box control with the right edges of the Reason and Comments text box controls.

2. Drag the selected controls to a position above the VisitID controls. Do not try to align them.

3. Click in a blank area of the screen to deselect the selected controls.

4. Press and hold the **Shift** key while you click the **Animal ID** label, the **Visit ID** label, **Date of Visit** label, **Reason/Diagnosis** label, and the **Comments** label, and then release the **Shift** key.

5. Click the **Form Design Tools Arrange** tab, in the Sizing & Ordering group, click the **Align** button, and then click **Left**. The selected controls are left-aligned.

6. Repeat Steps 4 and 5 to left-align the AnimalID combo box, VisitID text box, VisitDate text box, Reason text box, and the Comments text box.

7. Click the **Off-Site Visit?** label, press and hold the **Shift** key, click the **OffSite** check box, the **Reason** text box, and **Comments** text box, and then release the **Shift** key.

8. In the Sizing & Ordering group, click the **Align** button, and then click **Right**. The selected controls are right-aligned.

9. Switch to Form view, and then click the **AnimalID** arrow to open the combo box control's list box. Note that the column is not wide enough to show the full data values. See Figure 6-28.

| Figure 6-28 | AnimalID combo box and updated label in Form view |

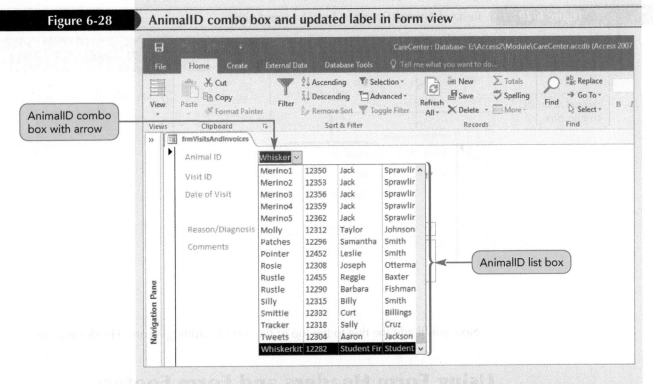

You need to widen the AnimalID combo box so that that the widest value in the list is displayed in the combo box. You can widen the combo box in Layout view or in Design view. Because Form view and Layout view display actual data from the table rather than placeholder text in each bound control, these views let you immediately see the effects of your layout changes. You'll use Layout view instead of Design view to make this change because you can determine the proper width more accurately in Layout view.

10. Switch to Layout view, and then navigate to record 1 (if necessary). Whiskerkitty, which is the animal name for this record, is one of the widest values that is displayed in the combo box. You want to widen the combo box so that it is a little bit wider than the value in record 1.

11. Make sure that only the combo box is selected, and then drag the right border to widen the combo box until the entire name of the animal is visible. See Figure 6-29.

Figure 6-29   Resized AnimalID combo box in Layout view

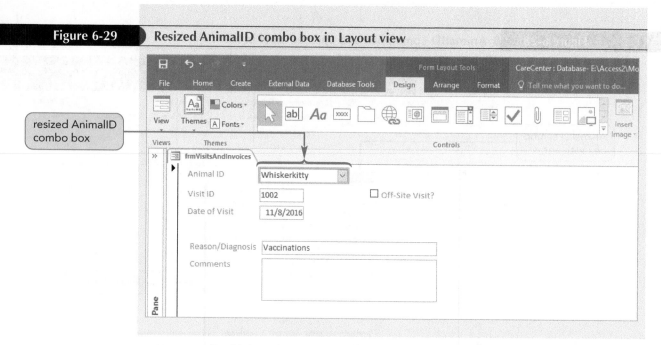

Now you'll add the title to the top of the form by adding a Form Header section.

Using Form Headers and Form Footers

The **Form Header** and **Form Footer sections** let you add titles, instructions, command buttons, and other controls to the top and bottom of your form, respectively. Controls placed in the Form Header or Form Footer sections remain on the screen whenever the form is displayed in Form view or Layout view; they do not change when the contents of the Detail section change as you navigate from one record to another record.

To add either a form header or footer to your form, you must first add both the Form Header and Form Footer sections as a pair to the form. If your form needs one of these sections but not the other, you can remove a section by setting its height to zero, which is the same method you would use to remove any form section. You can also prevent a section from appearing in Form view or in Print Preview by setting its Visible property to "No." The **Visible property** determines if a control or section appears in Form view, in Print Preview, or when printed. You set the Visible property to Yes to display the control or section, and set the Visible property to No to hide it.

If you've set the Form Footer section's height to zero or set its Visible property to No and a future form design change makes adding controls to the Form Footer section necessary, you can restore the section by using the pointer to drag its bottom border back down or by setting its Visible property to Yes.

In Design view, you can add the Form Header and Form Footer sections as a pair to a form by right-clicking the Detail section selector, and then clicking Form Header/ Footer. You also can click the Logo button, the Title button, or the Date and Time button in the Header/Footer group on the Form Design Tools Design tab or the Form Layout Tools Design tab. Clicking any of these three buttons adds the Form Header and Form Footer sections to the form and places an appropriate control in the Form Header section only. A footer section is added to the form, but with a height set to zero to one-quarter inch.

Daksha's design includes a title at the top of the form. Because the title will not change as you navigate through the form records, you will add the title to the Form Header section in the form.

Adding a Title to a Form

You'll add the title to Daksha's form in Layout view. When you add a title to a form in Layout view, a Form Header section is added to the form and contains the form title. At the same time, a Page Footer section with a height setting of zero is added to the form.

To add a title to the form:

▶ **1.** On the Form Layout Tools Design tab, in the Header/Footer group, click the **Title** button. A title consisting of the form name is added to the form and is selected.

You need to change the title.

▶ **2.** Type **Visits and Invoices** to replace the selected default title text. See Figure 6-30.

Figure 6-30   Title added to the form in the Form Header section

The title is a larger font size than the font used for the form's labels and field value boxes, but Daksha would like you to apply bold to increase its prominence.

▶ **3.** Select the title control, click the **Form Layout Tools Format** tab, and then in the Font group, click the **Bold** button B. The title is displayed in 18-point, bold text.

It is not obvious in Layout view that the title is displayed in the Form Header section, so you'll view the form design in Design view.

▶ **4.** Switch to Design view, click a blank area of the screen to deselect all controls. The title is displayed in the Form Header section. See Figure 6-31.

Figure 6-31 **Form Header and Form Footer sections in Design view**

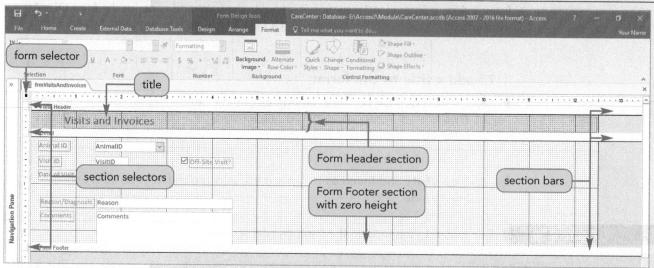

Figure 6-31 **Form Header and Form Footer sections in Design view**

The form now contains a Form Header section that displays the title, a Detail section that displays the bound controls and labels, and a Form Footer section that is set to a height of zero. Each section consists of a **section selector** and a section bar, either of which you can click to select and set properties for the entire section, and a grid or background, which is where you place controls that you want to display in the form. The **form selector** is the selector at the intersection of the horizontal and vertical rulers; you click the form selector when you want to select the entire form and set its properties. The vertical ruler is segmented into sections for the Form Header section, the Detail section, and the Form Footer section.

A form's total height includes the heights of the Form Header, Detail, and Form Footer sections. If you set a form's total height to more than the screen size, users will need to use scroll bars to view the content of your form, which is less productive for users and isn't good form design.

5. Save the design changes to the form, and then, if you are not continuing on to the next session, close the CareCenter database.

So far, you've added controls to the form and modified the controls by selecting, moving, aligning, resizing, and deleting them. You've added and modified a combo box and added a title in the Form Header section. In the next session, you will continue your work with the custom form by adding a combo box control for use in finding records, adding a subform, adding calculated controls, changing form and section properties, and changing control properties.

Session 6.2 Quick Check

REVIEW

1. What is a bound form, and when do you use bound forms?
2. What is the difference between a bound control and an unbound control?
3. The _____ consists of the dotted and solid lines that appear in the Header, Detail, and Footer sections in Design view to help you position controls precisely in a form.
4. The larger handle in a selected object's upper-left corner is the _____ handle.
5. How do you move a selected field value box and its label at the same time?
6. How do you resize a control?
7. A(n) _____ control provides the features of a text box and a list box.
8. How do you change a label's caption?
9. What is the purpose of the Form Header section?

Session 6.3 Visual Overview:

The label control has a shadow effect and uses a bold, red font.

You use the Line tool in Design view to add a line to a form or report.

These text box controls have a sunken effect.

This calculated control uses the Count function, which determines the number of occurrences of an expression; its general format as a control in a form or report is =Count(expression).

The labels are formatted with bold, blue text and the same background color as the Detail section.

You use the Rectangle tool to add a rectangle to a layout. This rectangle groups these controls and their labels visually.

This calculated control uses the Sum function, which calculates the total of an expression; its general format as a control in a form or report is =Sum(expression).

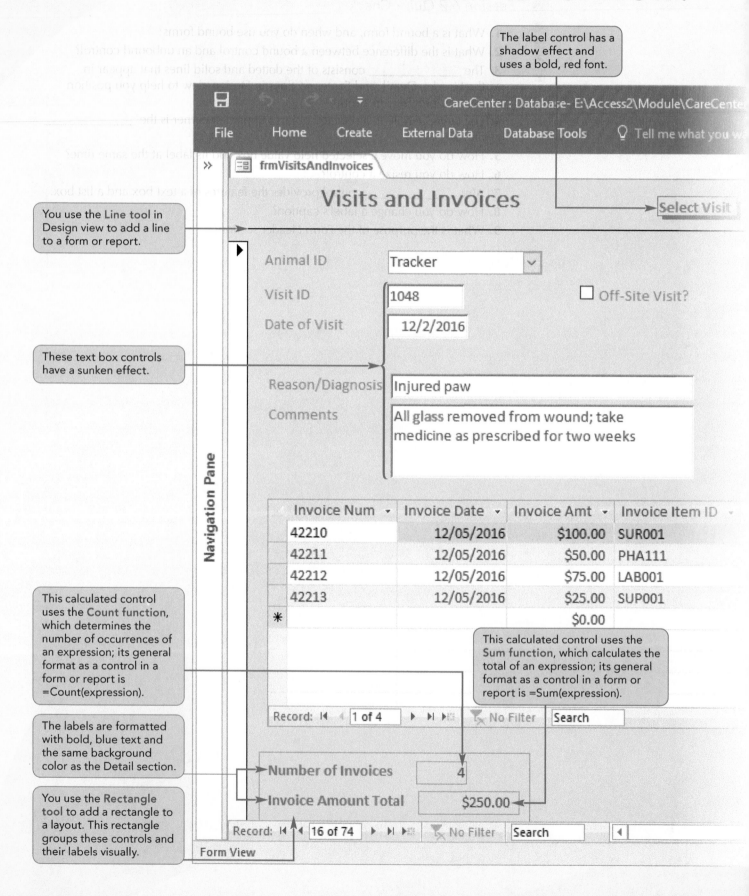

Custom Form in Form View

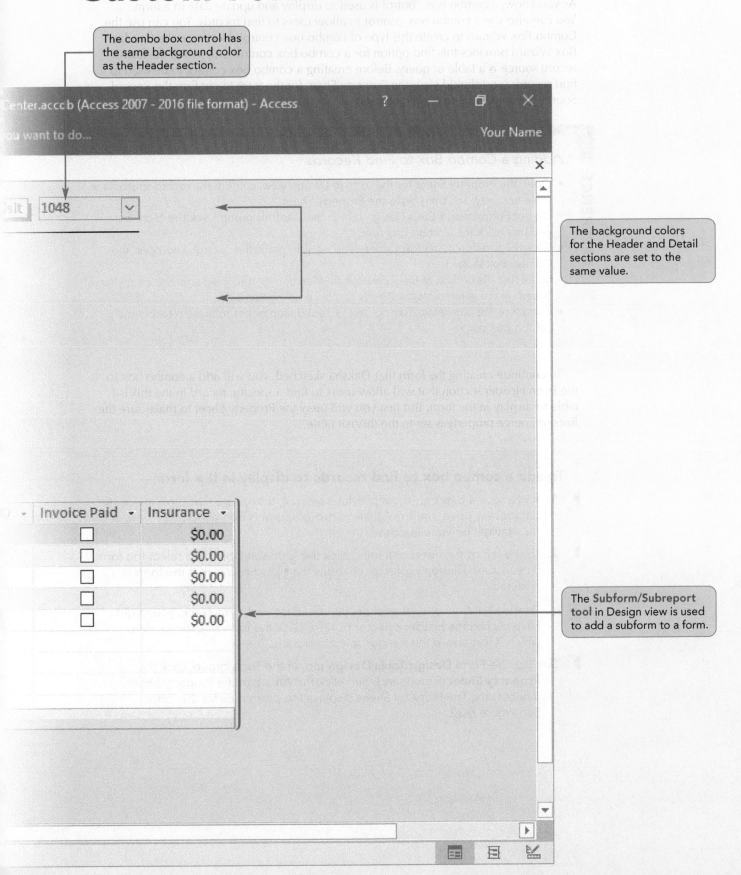

The combo box control has the same background color as the Header section.

Center.accdb (Access 2007 - 2016 file format) - Access   ? — □ ×

ou want to do...   Your Name

1048

The background colors for the Header and Detail sections are set to the same value.

Invoice Paid	Insurance
☐	$0.00
☐	$0.00
☐	$0.00
☐	$0.00
☐	$0.00

The **Subform/Subreport** tool in Design view is used to add a subform to a form.

Adding a Combo Box to Find Records

As you know, a combo box control is used to display and update data in a form. You can also use a combo box control to allow users to find records. You can use the Combo Box Wizard to create this type of combo box control. However, the Combo Box Wizard provides this find option for a combo box control only when the form's record source is a table or query. Before creating a combo box control to be used to find records, you should view the Property Sheet for the form to confirm the Record Source property is set to a table or query.

Adding a Combo Box to Find Records

- Open the Property Sheet for the form in Design view, confirm the record source is a table or query, and then close the Property Sheet.
- On the Form Design Tools Design tab, in the Controls group, click the More button, and then click the Combo Box tool.
- Click the location in the form where you want to place the control, and open the Combo Box Wizard.
- In the first dialog box of the Combo Box Wizard, click the "Find a record on my form based on the value I selected in my combo box" option button.
- Complete the remaining Combo Box Wizard dialog boxes to finish creating the combo box control.

To continue creating the form that Daksha sketched, you will add a combo box to the Form Header section that will allow users to find a specific record in the tblVisit table to display in the form. But first you will view the Property Sheet to make sure the Record Source property is set to the tblVisit table.

To add a combo box to find records to display in the form:

1. If you took a break after the previous session, make sure that the CareCenter database is open, the frmVisitsAndInvoices form is open in Design view, and the Navigation Pane is closed.

2. To the left of the horizontal ruler, click the form selector ▢ to select the form, if necessary. The form selector changes to ▣, indicating that the form is selected.

   Trouble? If the Form Header section head instead turns black, you might have clicked the header selector button. Click the form selector button, which is just above the header selector button.

3. Click the **Form Design Tools Design** tab, in the Tools group, click the **Property Sheet** button, and then click the **All** tab in the Property Sheet, if necessary. The Property Sheet displays the properties for the form. See Figure 6-32.

Figure 6-32 **Property sheet for the form**

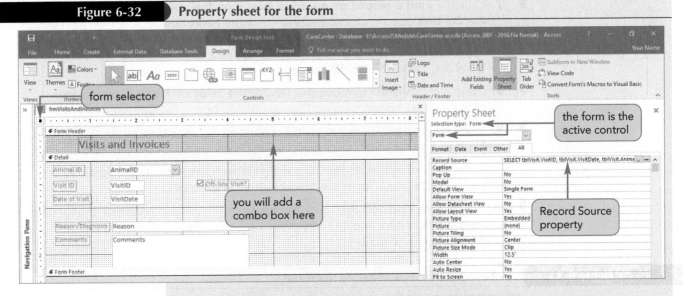

The Record Source property is set to an SQL SELECT statement, which is code that references a table. You need to change the Record Source property to a table or query, or the Combo Box Wizard will not present you with the option to find records in a form. You'll change the Record Source property to the tblVisit table because this table is the record source for all the bound controls you have added to the Detail section of the form.

4. In the Record Source box, click the **Record Source** arrow, click **tblVisit** in the list, and then close the Property Sheet.

   You'll now use the Combo Box Wizard to add a combo box to the form's Form Header section, which will enable a user to find a record in the tblVisit table to display in the form.

5. On the Form Design Tools Design tab, in the Controls group, click the **More** button to open the Controls gallery, and then click the **Combo Box** tool 🔲.

6. Position the plus symbol pointer at the top of the Form Header section at the 5-inch mark on the horizontal ruler (see Figure 6-32), and then click the mouse button. A combo box control appears in the Form Header section of the form, and the first Combo Box Wizard dialog box opens.

   Trouble? If the Combo Box Wizard dialog box does not open, delete the new controls and try again, ensuring the plus symbol pointer is very near the top of the Form Header grid.

   You will recall seeing this dialog box when you used the Combo Box Wizard in the previous session. The first dialog box in the Combo Box Wizard this time displays an additional option than what was available previously. This additional option, "Find a record on my form based on the value I selected in my combo box," is what you need to use for this combo box. (Recall in the last session you selected the first option, "I want the combo box to get the values from another table or query" when you used the Combo Box Wizard to create the AnimalID combo box, allowing the user to select a value from a list of foreign key values from an existing table or query.) You would choose the second option if you wanted users to select a value from a short fixed list of values that don't change. For example, if Riverview Veterinary Care Center wanted to include a field in the tblAnimal table to identify the state in which the animal resides, you could use a combo box with this second option to display a list of states.

7. Click the **Find a record on my form based on the value I selected in my combo box** option button, and then click the **Next** button. The next Combo Box Wizard dialog box lets you select the fields from the tblVisit table to appear as columns in the combo box. You need to include only one column of values, listing the VisitID values.

8. Double-click **VisitID** to move this field to the Selected Fields box, and then click the **Next** button to open the next dialog box in the Combo Box Wizard.

9. In the dialog box, resize the VisitID column to its best fit, and then click the **Next** button.

In the last dialog box in the Combo Box Wizard, you specify the name for the combo box's label. You'll use "Select Visit" as the label.

10. Type **Select Visit** and then click the **Finish** button. The completed unbound combo box control and its corresponding Select Visit label appear in the form. See Figure 6-33.

Figure 6-33	Unbound combo box added to the form

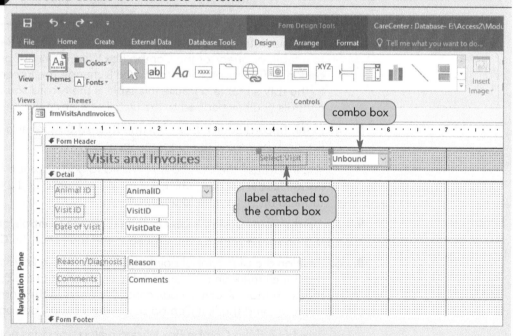

You'll move the attached label closer to the combo box control, and then you'll align the bottoms of the combo box control and its attached label with the bottom of the title in the Form Header section.

11. Click the **Select Visit** label, point to the label's move handle on the upper-left corner of the orange selection border, and then drag the label to the right until its right edge is two grid dots to the left of the combo box.

12. With the Select Visit label still selected, press and hold the **Shift** key, click the **combo box**, and then click the **Visit and Invoices** form title.

13. Right-click the selected controls, point to **Align** on the shortcut menu, and then click **Bottom**. The three selected controls are bottom-aligned. See Figure 6-34.

Figure 6-34   Aligned combo box control and form title

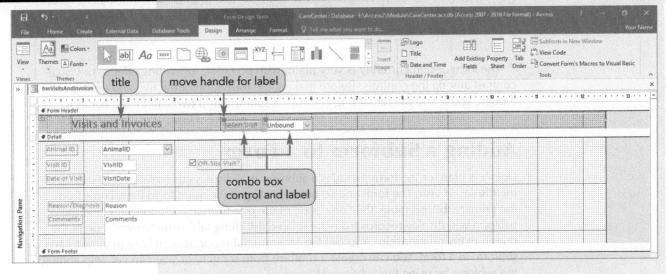

You'll save your form changes and view the new combo box control in Form view.

To save the form and view the Select Visit combo box control:

1. Save the form design changes, and then switch to Form view.

2. Click the **Select Visit** arrow to display the list of Visit ID numbers. See Figure 6-35.

Figure 6-35   List of Visit IDs in the combo box

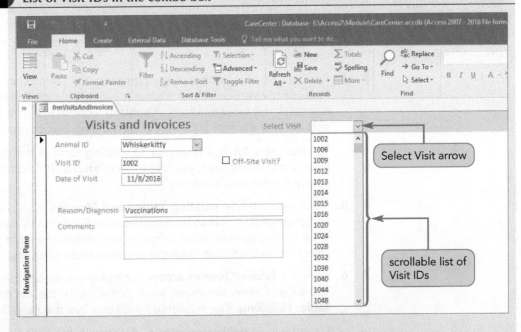

3. Scroll down the list, and then click **1048**. The current record changes from record 1 to record 16, which is the record for visit ID 1048.

Trouble? If you see the data for record 1, the navigation combo box is not working correctly. Delete the combo box, check to ensure that you have set the Record Source for the form object correctly, and repeat the previous set of steps to re-create the combo box.

The form design currently is very plain, with no color, formatting effects, or visual contrast among the controls. Before making the form more attractive and useful, though, you'll add the remaining controls: a subform and two calculated controls.

Adding a Subform to a Form

Daksha's plan for the form includes a subform that displays the related invoices for the displayed visit. The form you've been creating is the main form for records from the primary tblVisit table (the "one" side of the one-to-many relationship), and the subform will display records from the related tblBilling table (the "many" side of the one-to-many relationship). You use the Subform/Subreport tool in Design view to add a subform to a form. You can create a subform from scratch, or you can get help adding the subform by using the SubForm Wizard.

You will use the SubForm Wizard to add the subform for displaying tblBilling table records to the bottom of the form. First, you'll increase the height of the Detail section to make room for the subform.

To add the subform to the form:

1. Switch to Design view.

TIP

Drag slightly beyond the desired ending position to expose the vertical ruler measurement, and then decrease the height back to the correct position.

2. Position the pointer on the bottom border of the Detail section until the pointer changes to ✛, and then drag the border down to the 5-inch mark on the vertical ruler.

3. On the Form Design Tools Design tab, in the Controls group, click the **More** button to open the Controls gallery, and then click the **Subform/Subreport** tool ▦.

4. Position the plus symbol of the pointer in the Detail section at the 2.5-inch mark on the vertical ruler and at the 1-inch mark on the horizontal ruler, and then click the mouse button. A subform control appears in the form's Detail section, and the first SubForm Wizard dialog box opens.

   You can use a table, a query, or an existing form as the record source for a subform. In this case, you'll use the related tblBilling table as the record source for the new subform.

5. Make sure the **Use existing Tables and Queries** option button is selected, and then click the **Next** button. The next SubForm Wizard dialog box opens, in which you select a table or query as the record source for the subform and select the fields to use from the selected table or query.

6. Click the **Tables/Queries arrow** to display the list of tables and queries in the CareCenter database, scroll to the top of the list, and then click **Table: tblBilling**. The Available Fields box lists the fields in the tblBilling table.

   Daksha's form design includes all fields from the tblBilling table in the subform, except for the VisitID field, which you already placed in the Detail section of the form from the tblVisit table.

7. Click the >> button to move all available fields to the Selected Fields box, click **VisitID** in the Selected Fields box, click the < button, and then click the **Next** button to open the next SubForm Wizard dialog box. See Figure 6-36.

Figure 6-36 **Selecting the linking field**

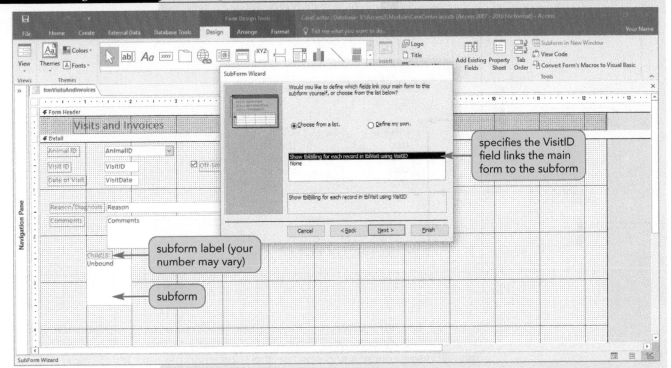

In this dialog box, you select the link between the primary tblVisit table and the related tblBilling table. The common field in the two tables, VisitID, links the tables. The form will use the VisitID field to display a record in the main form, which displays data from the primary tblVisit table, and to select and display the related records for that contract in the subform, which displays data from the related tblBilling table.

8. Make sure the **Choose from a list** option button is selected, make sure **"Show tblBilling for each record in tblVisit using VisitID"** is selected in the list, and then click the **Next** button. In the last SubForm Wizard dialog box, you specify a name for the subform.

9. Type **frmBillingSubform** and then click the **Finish** button. The completed subform appears in the Details section of the Form window; its label appears above the subform and displays the subform name.

10. Click a blank area of the screen, and then save the form.

11. Switch to Form view, click the **Select Visit** arrow, and then click **1048**. The subform displays the four invoices related to visit ID 1048. See Figure 6-37.

Figure 6-37	The subform in Form view

subform label

subform

Trouble? It is not a problem if the widths of the columns in your datasheet differ or the position of your subform is not exactly as shown in Figure 6-37. You will resize columns and position the subform in the next set of steps.

After viewing the form, Daksha identifies some modifications he wants you to make. He wants you to resize the subform and its columns so that all columns in the subform are entirely visible and the columns are sized to best fit. Also, he asks you to delete the subform label, because the label is unnecessary for identifying the subform contents. You'll use Design view and Layout view to make these changes.

To modify the subform's design and adjust its position in the form:

1. Switch to Design view. Notice that in Design view, the data in the subform control does not appear in a datasheet format as it does in Form view. That difference causes no problem; you can ignore it.

   First, you'll delete the subform label control.

2. Deselect all controls (if necessary), right-click the **frmBillingSubform** subform label control to open the shortcut menu, and then click **Delete**.

   Next, you'll align the subform control with the Comments label control.

3. Click the border of the subform control to select it, press and hold the **Shift** key, click the **Comments** label control, and then release the **Shift** key. The subform control and the Comments label control are selected. Next you'll left-align the two controls.

4. Right-click the **Comments** label control, point to **Align** on the shortcut menu, and then click **Left**. The two controls are left-aligned. Next, you'll resize the subform control in Layout view so that you can observe the effects of your changes as you make them.

5. Switch to Layout view, click the border of the subform to select it, and then drag the right border of the subform to the right until the Insurance column arrow is fully visible.

   Before resizing the columns in the subform to best fit, you'll display record 16 in the main form. The subform for this record contains the related records in the tblBilling table with one of the longest field values.

6. Use the record navigation bar for the main form (at the bottom left of the form window) to display record 16, for visit number 1048, and then resize each column in the subform to its best fit.

   Next, you'll resize the subform again so that its width matches the width of the five resized columns.

7. Resize the subform so that its right border is aligned with the right border of the Insurance column. See Figure 6-38.

Figure 6-38	Moved and resized subform

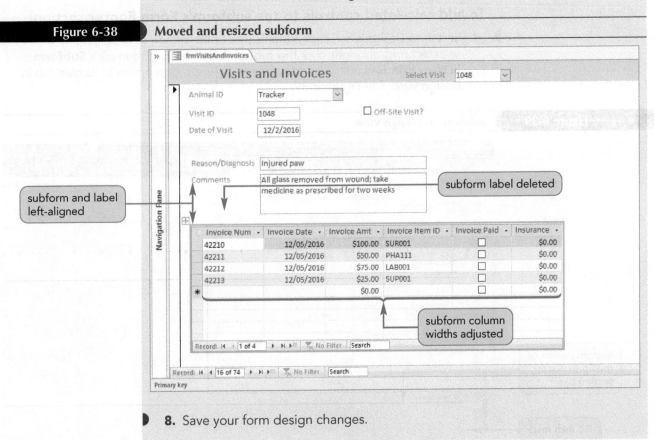

8. Save your form design changes.

You've finished your work with the subform. Now you need to add two calculated controls to the main form.

Displaying a Subform's Calculated Controls in the Main Form

Daksha's form design includes the display of calculated controls in the main form that tally the number of invoices and the total of the invoice amounts for the related records displayed in the subform. To display these calculated controls in a form or report, you use the Count and Sum functions. The Count function determines the number of occurrences of an expression; its general format as a control in a form or report is =Count(*expression*). The Sum function calculates the total of an expression, and its general format as a control in a form or report is =Sum(*expression*). The number of invoices and total of invoice amounts are displayed in the subform's Detail section, so you'll need to place the calculated controls in the subform's Form Footer section.

Adding Calculated Controls to a Subform's Form Footer Section

First, you'll open the subform in Design view in another window and add the calculated controls to the subform's Form Footer section.

To add calculated controls to the subform's Form Footer section:

1. Switch to Design view, click a blank area of the screen to deselect any selected controls, right-click the subform's border, and then click **Subform in New Window** on the shortcut menu. The subform opens in its own tab in Design view. See Figure 6-39.

Figure 6-39	Subform in Design view

The subform's Detail section contains the tblBilling table fields. As a subform in the main form, the fields appear in a datasheet even though the fields do not appear that way in Design view. The heights of the subform's Form

Header and Form Footer sections are zero, meaning that these sections have been removed from the subform. You'll increase the height of the Form Footer section so that you can add the two calculated controls to the section.

▶ 2. Click the **Form Footer** section bar, position the pointer on the bottom border of the Form Footer section bar until the pointer changes to ✛, and then drag the bottom border of the section down to the 0.5-inch mark on the vertical ruler.

Now you'll add the first calculated control to the Form Footer section. To create the text box for the calculated control, you use the Text Box tool in the Controls group on the Form Design Tools Design tab. Because the Form Footer section is not displayed in a datasheet, you do not need to position the control precisely.

▶ 3. On the Form Design Tools Design tab, in the Controls group, click the **Text Box** tool ab|.

▶ 4. Position the plus symbol of the pointer near the top of the Form Footer section and aligned with the 1-inch mark on the horizontal ruler, and then click the mouse button. A text box control and an attached label control appear in the Form Footer section. The text "Unbound" appears in the text box, indicating it is an unbound control.

Next, you'll set the Name and Control Source properties for the text box. Recall that the Name property specifies the name of an object or control. Later, when you add the calculated control in the main form, you'll reference the subform's calculated control value by using its Name property value. The **Control Source property** specifies the source of the data that appears in the control; the Control Source property setting can be either a field name or an expression.

▶ 5. Open the Property Sheet for the text box in the Form Footer section, click the **All** tab (if necessary), select the value in the Name box, type **txtInvoiceAmtSum** in the Name box, and then press the **Tab** key to move to the Control Source box.

▶ 6. In the Control Source box, type **=Sum(Inv**, press the **Tab** key to accept the rest of the field name of InvoiceAmt suggested by Formula AutoComplete, type **)** (a right parenthesis), and then press the **Tab** key. InvoiceAmt is enclosed in brackets in the expression because it's a field name. See Figure 6-40.

Figure 6-40   **Setting properties for the subform calculated control**

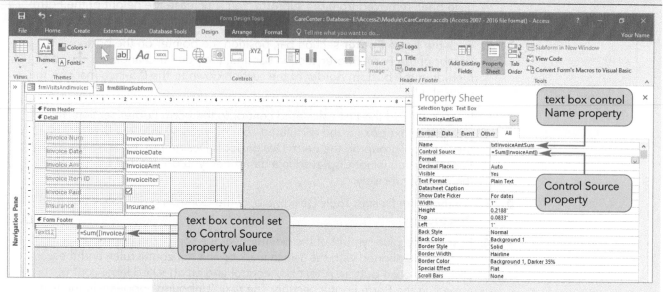

You've finished creating the first calculated control; now you'll create the other calculated control.

TIP

In the Name property, txtInvoiceNumCount, txt identifies the control type (a text box), InvoiceNum is the related field name, and Count identifies the control as a count control.

7. Repeat Steps 3 through 6, positioning the calculated field text box near the top of the Form Footer section aligned to the 3.5-inch mark on the horizontal ruler, setting the Name property value to **txtInvoiceNumCount**, and setting the Control Source property value to **=Count([InvoiceNum])**.

    When you use the Count function, you are counting the number of displayed records—in this case, the number of records displayed in the subform. Instead of using InvoiceNum as the expression for the Count function, you could use any of the other fields displayed in the subform.

    You've finished creating the subform's calculated controls.

8. Close the Property Sheet, save your subform changes, and then close the subform. The active object is now the main form in Design view.

    Trouble? The subform in the frmContractsAndInvoices form might appear to be blank after you close the frmInvoiceSubform form. This is a temporary effect; the subform's controls do still exist. Switch to Form view and then back to Design view to display the subform's controls.

9. Switch to Form view. The calculated controls you added in the subform's Form Footer section are *not* displayed in the subform.

10. Switch to Design view.

Next, you'll add two calculated controls in the main form to display the two calculated controls from the subform.

Adding Calculated Controls to a Main Form

The subform's calculated controls now contain a count of the number of invoices and a total of the invoice amounts. However, notice that Daksha's design has the two calculated controls displayed in the main form, *not* in the subform. You need to add two calculated controls in the main form that reference the values in the subform's calculated controls. Because it's easy to make a typing mistake with these references, you'll use Expression Builder to set the Control Source property for the two main form calculated controls.

To add a calculated control to the main form's Detail section:

▶ 1. Adjust the length of the Detail section if necessary so that there is approximately 0.5 inch below the frmBillingSubform control. The Detail section should be approximately 5.5 inches.

▶ 2. On the Form Design Tools Design tab, in the Controls group, click the **Text Box** tool [ab].

▶ 3. Position the pointer's plus symbol below the frmBillingSubform at the 5-inch mark on the vertical ruler and aligned with the 1-inch mark on the horizontal ruler, and then click to insert the text box control and label in the form. Don't be concerned about positioning the control precisely because you'll resize and move the label and text box later.

▶ 4. Open the Property Sheet, click the label control for the text box, set its Caption property to **Number of Invoices**, right-click the border of the label control, point to **Size** on the shortcut menu, and then click **To Fit**. Don't worry if the label control now overlaps the text box control.

You'll use Expression Builder to set Control Source property for the text box control.

▶ 5. Click the unbound text box control to select it, click the **Control Source** box in the Property Sheet, and then click the property's **Build** button [...] to open Expression Builder.

▶ 6. In the Expression Elements box, click the **expand indicator** [+] next to frmVisitsAndInvoices, and then click **frmBillingSubform** in the Expression Elements box.

▶ 7. Scroll down the Expression Categories box, and then double-click **txtInvoiceNumCount** in the Expression Categories box. See Figure 6-41.

| Figure 6-41 | Text box control's expression in the Expression Builder dialog box |

Instead of adding txtInvoiceNumCount to the expression box at the top, the Expression Builder changed it to [frmBillingSubform]. Form![txtInvoiceNumCount]. This expression displays the value of the txtInvoiceNumCount control that is located in the frmBillingSubform form, which is a form object.

You need to add an equal sign to the beginning of the expression.

▶ **8.** Press the **Home** key, type **=** (an equal sign), and then click the **OK** button. The Expression Builder dialog box closes, and the Control Source property is set.

Next, you'll add a second text box control to the main form, set the Caption property for the label control, and use Expression Builder to set the text box's Control Source property.

Be sure you resize the label to its best fit.

▶ **9.** Repeat Steps 2 through 4 to add a text box to the main form, positioning the text box at the 3.5-inch mark on the horizontal ruler and approximately the 5-inch mark on the vertical ruler, and setting the label's Caption property to **Invoice Amount Total**.

▶ **10.** Click the unbound text box control to select it, click the **Control Source** box in the Property Sheet, and then click the property's **Build** button [···] to open Expression Builder.

▶ **11.** In the Expression Builder dialog box, type **=** (an equal sign), in the Expression Elements box, click the **expand indicator** [+] next to frmVisitsAndInvoices, click **frmBillingSubform** in the Expression Elements box, scroll down the Expression Categories box, and then double-click **txtInvoiceAmtSum** in the Expression Categories box.

▶ **12.** Click the **OK** button to accept the expression and close the Expression Builder dialog box, close the Property Sheet, and save the form.

▶ **13.** Click the **Collapse the Ribbon** button [⌃], switch to Form view, and then display the record for VisitID 1048. See Figure 6-42.

Figure 6-42   Form with calculated controls

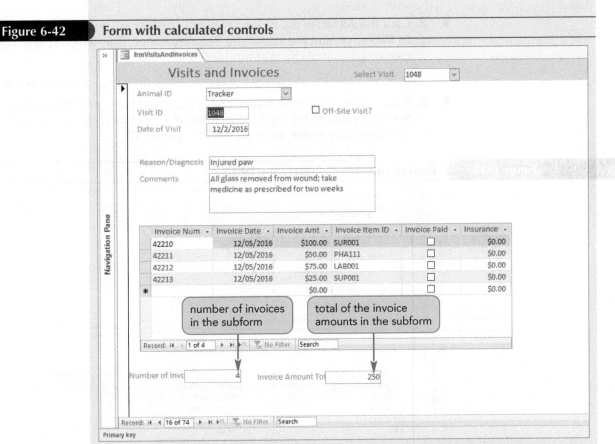

Now that the calculated controls are in the form, you will modify their appearance. You also will set additional properties for the calculated controls.

Resizing, Moving, and Formatting Calculated Controls

In addition to resizing and repositioning the two calculated controls and their attached labels, you need to change the format of the rightmost calculated control to Currency and to set the following properties for both calculated controls.

- Set the Tab Stop property to a value of No. The **Tab Stop property** specifies whether users can use the Tab key to navigate to a control on a form. If the Tab Stop property is set to No, users can't tab to the control.
- Set the ControlTip Text property to a value of "Calculated total number of invoices for this animal visit" for the calculated control on the left and "Calculated invoice total for this animal visit" for the calculated control on the right. The **ControlTip Text property** specifies the text that appears in a ScreenTip when users position the mouse pointer over a control in a form.

Now you'll resize, move, and format the calculated controls and their attached labels.

To size, move, and format the calculated controls and their attached labels:

▶ 1. Switch to Layout view, right-click the **Invoice Amount Total** calculated control, and then click **Properties** on the shortcut menu to open the Property Sheet.

2. Click the **All** tab in the Property Sheet (if necessary), set the Format property to **Currency**, and then close the Property Sheet. The value displayed in the calculated control changes from 250 to $250.00.

Now you'll resize and move the controls into their final positions in the form.

3. Individually, reduce the widths of the two calculated controls by dragging the left border to the right to decrease the text box width so that they approximately match those shown in Figure 6-43.

| Figure 6-43 | Resized calculated controls and labels |

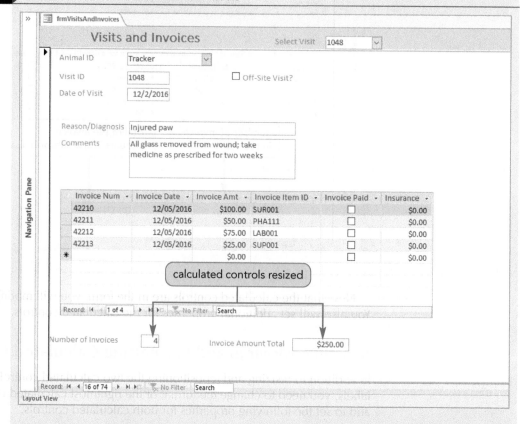

4. Switch to Design view, select the **Number of Invoices** label and its related calculated control, and then use the → key to move the label and its related text box to the right, aligning the left edge of the label with the left edge of the Comments label as closely as possible.

5. Press the ↑ key four times to move the selected calculated control and its label until it is two grid dots from the bottom of the subform control.

6. Lengthen the Detail section to approximately the 6-inch marker on the vertical ruler.

7. Click the **Invoice Amount Total** label control, press the **Shift** key, click the corresponding calculated control text box, release the **Shift** key, and then drag the selected calculated control and its label to position them below and left-aligned with the Number of Invoices label control and its calculated control.

TIP

In Design view you must use the move handle to move only a text box or its label, while in Layout view you can use either the move handle or the arrow keys.

8. Switch to Layout view.

9. Click the **Invoice Amount Total** label control, and use the arrow keys to left-align the label control with the Number of Invoices label, select the **Invoice Amount Total** text box, and then use the arrows to left-align the calculated control text box with the Number of Invoices calculated control text box.

10. Deselect all controls, switch to Form view, and then select record 1048. See Figure 6-44.

Figure 6-44	Calculated controls and labels aligned

modified calculated controls and labels

The calculated controls and their labels are properly placed in the form. Next you will set the Tab Stop Property and the ControlTip Text property for both controls, which you can do on the Other tab in the control's Property Sheet.

To set the Tab Stop Property and the ControlTipText property for the calculated controls:

1. Switch to Layout view, right-click the **Invoice Amount Total** calculated control, click **Properties** on the shortcut menu, and then click the **Other** tab in the Property Sheet.

2. Set the Tab Stop property to **No**, and then set the ControlTip Text property to **Calculated invoice total for this animal visit**.

3. Click the **Number of Invoices** calculated control to display this control's properties in the Property Sheet, set the Tab Stop property to **No**, and then set the ControlTip Text property to **Calculated total number of invoices for this animal visit**.

4. Close the Property Sheet, save your form design changes, switch to Form view, and then display visit 1048.

5. Position the pointer on the **Number of Invoices** box to display its ScreenTip, and then position the pointer on the **Invoice Amount Total** box to display its ScreenTip. You may have to pause while you position the pointer over the box, until the ScreenTip appears. See Figure 6-45.

Figure 6-45 ▶ **ScreenTip for the calculated control**

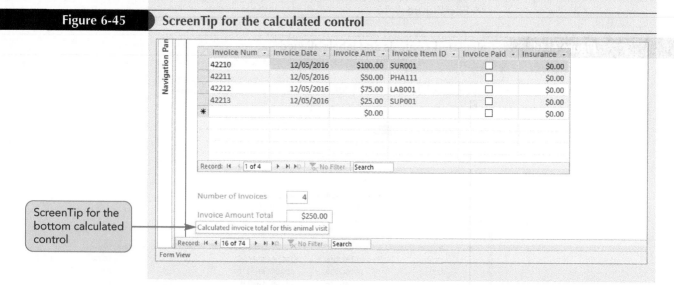

ScreenTip for the bottom calculated control

Daksha asks you to verify that users can't update the calculated controls in the main form and that when users tab through the controls in the form, the controls are selected in the correct order.

Changing the Tab Order in a Form

Pressing the Tab key in Form view moves the focus from one control to another. A control is said to have **focus** when it is active and awaiting user action. The order in which the focus moves from control to control when a user presses the Tab key is called the **tab order**. Setting a logical tab order enables the user to keep his or her hands on the keyboard without reaching for the mouse, thereby speeding up the process of data entry in a form. Daksha wants to verify that the tab order in the main form is top-to-bottom, left-to-right. First, you'll verify that users can't update the calculated controls.

To test the calculated controls and modify the tab order:

1. Select the value in the Number of Invoices box, and then type **8**. The Number of Invoices value remains unchanged, and the message "Control can't be edited; it's bound to the expression '[frmBillingSubform]. [Form]![txtInvoiceNumCount]'" is displayed on the status bar. The status bar message warns you that you can't update, or edit, the calculated control because it's bound to an expression. The calculated control in the main form changes in value only when the value of the expression changes in the subform.

2. Click the Invoice Amount Total box, and then type **8**. The value remains unchanged, and a message again displays on the status bar because you cannot edit a calculated control.

Next, you'll determine the tab order of the fields in the main form. Daksha wants the tab order to be down and then across.

3. Select the value in the Visit ID box, press the **Tab** key to advance to the Date of Visit box, and then press the **Tab** key five more times to advance to the Reason/Diagnosis box, Comments text box, OffSite check box, and AnimalID combo box, in order, and then to the subform.

Access sets the tab order in the same order in which you add controls to a form, so you should always check the form's tab order when you create a custom form in Layout or Design view. In this form you can see that the tab order is set such that the user will tab through the field value boxes in the main form before tabbing through the fields in the subform. In the main form, tabbing bypasses the two calculated controls because you set their Tab Stop properties to No, and you bypass the Select Visit combo box because it's an unbound control. Also, you tab through only the field value boxes in a form, not the labels.

The tab order Daksha wants for the field value boxes in the main form (top-to-bottom, left-to-right) should be the following: AnimalID, VisitID, OffSite, VisitDate, Reason, Comments, and then the subform. The default tab order doesn't match the order Daksha wants, so you'll change the tab order. You can change the tab order only in Design view.

4. Double-click the **Home** tab to restore the ribbon, switch to Design view, and then on the Form Design Tools Design tab, in the Tools group, click the **Tab Order** button. The Tab Order dialog box opens. See Figure 6-46.

Figure 6-46	Tab Order dialog box

Because you did not set the Name property for the combo box control and the calculated controls, Access assigned them names that consist of the type of control and number; for example Combo12 for the AnimalID combo box, Text24 for the Number of Invoices calculated control, and Text26 for the Invoice Amount Total calculated control as shown in Figure 6-46. (The numbers assigned to your controls might differ.) The Auto Order button lets you create a left-to-right, top-to-bottom tab order automatically, which is not the order Daksha wants. You need to move the Combo12 entry above the VisitID entry.

TIP

Setting the Name property for all your controls to meaningful names avoids having to guess which control a name references in this and similar situations.

5. Click the **row selector** to the left of the Combo12 item (your number might differ), and then drag the row selector up to position it above the VisitID entry.

6. Click the row selector to the left of the OffSite item, and then drag the row selector up to position it above VisitDate. The entries are now correct and in the correct order. See Figure 6-47.

Figure 6-47   **Tab Order dialog box with corrected order**

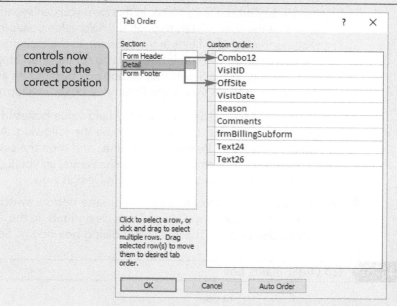

controls now moved to the correct position

7. Click the **OK** button to close the Tab Order dialog box, save your form design changes, and then switch to Form view.

8. Tab through the controls in the main form to make sure the tab order is correct, moving from the Animal ID box, to the Visit ID box, then to the Off-Site Visit checkbox, then to Date of Visit box, the Reason/Diagnosis box, to the Comments box, and then finally to the subform.

   Trouble? If the tab order is incorrect, switch to Design view, click the Tab Order button in the Tools group, change your tab order in the Tab Order dialog box to match the order shown in Figure 6-47, and then repeat Steps 7 and 8.

Written Communication: Enhancing Information Using Calculated Controls

For a small number of records in a subform, it's easy for users to quickly count the number of records and to calculate numeric total amounts when the form doesn't display calculated controls. For instance, when students have completed few courses or when people have made few tax payments, it's easy for users to count the courses and calculate the student's GPA or to count and total the tax payments. But for subforms with dozens or hundreds of records—for instance, students with many courses, or people with many tax payments—displaying summary calculated controls is mandatory. By adding a few simple calculated controls to forms and reports, you can increase the usefulness of the information presented and improve the ability of users to process the information, spot trends, and be more productive in their jobs.

You've finished adding controls to the form, but the form is plain looking and lacks visual clues organizing the controls in the form. You'll complete the form by making it more attractive and easier for Kimberly and her staff to use.

Improving a Form's Appearance

The frmVisitsAndInvoices form has four distinct areas: the Form Header section containing the title and the Select Visit combo box, the six bound controls in the Detail section, the subform in the Detail section, and the two calculated controls in the Detail section. To visually separate these four areas, you'll increase the height of the Form Header section, add a horizontal line at the bottom of the Form Header section, and draw a rectangle around the calculated controls.

Adding a Line to a Form

You can use lines in a form to improve the form's readability, to group related information, or to underline important values. You use the Line tool in Design view to add a line to a form or report.

Adding a Line to a Form or Report

- Display the form or report in Design view.
- On the Form Design Tools Design tab, in the Controls group, click the More button, and then click the Line tool.
- Position the pointer where you want the line to begin.
- Drag the pointer to the position for the end of the line, and then release the mouse button. If you want to ensure that you draw a straight horizontal or vertical line, press and hold the Shift key as you drag the pointer to draw the line.

You will add a horizontal line to the Form Header section to separate the controls in this section from the controls in the Detail section.

To add a line to the form:

1. Switch to Design view, and then drag the bottom border of the Form Header section down to the 1-inch mark on the vertical ruler to make room to draw a horizontal line at the bottom of the Form Header section.

2. On the Form Design Tools Design tab, in the Controls group, click the **Line** tool .

3. Position the pointer's plus symbol at the left edge of the Form Header section just below the title.

4. Press and hold the **Shift** key, drag right to the 6-inch mark on the vertical ruler, release the mouse button, and then release the **Shift** key. See Figure 6-48.

Figure 6-48   Line added to the form

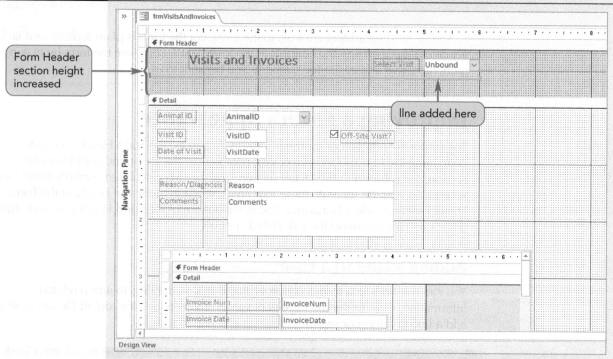

Trouble? If the line is not straight or not positioned correctly, click the Undo button on the Quick Access Toolbar, and then repeat Steps 2 through 4. If the line is not the correct length, be sure the line is selected, press and hold the Shift key, and press the left or right arrow key until the line's length is the same as that of the line shown in Figure 6-48.

5. Drag the bottom border of the Form Header section up to just below the line.

6. Save your form design changes.

Next, you'll add a rectangle around the calculated controls in the Detail section.

Adding a Rectangle to a Form

You can use a rectangle in a form to group related controls and to visually separate the group from other controls. You use the **Rectangle tool** in Design view to add a rectangle to a form or report.

Adding a Rectangle to a Form or Report

REFERENCE

- Display the form or report in Design view.
- On the Form Design Tools Design tab, in the Controls group, click the More button, and then click the Rectangle tool.
- Click in the form or report to create a default-sized rectangle, or drag a rectangle in the position and size you want.

You will add a rectangle around the calculated controls and their labels to separate them from the subform and from the other controls in the Detail section.

To add a rectangle to the form:

1. On the Form Design Tools Design tab, in the Controls group, click the **More** button to open the Controls gallery, and then click the **Rectangle** tool ☐.

2. Position the pointer's plus symbol approximately two grid dots above and two grid dots to the left of the Number of Invoices label.

3. Drag the pointer down and to the right to create a rectangle that that has all four sides approximately two grid dots from the two calculated controls and their labels. See Figure 6-49.

Figure 6-49 **Rectangle added to the form**

rectangle grouping the controls

Trouble? If the rectangle is not sized or positioned correctly, use the sizing handles on its selection border to adjust its size and the move handle to adjust its position.

Next, you'll set the thickness of the rectangle's lines.

> **4.** Click the **Form Design Tools Format** tab.

> **5.** In the Control Formatting group, click the **Shape Outline button arrow**, point to **Line Thickness** at the bottom of the gallery, and then click **1 pt** line (second line from the top).

> **6.** Click a blank area of the Form window to deselect the control.

Next, you'll add color and visual effects to the form's controls.

Modifying the Visual Effects of the Controls in a Form

Distinguishing one group of controls in a form from other groups is an important visual cue to the users of the form. For example, users should be able to distinguish the bound controls in the form from the calculated controls and from the Select Visit control in the Form Header section. You'll now modify the controls in the form to provide these visual cues. You'll start by setting font properties for the calculated control's labels.

To modify the format of the controls in the form:

> **1.** Select the **Number of Invoices** label and the **Invoice Amount Total** label, using the Shift key to select multiple controls.

> **2.** On the Form Design Tools Format tab, in the Font group, click the **Font Color button arrow** $\boxed{\text{A} \cdot}$, click the **Blue** color (row 7, column 8 in the Standard Colors palette), and then in the Font group, click the **Bold** button $\boxed{\text{B}}$. The labels' captions now appear in bold, blue font.

> Next, you'll set properties for the Select Visit label in the Form Header section.

> **3.** Select the **Select Visit** label in the Form Header section, change the label's font color to **Red** (row 7, column 2 in the Standard Colors palette), and then apply bold formatting.

> Next, you'll set the label's Special Effect property to a shadowed effect. The **Special Effect property** specifies the type of special effect applied to a control in a form or report. The choices for this property are Flat, Raised, Sunken, Etched, Shadowed, and Chiseled.

> **4.** Open the Property Sheet for the Select Visit label, click the **All** tab (if necessary), set the Special Effect property to **Shadowed**, and then deselect the label. The label now has a shadowed special effect, and the label's caption now appears in a red, bold font.

> Next, you'll set the Special Effect property for the bound control text boxes to a sunken effect.

> **5.** Select the **VisitID** text box, the **VisitDate** text box, the **Reason** text box, and the **Comments** text box, set the controls' Special Effect property to **Sunken**, close the Property Sheet, and then deselect the controls.

> Finally, you'll set the background color of the Form Header section, the Detail section, the Select Visit combo box, and the two calculated controls. You can use the **Background Color button** in the Font group on the Form Design Tools Format tab to change the background color of a control, section, or object (form or report).

6. Click the **Form Header** section bar.

7. On the Form Design Tools Format tab, in the Font group, click the **Background Color button arrow** 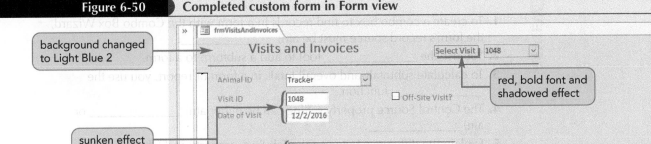, and then click the **Light Blue 2** color (row 3, column 5 in the Standard Colors palette). The Form Header's background color changes to the Light Blue 2 color.

8. Click the **Detail** section bar, and then in the Font Group, click the **Background Color** button to change the Detail section's background color to the **Light Blue 2** color.

9. Select the **Select Visit** combo box, **Number of Invoices** calculated control box, and the **Invoice Amount Total** calculated control box, set the selected controls' background color to the **Light Blue 2** color, and then deselect all controls by clicking to the right of the Detail section's grid.

10. Save your form design changes, switch to Form view, click the **Select Visit** arrow, and then click **1048** in the list to display this visit record in the form. See Figure 6-50.

TIP

To set a background image instead of a background color, click the Background Image button in the Background group on the Form Design Tools Format tab.

Figure 6-50   Completed custom form in Form view

11. Test the form by tabbing between fields, navigating between records, and using the Select Visit combo box to find records, making sure you don't change any field values and observing that the calculated controls display the correct values.

12. Close the form, make a backup copy of the database, compact and repair the database, and then close the database.

Applying Styles to Form and Report Controls

You can use the Quick Styles gallery to apply a built-in style reflecting a combination of several formatting options to a control in a form or report. To do this, select the control in either Layout or Design view, and then, on the Form or Report Design Tools Format tab, click the Quick Styles button in the Control Formatting group to display the Quick Styles gallery. Click a style in the gallery to apply it to the selected control.

You can also change the shape of a control in a form or report by clicking the Change Shape button in the Control Formatting group to display the Change Shape gallery, and then clicking a shape to apply it to the selected control.

Kimberly is pleased with the forms you have created. She will show these to her staff, and determine which of the forms will be most effective for using and managing the CareCenter database.

Session 6.3 Quick Check

1. To create a combo box to find records in a form with the Combo Box Wizard, the form's record source must be a(n) _____.
2. You use the _____ tool to add a subform to a form.
3. To calculate subtotals and overall totals in a form or report, you use the _____ function.
4. The Control Source property setting can be either a(n) _____ or a(n) _____.
5. Explain the difference between the Tab Stop property and tab order.
6. What is focus?
7. The _____ property has settings such as Raised and Sunken.

Review Assignments

PRACTICE

Data File needed for the Review Assignments: Supplier.accdb (cont. from Module 5)

Kimberly wants you to create several forms, including a custom form that displays and updates companies and the products they offer. Complete the following steps:

1. Open the **Supplier** database you worked with in the previous module.
2. In the **tblProduct** table, remove the lookup feature from the SupplierID field, and then resize the Supplier ID column in the datasheet to its best fit. Save and close the table.
3. Edit the relationship between the primary tblSupplier and related tblProduct tables to enforce referential integrity and to cascade-update related fields. Create the relationship report, save the report as **rptRelationshipsForProducts**, and then close it.
4. Use the Documenter to document the qryCompanyContacts query. Select all query options; use the Names, Data Types, and Sizes option for fields; and use the Names and Fields option for indexes. Print the report produced by the Documenter, and then close it.
5. Use the Datasheet tool to create a form based on the tblProduct table, save the form as **frmProductDatasheet**, and then close it.
6. Use the Multiple Items tool to create a form based on the qryDuplicateProduct Types query, save the form as **frmProductTypeMultipleItems**, and then close it.
7. Use the Split Form tool to create a split form based on the tblProduct table, and then make the following changes to the form in Layout view:
   a. Remove the two Units controls from the stacked layout, reduce the width of the Units field value box by about half, and then anchor the two Units controls to the bottom left. Depending on the size of your window, the two Units controls may be positioned at the bottom left of the right column.
   b. Remove the four control pairs in the right column from the stacked layout, and then anchor the group to the bottom right. You may see a dotted border outlining the location of the previously removed controls. This may be automatically selected as well.
   c. Remove the ProductName control pair from the stacked layout, move them to the top right, and then anchor them to the top right.
   d. Reduce the widths of the ProductID and SupplierID field value boxes to a reasonable size.
   e. Change the title to **Product**, save the modified form as **frmProductSplitForm**, and then close it.
8. Use Figure 6-51 and the following steps to create a custom form named **frmSuppliersWithProducts** based on the tblSupplier and tblProduct tables.

Figure 6-51   **Supplier database custom form design**

a. Place the fields from the tblSupplier table at the top of the Detail section. Delete the Contact Last Name label, and change the caption for the Contact First Name label to Contact Name.

b. Move the fields into two columns in the Detail section, as shown in Figure 6-51, resizing and aligning controls, as necessary, and increasing the width of the form.

c. Add the title in the Form Header section.

d. Make sure the form's Record Source property is set to tblSupplier, and then add a combo box in the Form Header section to find Company field values. In the Combo Box Wizard steps, select the Company and SupplierID fields, and hide the key column. Resize and move the control. Ensure the label displays the text "Company Name". Make sure the size of the Company Name field value box can accommodate the largest company name.

e. Add a subform based on the tblProduct table, include only the fields shown in Figure 6-51, link with SupplierID, name the subform **frmPartialProductSubform**, delete the subform label, resize the columns in the subform to their best fit, and resize and position the subform.

f. Add a calculated control that displays the number of products displayed in the subform. Set the calculated control's Tab Stop property to No, and the ControlTip Text property to Calculated number of products.

g. Add a line in the Form Header section, and add a rectangle around the calculated control and its label, setting the line thickness of both controls to 3 pt. Set the rectangle's color the same as the line's color.

h. In the main form, use the Light Gray 1 fill color (row 2, column 1 in the Standard Colors palette) for all form sections, and use the Black font color (row 1, column 2 in the Standard Colors palette) for all the label text, the calculated control, Company Name combo box, and the Title.

i. Make sure the tab order is top-to-bottom, left-to-right for the main form text boxes.

9. Make a backup copy of the database, compact and repair the database, and then close the database.

Case Problem 1

Data File needed for this Case Problem: MoreBeauty.accdb (cont. from Module 5)

APPLY

Beauty To Go   Sue Miller wants you to create several forms, including two custom forms that display and update data in the database. Complete the following steps:

1. Open the **MoreBeauty** database you worked with in the previous module.
2. Use the Documenter to document the qryMemberNames query. Select all query options; use the Names, Data Types, and Sizes option for fields; and use the Names and Fields option for indexes. Print the first page of the report produced by the Documenter.
3. Use the Datasheet tool to create a form based on the tblOption table, and then save the form as **frmOptionDatasheet**.
4. Create a custom form based on the qryUpcomingExpirations query. Display all fields from the query in the form. Create your own design for the form. Add a label to the bottom of the Detail section that contains your first and last names. Change the label's font so that your name appears in bold, red font. Change the OptionEnd text box format so that the field value displays in bold, red font. Save the form as **frmUpcomingExpirations**.
5. Use Figure 6-52 and the following steps to create a custom form named **frmPlansWithMembers** based on the tblOption and tblMember tables.

Figure 6-52   **Plans custom form design**

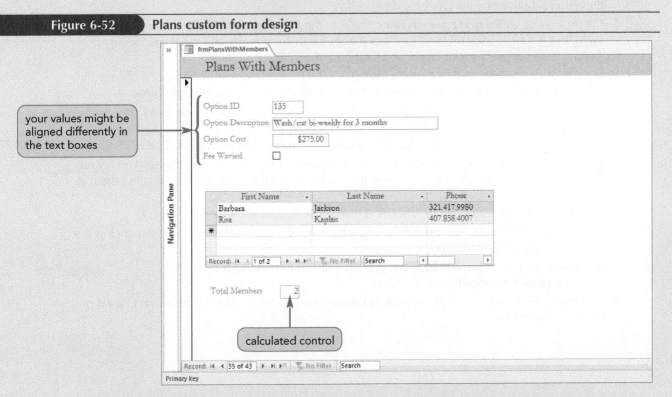

a. Place the fields from the tblOption table at the top of the Detail section, and edit the captions in the associated label controls as shown.
b. Selected fields from the tblMember table appear in a subform named **frmPlansWithMembersSubform**.
c. The calculated control displays the total number of records that appear in the subform. Set the calculated control's ControlTip Text property to Total number of members in this plan. Set the calculated control's Tab Stop property to No.

    d. Apply the Organic theme to the frmPlansWithMembers form only.

    e. Save and close the form.

6. Make a backup copy of the database, compact and repair the database, and then close the database.

Case Problem 2

APPLY

Data File needed for this Case Problem: Tutoring.accdb (cont. from Module 5)

Programming Pros   Brent Hovis wants you to create several forms, including a custom form that displays and updates the tutoring service's contracts with students. Complete the following steps:

1. Open the **Tutoring** database you worked with in the previous module.

2. Remove the lookup feature from the TutorID field in the tblContract table, and then resize the Tutor ID column to its best fit. Save and close the table.

3. Define a one-to-many relationship between the primary tblTutor table and the related tblContract table. Select the referential integrity option and the cascade updates option for this relationship.

4. Use the Documenter to document the tblContract table. Select all table options; use the Names, Data Types, and Sizes option for fields; and use the Names and Fields option for indexes. Print the report produced by the Documenter.

5. Create a query called **qryLessonsByTutor** that uses the tblTutor and tblContract tables and includes the fields FirstName and LastName from the tblTutor table, and the fields StudentID, ContractDate, SessionType, Length, and Cost from the tblContract table.

6. Use the Multiple Items tool to create a form based on the qryLessonsByTutor query, change the title to **Lessons by Tutor**, and then save the form as **frmLessonsByTutorMultipleItems**.

7. Use the Split Form tool to create a split form based on the qryLessonsByTutor query, and then make the following changes to the form in Layout view.

    a. Size the field value boxes in variable lengths to fit a reasonable amount of data.

    b. Remove the SessionType, Length, and Cost controls and their labels from the stacked layout, move these six controls to the right and then to the top of the form, and then anchor them to the top right.

    c. Select the Cost control and its label, and then anchor them to the bottom right.

    d. Remove the Contract Date control and its label from the stacked layout, and then anchor the pair of controls to the bottom left.

    e. Change the title to **Lessons by Tutor**, and then save the modified form as **frmLessonsByTutorSplitForm**.

8. Use Figure 6-53 and the following steps to create a custom form named **frmContract** based on the tblContract table.

Figure 6-53   Tutoring database custom form design

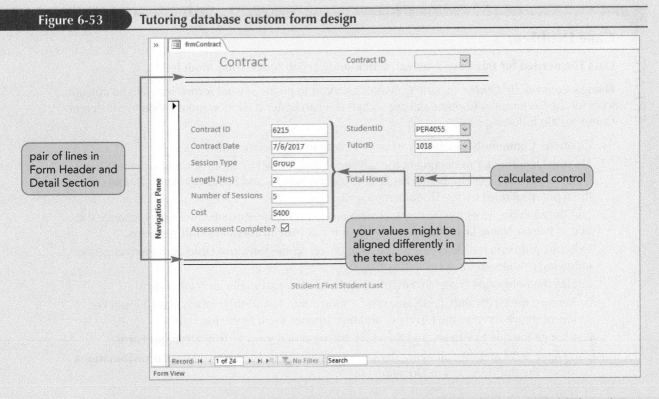

a. For the StudentID combo box, select the LastName, FirstName, and StudentID fields from the tblStudent table, in order, and sort in ascending order by the LastName field and then by the FirstName field.

b. For the TutorID combo box, select the LastName, FirstName, and TutorID fields from the tblTutor table, in order, and sort in ascending order by the LastName field and then by the FirstName field.

c. Make sure the form's Record Source property is set to tblContract, and then add a combo box in the Form Header section to find ContractID field values.

d. Add a calculated control that displays the total number of hours (length multiplied by sessions). *Hint*: Use the * symbol for multiplication. Set the calculated control's Tab Stop property to No, and set the number of decimal places to Auto.

e. Add a line in the Form Header section, add a second line below it, and then add a second pair of lines near the bottom of the Detail section. Set the line thickness of all lines to 1 pt.

f. Use the Label tool to add your name below the pair of lines at the bottom of the Detail section.

g. For the labels in the Detail section, except for the Total Hours label and the label displaying your name, use the Red font color (row 7, column 2 in the Standard Colors palette).

h. For the title and Contract ID label, use the Dark Red font color (row 7, column 1 in the Standard Colors palette).

i. Apply bold to the calculated control and its label.

j. For the background fill color of the sections, the calculated control, and the Contract ID combo box, apply the Medium Gray color (row 1, column 3 in the Standard Colors palette).

k. Make sure the tab order is top-to-bottom, left-to-right for the main form field value boxes.

9. Make a backup copy of the database, compact and repair the database, and then close the database.

CREATE

Case Problem 3

Data File needed for this Case Problem: Community.accdb (cont. from Module 5)

Diane's Community Center Diane Coleman asks you to create several forms, including a custom form for the Community Center database so that she can better track donations made to the center. Complete the following steps:

1. Open the **Community** database you worked with in the previous module.
2. Use the Documenter to document the tblPatron table. Select all table options; use the Names, Data Types, and Sizes option for fields; and use the Names and Fields option for indexes. Print the report produced by the Documenter.
3. Use the Multiple Items tool to create a form based on the qryPatronNames query, change the title to **Patron Name List**, and then save the form as **frmPatronNamesMultipleItems**.
4. Use the Split Form tool to create a split form based on the tblPatron table, and then make the following changes to the form in Layout view.
   a. Size the field value boxes in variable lengths to fit a reasonable amount of data.
   b. Remove the FirstName, LastName, and Phone controls and their labels from the stacked layout, move them to the top right, and then anchor them to the top right.
   c. Change the title to **Patron**, and then save the modified form as **frmPatronSplitForm**.
5. Use Figure 6-54 and the following steps to create a custom form named **frmPatronDonations** based on the tblPatron and tblDonation tables.

Figure 6-54 Community database custom form design

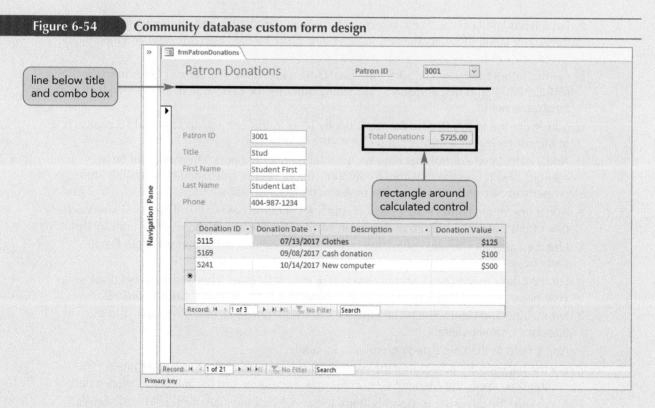

a. Add the title Patron Donations in the Form Header section.
b. Make sure the form's Record Source property is set to tblPatron, and then add a combo box in the Form Header section to find PatronID field values. In the Combo Box Wizard steps, select the PatronID field. Format the label using the Red font (row 7, column 2 in the Standard Colors palette), bold, and the Chiseled special effect.

c. Add a subform based on the tblDonation table, name the subform **frmPatronDonationsSubform**, delete the subform label, and resize the columns in the subform to their best fit, and resize and position the subform.

d. Add a calculated control that displays the total of the DonationValue field displayed in the subform with the Currency format. Set the calculated control's Tab Stop property to No and the Border Style property to Transparent.

e. Add a line in the Form Header section, and add a rectangle around the calculated control and its label, setting the line thickness of both controls to 3 pt. Set the rectangle color to Black (row 1, column 2 in the Standard Colors section) using the Shape Outline button in the Control Formatting group on the Form Design Tools Format tab.

f. Use the background color Aqua Blue 2 (row 3, column 9 in the Standard Colors palette) for the sections, the calculated control, and the Patron ID combo box.

g. Make sure the tab order is top-to-bottom for the main form text boxes.

6. Make a backup copy of the database, compact and repair the database, and then close the database.

Case Problem 4

CREATE

Data File needed for this Case Problem: AppTrail.accdb (cont. from Module 5)

Hike Apalachia   Molly and Bailey Johnson want you to create several forms, including a custom form that displays and updates guest and reservation data in the AppTrail database. Complete the following steps:

1. Open the **AppTrail** database you worked with in the previous module.

2. Remove the lookup feature from the TourID field in the tblReservation table. Size the TourID field, and save and close the table.

3. Edit the relationship between the primary tblTour and related tblReservation tables to enforce referential integrity and to cascade-update related fields. Create the relationship report, and then save the report as **rptRelationshipsForAppTrail.pdf**, without exporting steps.

4. Use the Documenter to document the qrySelectedStates query. Select all query options; use the Names, Data Types, and Sizes option for fields; and use the Nothing option for indexes. Print the report produced by the Documenter.

5. Use the Datasheet tool to create a form based on the qryHikerLastNameS query, and then save the form as **frmHikerLastNameS**.

6. Create a custom form based on the qryNonHikingTours query. Display all fields in the form. Use your own design for the form, but use the title **Tours with No Hiking** in the Form Header section, and use the Label tool to add your name to the Form Header section. Save the form as **frmNonHikingTours**.

7. Use Figure 6-55 and the following steps to create a custom form named **frmHikersWithReservations** based on the tblHiker and tblReservation tables.

Figure 6-55 AppTrail database custom form design

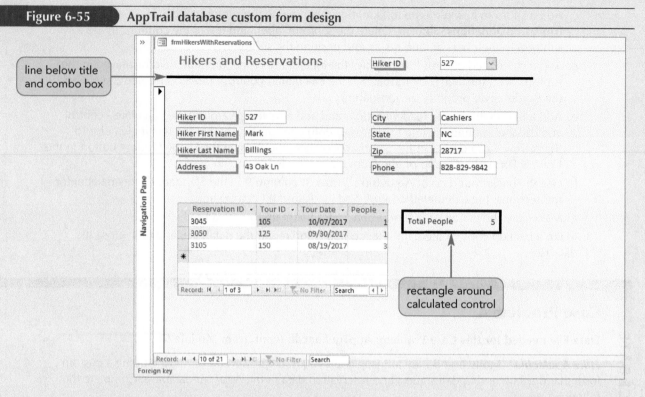

a. Add the title Hikers and Reservations in the Form Header section, and apply bold formatting.

b. Add the fields from the tblHiker table. Size the associated labels so that they're all the same length. Size the field value boxes in variable lengths to fit a reasonable amount of data, as shown in Figure 6-55.

c. Make sure the form's Record Source property is set to tblHiker, and then add a combo box in the Form Header section to find HikerID field values.

d. Add a subform based on the tblReservation table, name the subform **frmHikersWithReservationsSubform**, delete the subform label, resize the columns in the subform to their best fit, and then resize and position the subform.

e. Add a calculated control that displays the total of the People field displayed in the subform. Set the calculated control's Tab Stop property to No, and set the calculated control's Border Style property to Transparent.

f. Add a line in the Form Header section, and add a rectangle around the calculated control and its label, setting the line thickness of both controls to 3 pt. Set the rectangle color to Black (row 1, column 2 in the Standard Colors section) using the Shape Outline button in the Control Formatting group on the Form Design Tools Format tab.

g. Apply the black font color for all controls, including the controls in the subform.

h. Apply the Green 1 fill color (row 2, column 7 in the Standard Colors palette) for the sections and the calculated control.

i. Use the Shadowed special effect for the labels in the Detail section, except for the calculated control label, and the Form Header section, except for the title.

j. Make sure the tab order is top-to-bottom and left-to-right for the main form field value boxes.

8. Make a backup copy of the database, compact and repair the database, and then close the database.

MODULE **7**

Creating Custom Reports

ACCESS

OBJECTIVES

Session 7.1
• Modify a report in Design view

Session 7.3
• Creating mailing labels

STARTING DATA FILES

Access2 →

Module
CareCenter.accdb (*cont.*)

Review
Supplier.accdb (*cont.*)

Case1
MoreBeauty.accdb (*cont.*)

Case2
Tutoring.accdb (*cont.*)

Case3
Community.accdb (*cont.*)

Case4
AppTrail.accdb (*cont.*)

Modifying a Report in Design View

Design view for reports is similar to Design view for forms, which you used in the previous module to customize forms. When you open a report in Design view, the Report Design Tools contextual tabs—Design, Arrange, Format, and Page Setup—appear on the ribbon. A report in Design view is divided into seven sections:

• **Report Header section**—appears once at the beginning of a report and is used for report titles, company logos, report introductions, dates, visual elements such as lines, and cover pages.
• **Page Header section**—appears at the top of each page of a report and is used for page numbers, column headings, report titles, and report dates.

- **Group Header section**—appears before each group of records that share the same sort field value, and usually displays the group name and the sort field value for the group.
- **Detail section**—contains the bound controls to display the field values for each record in the record source.
- **Group Footer section**—appears after each group of records that share the same sort field value, and usually displays subtotals or counts for the records in that group.
- **Page Footer section**—appears at the bottom of each page of a report and is used for page numbers, brief explanations of symbols or abbreviations, or other information such as a company name.
- **Report Footer section**—appears once at the end of a report and is used for report totals and other summary information.

As Kimberly requested, you need to move the page number in the report, and you need to insert a line below the column headings. To do this, you will work in Design view to move the page number control in the Page Footer section to the left and then create a line control below the column headings in the Page Header.

To view and modify the report in Design view:

1. Switch to Design view, and click the **Report Design Tools Design** tab, if necessary. See Figure 7-10.

| Figure 7-10 | rptVisitsAndInvoices report in Design view |

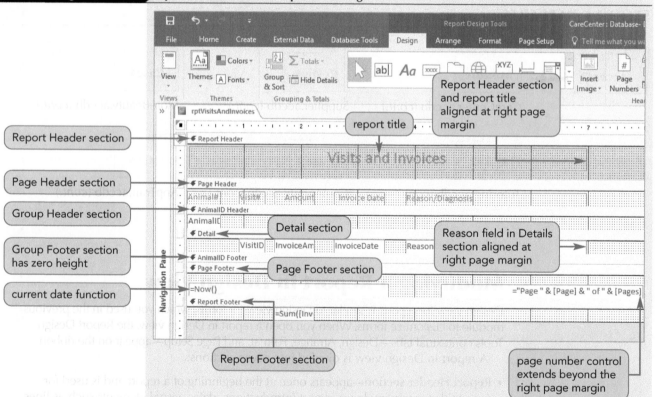

Notice that Design view for a report has most of the same components as Design view for a form. For example, Design view for forms and reports includes horizontal and vertical rulers, grids in each section, and similar buttons in the groups on the Report Design Tools Design tab.

Design view for the rptVisitsAndInvoices report displays seven sections: the Report Header section contains the report title; the Page Header section contains the column heading labels; the Group Header section (AnimalID Header) contains the AnimalID grouping field; the Detail section contains the bound controls to display the field values for each record in the record source (tblVisit); the Group Footer section (AnimalID Footer) isn't displayed in the report; the Page Footer section contains the current date and the page number; and the Report Footer section contains the Sum function, which calculates the grand total of the InvoiceAmt field values.

You will now move the page number control in the Page Footer section so that it is within the report's right page margin. To guide you in this, recall you earlier resized and repositioned the Reason/Diagnosis column in Layout view so it aligned to the right margin of the page. Therefore, you will right-align the page number control to the Reason field value box in the Detail section.

2. Click the **Page Number** control to select it (the control on the right side of the Page Footer section), and then press the ← key to move the control to the left until the right border of its selection box is roughly aligned with the right edge of the Reason field value control box in the Detail section.

   Trouble? If the page number control overlaps the date control in the Report Footer section, don't worry about it. The contents of both will still be displayed.

3. With the Page Number control still selected, press and hold the **Shift** key, click the **Reason** field value control box in the Detail section, and then release the **Shift** key. Both controls are now selected.

4. Right-click one of the selected controls, point to **Align** on the shortcut menu, and then click **Right**. Both controls are now right-aligned.

   Finally, you'll create the line in the Page Header section.

5. Drag the bottom border of the Page Header section down to increase the height approximately half an inch. You'll resize this again after the line is created.

6. On the Report Design Tools Design tab, in the Controls group, click the **More** button, and then click the **Line** tool 🔲.

7. In the Page Header section, position the plus symbol of the Line tool pointer approximately two grid dots below the column header boxes, press and hold the **Shift key**, drag to the right page margin, and then release the **Shift** key to create a horizontal line that spans the width of the page. Holding the Shift key while drawing or extending a line snaps the line to either horizontal or vertical—whichever is nearest to the angle at which the line is drawn.

8. If necessary, drag the lower edge of the Page Header section up so it is approximately two grid dots below the line. See Figure 7-11.

9. Save your report changes, switch to Print Preview, and then scroll and use the navigation buttons to page through the report, paying particular attention to the placement of the line in the Page Header section and the page number in the Page Footer section. The page number is right-aligned in the control box, so the text appears flush with the right margin. The data in the Reason field value text boxes are left-aligned, so this data does not appear flush with the right margin.

Figure 7-11   Modified report in Design view

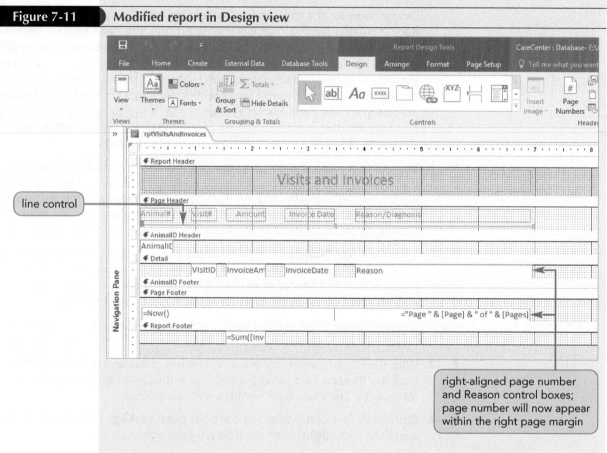

line control

right-aligned page number and Reason control boxes; page number will now appear within the right page margin

Trouble? If you resize a field to position it outside the current margin, the report may widen to accommodate it, triggering a dialog box about the section width being greater than the page width. If this dialog box opens, click OK, manually move form elements as necessary so that no elements extend past 7 inches, and then adjust the report width to 7 inches.

10. Save and close the report.

11. If you are not continuing on to the next session, close the CareCenter database.

Kimberly is happy with the changes you've made to the rptVisitsAndInvoices report. In the next session, you create a new custom report for her based on queries instead of tables.

Session 7.1 Quick Check

REVIEW

1. What is a custom report?

2. Can a report be modified in Layout view?

3. Besides viewing a report, what other actions can you perform in Report view?

4. What is a grouping field?

5. List and describe the seven sections of an Access report.

Creating Mailing Labels

Kimberly needs a set of mailing labels printed for all pet owners so she can mail a marketing brochure and other materials to them. The tblOwner table contains the name and address information that will serve as the record source for the labels. Each mailing label will have the same format: first name and last name on the first line; address on the second line; and city, state, and zip code on the third line.

You could create a custom report to produce the mailing labels, but using the Label Wizard is an easier and faster way to produce them. The **Label Wizard** provides templates for hundreds of standard label formats, each of which is uniquely identified by a label manufacturer's name and product number. These templates specify the dimensions and arrangement of labels on each page. Standard label formats can have between one and five labels across a page; the number of labels printed on a single page also varies. Kimberly's mailing labels are manufactured by Avery and their product number is C2163. Each sheet contains 12 labels; each label is 1.5 inches by 3.9 inches, and the labels are arranged in two columns and six rows on the page.

REFERENCE

Creating Mailing Labels and Other Labels

- In the Navigation Pane, click the table or query that will serve as the record source for the labels.
- On the Create tab, click the Labels button in the Reports group to start the Label Wizard and open its first dialog box.
- Select the label manufacturer and product number, and then click the Next button.
- Select the label font, color, and style, and then click the Next button.
- Construct the label content by selecting the fields from the record source and specifying their placement and spacing on the label, and then click the Next button.
- Select one or more optional sort fields, click the Next button, specify the report name, and then click the Finish button.

You'll use the Label Wizard to create a report Kimberly can use to print mailing labels for all animal owners.

To use the Label Wizard to create the mailing label report:

1. Open the Navigation Pane, click **tblOwner** to make it the current object that will serve as the record source for the labels, close the Navigation Pane, and then click the **Create** tab.

2. In the Reports group, click the **Labels** button. The first Label Wizard dialog box opens and asks you to select the standard or custom label you'll use.

3. In the Unit of Measure section make sure that the **English** option button is selected, in the Label Type section make sure that the **Sheet feed** option button is selected, in the Filter by manufacturer box make sure that **Avery** is selected, and then in the Product number box, click **C2163**. See Figure 7-34.

Figure 7-34   Label Wizard dialog box

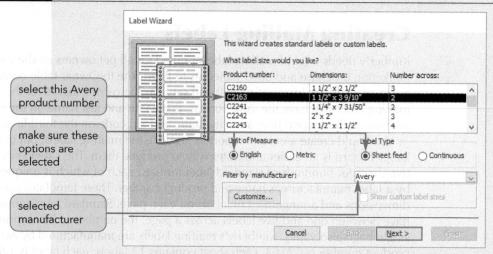

select this Avery product number

make sure these options are selected

selected manufacturer

The top box shows the Avery product number, dimensions, and number of labels across the page for each of its standard label formats. You can display the dimensions in the list in either inches or millimeters by choosing the appropriate option in the Unit of Measure section. You specify in the Label Type section whether the labels are on individual sheets or are continuous forms.

4. Click the **Next** button to open the second Label Wizard dialog box, in which you choose font specifications for the labels.

Kimberly wants the labels to use 10-point Arial with a medium font weight and without italics or underlines. The font weight determines how light or dark the characters will print; you can choose from nine values ranging from thin to heavy.

5. If necessary, select **Arial** in the Font name box, **10** in the Font size box, and **Medium** in the Font weight box, make sure the Italic and the Underline check boxes are not checked and that black is the text color, and then click the **Next** button. The third Label Wizard dialog box opens, in which you select the data to appear on the labels.

Kimberly wants the mailing labels to print the FirstName and LastName fields on the first line, the Address field on the second line, and the City, State, and Zip fields on the third line. A single space will separate the FirstName and LastName fields, the City and State fields, and the State and Zip fields.

6. In the Available fields box, click **FirstName**, click the > button to move the field to the Prototype label box, press the **spacebar**, in the Available fields box click **LastName** (if necessary), and then click the > button. As you select fields from the Available fields box or type text for the label, the Prototype label box shows the format for the label. The braces around the field names in the Prototype label box indicate that the name represents a field rather than text that you entered.

Trouble? If you select the wrong field or type the wrong text, click the incorrect item in the Prototype label box, press the Delete key to remove the item, and then select the correct field or type the correct text.

7. Press the **Enter** key to move to the next line in the Prototype label box, and then use Figure 7-35 to complete the entries in the Prototype label box. Make sure you type a comma and press the spacebar after selecting the City field, and you press the spacebar after selecting the State field.

Figure 7-35	Completed label prototype

completed label format

insert a comma and
a space here

insert a space here

8. Click the **Next** button to open the fourth Label Wizard dialog box, in which
you choose the sort fields for the labels.

Kimberly wants Zip to be the primary sort field and LastName to be the
secondary sort field.

9. In the Available fields list, click the **Zip** field, click the ﹥ button to select Zip
as the primary sort field, click the **LastName** field, click the ﹥ button to select
LastName as the secondary sort field, and then click the **Next** button to open
the last Label Wizard dialog box, in which you enter a name for the report.

10. Change the report name to **rptOwnerMailingLabels**, and then click the
Finish button. The report is saved, and the first page of the report appears
in Print Preview. Note that two columns of labels appear across the page.
See Figure 7-36.

Figure 7-36	Print Preview of mailing labels

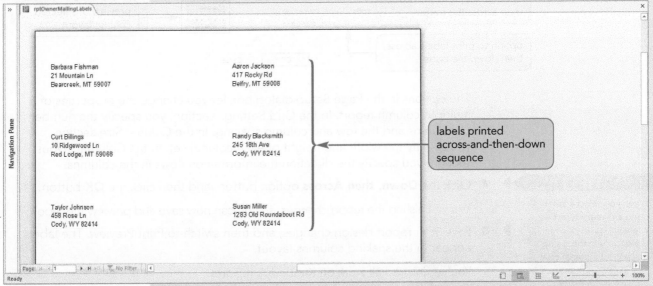

labels printed
across-and-then-down
sequence

The rptOwnerMailingLabels report is a multiple-column report. The labels will be printed in ascending order by zip code and, within each zip code, in ascending order by last name. The first label will be printed in the upper-left corner on the first page, the second label will be printed to its right, the third label will be printed below the first label, and so on. This style of multiple-column report is the "across, then down" layout. Instead, Kimberly wants the labels to print with the "down, then across" layout because she prefers to pull the labels from the sheet in this manner. In this layout, the first label is printed, the second label is printed below the first, and so on. After the bottom label in the first column is printed, the next label is printed at the top of the second column. The "down, then across" layout is also called **newspaper-style columns** or **snaking columns**.

To change the layout of the mailing label report:

1. Switch to Design view. The Detail section, the only section in the report, is sized for a single label.

   First, you'll change the layout to snaking columns.

2. On the ribbon, click the **Report Design Tools Page Setup** tab.

3. In the Page Layout group, click the **Page Setup** button to open the Page Setup dialog box, and then click the **Columns** tab. The Page Setup dialog box displays the column options for the report. See Figure 7-37.

| Figure 7-37 | Columns tab in the Page Setup dialog box |

The options in the Page Setup dialog box let you change the properties of a multiple-column report. In the Grid Settings section, you specify the number of columns and the row and column spacing. In the Column Size section, you specify the width and height of each column set. In the Column Layout section, you specify the direction the information flows in the columns.

4. Click the **Down, then Across** option button, and then click the **OK** button.

   You've finished the report changes, so you can now save and preview the report.

5. Save your report design changes, and then switch to Print Preview. The labels appear in the snaking columns layout.

   You've finished all work on Kimberly's reports.

6. Close the report, make a backup copy of the database, compact and repair the database, and then close it.

INDEX

A

abbreviations, using consistently, AC 12
.accdb files, AC 9
Access
  backward compatibility, AC 9
  comparison operators (fig.), AC 142
  converting database to SQL Server, Oracle, AC 263
  data limits, AC 7
  described, AC 1
  vs. Excel, when to use which, AC 44
  exiting, AC 22–23
  exporting queries to HTML documents, AC 446–448
  exporting tools, AC 444
  Help, AC 40–41
  integrating with other applications, AC 485–490
  maintaining databases, AC 42–43
  starting, AC 7–8
  table exported as HTML file, AC 445
Access 2016 Help, AC 25
Access window (visual overview), AC 2–3
Add & Delete group, AC 2, AC 14
adding. See inserting
Address Quick Start selection, AC 87
advanced Query Wizards (visual overview), AC 254–255
aggregate functions, AC 161
  frequently used (fig.), AC 161
  query with (fig.), AC 165
  used in crosstab queries (fig.), AC 256
  using record group calculations, AC 166–167
  working with using Total row, AC 162–163
aligning form controls, AC 331–333
alignment of field values in reports, changing, AC 213–214
All Access Objects, Navigation Pane, AC 40, AC 167, AC 169
alternate colors, AC 415–416
Alternate Row Color, report layout, AC 392–393
ampersand (&) operator, AC 245–249
Anchor property, AC 303
anchoring
  controls (visual overview), AC 302–303
  controls in forms, AC 319–321
Anchoring gallery, AC 303, AC 319
And logical operator
  described, AC 149–151
  vs. Or logical operator, AC 153
animation emphasis effects, PA-8
annotating webpages (Microsoft Edge), PA-15
Apple Safari, AC 446
application parts
  described, AC 479
  templates and, AC 479–483
Application Parts gallery, AC 482–483
applications, integrating Access with other, AC 485–490
apps, productivity, PA-1–4
arithmetic. See aggregate functions
Ascending sort order, AC 134
ascending sort order, AC 400, AC 404
assigning conditional values to calculated fields, AC 245–249
asterisks (*) as wildcards, AC 237
AutoFilter, AC 131
  filtering data with, AC 242–244
  sorting data using, AC 131–132

AutoNumber, AC 13
Available Fields box, Simple Query Wizard dialog box, AC 31
Average aggregate function, AC 163

B

background colors, AC 347
backing up
  databases, AC 43
  described, AC 43
backslash (\), literal display characters, AC 271
Backstage view, AC 8
  Recent screen in (fig.), AC 8
  Save As options in (fig.), AC 481
bolding
  label controls, AC 412–413
  text, AC 191
borders, removing, AC 415–416
bound controls, AC 322, AC 326, AC 328, AC 333, AC 405–406
bound forms, AC 325
browsers. See Microsoft Edge
buttons
  See also specific button
  on ribbon, AC 13
  window, AC 2

C

calculated controls
  adding to main form, AC 358–361
  adding to subform's Form Footer section, AC 356–358
  aligned (fig.), AC 363
  enhancing information using, AC 367
  form with (fig.), AC 361
  resized, and labels (fig.), AC 362
  resizing, moving, formatting, AC 361–364
calculated fields, AC 156
  assigning conditional values to, AC 245–249
  completed (fig.), AC 248
  creating, using, AC 156–160
  creating using Expression Builder, AC 157
  formatting, AC 160
  IIf function inserted for (fig.), AC 246
  vs. using calculated field data type, AC 161
  visual overview, AC 234–235
calculating average, and maximum amounts, AC 164–165
Caption property, setting for fields, AC 58, AC 91–92
caption property values, and importing, AC 80
captions, label, AC 338–339
capturing video clips, PA-11
cards (Sway), PA-6–7
Cascade Delete Related Records option, AC 99
Cascade Update Related Fields option, AC 99
case of Riverview Veterinary Care Center
  creating and modifying tables, AC 51
  creating database, AC 1
  creating forms, AC 301
  custom reports, AC 381
  importing, exporting, linking, AC 443
  sophisticated queries, AC 233
  updating tables, retrieving information, AC 115
  using forms, reports

centering report titles, AC 392
characters
  input mask (fig.), AC 278
  wildcard (fig.), AC 195
Chart Wizard, AC 473–476
charts
  creating with Chart Wizard, AC 473–476
  embedding in forms, reports, AC 473
  in Microsoft Graph window (fig.), AC 476
  tab control with (visual overview), AC 466–467
  types, AC 474, AC 477
check boxes in reports, yes/no or true/false field, AC 401
Click to Add column, AC 2
Clipboard, AC 386–387
clips, PA-11
Close (relationships) button, AC 76
closed-captioning tools, Office Mix, PA-11
closing
  databases, AC 28
  Print Preview, AC 207
  reports, AC 39
  tables, AC 22–23
collapsing ribbon, AC 310
colors
  background, AC 347
  changing font, in reports, AC 217–218
  changing of text on forms, AC 191–192
  report row, alternate, AC 392–393
column selector, AC 16
Columnar form layout, AC 180, AC 183–184
columns
  datasheet, AC 2
  modifying in reports, AC 390–392
  newspaper-style, snaking, AC 433
  resizing report, AC 36–37, AC 406–407
combo box controls, AC 322
  adding to forms, AC 336–342
  background color, AC 347
  finding records using, AC 348–351
Combo Box tool, AC 337
Combo Box Wizard, AC 348, AC 349
combo boxes
  described, AC 304
  modifying, AC 340–342
commands. See specific command
Commands text box, AC 303
Comments field value box, AC 322
comments for records, AC 287
common field, AC 4
Compact & Repair Database button, File tab, AC 42
Compact on Close option, AC 42–43
compacting
  described, AC 42
  and repairing databases, AC 42–43
comparison operators, AC 140
  described (fig.), AC 142
  In, AC 240
  Like, AC 237
  using to match range of values, AC 147–149
concatenation described, AC 245
conditional formatting
  described, AC 218
  using in reports, AC 218–220
conditional values, assigning to calculated fields, AC 245–249

conditions described, AC 140
contextual tabs, AC 13
control layouts
    described, AC 190
    selected in form (fig.), AC 316
Control Margins Property, AC 303
Control Source property, AC 357
Control Wizard, AC 336
controls
    See also specific type
    adding combo box, to forms, AC 336–342
    adding styles to form and report, AC 372
    anchoring (visual overview), AC 302–303
    anchoring in forms, AC 319–321
    bound. See bound controls
    modifying visual effects in forms, AC 370–371
    moving, AC 322
    moving, resizing on reports, AC 413–415
    removing from control layouts, AC 411
    sizing, deleting, AC 333–335
    unbound. See unbound controls
    working with in Design view, AC 412–417
Controls gallery (fig.), AC 337
ControlTip Text property, AC 361, AC 363–364
converting
    Access database to SQL Server, Oracle, AC 263
    handwriting to text, PA-3–4
copying
    and pasting reports into Word, AC 386–387
    records from another Access database, AC 26–29
Cortana, locating information with, PA-14–15
Count function, AC 346
Create New Template from This Database dialog box
(fig.), AC 481
Create Relationship dialog box (fig.), AC 483
Create tab illustrated (fig.), AC 24
Create tab options (visual overview), AC 24–25
creating
    application parts, AC 479–481
    calculated fields, AC 156–160
    calculated fields vs. using calculated field data type,
    AC 161
    charts with Chart Wizard, AC 473–476
    crosstab queries, AC 256–262
    custom forms, AC 324–328
    custom reports, AC 405–412
    databases, AC 7–9
    expressions, AC 156
    find duplicates queries, AC 263–265
    find unmatched queries, AC 265–266
    form with main form and subform, AC 200–204
    forms, AC 33–35
    forms using Datasheet Tool, AC 311–313
    forms using Form Wizard, AC 182–185
    forms using Split Form tool, AC 314–315
    labels, mailing labels, AC 430–434
    larger databases, AC 104
    lookup fields, AC 272–275
    multiple forms, reports, AC 311
    multitable queries, AC 129–130
    parameter queries, AC 249–253
    queries, AC 30–33, AC 125–127
    queries for custom reports, AC 403–404
    queries using Not logical operator,
    AC 241–242
    queries using pattern matches, AC 237–239
    queries with aggregate functions, AC 163–165
    queries with Group By operator, AC 166–167
    Relationship report, AC 307–310
    report based on query, AC 208
    reports, AC 35–39
    subforms, AC 201–204

Sway presentations, PA-6–7
tables by importing existing table, table structure,
AC 83–86
tables in Datasheet view, AC 11
tables in Design view, AC 59–68
top values queries, AC 267–269
Creative Commons license, PA-7
crosstab queries, AC 254
    completed design (fig.), AC 260
    creating, AC 256–262
    IIf function for column headings (fig.), AC 262
    recordset (fig.), AC 261
    vs. select queries (fig.), AC 257
Crosstab Query Wizard
    described, AC 254, AC 258
    using, AC 258–260
CSV (comma-separated values) file, AC 449
CSV files, importing as Access tables, AC 449–452
currency format, AC 160
Current Record box, AC 22, AC 29
custom forms, AC 304
    creating, AC 324–328
    in Design view (visual overview), AC 322–323
    planning, designing, AC 324
    visual overview, AC 346–347
custom reports
    creating, AC 405–412
    creating queries for, AC 403–404
    in Layout view (visual overview), AC 382–383
    planning, designing, AC 402–403
    in Print Preview (visual overview), AC 400–401
customizing existing reports, AC 384

D
data
    adding to tables by importing text files, AC 95–97
    filtering, AC 136–138
    filtering with AutoFilter, AC 242–244
    finding in datasheets, AC 194
    finding using forms, AC 194–196
    importing and exporting, AC 465
    importing from Excel worksheets, AC 80–83
    importing from XML files, AC 455–456
    linking from Excel worksheets, AC 487–489
    maintaining table data using forms, AC 197–198
    organizing, AC 4
    quality, perfecting, AC 286
    searching in tables for, AC 121–122
    sorting in queries, AC 131–135
    storing in separate tables, AC 6
    updating in linked table, AC 489–490
    updating using queries, AC 128–129
data markers, AC 467
data redundancy
    avoiding, AC 55
    described, AC 55
Data Type column, Table window, AC 52
Data Type gallery
    adding fields using, AC 86–88
    described, AC 86–88
data types, AC 13
    assigning field, AC 56–57
    calculated field, vs. using calculated field, AC 161
    changing for fields in Design view, AC 90
    changing for lookup fields, AC 305
    changing of primary key field, AC 13–14
    common (fig.), AC 57
    sorting results for different (fig.), AC 131
data validation rules, defining, AC 282–285
database concepts, AC 4–7
database management system (DBMS), AC 6–7

database objects
    See also objects
    applying themes to, AC 185–188
    saving, AC 35
    viewing in Navigation pane, AC 221
databases, AC 4
    backing up and restoring, AC 43
    closing, AC 28
    copying records from another Access database,
    AC 26–29
    creating, AC 7–9
    creating larger, AC 104
    design guidelines, AC 54–56
    file types, AC 9
    forms. See forms
    maintaining, AC 41–43
    opening, AC 26
    and relationships, AC 4–5
    reviewing, AC 236
    saving, AC 23
    tables. See tables
    updating, AC 118–124
Datasheet form layout, AC 183
Datasheet Tool, AC 311
    creating forms using, AC 311–313
    view options for form created with (fig.), AC 312
Datasheet view, AC 2
    changing format properties in, AC 71–73
    creating tables in, AC 11
    form displayed in (fig.), AC 302–303
    modified table in (visual overview), AC 76–77
    selectors in, AC 16
    viewing Long Text fields with large contents in,
    AC 288
Datasheet View button, AC 117
datasheets, AC 2
    changing alternate row colors in, AC 154–156
    changing appearance of, AC 154–155
    displayed after running query (fig.), AC 127
    displaying calculated field (fig.), AC 160
    displaying selected fields, records (fig.), AC 144
    finding data in, AC 194
    freezing columns, AC 287
    navigating, AC 29–30
    with records added (fig.), AC 21
    sorted on two fields (fig.), AC 135
    sorting query, AC 133
    viewing, AC 96–97
Date and Time dialog box (fig.), AC 424
date format symbols (fig.), AC 65
Date function, AC 420, AC 422, AC 424
dates
    adding to reports, AC 422–425
    in Page Footer section, AC 382
    symbols for some custom formats (fig.), AC 65
Date/Time fields, displaying available formats (fig.),
AC 64
decision making
    Access vs. Excel, when to use which, AC 44
    creating multiple forms, reports, AC 311
    importing, embedding, linking data, AC 486
    methods of adding fields to design grid, AC 128
    Page Header section effective content, AC 422
    specifying field size property for number fields, AC 58
    using both select and crosstab queries, AC 258
Default Value property
    described, AC 93
    setting for a field, AC 93–94
defining
    data validation rules, AC 282–285
    database table fields, AC 59–66
    table validation rules, AC 284–285

deleting
  controls, AC 333–335
  fields from table imported structures, AC 88–89
  records, AC 122–124
dependencies, identifying object, AC 281–282
Descending sort order, AC 134
Description property, AC 53
design grid, AC 116
  after adding fields from two tables (fig.), AC 143
  columns in, AC 117
  field added to (fig.), AC 126
  on forms, AC 322
  methods of adding fields to, AC 128
  moving fields in, AC 145–146
  queries and, AC 234
  Total row inserted in (fig.), AC 164
Design view, AC 52
  adding fields in, AC 69–71
  blank form in (fig.), AC 326
  changing field properties in, AC 73–74
  changing field's data types, AC 90
  creating custom forms, AC 324–328
  creating queries in, AC 237–239
  creating tables in, AC 59–68
  criteria entry (fig.), AC 140
  defining fields, AC 59
  Form Header, Form Footer sections, AC 343–344
  Form window, AC 325–327
  modifying reports in, AC 395–398
  moving fields in, AC 69
  Query window in (visual overview),
    AC 116–117
  renaming fields in, AC 90
  selecting two sort fields in (fig.), AC 134
  sorting on multiple fields in, AC 132–133
  specifying primary key in, AC 67
  Table window in (visual overview), AC 52–53
  working with controls in, AC 412–417
Design view button, AC 323
designing
  custom forms, AC 324
  databases, AC 54–56
  forms, AC 183–193, AC 304–306, AC 335
  reports, AC 212–218, AC 402–403
destination files, AC 486
detail records, AC 207, AC 210
detail reports, AC 402
Detail section bar, AC 322
Detail section of forms, AC 323
Detail section of reports, AC 396, AC 421
displaying
  See also viewing
  available Date/Time field formats (fig.), AC 64
  forms with grid, AC 323
  object names, AC 262
  selected records, AC 142
  subform's calculated controls in main form,
    AC 356–364
Docs.com public gallery, PA-8
Documenter
  described, AC 307
  dialog box (fig.), AC 309
dragging and dropping outlines into Sway, PA-7
Draw tab tools (fig.), PA-3
drawing canvas, PA-3

E
Edge
  See also Microsoft Edge
  browser, AC 446, AC 448
Edit Relationships dialog box (fig.), AC 101

editing
  mode, keyboard shortcuts (fig.), AC 118
  Sway presentations, PA-8
embed described, AC 486
embedding
  charts in forms, reports, AC 473
  data vs. importing or linking, AC 486
Enter Parameter Value dialog box (fig.), AC 250
entity integrity, AC 68
equal sign (=) and expressions, AC 356, AC 422
exact matches
  and pattern matches, AC 237–239
  specifying, AC 142–144
Excel vs. Access, when to use which, AC 44
Excel worksheets
  importing data from, AC 80–83
  linking data from, AC 487–489
exiting Access, AC 22–23
Export—HTML Document dialog box, AC 446–447
Export to HTML tool, AC 445
Export to XML tool, AC 445
Export XML dialog box
  Data tab, AC 460
  Schema tab, AC 461
exporting
  Access queries to HTML documents, AC 446–448
  Access tables as XML files, AC 459–462
  data, AC 465
  data to XML, HTML (visual overview), AC 444–445
  reports to PDF files, AC 484–485
  saving export specifications, AC 462–465
Expression Builder, AC 156, AC 235
  creating calculated fields with, AC 157
  dialog box (fig.), AC 359
  opening, AC 246
expressions, AC 156
  for calculated field (fig.), AC 158
  in calculated fields, AC 234
  creating using Expression Builder, AC 157
  equal sign (=) and, AC 356
Extensible Markup Language (XML), AC 444

F
F1 Help, AC 40–41
F2 key, AC 118
falsepart of IIf function, AC 235, AC 247
field heading labels, AC 401
field list, Relationships window, AC 77
field lists, Query window, AC 116
Field Name column, Table window, AC 52
field properties
  determining, AC 56
  modifying, AC 71–74
  setting, AC 56–58
Field Properties pane
  described, AC 53
  moving from Table Design grid to, AC 52
field selector, AC 16
Field Size property, AC 57–58
field validation rules, AC 283
field value, AC 4
fields
  adding in Design view, AC 69–71
  adding to design grid, AC 128
  adding to forms, AC 327–328
  adding to tables, AC 14–16
  adding using Data Type gallery, AC 86–88
  calculated. See calculated fields
  Caption property, AC 58
  changing alignment of values, AC 213–214

condition for (fig.), AC 140
  defining, AC 59–66
  Description property, AC 53
  Field Size property, AC 57–58
  field validation rules, defining, AC 283–284
  filter options for, in Report view (fig.), AC 385
  group band, AC 400
  grouping related, into tables, AC 54
  hiding, AC 119
  hiding duplicate field values, AC 400
  identifying all needed, AC 54
  including common, in related tables, AC 55
  Long Text, AC 286–289
  Lookup Wizard, AC 272
  modifying properties, AC 71–74
  moving, AC 69
  moving, resizing on reports, AC 214–216
  moving in design grid, AC 145–146
  for pattern match queries (fig.), AC 238
  Quick Start selection, AC 87
  renaming in Design view, AC 90
  secondary sort, AC 133
  setting Default Value property, AC 93–94
  sort, AC 131
  unhiding, AC 119
  using Input Mask Wizard, AC 276–280
Fields tab, AC 2
file types, database, AC 9
Filter By Form, AC 136
Filter By Selection
  described, AC 136
  using, AC 136–138
filter options for field in Report view (fig.), AC 385
filtering
  data, AC 136–138
  data with AutoFilter, AC 242–244
filters described, AC 136
Find and Replace dialog box (fig.), AC 121, AC 195
Find button, AC 181
Find command, AC 121
Find Duplicate Query Wizard, AC 255, AC 263–265
find duplicates queries, creating, AC 263–265
find unmatched queries, creating, AC 265–266
Find Unmatched Query Wizard
  described, AC 255
  using, AC 265–267
finding
  See also searching
  data in tables, AC 121–122
  data using forms, AC 194–196
  records with combo box control, AC 348–351
First record button, AC 30
focus, AC 364
folders, designating trusted, AC 289–291
font color on reports, AC 217–218
font size, changing, AC 154
footers and headers in reports (visual overview),
  AC 420–421
foreign key, AC 5
form controls
  aligning, AC 331–333
  moving, AC 330–331
  selecting, AC 329
form design, AC 193
Form Footer section, AC 323, AC 342
  adding calculated controls to, AC 356–358
  using, AC 342
Form Header section, AC 323
  described, AC 342
  using, AC 342
form objects, name displayed on tab for the form, AC 180

form records
    displayed in Print Preview (fig.), AC 199
    previewing and printing selected, AC 198–200
form titles, AC 180
Form tool
    creating forms using, AC 33–35
    described, AC 24
Form view
    completed custom form in (fig.), AC 371
    custom forms (visual overview), AC 346–347
    form displayed in (fig.), AC 332
    forms displayed in (visual overview), AC 180–181
    main form with subform in (fig.), AC 202
    subform in (fig.), AC 354
Form window, Design view, AC 325–327
Form Wizard, AC 24, AC 310, AC 324
    creating forms using, AC 182–185, AC 200–204
    described, AC 181
Form Wizard dialog box (fig.), AC 182
Format Data Series dialog box, Microsoft Graph,
AC 477–478
formats
    currency, AC 160
    displaying available Date/Time field (fig.), AC 64
    symbols for some custom date (fig.), AC 65
formatting
    calculated fields, AC 160
    conditional, in reports, AC 218–220
    forms, subforms, AC 201
    reports, AC 402
    values, AC 445
forms, AC 24
    adding calculated controls, AC 358–361
    adding combo box control, AC 336–342
    adding fields to, AC 327–328
    adding line to, AC 367–368
    adding pictures to, AC 189–191
    adding rectangle to, AC 368–370
    adding subform to, AC 352–355
    adding titles, AC 343–344
    anchoring controls in, AC 319–321
    applying themes to, AC 185–188
    bound and unbound, AC 325
    bound controls added to (fig.), AC 328
    changing color of text on, AC 191–192
    changing tab order, AC 364–366
    created by Form tool (fig.), AC 34
    creating main, with subform, AC 200–204
    creating multiple, AC 311
    creating simple, AC 33–35
    creating using Datasheet Tool, AC 311–313
    creating using Form Wizard, AC 182–185
    custom. See custom forms
    designing, AC 304–306
    displayed in Form view (visual overview), AC 180–181
    displayed in Layout view (fig.), AC 186
    displaying subform's calculated controls in main,
    AC 356–364
    embedding charts in, AC 473
    finding data using, AC 194–196
    icon (fig.), AC 40
    importance of design, AC 193
    improving appearance of, AC 367–371
    large, working with, AC 468
    maintaining table data using, AC 197–198
    making design changes, AC 335
    modifying design in Layout view, AC 185–193
    modifying split, AC 315–317
    modifying visual effects in controls of, AC 370–371
    navigating, AC 34–35, AC 193–194
    object prefix tag, AC 236
    with picture added (fig.), AC 190
    property sheet for (fig.), AC 349

Record Source property, AC 304
    rectangle added to (fig.), AC 369
    saving, AC 35
    strategies for building, AC 329
    tab controls in, AC 468–470
    text box controls, AC 302
    themes, working with, AC 189
    unbound control added to (fig.), AC 350
Forms group, AC 24
Formula AutoComplete menu, AC 239
free-response quizzes, PA-12
freezing datasheet columns, AC 287
functions, aggregate. See aggregate functions

G
General tab, AC 52
Get External Data - Excel Spreadsheet dialog box (fig.),
AC 81
Get External Data - Text File dialog box (fig.), AC 450
Get External Data - XML File Wizard, AC 456–457
Google Chrome, AC 446
grand totals, adding to reports, AC 393–395
graphic elements, adding, AC 180
Group, Sort, and Total pane in Layout view (fig.), AC 389
group band fields, AC 400, AC 409–410
Group By operator, AC 166–167
Group Footer section of reports, AC 396, AC 401,
AC 407, AC 412, AC 420
Group Header section of reports, AC 396, AC 407, AC 412
grouped reports, AC 206
grouping
    data in reports, AC 407–410
    objects, AC 167–169
    related fields into tables, AC 54
    in reports, AC 382

H
handles
    move, AC 322
    sizing, AC 323
handwriting, converting to text, PA-3–4
headers and footers in reports (visual overview),
AC 420–421
Help
    accessing, AC 25
    using, AC 40–41
    windows (fig.), AC 25
Hide Fields command, AC 119
hiding
    display of group's objects in Navigation Pane, AC 167
    duplicate field values, AC 400
    duplicate values in reports, AC 418–419
    and unhiding fields, AC 119
Hoisington, Corinne, PA-1
HTML documents
    described, AC 445
    exporting Access queries to, AC 446–448
    viewing in Edge, AC 448–449
HTML Output Options dialog box, AC 446–448

I
ID field (primary key field), AC 2
identifying object dependencies, AC 281–282
IIf function
    described, AC 235
    for crosstab query columns headings (fig.), AC 262
import described, AC 80
Import Objects dialog box (fig.), AC 85

Import Spreadsheet Wizard, AC 449
Import Spreadsheet Wizard dialog box (fig.), AC 82
Import Text Wizard, AC 449, AC 451–452
Import Wizard dialog box (fig.), AC 96
importing
    CSV files as Access tables, AC 449–452
    data, AC 465
    data from Excel worksheets, AC 80–83
    data from XML files, AC 455–456
    data vs. embedding, linking, AC 486
    saving and running import specifications,
    AC 456–459
    tables, table structures, AC 83–86
    text files to add data to tables, AC 95–97
In comparison operator, AC 240, AC 241
Ink to Text button, Convert group, Drawing tab, PA-3
inked handwriting, PA-3
inking toolbar, Make a Web Note button (Microsoft
Edge), PA-15
input mask characters (fig.), AC 278
Input Mask Wizard
    dialog box (fig.), AC 276
    using, AC 276–280
input masks, AC 271
    using Input Mask Wizard, AC 276–280
    visual overview, AC 270–271
    when to use, AC 280
inserting
    pictures in reports, AC 217–218
    table rows, AC 70–71
    videos into OneNote notebooks, PA-4
integrating Access with other applications, AC 485–490
Internet Explorer, PA-14
IsNull function, AC 235
italicizing text, AC 191

J
join line (fig.), AC 77

K
Keep Together property, AC 412
key symbol, AC 76
keyboard shortcuts, AC 79, AC 118

L
Label Wizard, AC 430–434
Label Wizard dialog box (fig.), AC 431
labels
    aligned (fig.), AC 363
    changing caption, AC 338–339
    creating mailing, AC 430–434
    formatting, AC 346
    moving, resizing on reports, AC 214–216
    resizing field value, AC 317–319
    on ribbon, AC 13
landscape orientation, AC 207
Last record button, AC 30, AC 204
Layout view, AC 34, AC 302–303
    creating blank report, adding bound controls,
    AC 405–412
    custom reports in (visual overview), AC 382–383
    displaying forms in, AC 181
    form displayed in (fig.), AC 186
    Group, Sort, and Total pane in (fig.), AC 389
    modifying design of forms in, AC 185–193
    modifying forms in, AC 202–204
    modifying report design in, AC 212–218
    modifying reports in, AC 388–395
    removing controls from control layouts, AC 411

layouts
adding rectangle to, AC 346
choosing for forms, AC 183–184
control, AC 190, AC 316
stacked, AC 302
tabular, AC 303
lectures, recording, PA-4
Like comparison operator, AC 237
Line tool, AC 346, AC 416–417
lines
adding to forms, AC 367–368
totals, adding to reports, AC 416–417
link described, AC 486
Link Spreadsheet Wizard dialog box (fig.),
AC 489
linking
data from Excel worksheets, AC 487–489
data vs. importing, embedding, AC 486
record sources, AC 475
list-of-values match
described, AC 240
queries, AC 240–241
live webpages, PA-12
logical operators, AC 149
Long Text fields, working with, AC 286–289
lookup fields, AC 270
changing to Short Text fields, AC 304–306
creating, AC 272–275
selecting (fig.), AC 273
visual overview, AC 270–271
lookup properties, AC 305–306
Lookup Wizard field, AC 272

M
mailing labels, creating, AC 430–434
main form, AC 200
maintaining, AC 118
databases, AC 41–43
table data using forms, AC 197–198
Manage Data Tasks dialog box
Saved Exports tab, AC 464
Saved Imports tab, AC 458
margins
changing report's, AC 212
report guidelines, AC 383
matches
of range of values, AC 147–149
specifying exact, AC 142–144
Maximum aggregate function, AC 163
menus
See also specific menu
shortcut, AC 12
Microsoft Access 2016, AC 1
See also Access
.accdb files, AC 9
Microsoft Access Help button, AC 25
Microsoft Edge, AC 446
browsing the web with, PA-14
described, PA-14
tools (fig.), PA-14
Microsoft Excel. See Excel
Microsoft Graph, AC 473
Microsoft Graph Chart Type dialog box (fig.),
AC 477
Microsoft Graph tools, AC 476–479
Microsoft Office 365, AC 473
Microsoft OneNote Mobile app, PA-2, PA-3
Minimum aggregate function, AC 163
Mouse Mode, switching between Touch Mode and, AC 10

move handle, AC 322
moving
controls, AC 322
controls on reports, AC 413–415
fields in design grid, AC 145–146
fields in Design view, AC 69
fields in reports, AC 214–216
form controls, AC 330–331
from one fields to another, AC 18
Multiple Items tool, AC 313
creating forms using, AC 313–314
view options for form created with (fig.),
AC 314
multiple selection criteria, defining queries for,
AC 149–153
multitable queries, creating, AC 129–130

N
naming
See also renaming
fields, AC 12, AC 56
fields vs. setting Caption property, AC 57
objects, AC 56
queries, AC 116
tables, AC 2
naming conventions, AC 237
navigating
datasheets, AC 29–30
forms, AC 34–35, AC 193–194
navigation buttons, AC 29, AC 180, AC 203, AC 206
Navigation Caption property, AC 470–472
navigation mode
described, AC 118
keyboard shortcuts (fig.), AC 118
Navigation Pane, AC 2
displaying object names, AC 262
menu (fig.), AC 168
renaming objects, AC 241
tables listed in, AC 22
viewing database objects in, AC 221
viewing objects in, AC 40
working with, AC 167–169
New Formatting Rule dialog box (fig.), AC 219
newspaper-style columns, AC 433
Next record button, AC 30, AC 203
nonunique (sort field), AC 132
Not logical operator
described, AC 241
using in queries, AC 241–242
notebooks, OneNote, PA-2–3
Notepad, AC 464–465
notes, taking, PA-3
null value, AC 68
number symbols (#) as wildcards, AC 237

O
Object Definition report, creating, AC 308–310
object dependencies, identifying, AC 281–282
Object Dependencies pane, opening and using,
AC 281–282
object prefix tags, AC 236
Object Type, Navigation Pane, AC 167
objects
See also specific object
database. See database objects
dependencies. See object dependencies
displaying names, AC 262
exporting Access, as XML files, AC 459
grouping, AC 167–169

opening Access, AC 22
renaming, AC 241
Office accounts, Sign in link, AC 2
Office Mix, PA-10
OneDrive
database backups, AC 43
storing Sway sites on, PA-6
syncing with OneNote notes, PA-2
OneNote, PA-2
creating notebook, PA-2
syncing notebooks to the cloud, PA-2–3
one-to-many relationships, AC 98–99, AC 200
defining, AC 102
described, AC 76
opening
Access objects, AC 22
databases, AC 26
Expression Builder, AC 246
Query window in Design view, AC 125
tables, AC 22, AC 119
operators
See also specific operator
comparison. See comparison operators
logical. See logical operators
Or logical operator, AC 149, AC 152–153
Oracle
converting Access database to, AC 263
and object field names, AC 236
organizing
data, AC 4
data into smallest part(s), AC 54
outlines, dragging into Sway, PA-7
OwnerData form, AC 181, AC 184

P
Page Footer section
inserting date, AC 382
page numbers in, AC 383
of reports, AC 396, AC 420
understanding, AC 422–429
Page Header section, AC 421
adding report titles, AC 428–429
column headings in, AC 383
of reports, AC 395
understanding, AC 422–429
Page Number control, AC 397
page number expression, AC 421
page numbers
adding to reports, AC 426–428
in Page Footer section, AC 383
in Report Footer section, AC 396–397
on reports, AC 37–38
Page Numbers dialog box (fig.), AC 427
page orientation
changing report's, AC 212
portrait and landscape, AC 207
Page Setup dialog box (fig.), AC 433
parameter queries
described, AC 249
using, AC 249–253
password-protecting OneNote notebooks, PA-4
pasting records into databases, AC 28
pattern match queries, AC 237–239
pattern matches
described, AC 237
using in queries, AC 237–239
PDF (portable document format), AC 484
PDF file export, Options dialog box (fig.),
AC 485
PDF files, exporting reports to, AC 484–485

pencil symbol, AC 17
pictures
    adding to forms, AC 189–191
    inserting in reports, AC 217–218
pie chart in tab control (fig.), AC 475
planning
    custom forms, AC 324
    custom reports, AC 402–403
    database backups, AC 43
    tables, AC 11–12
portrait orientation, AC 207
PowerPoint, adding Office Mix to, PA-10
prefix tags, AC 234
prefix tags for objects. See object prefix tags
presentations
    creating Sway, PA-6–7
    Office Mix, PA-12
    publishing Sway, PA-8
previewing
    reports, AC 220
    selected form records, AC 198–200
Previous record button, AC 30, AC 204
primary key, AC 5
    changing data types of, AC 13–14
    determining each table's, AC 54–55
    importance of, AC 68
    renaming default field, AC 12–13
    specifying, AC 67
primary sort field, AC 133
primary tables, AC 77
Print Preview
    closing, AC 207
    custom reports in (visual overview), AC 400–401
    finished report in (fig.), AC 220
    first page of report in (fig.), AC 38
    form records displayed in (fig.), AC 199
    of mailing labels (fig.), AC 432
    of Object Definition report (fig.), AC 310
    report changes in (fig.), AC 415
    report displayed in (visual overview), AC 206–207
Print Table Definition dialog box (fig.), AC 309
printing
    options, AC 309
    reports, AC 39–40, AC 220–221
    selected form records, AC 198–200
productivity apps
    creating OneNote notebook, PA-2
    recording lectures, PA-4
    syncing OneNote notebooks to the cloud, PA-2–3
prompts, specifying for parameter query, AC 250
properties, AC 56
    determining field, AC 56
    setting field, AC 56–58
    setting table validation (fig.), AC 285
property sheet
    for calculated field (fig.), AC 159, AC 248
    for form (fig.), AC 349
Property Update Options button menu (fig.), AC 279
Publish as PDF or XPS file dialog box (fig.), AC 484
publishing Swap presentations, PA-8

Q
queries, AC 24
    with aggregate functions entered (fig.), AC 165
    creating, for custom reports, AC 403–404
    creating and running, AC 125–127
    creating multitable, AC 129–130
    creating new, AC 157–158
    creating reports based on, AC 208
    creating simple, AC 30–33
    creating with aggregate functions, AC 163–165

    creating with And logical operator, AC 149–151
    creating with Group By operator, AC 166–167
    creating with Or logical operator, AC 152–153
    crosstab. See crosstab queries
    defining multiple selection criteria for, AC 149–153
    defining record selection criteria for, AC 142–149
    designing, vs. using Query Wizard, AC 124
    exporting Access, to HTML document, AC 446–448
    filtering records with AutoFilter (fig.), AC 243
    find unmatched. See find unmatched queries
    icon (fig.), AC 40
    introduction, AC 124–125
    limiting records in, AC 267
    matches, specifying exact, AC 142–144
    modifying, AC 144–147
    naming, AC 116
    object prefix tag, AC 236
    parameter. See parameter queries
    results (fig.), AC 141
    saving, AC 35
    selection criteria in (visual overview), AC 140–141
    setting sort fields, AC 404
    sorting data in, AC 131–135
    updating data using, AC 128–129
    using list-of-values match in, AC 240–241
    using Not logical operator in, AC 241–242
    using pattern matches in, AC 237–239
Queries group, AC 24
query by example (QBE), AC 117
query datasheets, sorting, AC 133
query results (fig.), AC 32, AC 141, AC 165
Query Tools Design tab, on ribbon, AC 117
Query Type group, active Select button, AC 116
Query window
    in Design view (visual overview), AC 116–117
    opening in Design view, AC 125
    with Or logical operator (fig.), AC 152
Query Wizard button, AC 24
Query Wizard vs. designing queries, AC 124
Query Wizards (visual overview), AC 254–255
question marks (?) as wildcards, AC 237
Quick Access Toolbar
    described, AC 2
    Save button on, AC 23, AC 74
Quick Print, AC 39
Quick Start selection, AC 87
quizzes, adding to slides, PA-12

R
Reading view (Microsoft Edge), PA-14
Recent screen in Backstage view (fig.), AC 8
record selector, AC 16
Record Source property, AC 304
recording lectures, PA-4
records, AC 4
    adding to new tables, AC 78–80
    adding to tables, AC 94
    adding using forms, AC 198
    comments, AC 287
    copying from another Access database, AC 26–29
    creating based on query, AC 208
    defining record selection criteria for queries,
        AC 142–149
    deleting, AC 122–124
    detail, AC 207, AC 210
    display, and primary key, AC 68
    entering, AC 16–19
    entering new (fig.), AC 20
    finding using wildcard characters, AC 195–196
    limiting in queries, AC 267
    linking sources, AC 475

    modifying, AC 118–119
    previewing and printing selected form, AC 198–200
    selection based on list-of-values match (fig.), AC 242
    selection based on pattern match (fig.), AC 239
    sorting with AutoFilter, AC 131–132
recordsets, AC 124
    crosstab query (fig.), AC 261
    query, for duplicate visit dates (fig.), AC 264
    top values query (fig.), AC 269
Rectangle tool, AC 346, AC 368
rectangles, adding to forms, AC 368–370
redundancy. See data redundancy
referential integrity, AC 99, AC 101, AC 103
related tables, AC 77
relational database management system, AC 6
relational databases, AC 4
Relationship report, creating, AC 307–310
relationships
    defining between two tables, AC 99–103
    one-to-many, AC 76
    viewing table, in Relationships window, AC 306
Relationships window, AC 76
    adding tables to, AC 100
    defined relationship in (fig.), AC 102
    viewing table relationships in, AC 306
removing. See deleting
renaming
    See also naming
    default primary key field, AC 12–13
    fields in Design view, AC 90
    objects, AC 241
    report columns, AC 406–407
repairing databases, AC 42–43
Report Footer section, AC 396, AC 420
Report Header section, AC 395, AC 420
report titles, AC 206
Report tool, AC 25, AC 422
Report view, AC 384–387
Report Wizard, AC 25, AC 207, AC 422
    creating report using, AC 208–212
    starting, AC 208
reports
    adding line to, AC 367–368
    adding rectangle to, AC 369
    bound controls, adding, AC 405–406
    changing page orientation, margins, AC 212
    conditional formatting, using, AC 218–220
    copying and pasting into Word, AC 386–387
    created by Report tool (fig.), AC 36
    creating, AC 35–39
    creating multiple, AC 311
    creating Relationship, AC 307–310
    creating using Report Wizard, AC 208–212
    custom. See custom reports
    customizing existing, AC 384
    dates, adding, AC 422–425
    design modifications, AC 405
    detail, summary, AC 402
    displayed in Print Preview (visual overview),
        AC 206–207
    embedding charts in, AC 473
    exporting to PDF files, AC 484–485
    finding with combo box control, AC 348–351
    finished, in Print Preview (fig.), AC 220
    first page, in Print Preview (fig.), AC 38
    formatting, AC 402
    grand totals, adding to, AC 393–395
    grouped, AC 206
    headers and footers (visual overview), AC 420–421
    hiding duplicate values in, AC 418–419
    inserting pictures, AC 217–218
    mailing label, AC 430–434

modifying columns in, AC 390–392
modifying design in Layout view, AC 212–218
modifying in Design view, AC 395–398
modifying in Layout view, AC 388–395
object prefix tag, AC 236
page numbers, adding, AC 426–428
previewing, AC 220
printing, AC 39–40, AC 220–221
printing options, AC 309
saving, AC 35
sorting and grouping data in, AC 407–410
themes, applying to, AC 212–213
titles, AC 382, AC 428–429
viewing in Report view, AC 384–386
views, choosing to use, AC 384
Reports group, AC 25
resizing
See also sizing
columns, AC 36–37
controls on reports, AC 413–415
fields in reports, AC 214–216
form's field value labels and boxes, AC 317–319
report columns, AC 406–407
responsive design, PA-6
restoring databases, AC 43
reviewing
databases, AC 236
property settings of Long Text field, AC 288–289
ribbon, AC 2
buttons and labels on, AC 13
collapsing, AC 310
displayed in Touch Mode (fig.), AC 10
Riverview Veterinary Care Center (case)
creating and modifying tables, AC 51
creating database, AC 1
creating forms, AC 301
custom reports, AC 381
importing, exporting, linking, AC 443
sophisticated queries, AC 233
updating tables, retrieving information, AC 115
using forms, reports
row selector, AC 16
rows
alternate colors, AC 392–393
datasheet, AC 2
inserting table, AC 70–71
ruler, vertical, AC 352
rules
conditional formatting, AC 218–220
data validation, defining, AC 282–285
table validation, defining, AC 284–285
Run button, AC 116
running queries, AC 125–127, AC 147

S

sandbox (Microsoft Edge), PA-15
Save As options in Backstage view (fig.), AC 481
Save button, Quick Access Toolbar, AC 23
saving
database objects, AC 35
databases, AC 23
export specifications, AC 462–465
import specifications, AC 456–459
table structures, AC 68
tables, AC19–20, AC 74
school, productivity apps for, PA-1–4
screen recordings, PA-11
ScreenTips
for calculated control (fig.), AC 364
displaying object names, AC 262

Search box, AC 25, AC 180
searching
See also finding
Cortana, locating information with, PA-14–15
the web with Microsoft Edge, PA-14
secondary sort field, AC 133
section tabs, OneNote, PA-2
select queries
vs. crosstab queries (fig.), AC 257
described, AC 234
selecting multiple objects, AC 383
selection criteria in queries (visual overview), AC 140–141
shading, AC 207, AC 211
shadow effects, AC 346
sharing
Office Mix presentations, PA-12
Sway sites, PA-8
Short Text data type, AC 13, AC 14, AC 57, AC 60,AC 61
Short Text fields, AC 304–306
shortcut menus
for applying themes (fig.), AC 188
described, AC 12
shortcuts, keyboard, AC 79
Show Table button, AC 76
Show Table dialog box (fig.), AC 100, AC 125
Shutter Bar Open/Close Button, AC 2
Sign in link, AC 2
Simple Query Wizard, AC 403
described, AC 24, AC 254
using, AC 31–33
Simple Query Wizard dialog box (fig.), AC 31
size, changing font, AC 154
sizing
See also resizing
controls, AC 333–335
tab controls, AC 466
sizing handles, AC 323
Slide Notes, PA-11
slide recordings, PA-11
snaking columns, AC 433
sort field, AC 131
sort order, AC 209
sorting
ascending sort order, AC 400
data in queries, AC 131–135
data in reports, AC 407–410
query datasheets, AC 133
source files, AC 486
spaces in field names, AC 12
Split Form Tool, AC 302, AC 315–317
split forms, AC 315–317
spreadsheet programs vs. DBMSs, AC 7
SQL (Structured Query Language), AC 263
SQL Server
converting Access database to, AC 263
and object field names, AC 236
Standard Colors, AC 155
star symbol, AC 17
starting
Access, AC 7–8
Form Wizard, AC 182
Report Wizard, AC 208
Simple Query Wizard, AC 31
status bar, AC 2
status bar view buttons, AC 117
Storylines (Sway), PA-6

styles, adding to form and report controls, AC 372
Subform Wizard, AC 352–355
subforms, AC 200–204
adding to forms, AC 347, AC 352–355
creating, AC 201–204
in tab control (fig.), AC 469
in tab control in Form view (fig.), AC 470
Subform/Subreport tool, AC 347
subtotals, AC 382
Sum function, AC 346, AC 397, AC 401, AC 421
summary reports, AC 402
sunken effects, AC 346
Sway
adding content to build stories, PA-7
creating presentations, PA-6–7
Sway sites, PA-6, PA-8
Sways, PA-2
switching
between navigation and editing mode, AC 118
between Touch Mode and Mouse Mode, AC 10
symbols for some custom date formats (fig.), AC 65
syncing
described, PA-2
OneNote notebooks to the cloud, PA-2–3

T

Tab Control tool, AC 468
tab controls, AC 466, AC 470
with chart (visual overview), AC 466–467
pie chart in (fig.), AC 475
subform in (fig.), AC 469–470
using in forms, AC 468–470
tab order
changing in forms, AC 364–366
described, AC 364
Tab Order dialog box (fig.), AC 365, AC 366
Tab Stop property, AC 361, AC 363–364
Table Analyzer, using, AC 453
Table Analyzer Wizard, AC 452
table data, maintaining using forms, AC 197–198
Table Design grid, AC 52
table relationships
introduction, AC 97–98
one-to-many, AC 98–99
table structures
creating by importing existing, AC 84–86
deleting fields from, AC 88–89
modifying imported, AC 88–92
table validation rules, AC 284
Table window in Design view (visual overview), AC 52–53
Table window, table with three fields (fig.), AC 63
tables, AC 4
adding data from imported text files, AC 95–97
adding fields to, AC 14–16, AC 86–88
adding records to, AC 94
adding records to new, AC 78–80
with all fields entered (fig.), AC 16
analyzing with Table Analyzer, AC 453
closing, AC 22–23
creating by importing existing, AC 83–86
creating in Datasheet view, AC 11
creating in Design view, AC 59–68
in database (fig.), AC 27
in Datasheet view (visual overview, AC 76–77
default name of, AC 2
defining relationship between two, AC 99–103
entering tables, AC 16–19

exporting Access, as XML files, AC 459–462
field validation rules, defining, AC 284–285
finding data in, AC 121–122
icon (fig.), AC 40
importing, AC 86
after importing data (fig.), AC 83
importing XML files as Access
lookup fields. *See* lookup fields
modifying field properties, AC 71–74
modifying structures of, AC 68–71
modifying structures of Access, AC 68–71
naming, AC 52
object prefix tag, AC 236
opening, AC 22
organizing related fields into, AC 54
planning, AC 11–12
primary. *See* primary tables
related, AC 77
renaming default primary key field, AC 12–13
saving, AC19–20
saving structure, AC 68
storing data in separate, AC 6
updating data in linked, AC 489–490
Tables group options, AC 24
tabs
    See also specific tab
    contextual, AC 13
    OneNote section, PA-2
Tabular form layout, AC 183
tabular layout, AC 303
<tblReferral> tags, AC 444
teamwork
    exchanging data between programs, AC 454
    following naming conventions, AC 237
templates, AC 8, AC 479
    and application parts, AC 479–483
    meeting notes, PA-3
    OneNote, PA-2
testing
    calculated controls, AC 364–365
    parameter queries, AC 252–253
    queries, forms, reports, AC 286
text
    bolding, italicizing, underlining, AC 191
    changing color of on forms, AC 191–192
    converting handwriting to, PA-3–4
text box controls, AC 302–303
text boxes
    described, AC 304
    resizing, AC 333–335
text files, adding data to tables by importing,
AC 95–97
Theme Colors, AC 155
themes, AC 154, AC 181
    adding to reports, AC 212–213
    applying to database objects, AC 185–188
    applying to forms, AC 181
    changing alternate row colors in datasheets,
    AC 154–156
    working with, AC 189

Themes gallery (fig.), AC 187
time, adding to reports, AC 423
title bar, AC 2
titles
    adding to forms, AC 343–344
    chart, AC 467
    report, AC 382, AC 428–429
To Do tags, PA-2
To Fit command, AC 414
Top Values property, AC 267
top values queries, AC 267–269
Total row
    and aggregate functions, AC 162–163
    inserted in design grid (fig.), AC 164
Touch Mode
    ribbon in (fig.), AC 10
    switching to, AC 10
    working in, AC 9
truepart of Ilf function, AC 235, AC 247
trusted folders, designating, AC 289–291

U

unbound controls
    added to form (fig.), AC 350
    described, AC 326
unbound forms, AC 325
underlining text, AC 191
Unhide Columns dialog box (fig.), AC 120
Unhide Fields command, AC 119
unhiding fields, AC 119
unique (sort field), AC 132
Update Properties dialog box (fig.), AC 279
updating, AC 118
    data in linked table, AC 489–490
    data using queries, AC 128–129
    databases, AC 118–124
user documentation requirements, satisfying, AC 307

V

Validation Rule property, AC 283
Validation Text property, AC 283
vertical ruler, AC 352
video clips, capturing, PA-11
videos, inserting into OneNote notebooks, PA-4
View button, AC 116
view buttons on status bar, AC 117
viewing
    See also displaying
    datasheets, AC 96–97
    HTML documents in web browser, AC 448–449
    Long Text fields with large contents in Datasheet
    view, AC 288
    objects in Navigation Pane, AC 40
    reports in Print Preview, AC 211–213
    reports in Report view, AC 384–386
    table relationships in Relationships window, AC 306
    tables in Datasheet view, AC 74–75
Visible property, AC 342

visual overviews
    Access window, AC 2–3
    advanced Query Wizards, AC 254–255
    anchoring controls, AC 302–303
    calculated fields, AC 234–235
    Create tab options, AC 24–25
    custom forms in Form view, AC 346–347
    custom reports in Layout view, AC 382–383
    custom reports in Print Preview, AC 400–401
    forms displayed in Form view, AC 180–181
    lookup fields and input masks, AC 270–271
    modified Visit table in Datasheet view, AC 76–77
    Query window in Design view, AC 116–117
    report displayed in Print Preview, AC 206–207
    selection criteria in queries, AC 140–141
    tab control with chart, AC 466–467
    Table window in Design view, AC 52–53

W

warning messages for existing table relationship (fig.),
AC 272
Web Note tools (Microsoft Edge), PA-15
webpages
    annotating, PA-15
    live, PA-12
wildcard characters, AC 195, AC 237
window, Access (visual overview), AC 2–3
window buttons, AC 2
wizards. *See specific wizard*
Word
    See also specific feature
    copying and pasting reports into, AC 386–387
    dragging outlines into Sway, PA-7
work, productivity apps for, PA-1–4
worksheet, importing Excel, AC 80–83
written communication
    enhancing information using calculated controls, AC 367
    formatting reports, AC 402
    satisfying user documentation requirements, AC 307

X

x-axis, AC 467
XML (Extensible Markup Language), AC 454
XML files
    exporting Access tables as, AC 459–462
    importing data from, AC 455–456
    working with, AC 454–465
XML tags, AC 444
XSD (XML Structure Definition), AC 461
XSL (Extensible Stylesheet Language), AC 462

Y

y-axis, AC 467

Z

Zoom box, AC 156
Zoom dialog box, AC 252